Psychology for Social Care

An Irish Perspective

Psychology for Social Care

An Irish Perspective

EMMA O'BRIEN

GILL & MACMILLAN

Gill & Macmillan
Hume Avenue
Park West
Dublin 12
with associated companies throughout the world
www.gillmacmillan.ie

© Emma O'Brien 2011

978 07171 4999 5

Index compiled by Cliff Murphy
Print origination by Carole Lynch
Printed by GraphyCems, Spain

The paper used in this book is made from the wood pulp of managed forests. For every tree felled, at least one is planted, thereby renewing natural resources.

A CIP catalogue record is available for this book from the British Library.

For permission to reproduce photographs, the author and publisher gratefully acknowledge the following:

© Press Association: 12; © Mark Stivers: 58; © Science Photo Library: 27, 45, 64; Courtesy of The National Academies Press: 91; Courtesy of oxfordschoolblogs.co.uk: 59.

The author and publisher have made every effort to trace all copyright holders, but if any have been inadvertently overlooked we would be pleased to make the necessary arrangements at the first opportunity.

Contents

*This book is dedicated to
my mother, Paula O'Kelly,
my son, Ultan O'Brien, and
Mark J. Daly, with love forever.*

Acknowledgments

I wish to thank Michele Savage of Fetal Alcohol Spectrum Disorders Ireland for her contribution to the book on this vital topic that really hasn't received the exposure it should. Another note of gratitude is due to Margaret Prangnell, who contributed an insightful piece on the area of child protection. I'm grateful to both for the expertise they bring to this book. Many thanks to my colleagues Dr Paula Faller and Garett Evers for their feedback, which proved immensely helpful. On a personal note, I wish to thank Mark for his unending support and wisdom while writing the book. Finally, any mistakes in this book are mine and mine alone.

1
Introduction

THE STRUCTURE OF THIS BOOK

The topics and material dealt with in this book are confined to those that are of direct importance to the field of social care. An emphasis is placed on the use of Irish statistics, research, policy and interventions to highlight what is current in Ireland today. The first chapters deal with the brain and its role in behaviour (Chapter 2) and theories of psychology, including developmental psychology (Chapter 3). Chapter 4 provides an overview of the individual's psychological development across their lifespan. Chapters 5 to 10 deal with more specific topics such as disability, abuse, social psychology, counselling and health and well-being. Each of these chapters has an obvious and direct relevance to the area of social care practice. In each chapter, theory, research and practice elements are blended to demonstrate the relevance of psychology in supporting the work of social care practitioners. The final chapter looks at the area of research and explains different methodologies and examples of Irish research as well as issues relevant to conducting and writing research.

Where links to websites are given in the text, a short URL is given. For the full link, see 'Websites', p.322.

Student resources are available online at www.gillmacmillan.ie. Search for *Psychology for Social Care* and click on the link in the right-hand column.

LIFE HAPPENS

> *Even the monkeys fall out of the trees.*
> – Old Japanese proverb

I have always liked that proverb because it reminds me that 'life' happens! The proverb reminds us that sometimes we fall off the tracks or get sidelined. Monkeys sometimes fall out of trees even though that is not their 'natural' behaviour; people can be similarly unlucky or unpredictable. This is what appeals to me every time I think of this proverb; that 'stuff' happens, events can sidetrack us and we can end up in situations we never imagined. It's a good lesson in humility, I often think.

Those of us who work in the social care arena encounter people who are vulnerable, people who need support. Yet how do we support them to ensure the best outcomes possible?

In this book we will be looking at the relationship between research, policy and practice. In Chapter 11 we will discuss the importance of evidence-based interventions, and practice elements will be addressed throughout the book where appropriate.

I originally stumbled into psychology because I was curious as to how some people were able to overcome extreme adversity and have successful lives, while others were not. Why the different outcomes? There are no easy answers – I doubt there will ever be answers that are conclusive – but the quest to understand human behaviour is a fascinating one. The question of how we become who we are is not recent; it has exercised the minds of humans since they could reason. Before we look at that and other issues pertinent to the study of psychology, we should address what is meant by social care practice and the relationship between psychology and social care.

WHAT IS SOCIAL CARE PRACTICE?

Lalor and Share (2009, p.5) note that it is difficult to define social care but offer the following key terms 'that help mark out the territory of social care practice':

- *A profession*
  Social care practice is not just an ordinary job, nor is it something done on a voluntary or amateur basis. This distinguishes it from the vast bulk of (equally valuable) care that is carried out informally in society by family and community members. The notion of 'professionalism' also implies that this is an occupation with some status and one that requires access to a specific body of skills and knowledge.

- *Planning and delivery*
  Social care is not just about providing services, but also about devising and planning them. It thus requires at least two types of skill and understanding: the ability to provide hands-on care and support to people as well as the ability to identify what people require and the ability to be able to plan accordingly, preferably drawing on available evidence and policy guidance. This dual role makes social care practice difficult and challenging, yet also rewarding.

- *Quality care and other support services*
  Social care is indeed about care and it requires qualities of compassion, empathy, patience and resilience. Yet it is also about providing other supports, which may include advocating on behalf of another, turning up in court to

speak before a judge and knowing where to refer a person who has particular problems.

- *Individuals and groups*
  Social care can be, and often is, provided in a one-to-one situation, but it can also mean working with small or large groups of people. As a result, both well-developed interpersonal communication skills and a good knowledge of group dynamics are required.

- *With identified needs*
  The traditional 'client group' of social care practitioners in Ireland (and many other countries) has been children in the care of state or other voluntary organisations. While caring for this group remains an important task, social care practitioners may now find work with a broad range of groups of all ages that have special 'needs' or vulnerabilities identified, or indeed with individuals and groups in what we might think of as 'mainstream' society, such as young people in suburban housing estates. The needs and the groups are various.

Lalor and Share also list working in partnership, marginalisation or disadvantage, children and their families and people with disabilities, those who are homeless, those with addiction, older people and recent immigrants as other important areas that can be included in defining social care practice. As you can see, defining social care and its practice is complex as it encompasses such a wide variety and scope and yet this is what makes it a challenging and interesting field to work in. Psychology is, at its most simplistic, the study of the human mind and behaviour. The link is quite apparent that exists between (applied) psychology, which strives to understand, explain and improve people's lives, and social care practice, which involves working with people, particularly those who are vulnerable and have 'needs' that require support.

THE ROLE OF PSYCHOLOGY IN SOCIAL CARE

Seligman and Csikszentmihalyi (2000, p.1) articulate their vision for the role of psychology in shaping people's lives and improving them:

> At this juncture, the social and behavioural sciences can play an enormously important role. They can articulate a vision of the good life that is empirically sound while being understandable and attractive. They can show what actions lead to well-being, to positive individuals, and to thriving communities. Psychology should be able to help document what kinds of families result in children who flourish, what work settings support the greatest satisfaction among workers, what policies result in the strongest civic engagement, and how people's lives can be most worth living.

Until recently psychologists concerned themselves only with how people survive and endure adversity. Seligman identifies the emphasis in psychology on the study of psychopathology, when people develop maladaptive behaviours and become 'mentally unwell'. Seligman states that most psychologists have 'scant knowledge of what makes life worth living'. He eloquently identifies the potential that psychology has to benefit the field of social care through improving the lives of others. Throughout this book the role of psychology within social care will become clear, from psychological theory to informed evidence-based interventions.

So what is psychology? We need to know something of its history, its goals and current debates within the field.

PSYCHOLOGY

The historical perspective

Throughout history there have been attempts to understand what makes us human, what shapes our thoughts and behaviour. Religion played an early part in attempting to unravel human behaviour; for example, there was the Christian assertion of 'original sin', the idea that people are born flawed and susceptible to undesirable behaviour. Philosophers added to the debate as the centuries unfolded. John Locke, for instance, suggested that a person was born a 'blank slate' or 'tabula rasa' and that life experiences shaped who we became. Jean-Jacques Rousseau, in contrast to the Christian view, believed in the innate goodness of humans striving to reach their full potential. Of course these arguments are best left to theologians and philosophers, but the study of psychology is really not much different in that, put simply, it attempts to gain understanding of humans, their development and behaviours.

What is psychology?

Psychology is the study of people: how they think, act, react and interact. Psychology is concerned with all aspects of behaviour and the thoughts, feelings and motivations underlying behaviour. In their search for the causes of diverse forms of behaviour, psychologists take into account biological, psychological and environmental factors. Psychology is different from psychiatry, which requires a medical degree and examines mental illness.

The history of psychology

Within the history of psychology several approaches have been used to gain a greater understanding of human behaviours, beginning in the early 1800s with:

Introspection: As the name indicates this approach relied on 'inspection' where an individual would be asked to report on their feelings and thoughts. William

James, considered one of the forefathers of psychology, was an exponent of this method, as was William Wundt.

Psychodynamic: Originating in the late 1800s, this movement is best known through the work of Freud. It placed emphasis upon the 'unconscious' mind, believing that a person had awareness of only a fraction of his thoughts and mental processes. Freud believed that unconscious urges were responsible for behaviour. Techniques such as hypnosis and dream analysis were used to access these unknown recesses of the mind.

Behaviourism: This approach was very popular in America in the 1920s. Those best known for their work in this field are Skinner and Pavlov. Behaviourists believed that, while the inner workings of the mind could not be observed, a person's behaviour could. Their work still has some relevance in the area of learning.

Humanism: This approach was, it could be argued, a reaction against the behaviourist picture of a human as almost a robot merely responding to outside influence (external stimuli) or the Freudian image of humans driven by their unconscious urges. Humanists such as Carl Rogers and Abraham Maslow promoted the view that within a person is an active desire to reach their full potential, or 'self-actualisation'. Their work has been important in the area of personality.

Socio-cultural: No person is an island. We are social creatures and this perspective recognises this and suggests that our thoughts and behaviours are influenced through our interactions with others. Importantly, it highlights how we are embedded in the culture we are raised or live in and how the views of that culture in turn influence us. In the past psychology tended to look at the individual to gain a greater understanding of them, without looking outside of the person to gauge external influences on them. The socio-cultural approach examines how culture is transmitted to the members of a society and investigates the differences and similarities of people from differing cultures.

Scientific: The predominant approach within psychology at present is the scientific method, or science of behaviour. This approach is less interested in human behaviour *per se*, focusing instead on *why* that behaviour occurs. Thus, if a child exhibits aggressive behaviour the psychologist would not focus on the behaviour itself but rather would want to know why the child is behaving in such a fashion. Methods of research (methodology) include statistics and experiments.

The goals of psychology

1. to *describe* how people and other animals behave
2. to *understand* the causes of these behaviours
3. to *predict* how people and animals will behave under certain conditions
4. to *control* behaviour through knowledge and control of its causes.

Recent developments in psychology

Dissatisfaction has been voiced regarding the use of the scientific approach within psychology as critics claim that it cannot capture the complexity of human behaviour. Reactionary approaches include that of community psychology, which examines individuals within their social world. Community psychology explores social issues and how they influence individuals, groups and society at large. Nonetheless the scientific approach maintains its dominant position within psychology.

SOME KEY DEVELOPMENTAL ISSUES

Nature versus nurture

The nature–nurture debate is one of the key issues in psychology and, more particularly, in understanding human development. Its origins can be traced to the early philosophers who discussed the nature of humans: are we 'blank slates' as Locke believed, shaped by those around us and the society we live in? Or in keeping with the doctrine of 'original sin', are we born the way we are? These positions reflect the nature versus nurture argument. Nature refers to biological processes, genes and our brain as determinants of our behaviour. Nurture relates to the influence of our environment in our development. The culture we are born into influences how we see ourselves and others and also influences our behaviour. Other environmental influences are child-rearing practices, education and so on.

In the early twentieth century the nature position dominated and this fuelled a belief in racial superiority and differences. By the 1960s this position had changed to a nurture stance, which postulated the importance of environment on a person's development, and can be best seen in the explosion of literature on child-rearing practices.

Nowadays a more reasonable position is generally maintained, recognising the influence of both nature and nurture in human development. Debates continue regarding the degree to which either is involved, their role and the interaction between the two elements. Urie Bronfenbrenner's revised 'bioecological' theory (see Chapter 3) best captures this new position as he demonstrates the many influences that interact to shape development. We still do not understand the complexity of the interaction between nature and nurture and it remains an issue of great interest and importance.

Critical versus sensitive periods

We will look at examples of extreme deprivation in the early years to explore the issue of critical versus sensitive periods of development. Does a *critical* period exist in development, meaning that if development does not occur during this stage then the opportunity is lost? Or does a *sensitive* period exist where it is preferable for development to occur, but if it does not, development can occur at a later date? In Chapter 2 Dr Sunderland makes clear her view that early experiences have a fundamental role in shaping a child's brain development, yet some people show greater resilience to adverse events than others who are badly affected by them. The following discussion illustrates the complexity of human behaviour and that there are no easy answers to be had.

In focus: Critical versus sensitive period debate – extreme deprivation

Development in infancy encompasses social, emotional, cognitive and physical growth. What is the difference between critical and sensitive periods? Let's take the example of language. If you believe in a 'critical period' for the acquisition of language, then you would believe that if language is not acquired during a particular period, it would not be possible to acquire language at a later date.

If you believe in a 'sensitive period' of development then you might believe that if you do not acquire language in the early years, it is possible to do so at a later time. In the debate between critical vs. sensitive periods of development, infancy is often examined, as it is a time of huge growth in many areas. The critical vs. sensitive period debate is one of the most active in psychology, and cases of extreme deprivation are often examined in an effort to illuminate this debate. Recent examples of children who have suffered extreme deprivation include Romanian orphans whose images shocked us in the early 1990s. Extreme deprivation in infancy offers us an insight as to whether children can recover from adverse experiences in their early years and develop normally with caring and appropriate interventions or whether there is in fact a 'critical period' which cannot be recovered from, leaving the individual permanently and irreversibly affected.

Clarke and Clarke (1976) support the idea of a sensitive period, after which experienced adversity and resulting deficits can be compensated for – an 'initial step in an ongoing life path'. On the other hand, Freud, and later Bowlby, argued that early experience determines later development. Bowlby's work with children in institutional care led him to believe that negative early experiences cannot be reversed in later years, especially in the area of attachment (Bowlby, 1951).

However, in more recent decades this position has been questioned. Cases of extreme deprivation have had quite different outcomes, suggesting that the debate surrounding critical vs. sensitive periods isn't quite as clear cut as earlier presumed. Rutter (1989, p.24) argues that 'even markedly adverse experiences in infancy carry few risks for later development if the subsequent rearing environment is a good one'. Let's consider how true this is by examining some cases of extreme deprivation and their subsequent outcomes.

Skuse (1984) explored case studies of children who spent their early years in conditions of extreme adversity and deprivation, hoping to explore specific questions.

- Are some psychological qualities more sensitive to deprivation than others?
- At what pace does recovery take place and what course does it follow?
- What interventions are necessary to optimise recovery?

Anna was discovered in 1938 at nearly six years of age, having spent her life in a storage room tied to a chair with her arms above her head. Severely malnourished, she was skeletal, expressionless, lacking speech with severe motor retardation. While Anna showed some improvement, she never integrated successfully into her peer group even though she was now living with a foster family. Anna received no specialist intervention and while she made some improvement she remained severely retarded until her death at the age of 10 (Clarke and Clarke, p.28).

Isabelle was discovered at six years locked in a dark room with her 'deaf-mute' mother. Isabelle was suffering from severe malnourishment, her behaviour was either infantile or like that of a wild animal and she did not seem to possess speech. Experts decided she was 'feeble-minded' (Clarke and Clarke, p.42). Within two years of intensive speech and educational therapy she had achieved a normal level of speech and cognitive function.

Language

Let's examine a specific area of development, that of language, to see if we can come closer to a conclusion in this debate of critical vs. sensitive periods.

Skuse concludes that the development of language appears to be the most vulnerable to deprivation, but much debate surrounds the question of whether there is a critical period for language exposure and/or acquisition. Hall (1985) replied to Skuse with the suggestion that 'some exposure to language and communication is essential at a very early stage, even if only for a very brief period' (p.825), while Lenneberg's 'critical age hypothesis' (cited in Curtiss, 1977, p.208) states that the critical period runs from two years to puberty.

Genie was confined in total isolation from 20 months until her discovery at 13 years of age; although intensive language therapy suggested initial promising acquisition, her capacity remained severely limited and she was capable of 'few normal or appropriate acts of communication at 18 years' (Skuse, 1984, p.562), although Isabelle, confined with a 'deaf-mute' mother, developed normal language skills.

Or we could consider the case of the Koluchova twins, grossly deprived and confined from 18 months to nearly seven years, who went on to develop normally with respect to language (as well as in every other facet of life) (Skuse, 1984). Was this due to their early normal language exposure before they were confined? Was it because they had each other for company and developed ways of communicating? Or was it due to their later intensive care within a foster family?

English and Romanian adoptees (ERA)

Thus we will turn to the work of the English and Romanian adoptees (ERA) study team and their ongoing research comparing UK adoptees with those adopted into the UK from Romania. The fall of the Ceaușescu regime in Romania created a unique research opportunity through the humanitarian endeavour of removing infants and children from orphanages in which they had suffered severe deprivation.

Study

The research (Rutter *et al.*, 1998) studied 324 children who were adopted into the UK. The conditions in which the children had lived in Romania varied from 'poor to appalling' (Rutter *et al.*, 1998, p.467). They were confined to cots, had few, if any playthings and barely any stimulation through talk or play; were poorly nourished and often endured harsh physical conditions. Nearly half had been reared entirely in institutions; 18 had had family rearing with only two weeks' institutional care; the rest had spent about half their lives in institutions. Half were severely malnourished and suffering from chronic infections.

Findings

- The catch-up with respect to these norms was nearly complete at age four (Rutter *et al.*, 1998).
- Age on adoption was a strong predictor of more positive outcomes with no measurable deficit in those adopted before six months. Those adopted after six months were more likely to show evidence of deficits.
- Children who had received better individualised care in institutions tended to have higher cognitive scores at age six.

Rutter *et al.* conclude that 'children who had experienced prolonged privation in poor-quality institutions tended to show a less complete cognitive recovery, although even with prolonged institutional care, cognitive catch-up was very substantial indeed'.

Irish findings

Dr Sheila Greene of the Children's Research Centre, Trinity College Dublin, presented a paper entitled 'Children's recovery after early adversity: lessons from inter-country adoption'. The findings were based on research conducted by the Children's Research Centre on inter-country adoption in Ireland. Dr Greene concludes:

- Inter-country adoption provides many striking examples of resilience.
- Pervasive environmental change from very poor to very positive circumstances can bring about remarkable levels of recovery in children suffering the effects of adversity – by any standard.

- Most children demonstrate a capacity to recover when their circumstances change dramatically; a minority do not.
- Some children who have been subjected to long periods of very intense deprivation will show some recovery but may never be normal in their functioning (p.14).

Source: www.tcd.ie/childrensresearchcentre

Our understanding has certainly extended far beyond early simplistic suggestions that early experience determines all future development. What can cause these differences in outcomes? This question is one that will arise repeatedly throughout this book.

SPECIALTIES IN PSYCHOLOGY

Clinical psychology is the application of psychological theories, models and research to a range of psychological, psychiatric, mental health and developmental problems. Clinical psychologists provide a variety of services, including assessment, therapy and consultancy services. They work primarily, but not exclusively, in child and/or adult and learning disability services where emotional, behavioural, psychiatric or developmental difficulties are addressed.

Counselling psychology, as a psychological specialty, facilitates personal and interpersonal functioning across the lifespan with a focus on emotional, social, vocational, educational, health-related and developmental concerns. Therefore, counselling psychologists can be found working in such diverse areas as schools and colleges, industrial workplaces and health services. Counselling psychology encompasses a broad range of practices that help people improve their well-being, alleviate distress and maladjustment, resolve crises and increase their ability to live more highly functioning lives. Counselling psychologists work with people who have experienced a range of emotional and psychological difficulties. These include problems of identity and bereavement, relationship problems, sexual abuse, emotional abuse and neglect.

Educational psychologists deal with the psychological and educational development of people in the education system. This may include students of any age, their parents or guardians and the people who work with them. Their work can involve both assessment and intervention within the education setting. They are also likely to be involved in training and research on related issues.

Forensic psychologists work in a variety of areas, including prisons, probation services, special secure hospitals, rehabilitation units and in private practice. Responsibilities include the assessment of offenders prior to sentencing, management of offenders during sentence and in the community upon release, risk assessment and sex offender treatment programmes. Forensic psychologists also act as expert witnesses and give evidence in court.

Health psychology involves an examination of the way in which biological, psychological and social factors affect health and illness. Health psychologists are concerned with studying the relationship between psychological factors (for example, proneness to hostility), social/psychological factors (for example, psychological stress) and illness (for example, heart disease). Areas of practice include health-risk behaviours and developing better ways of helping people to change their behaviours. Health psychologists are also involved in helping individuals to improve their health or to cope with chronic illness or unpleasant medical procedures.

Neuropsychology is the scientific study of brain–behaviour relationships, and the clinical application of that knowledge to human problems. A clinical neuropsychologist is a professional psychologist who applies principles of assessment and intervention based upon the scientific study of human behaviour as it relates to normal and abnormal functioning of the central nervous system.

Organisational psychology involves the study of human behaviour in the workplace. It is also referred to as industrial or occupational psychology. Organisational psychologists recognise the importance of relationships between individuals, organisations and society. They deal with issues and problems involving people at work by serving as advisors in a variety of organisations.

Source: www.psihq.ie

SUMMARY

I hope this book will serve as a guide to walk the reader through some of the most fundamental aspects not just of social care but of human development in general. This book is intended to offer a foundation for further exploration of the topics touched on. Life is akin to a voyage; it can be said that it's not so much the destination that is important as the journey there – I wish you a fruitful one!

2

The brain and behaviour

This chapter outlines the basic structure and functions of the brain and its development across the lifespan. We will then consider brain damage and illness including acquired brain damage and dementia. The work of Margot Sunderland, whose interest lies in early brain development and its impact on the brain, will be discussed. We will also take a more philosophical approach in discussing what is a 'sense of self' and how the brain is tied up with this.

ROLE OF THE BRAIN

The role of the brain in behaviour has not always been obvious; it took an accident involving a man named Phineas Gage to demonstrate the integral role of the brain in regulating our behaviour. Phineas Gage worked on the railway lines in America in the mid-1800s. He was planting some explosives which detonated early, causing his tampering iron to enter under his cheekbone and exit through the top of his head as you can see in the image below.

The brain of Phineas Gage

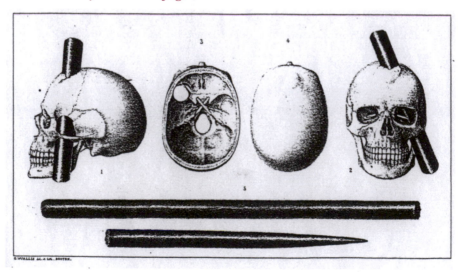

Amazingly he survived this injury, but most of the front part of his left brain had been destroyed, resulting in a complete change in his personality and behaviour. As his doctor noted, 'Gage was no longer Gage.' The old Phineas held the position of foreman and was considered diligent, conscientious and hard-working. The new Phineas became unreliable, nasty, used vulgar language in front of women (considered quite a *faux pas* then) and changed his mind from moment to moment. This dramatic change in behaviour gave the first indication that damage to the brain could affect behaviour, and this is why Phineas Gage holds an important place in the history of neuropsychology. The area of Gage's injury (frontal lobe) is significant because, as you will see, different parts of the brain are responsible for different functions (referred to as localisation). Modern day individuals with the same area of brain damage as Gage are affected similarly: they are unable to make effective personal or social decisions and they cannot plan ahead, demonstrating also how emotions are involved in our ability to reason.

As we have seen from the case of Phineas Gage, the role of the brain in human behaviour is now understood to be paramount. The brain is involved in all aspects of development: motor (movement), sensory, cognitive and social.

FUNCTIONS OF THE BRAIN

The four lobes of the brain

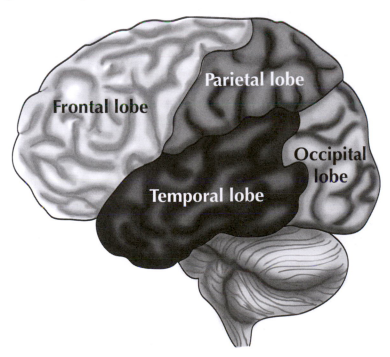

The brain consists of four lobes, which have different locations and functions.

Frontal lobe: located behind the forehead, this is the 'front' of the brain. This lobe does not develop fully until the teen years. It is possible to divide the frontal lobe into three distinct zones of functioning:

- **Motor cortex:** responsible for making movements
- **Premotor cortex:** selects the movements
- **Prefrontal cortex:** controls cognitive (thinking) processes so that appropriate movements are selected at the correct time and place. The prefrontal cortex is also responsible for selecting behaviour with respect to context (put plainly, appropriate behaviour). Gage was unable to perform this function.

Briefly, the frontal lobe's functions include higher forms of thinking, such as reasoning and also voluntary movements.

Parietal lobe: located behind the frontal lobe, around the top of the head. Its main responsibility is in somatosensory functions. Somatosensory means the sensation of the body and its movement, including sensations of pressure, warmth, cold, vibrations and limb position and movement. Briefly, the functions of this lobe include processing information about body sensations.

Occipital lobe: located at the back of the brain. One of its main functions is vision, including perception of form, colour and movement.

Temporal lobes: located at either side of the brain. They are involved in hearing and enable the processing of speech. The temporal lobes are also involved in the analysis of visual processing, especially recognition of form. Finally, these lobes play a role in long-term memory.

The brain is not one huge mass; it is divided into two halves or 'hemispheres'. These are connected by a bundle of nerves called the corpus callosum that allows each half to communicate with the other, thus ensuring that they are working in unison. Lateralisation is a term used to describe the specialisation of function in one or the other hemisphere. Put more plainly, it means that one hemisphere can be responsible for a particular function; for example, in most people the left side of the brain is generally responsible for language. However, this does not mean that the right side has no role at all in language – it does, but not the dominant role. It is generally accepted that lateralisation occurs between the ages of 2 and 12.

The nervous system

The main function of the nervous system is as the body's decision and communication centre. It consists of the central nervous system (CNS) and the peripheral nervous system. The central nervous system is made up of the brain and spinal cord. Its main function is to relay information to and from the brain. A healthy nervous system controls movement and co-ordination of the limbs. The peripheral nervous systems consists of nerves. Together, these systems control every part of our daily life: nerves connect the brain to the face, eyes, ears, nose and spinal cord and connect the spinal cord to the rest of the body.

Sensory nerves gather information from the environment through the senses (eyes, ears, etc.) and that information is transmitted to the spinal cord and relayed to the brain. The brain then deciphers the message and fires off a response. Motor neurons (neurons are nerve cells) take the instructions from the brain to the rest of the body. The spinal cord plays an essential role in the relationship between the brain and body as a transmitter, delivering and relaying messages to and from the brain.

STRUCTURES OF THE BRAIN

- cerebrum
- cerebellum
- limbic system
- brain stem

The **cerebrum** or cortex is the biggest part of the brain and is divided into four lobes: frontal, parietal, occipital and temporal as discussed above. The cerebral cortex is generally associated with higher thinking and brain function. As you might have noticed in the diagram of the brain, the surface of the cortex is wrinkled. If you take a piece of cloth and lay it down flat it will cover an area the size of the cloth; however, if you were to fold the fabric continually upon itself that same piece of cloth would take up a smaller surface area. The same principle can be applied to the brain; by folding in on itself to create this wrinkled surface it has a larger surface area; this allows the brain to have a higher density of neurons, which creates a much more powerful brain.

The **cerebellum**, or 'little brain' as it is sometimes called, is located deeper in the brain and is associated with regulation and co-ordination of movement, posture and balance.

The **limbic system** is found deep in the cerebrum and is often called the 'emotional brain' as it houses some of our basic emotions, such as rage and happiness. It contains the **thalamus**, which serves as a station that receives sensory information of all kinds (particularly pain and pleasure) and relays it to the cortex; it also receives information from the cortex. Drugs that shut down the thalamus are often used for anaesthetic effects.

The **hypothalamus** is a part of the limbic system that helps regulate hormone activity, directs autonomic nervous system functions and influences or manages many critical functions, including sleep.

The **amygdala** is a part of the limbic system that plays an important role in motivation and emotional behaviour.

The **hippocampus** is involved in controlling emotion (such as fear or happiness) and instinct (how we respond in certain situations). It is called the hippocampus because it is shaped a bit like a seahorse: 'hippocampus' is Greek for seahorse.

The **brain stem** is responsible for fundamental life functions such as breathing, heartbeat and blood pressure. It is considered the earliest, simplest part of the human brain. Damage to this part of the brain is inevitably fatal as it supports the vital life functions.

Earlier in discussing the case of Phineas Gage the important role played by emotions in our ability to reason was noted, so let's now look at the relationship between emotions and brain function.

EMOTIONS AND THE BRAIN

Emotions enable us to react to situations – for example, anger or fear will set your heart racing, and feeling happy will make you smile. One of the key areas of the brain that deals with showing, recognising and controlling the body's reactions to emotions is known as the limbic system.

Animal emotions

The limbic system is often thought of as a primitive part of the brain as it is present in lower mammals and is even found in reptiles. Animals need emotions to survive – they need fear as a trigger to escape predators and aggression to defend their territory, young and food. Charles Darwin thought emotions were merely left over from our animal past. However, we rely on our emotions to make quick, often complex, decisions.

Fear triggers immediate changes in humans just as in other animals – your hair stands on end, your heart beats faster and your body gets ready to either attack or run. When you recognise danger or feel afraid, you are using an area of your brain called the amygdala. People with damage to this area can no longer recognise fear in others.

Anger: danger can make you feel either angry or frightened and both these emotions are triggered by the same part of the brain – the amygdala. The amygdala in turn triggers a response in the hypothalamus, a key area for many of the functions your brain performs 'without thinking', including this 'fight or flight' response.

Happiness: enjoyment triggers areas in your brain known as 'pleasure centres'. They release 'feel-good' chemicals, in particular dopamine. All animals have this reward system, usually triggered by food or sex. However, the system can be affected by drugs, including nicotine and alcohol. At first these act in the same way as 'natural' rewards, producing pleasure. But with increased use, the drug is needed to stop unpleasant symptoms that appear when it is not available (withdrawal). These effects contribute to drug addiction.

BRAIN DEVELOPMENT ACROSS THE LIFESPAN

The brain at birth weighs 25 per cent of its eventual adult weight; by the child's second birthday the brain will have grown to 75 per cent of its adult weight. This gives us some insight into the rapid changes that occur in the brain during the first two years of life. An infant is born with reflexes that diminish as the brain develops and takes over from these reflexes.

The infant brain

An infant is born with all the brain cells it will need; in fact, it is born with more than it needs. As the brain develops it will cut back or 'prune' cells, synapses (cell connections) and pathways it does not need or use. Imagine a city that has hundreds of little roads: it comes to the mayor's attention that some of these roads are not very efficient or are not being used and that an overhaul is needed. So he orders that the inefficient or superfluous roads that aren't contributing to the smooth running of traffic are removed. When this is done the traffic moves more smoothly and quickly as it is easier and clearer to see how to get from one point to another. So although there are fewer roads, the roads that are left are the ones that work best and ensure traffic flows quickly and efficiently. This is similar to how the brain develops. Pruning away superfluous neural pathways and cells ensures that the brain works more efficiently. Interestingly the interaction of the child with its environment influences the development of the brain. As discussed in Chapter 1, the brain needs a stimulating environment. If a child is severely neglected, the brain does not develop normally. Pathways for language can be lost if no stimulation or access to language is available to the child. In fact, such a child's brain can weigh significantly less than the brain of an average child of similar age. So as we can see, the child's environment can influence the development of the brain.

Another process that occurs during the first two years of life is myelinisation, when the nerve fibres are insulated, improving and speeding up the nerve impulses.

In terms of early experience and brain development, modern neuroscience argues that our early experiences with primary carers are internalised and become an organising principle throughout our lives (Cozolino, 2002). Our patterns of communicating will be largely shaped by these early experiences with our primary carers. We will explore this issue later when discussing affective neuroscience.

Shaken baby syndrome

We've looked at how rapidly the brain develops. Young infants have weak neck muscles and are unable to support the weight of their heads. Further, the blood vessels in the developing brain are fragile. For these reasons it is essential that the baby's head is protected and care is taken to prevent falls, etc. Shaken baby syndrome is the result of abuse which involves the violent shaking of an infant, causing damage to the brain. Injuries can include blindness, seizures, developmental delay, brain damage and death.

Infancy to two years

While the brain at birth weighs 25 per cent of its eventual adult weight, by the child's second birthday the brain will have increased to 75 per cent of its adult weight. Clearly this period in a child's life is one of marked growth. It is therefore imperative that this development is supported and the child suitably stimulated to ensure the best outcomes possible.

Age two to five years

During this period the number and size of nerve endings increase. The process of myelinisation continues with a resulting increase in the speed of information transmission between cells. Finally, a rapid growth in the frontal lobes takes place.

Adolescence

The brain undergoes a major growth spurt, particularly in the frontal cortex at the front of the brain. You will recall that an infant has far more brain cells, synapses (cell connections) and pathways than it needs and that 'pruning' occurs to cut back the superfluous and inefficient cells and connections. Dr Jay Giedd (2004, p.2–9) has discovered that a second wave of synapse formation occurs just before puberty in the prefrontal cortex, whose functions include planning, memory and organisation. A maturing prefrontal cortex increases the teenager's ability to reason, to control their impulses and in general to make better judgements. During adolescence 'pruning' occurs again, with the brain discarding cells that are not stimulated and used. It's similar to the idea of pruning a tree and cutting back the dead or weak branches. It has been argued that the principle of 'use it or lose it' is important during adolescent brain development. If a teenager takes part in sport or plays a musical instrument, the brain connections that are stimulated by these experiences will survive and become 'hardwired' in the brain. If, on the other hand, the teenager watches television most of the day, a different set of cells and connections will be maintained. Further, an immature prefrontal cortex and its associated functions have been implicated in the risk-taking behaviours seen in some adolescents, as Dr Giedd (2004) explains:

> Now that MRI studies have cracked open a window on the developing brain, researchers are looking at how the newly detected physiological changes

might account for the adolescent behaviours so familiar to parents: emotional outbursts, reckless risk taking and rule breaking, and the impassioned pursuit of sex, drugs and rock 'n' roll. Some experts believe the structural changes seen at adolescence may explain the timing of such major mental illnesses as schizophrenia and bipolar disorder. These diseases typically begin in adolescence and contribute to the high rate of teen suicide. Increasingly, the wild conduct once blamed on 'raging hormones' is being seen as the by-product of two factors: a surfeit of hormones, yes, but also a paucity of the cognitive controls needed for mature behaviour.

Indeed it is suggested that the brain is not fully mature until 25 years of age. So we can see that as the physical brain develops and matures, we would expect to see the cognitive (thinking) functions increase and mature also.

The ageing brain

According to Carter (2009, p.206), 'the natural degeneration of the brain and the nervous system is not caused by disease, and so should not be confused with the pathology of dementia, which is associated with a pattern of specific brain changes. Recent research shows that most neurons actually remain healthy until you die, but brain volume and size decrease 5–10 per cent from the age of 20–90.' The ageing brain is a relatively recent phenomenon in the history of humankind as in the past most people did not live beyond the age of 50, so this issue was not relevant. Research on the ageing brain has much to catch up on, and the following section reflects much of the research conducted in this area.

Neuropsychology of ageing

The biggest threat to successful ageing is loss of mental function – memory, thinking, concentration, learning, problem-solving, alertness, error-proneness, vulnerability to crime/deception, etc. Changes in these mental abilities occur because the brain changes as we get older, and these alterations may accelerate in the fifties and sixties. In an unfortunate minority of people, they accelerate into dementia. Such difficulties are also linked to other common problems of age – depression, falls and social isolation. Finding how to keep older people's brains functioning well is one of the greatest challenges of the next decade. Ian Robertson and his group at the Trinity College Institute of Neuroscience are tackling this in a number of ways:

- Identifying early 'markers' of declining brain function, with a view to helping the pharmaceutical industry develop more effective drugs that can prevent brain disease before it causes irreversible damage to the brain.
- Finding ways of training the brains of healthy older people so as to help

them keep more mentally fit – and hence more independent – as they get older.

- Developing new technologies to help monitor brain function in the person's home environment, with a view to providing support and even therapy from such 'intelligent environments'.
- Providing older people themselves with better information and feedback about their cognitive and related function to allow them either to compensate for any problems, or to work on improving them.

For more information: www.tcd.ie

BRAIN DAMAGE AND DISORDERS

As we have seen, changes in the ageing brain can leave us susceptible to developing dementia. In this section we examine brain damage (acquired brain injury due to trauma), and the brain disorders of dementia, including Alzheimer's disease, and their causes.

Brain dysfunction

When the brain becomes damaged it can malfunction in many different ways, depending on the severity and location of the damage and the speed with which the damage progresses. Brain dysfunction can be diffuse (widespread) or localised (confined to a specific area). Causes of diffuse damage include infections, such as encephalitis and meningitis, and lack of oxygen. Localised brain dysfunction can be the result of a brain tumour or disorders, such as stroke, that decrease the blood (and thereby oxygen) supply to a specific area. The following three characteristics of the brain contribute to its ability to compensate for, and recover from, damage:

- Redundancy: many brain functions can be performed in more than one area in the brain
- Adaptation: areas with somewhat overlapping functions can sometimes compensate for lost functions
- Plasticity: certain areas of brain can adapt to perform new and different functions.

Neuroplasticity refers to the ability of neurons to change in structure and function. It allows the neurons to compensate for injury and disease and to adjust their activities in response to new situations or to changes in their environment. Two areas of interest in the realm of neuroplasticity are the role of early experience on brain development and recovery from brain damage.

It should be noted that while the brain maintains some level of plasticity throughout our lives, in the early years the brain is at its most malleable. This can be both hugely positive and negative, as we will see below in the discussion on Margot Sunderland and affective neuroscience.

Thus, undamaged areas of the brain can sometimes take over functions previously performed by a damaged area, aiding recovery. A fascinating case exists of a young boy, Nico, who had his right hemisphere removed and yet the other hemisphere took over many of its functions, leaving the boy functioning well.

> ### Nico: The boy with half a brain
> Nico's right hempishere was removed when he was three in an effort to control his severe and intractable epilepsy. Despite the removal of half his brain, he developed into a bright child with relatively minor physical and mental impairments; he had no significant cognitive or affective (emotional) disorder. It appeared that the left hemisphere had taken over the functioning of the right hemisphere.

Of course the fact that we know about this case indicates how unusual this level of recovery is, but it does demonstrate the potential capacity of the brain to recover functioning after a trauma or injury to it. Of course the fact that he was young was a major factor in his astounding recovery; as we age the brain becomes less able to shift functions from one area to another. As we grow older functions become more localised (fixed) and therefore the ability for other parts to take on new functions diminishes. Further, certain functions such as vision cannot be performed by any other part of the brain and thus damage to these functions generally results in permanent impairment.

Damage by location

Before we look at specific types of brain damage and disorders such as Alzheimer's disease, it is important to understand how damage to specific parts of the brain manifests itself. The side of the brain on which damage occurs is an important factor, despite the story of Nico above. Put simply the left side is dominant for language while the right is concerned with spatial awareness. Therefore, damage to one side (for example, the left) could result in the complete loss of a function (such as language). Other functions such as memory are performed by both hemispheres; therefore damage to one will not necessarily result in the complete loss of that function. It should be borne in mind that damage to a hemisphere affects the opposite side of the body; for example, a stroke in the right side of the brain affects the left side of the body (lateralisation).

Frontal lobe damage
Damage to the frontal lobe can result in the following difficulties:

- Loss of ability to solve problems and plan actions may be experienced.
- Concentration may be affected; apathy and inattentiveness may be noticed.
- A lack of inhibition may occur, including socially inappropriate behaviour and a disregard for the consequences of the behaviour.

Parietal lobe damage

Features of damage in this area can include:

- Numbness and impaired sensation can occur on the side of the body opposite the area of damage in the brain.
- Affected individuals can have difficulty identifying a sensation's location and type (pain, heat, etc.).
- Damage to the right side of this lobe can result in apraxia – a loss of intentional movements. Apraxia results in the inability to perform simple skilled tasks, such as dressing or brushing the hair.

Temporal lobe damage

Damage to these lobes can have the following results:

- The ability to recognise sounds and shapes may be impaired.
- The memory may be impaired; there may be loss of ability to understand language (aphasia).
- Personality changes, such as extreme religiosity and humourlessness, may be noticed.

Occipital lobe damage

The following characteristics may be due to damage in this lobe:

- Visual impairment: this lobe's main function concerns the processing of visual information so that some will be left unable to see, even though the eyes themselves are functioning normally.
- Impairment of the ability to recognise familiar objects and faces and to interpret what is seen may occur.

Memory

The memory, implicated in disorders such as dementia, is a function that is located in many parts of the brain. Generally speaking, left-hemisphere damage leads to verbal memory problems while damage to the right results in non-verbal (visuospatial) memory problems.

Amnesia, put simply, is a failure to remember. There are two types of amnesia: retrograde and anterograde. Retrograde amnesia is an inability to recall events that occurred prior to the trauma, while anterograde amnesia involves difficulties in learning new material and forming new memories. Anterograde amnesia is far more common than retrograde and can result from a wide range of neurological trauma or insult. The best known case of severe anterograde amnesia is the case of H.M., who has no memory of anything that has happened to him since undergoing a brain operation for epilepsy in 1953, though he can recall everything before the operation.

The case of H.M.

It became apparent that the removal of H.M.'s hippocampus during an operation for epilepsy resulted in severe memory loss. H.M.'s main difficulty is the transfer of information from his short-term to his long-term memory. Carter (1998, p.278) remarks, 'Everything that went into his head stayed put for a few minutes, at most, then faded away. ... H.M. does not have the continuity that allows most of us to make meaning of our lives. He is permanently trapped in a single, frozen moment. The stream of his life stopped running when he was twenty-five, so, for him, his identity is suspended there with it. When asked, he tells people he is a young man. He talks about his brother and friends, long dead, as though they were still alive. When he is given a mirror to look in, his face registers horror as he sees an old man look back at him. The cruelty of inviting him to look at his reflection is mitigated only by the fact that within minutes he has clearly forgotten what he saw.' H.M.'s case had important ramifications; his was the first case to implicate the role of the hippocampus in memory and illustrated that different modes of storage exist for the short- and long-term memory.

Disorders and damage to the brain

- hydrocephalus
- acquired brain injury
- dementia and Alzheimer's disease.

As will become clear in the following chapters, the timing of illness or dysfunction can have an impact on a person's overall development through their lifespan. A person born with brain damage will experience a different impact on their life than another who acquires a brain injury later in life.

Early brain damage: hydrocephalus

Hydrocephalus is a condition where there is a build-up of fluid on the brain. The excess fluid can put pressure on the brain, which can damage it. This can result in a wide range of symptoms including:

- headache
- vomiting

- blurred vision
- difficulties in walking.

In the past, hydrocephalus was known as 'water on the brain', but this term is incorrect. The brain is surrounded not by water, but by a special fluid called cerebrospinal fluid (CSF).

CSF has three important functions:

- it protects the brain (and the spinal cord) from damage
- it removes waste products from the brain
- it provides the brain with the hormones it needs to function properly.

The brain is constantly producing new CSF (about a pint a day). The old CSF is released from the brain and is absorbed into blood vessels. However, if something interrupts this process, the level of CSF can quickly build up, placing pressure on the brain.

There are three main types of hydrocephalus:

- congenital hydrocephalus: present at birth
- acquired hydrocephalus: develops after birth
- normal pressure hydrocephalus: usually develops only in older people.

Congenital hydrocephalus

It is estimated that one in every 1,000 babies will be born with congenital hydrocephalus. The condition can be caused by birth defects such as spina bifida or as a result of an infection that the mother contracts during pregnancy, such as mumps or rubella (German measles).

Acquired hydrocephalus

Acquired hydrocephalus usually develops after a serious head injury or as a complication of a pre-existing medical condition, such as a stroke or brain tumour. It is difficult to estimate how widespread acquired hydrocephalus is because cases are not recorded in the same way as congenital hydrocephalus. Acquired hydrocephalus is a common complication of stroke, and may affect up to 11,000 people a year in England.

Normal pressure hydrocephalus

Normal pressure hydrocephalus (NPH) is a poorly understood condition that usually only affects people above 50 years of age. NPH can sometimes develop after an injury or a stroke, but in most cases the cause in unknown. NPH is a rare condition that affects about 2 in every 100,000 people each year in England.

Outlook

The outlook for all three types of hydrocephalus is good. However, congenital hydrocephalus does carry the risk of long-term mental and physical disabilities as a result of permanent brain damage. Hydrocephalus can usually be treated using a piece of equipment known as a shunt. This is a thin tube that is implanted in the brain and is used to drain away excess CSF.

Source: www.nhs.uk

Acquired brain injury

The Brain Injury Inpatient Rehabilitation Programme

The Brain Injury Inpatient Rehabilitation Programme (BI/IP) at the National Rehabilitation Hospital (NRH) provides specialised, individualised and goals-focused rehabilitation for people with acquired brain injury (ABI). It is the inpatient rehabilitation service provider for people with ABI in the Republic of Ireland. It strives to demonstrate the commitment, capabilities and resources to maintain itself as a specialised rehabilitation programme in the care for people with ABI.

An acquired brain injury may be caused by **traumatic injury** (for example, a fall, or a road traffic accident) or **non-traumatic injury** (for example, a tumour, stroke, or brain infection). The effects of a brain injury are usually very different for each individual. An injury to the brain may affect the person's abilities to pay attention and remember, to communicate, to undertake everyday tasks; and may affect their personality, behaviour and mood. And these changes may in turn have implications for the person's ability to live independently, to communicate effectively with others, drive a vehicle, use public transport, return to work or education, participate in leisure and social activities, perform family roles and maintain personal and family relationships. Some people living with a brain injury may need to acquire new skills and develop strategies to compensate and manage their changed ability.

Source: www.nrh.ie

The following link contains an interview with a woman and her partner on the effects of her brain damage upon her and her family:
http://www.nhs.uk/video/pages/medialibrary.aspx?Id={D095EF23-B14E-4CA9-A6DB-1490147F68A9}&Uri=video/2009/May/Pages/Personality changerealstory.aspx

Dementia

A woman in her early 50s was admitted to hospital because of increasingly odd behaviour. Her family reported that she had been exhibiting memory problems and strong feelings of jealousy. She also had become disoriented at home and was hiding objects. During a doctor's examination, the woman was unable to remember her husband's name, the year, or how long she had been at the hospital. She could read but did not seem to understand what she read, and she stressed the words in an unusual way. She sometimes became agitated and seemed to have hallucinations and irrational fears.

This account relates to the first known case of dementia presented in the early 1900s. Dementia is an umbrella term for a collection of symptoms that can result from a number of disorders that affect the brain. Those with dementia have significantly impaired cognitive (intellectual) functioning, with a consequent impact on relationships and daily activities. Symptoms can include:

- inability to solve problems
- personality changes, such as agitation, loss of emotional control and hallucinations
- memory loss, though this feature alone is not enough to warrant a diagnosis of dementia.

Doctors diagnose dementia only if two or more brain functions, such as memory, language skills, perception or cognitive skills, including reasoning and judgement, are significantly impaired without loss of consciousness.

- There are currently more than 44,000 people in Ireland with dementia, with the number expected to be in excess of 104,000 by 2036 unless there is a medical breakthrough.
- In 2009 there were an estimated 4,000 new cases of dementia in Ireland.
- Dementia can affect younger people; currently approximately 4,000 people in Ireland under the age of 65 have younger-onset dementia.
- By 2036 the number of people with dementia in Ireland is expected to have increased by 303 per cent since 2002, while the total population will have increased by less than 40 per cent.
- Dementia affects the lives of nearly 50,000 people in Ireland who are involved in caring for someone with one of the six symptoms of dementia.

Source: www.alzheimer.ie

Alzheimer's disease
Alzheimer's disease is the most common cause of dementia in people aged 65 and older. In most people, symptoms of Alzheimer's disease appear after age 60.

However, there are some early-onset forms of the disease, usually linked to a specific gene defect, which may appear as early as age 30. Alzheimer's disease typically causes a gradual decline in thinking abilities, usually during a span of 7 to 10 years. Nearly all brain functions, including memory, movement, language, judgement, behaviour and abstract thinking are eventually affected. Different types of dementia cause characteristic patterns of memory loss because they attack different parts of the brain. In Alzheimer's disease the first area to go tends to be the hippocampus, where personal memories are stored. The hippocampus is also involved in remembering one's way around, which is why people with Alzheimer's disease often get lost (Carter, 1998).

Alzheimer's disease is characterised by two abnormalities in the brain: amyloid plaques – clumps of protein found in the tissue between the nerve cells – and neurofibrillary tangles – bundles of twisted filaments found within neurons. These tangles are largely made up of a protein called tau. In healthy neurons, the tau protein helps the functioning of microtubules, which are part of the cell's structural support and deliver substances throughout the nerve cell. However, in Alzheimer's disease, tau is changed in a way that causes it to twist into pairs of helical filaments that collect into tangles. When this happens, the microtubules cannot function correctly and they disintegrate. This collapse of the neuron's transport system may impair communication between nerve cells and cause them to die.

The brain of a healthy person and the brain of a person with dementia

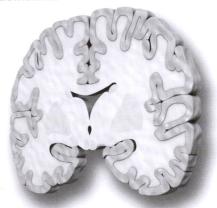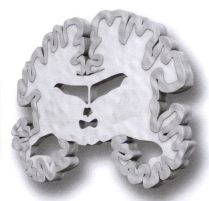

In the early stages of Alzheimer's disease, patients may experience memory impairment, lapses of judgement and subtle changes in personality. As the disorder progresses, memory and language problems worsen, and patients begin to have difficulty performing activities of daily living. They may become disoriented about places and times, may suffer delusions (such as the idea that someone is stealing from them or that their spouse is being unfaithful), and may become short-tempered and hostile. During the late stages of the disease, patients begin to lose the ability to control motor functions such as swallowing, bowel and bladder control. They eventually lose the ability to recognise family members and to speak. As the disease progresses it begins to affect the person's emotions and behaviour and they develop symptoms such as aggression, agitation, depression, sleeplessness and delusions. On average, patients with Alzheimer's disease live for 8 to 10 years after they are diagnosed. However, some people live as long as 20 years.

A SENSE OF SELF AND NEUROLOGICAL CONDITIONS

We have seen that dementia and Alzheimer's disease can affect the personality, and this raises the question 'What is the self?'. If personality reflects the core person, then changes to the personality can result in the person no longer being the person they once were, as in the case of Phineas Gage (Chapter 1).

What is a 'sense of self' and how is it acquired? Almost as importantly, if not more so, what does not having a 'sense of self' mean? This will be examined to better illustrate what it means to have a sense of self. Several theorists have suggested what 'sense of self' is and how it develops. Benson (2003) comments that for Harré it refers to 'the generally "centred" structure of experience'. This sense develops as the individual moves from 'impersonal' to 'personal' modes of psychological functioning. Yet what does this mean? Rochat (2001) charts the development of self-knowledge in infants from implicit self-knowledge towards explicit self-knowledge. There are two types of implicit self-knowledge. One is perceptual in origin and relates to the development of knowledge about an individual's own body through self-exploration and action on objects. The second type of implicit self-knowledge is social and relates to the development of specific knowledge through interactions and reciprocation with others. The development of a 'sense of self' can be witnessed through the use of language. Rochat (2001) contends that the use of 'me' refers to the early, implicit, stage of self-knowledge, while the use of 'I' is accomplished at the explicit stage of self-knowledge, when a self-concept is formed.

So what has this to do with neurologically based conditions? Neurological impairments have done much to improve our understanding of 'having a sense of self'. Indeed Damasio, who has been at the forefront of endeavours to unlock the mysteries of consciousness, was at his work as a neurologist when he witnessed an episode of epileptic autonism, where a patient, though able to continue drinking tea, which requires consciousness, was unresponsive and was in effect 'not there'. This episode sparked his interest in the nature of consciousness. Neurologists, neuroscientists and neuropsychologists, such as Damasio, play a pivotal role in the debate as to what a 'sense of self' is. Their focus tends to be on consciousness, which is considered the holy grail of the mind and, as we will explore, is obligatory to our understanding of self. As alluded to earlier, examining what it means not to have a 'sense of self' is revealing, and certain neurological conditions and disorders offer opportunities to do so.

Damasio (1999) posits that to lack a 'sense of self' requires having no core self or autobiographical self. He differentiates between proto-, core and autobiographical self. Damasio (p.154) proposes that 'the sense of self has a preconscious biological precedent, the "proto-self" which we are not conscious of and is defined as a . . . collection of neural patterns which map, moment by moment, the state of the physical structure of the organism in its many dimensions'. Core consciousness provides the individual with a sense of self about one moment; the here and now. Thus the sense of self that emerges in core consciousness is the core self. Our more traditional perception of self linked to identity is captured by autobiographical self, which forms part of extended consciousness and relies on memories of situations. Damasio refers to a patient 'L' who had suffered a stroke, damaging the frontal lobes of both hemispheres, rendering her speechless and motionless with a neutral expression on her face. Damasio relates that she appeared not to have much of a 'mind' at all and certainly nothing that resembled core and extended consciousness. 'L' appeared not to have 'any sense of self and surroundings, any sense of knowing'. The lack of a conscious mind resulted in an inability to formulate a plan or command even to move her limbs. In comparison, in the final degenerative stages of Alzheimer's disease, those afflicted still have 'mind' enough to be able to formulate commands to move limbs but their autobiographical self has been obliterated and their consciousness compromised so that in Damasio's words 'even the simple sense of self is no longer present'.

One of the keys to understanding the loss of a sense of self can be seen in the ability of the individual to access 'acts of knowing'. In the final stages, an Alzheimer's patient no longer knows or is aware that something is wrong with them. In those with anosognosia, an impairment of extended consciousness including autobiographical self but not core consciousness, those afflicted are unable to recognise a state of disease in their own organism. When asked how they are, they report that they're feeling fine, so total is their ignorance of their affliction. A common thread in the conditions of impaired consciousness discussed is that autobiographical self, key to our identity, is affected.

Thus we can begin to see that a 'sense of self' is constituted of several forms of consciousness and that disorders of consciousness demonstrate the subtle differences that exist between levels of consciousness and layers of self, which is clearly not a unitary construct but a multifaceted and interactional construct.

STRESS AND THE DEVELOPING BRAIN

The idea of who we are, what our sense of self is, is a vital one to how we conceive of ourselves and others. Early experiences shape the people we become and neurologists are very interested in the role of early experiences and their impact on brain development. In the last chapter we looked at the idea of critical periods of development and the impact of early experiences on all aspects of development.

We will now look at the work of Margot Sunderland of the Centre for Child Mental Health. Dr Sunderland has an interest in affective neuroscience which looks at the relationship between brain development and an individual's emotional content. This informs her work with children who have been traumatised and are suffering the effects. She offers some interesting insights into the nature of early experience and how it can shape the brain, thus having ramifications for later life.

According to Sunderland, modern science is now confirming the power of early relationships and their effects on the brain, which are long-lasting. One can think of a child's brain as an ice sculpture which is 'sculpted' through relational interactions for better or worse. Earlier we spoke of the brain's malleability, that is, it is flexible and can be 'shaped' accordingly. Sunderland (2006, p.27) makes a powerful case for the effects of stress on the developing brain and its long-term consequences for the child:

> The developing brain in those crucial first years of life is highly vulnerable to stress. It is so sensitive that the stress of many common parenting techniques can later upset delicate 'emotion chemical' balances and stress response systems in the infant's brain and body, and sometimes cause actual cell death in certain brain structures. ... There is a mass of scientific research showing that quality of life is dramatically affected by whether or not you established good stress-regulating systems in your brain in childhood. One of the most important alarm systems in the lower brain is called the amygdala. One of its main functions is to work out the emotional meaning of everything that happens to you. If the amygdala senses that something threatening is happening to you, it communicates with another structure called the hypothalamus, and this part of the brain actions the release of stress hormones, which can prepare your body for flight or fight. ... If you were left in childhood to manage your painful feelings on your own, and without counselling or therapy in later life, your higher brain may not have developed the necessary wiring to be able to perform these wonderful stress-managing functions. As a result, you can stay feeling stressed out for hours and sometimes days and even weeks. This can result in clinical depression.

Sunderland is clearly saying that if children are not met with responsive and attuned relationships in early life which teach them to manage what she calls the 'big feelings', then the cycle of flight or fight that we experience when we are stressed becomes literally ingrained in the brain; that is, it shapes and sculpts the brain, leaving the person unequipped to deal with stressful feelings in later life and in a state of permanent alert. This has devastating effects for later life. Sunderland reports that an individual who has not established effective stress-responsive systems in their brain can suffer from a range of difficulties in later life, including:

- depression
- persistent states of anxiety
- phobias and obsessions
- physical symptoms/illness
- being cut off emotionally
- lethargy and lack of get-up-and-go
- lack of desire and excitement
- lack of spontaneity (p.32).

In Chapter 1 we examined extreme deprivation and the lasting consequences that it had for most of the children who had suffered it. Some children are more resilient than others in overcoming such traumas, but this should not detract from the scientific research referred to by Sunderland that indicates that early experiences can affect brain development and have implications for later life experiences.

CARING FOR PEOPLE WITH DEMENTIA

Sometimes when we read the theory and research on dementia it can make for despairing reading, and we wonder what can be done practically to support sufferers. The good news is that there is plenty that we can do. This section examines some research on person-centred care and dementia, and will give you a practical perspective on how best to care for clients experiencing the disease.

Person-centred approach

Carl Rogers coined the term person-centred in terms of the therapeutic relationship that should be fostered between client and therapist (see Chapters 3 and 10). It puts an emphasis on the relationship and focuses on the individual. This approach has become very popular within health and social care, as it places a primary focus on the person, rather than on a disability, a service or some other particular issue. Brooker (2004) relates that the term 'person-centred approach' in the context of dementia was first used by Kitwood to differentiate ways of working with people with dementia that were not framed within a biological and technical model. At the heart of this approach is the recognition of the person with dementia as an individual with rights and a need for sensitive interactions, thus reflecting Rogers' emphasis on the individual and the quality of the relationship. Brooker (2004, p.219) offers the following four elements as integral to person-centred care:

V **valuing** people with dementia and those who care for them
I treating people as **individuals**
P looking at the world from the **perspective** of the person with dementia
S a positive **social** environment in which the person living with dementia can experience relative well-being.

These elements in turn form a model of person-centred care for people with dementia, as is illustrated in the table below.

Table 2.1: Towards a model of person-centred care for people with dementia

Underemphasis	Element	Overemphasis
Discrimination within care organisations and a policy agenda against people with dementia and those who care for them.	**V** **Valuing** people with dementia and those who care for them	Care evangelism. Platitudes that people agree with but don't know how to put into practice.
Chaotic and inappropriate assessments and care plans for people with complex needs and life histories.	**I** Treating people as **individuals**	Lots of paperwork. Care plans are all different from each other but meet individual needs only within a narrow range.
Care will not meet the priorities of the individual. High levels of challenging behaviour and learned helplessness.	**P** Looking at the world from the **perspective** of the person with dementia	Lots of information collected but never used appropriately.
Poor communication and lack of dementia-aware interpersonal skills by staff. Organisational emphasis on safety and aesthetics.	**S** A positive **social** environment	Slavish following of techniques. Frequent changes in direction as latest techniques are tried and discarded.

Source: Brooker, 2004, p.220

This model outlines the outcome when an underemphasis is placed on an element, for example, if the element of 'valuing' the individual with dementia is underemphasised, the result is discrimination. Similarly, it is possible to place an overemphasis upon an element. An overemphasis on 'valuing' has the consequence that we 'talk the talk' but are unable to apply it in our practice. So it is clear that skill and reflection are involved in ensuring not just that the elements within the care-centred model are met but that a balance is struck to ensure best practice outcomes.

Brooker details a number of activities that can be used to meet a care-centred approach in working with people with dementia, including life-story work, reminiscence, creativity, play, doll therapy, pet therapy, sensory therapies and psychotherapy. We will look briefly at one of those activities: reminiscence therapy.

Reminiscence therapy

Reminiscence therapy is an activity where the elderly person recalls various experiences from their past life and shares them with others. Through this process it is expected that emotional stability will be promoted and that the elderly person will benefit from being able to share their knowledge and areas of expertise. In the following study, the researchers compared outcomes between reminiscence therapy and general conversation with people with dementia.

Okumura *et al.* (2008, p.125) elaborate on the design of their study: 'There were four reminiscence themes: (i) childhood play; (ii) helping with housework; (iii) school memories and (iv) memories centered on the current session.' The authors conclude that reminiscence therapy performed over a short period of time in closed groups was shown to be more effective than everyday conversations in the treatment of elderly people with dementia. Further, they suggest that (2008, p.132), 'based on the results of the present study, it is concluded that reminiscence therapy is an effective method of providing care to a wide range of elderly people, including those with dementia. It could be introduced as a part of the daily exchange at care facilities. For example, it may be implemented quickly in group homes with the goal of improving care in accordance with the wishes of elderly with dementia. The present study revealed the usefulness of introducing such therapy over a short period of time.'

SUMMARY

By now you should have grasped something of the complexity of the brain and its implication for practice. Having some degree of knowledge and understanding of the brain when working with those who have brain dysfunction of some kind can inform practice. A care-centred approach to working with those with dementia or any other brain disorder or disease should form a fundamental part of daily practice. Finally, what should be apparent from the findings of Sunderland and those who study the effects of early experiences and their effect on brain development is the importance of supporting good development in the young to optimise their later outcomes in life. This theme will be developed in the following chapters.

3

Approaches to psychology

Sometimes it is hard for the practitioner to see the relevance of some psychological theories to the world of social care. In this chapter we will look at some of the more important theories that have been proposed to gain a greater understanding of human behaviour. Certainly the 'ecological' theories of, for example, Bronfenbrenner are more easily recognised as relevant, in that his theory attempts to place the individual in their context and extrapolate all the various interacting influences that shape a person's life. Within the developmental theories, some students struggle particularly with cognitive theories; the language can be off-putting and the direct relevance may be unclear; but it is essential that we, as practitioners, understand the 'typical' and expected development of a person in order to support that development. It is also important to be able to recognise when development becomes 'atypical' or is not in line with the expected developmental trajectories suggested by some developmental theorists. The acquisition of this knowledge is always with the goal of ensuring better outcomes for the people we work with.

This chapter covers:

- developmental theories
- behaviourism
- humanist theories
- ecological theories.

DEVELOPMENTAL THEORIES

Developmental theories hold a fundamental place not just in the arena of psychology but also in social care. A developmental theory is one which, according to Miller (2002, p.8), 'focuses on change over time'. When we consider an individual across their lifespan the one constant is change. At different times in the lifespan, such as in adolescence, this change may be more urgent than at other times. As we saw in the last chapter, there are within psychology two different approaches to understanding human development; cognitive (thinking) and social/emotional development. Taking this two-pronged approach, we will first consider the theories regarding social and emotional development, and in particular the work of Sigmund Freud (1856–1939), Erik Erikson (1902–1992) and John Bowlby and his work on attachment. We will then review the work of Jean Piaget (1896–1980) and his contemporary, Lev Vygotsky (1896–1934), and their insight into the development of thinking (cognitive).

Developmental psychology

Many theories have been proposed, some newer than others, that try to explain human development or aspects of it. These theories are generally constructed in an attempt to explain and predict behaviour. Some relate to specific areas such as cognitive development (Piaget), while others are influenced by a particular approach in psychology, such as the psychoanalytic movement (Freud, Erikson).

Social and emotional theories

Social and emotional theories relate to the development of our emotional side and our personality. Social development refers not just to our relationships with others and how we construe them; it also involves how we see ourselves in the eyes of or from the perspective of others. As an example of such social comparison, where we compare ourselves to another person, have you ever looked at a magazine with an image of an impossibly thin model and felt the urge to start a diet? That would be an example of social comparison!

So as you can see, social development has two aspects. The two theorists that we will examine both come from the psychoanalytic tradition, yet they have quite different explanations of this aspect of human development.

Sigmund Freud (1856–1939)

Sigmund Freud is considered the founder of the psychoanalytic movement, but what is psychoanalysis and how does it relate to human development? Freud believed that much of human behaviour, emotions and feelings emanated from the unconscious mind. Our behaviour was merely the tip or surface that one could see of the unconscious mind. In order to understand behaviour, Freud believed that the unconscious mind would need to be accessed through techniques such as word association and dream analysis. We are not aware of this part of our mind, yet Freud believed that it held powerful urges that had to be satisfied. This created the impetus for our behaviour. As you can see from the image below, there are three levels of the mind: unconscious, preconscious and conscious.

Iceberg of consciousness

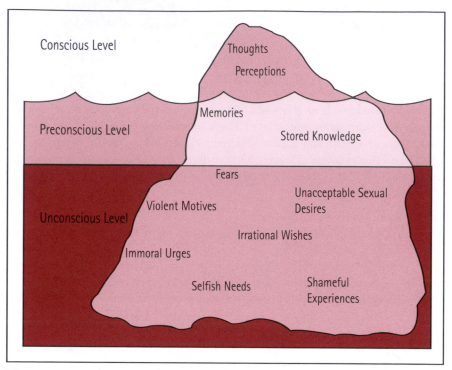

This interest in the unconscious drives that exist within an individual and their role in conscious behaviour is reflected in Freud's conceptualisation of personality. According to Freud, the personality consists of three components: the id, the ego and the superego.

Components of personality
- id
- ego
- superego.

The **id** is the only structure present at birth and exists solely in the unconscious mind. Freud (1964, p.106) describes the id as 'a chaos, a cauldron of seething excitations' and further that 'it is filled with energy reaching it from the instincts, but it has no organisation, produces no collective will, but only a striving to bring about the satisfaction of the instinctual pleasure principle'. The pleasure principle is solely concerned with instant gratification regardless of any other consideration. In order to control the impulses of the id another aspect of personality develops – the ego.

The **ego** operates primarily at a conscious level and is driven by the reality principle, which acts as a check on the id. The ego examines whether it is safe for the id to discharge its impulses and satisfy its instinctual needs. Finally, the last component comes to fruition: the superego, which in its barest form is the moral voice of the personality and endeavours to control the id, particularly with regard to sexual and aggressive needs.

The **superego** grows out of a child's internalisation of their parents' views of morality and is influenced by the cultural norms of the society of which the individual is a member or to which the individual belongs. The ego stands in the middle between the id and the superego.

Think of it another way. As we get older we are taught by parents, school and our culture that expectations of us exist and that our needs cannot always be satisfied. For example, stealing is prohibited and frowned upon in many cultures. I'm hungry and go into a shop to buy some food when I realise I've forgotten my purse. An id response would be to take and eat the food as the id is only interested in satisfying the hunger. However, I've been brought up to believe that stealing is wrong, so I put the food back – this is a superego response. The superego develops as we get older and learn more and more of what is acceptable and the rules we must obey (legal and moral).

Of course, both represent extremes, and that's where the ego comes in. Like the superego, it develops as we get older and acts as a kind of mediator between the id and the superego, trying to find an outcome that will satisfy both. Back in the shop, after I've discovered I've forgotten my money, the ego solution could be for me to ask my friend to lend me the money so I can buy the food. That way my hunger will be satisfied, keeping the id happy, and I won't have stolen anything, keeping my superego happy, and also my mother!

The ego stands in the middle between the id and the superego. As can be imagined, conflict occurs between the competing demands of the id for satisfaction at any cost and the superego attempting to constrain the id. Anxiety occurs when the ego confronts impulses, threatening to get out of control, or external danger.

Let's look at the concept of anxiety and the defence mechanism which springs from anxiety. Anxiety (Hall, 1962, as cited in Passer, 2001) is a painful emotional experience resulting from internal or external stimulation. When the ego is unable to produce realistic coping mechanisms in times of anxiety it resorts to what Freud terms 'defence mechanisms' to relieve the anxiety in a safe manner by denying, distorting or falsifying reality.

Defence mechanisms

Freud outlined several defence mechanisms that are utilised by the ego when it cannot produce realistic coping mechanisms powerful enough to cope with the anxiety being experienced by an individual. A number of defence mechanisms exist, including:

- repression
- denial
- projection.

Before considering the individual mechanisms a further discussion of their general characteristics is called for. As mentioned above, the defence mechanisms operate by distorting or denying reality in order to reduce anxiety; however, in doing so they impede psychological development by using up psychological energy that would otherwise serve the developing maturational process of the personality. The purpose of the defence mechanisms is a developmental one and, as such, they exist early on and are used by the infantile ego to cope with demands and as a protective measure. Freud claimed that defence mechanisms continue after the infantile stage if the ego has not developed sufficiently and has remained dependent on the mechanisms. Further, the individual's environment can contribute towards the maintenance and dominance of the defence mechanisms. Should a child's experiences be overwhelming in relation to their capacity to cope, the ego can become overly reliant upon defence mechanisms, which in turn leads to the dominance of defence mechanisms over the ego.

Repression is one of the most widely known of the defence mechanisms and was of primary interest to Freud. In the beginning Freud coined the term 'repression' to describe unacceptable or painful mental content that was excluded from awareness. Freud contended that bringing these repressed memories to consciousness would cure the hysteria he was witnessing. Defence mechanisms act to repress painful memories from entering consciousness. However Freud modified his view of repression to that of infantile-operated drives rather than on memories of actual events. These drives and memories trapped in the unconscious strive for release and will occasionally be released in the form of a slip of the tongue, a 'Freudian slip'. An example of repression would be where an individual abused as a child develops amnesia of the event. Sublimation is a component of repression, consisting of a repressed impulse released through a desirable form. An individual with hostile impulses channels those impulses by becoming a prosecuting lawyer; this would be an example of sublimation. Freud is never clear as to whether repression is a fully unconscious act or if there is some degree of awareness on the part of the person.

Denial is another well-known defence mechanism. It involves the denial of an event or emotions associated with an event that is painful and generating high levels of anxiety. Whereas with repression the individual is rendered unaware of an event or of an internal or external stimulation, denial differs in that the person is aware but refuses to acknowledge the reality, in fact denies it in an attempt to avoid acknowledging the extent of the threat. An alcoholic when challenged that they have a drink problem will deny that to be the case. Freud and his supporters contend that denial through a refusal to acknowledge the reality of a situation is necessarily a bad thing as it impedes good mental health, and purport 'reality orientation' as essential to mental health. However, one has to question the validity of this in certain circumstances. Steiner (1966) reported that Jews held in the Treblinka concentration camp, who were witnessing death on an unimaginable scale, adopted a belief that death did not exist despite the obvious evidence to the contrary. Could these people really have coped with the reality of the situation they were in and the reality that they could be next? That is the purpose of the defence mechanism: to protect and enable the individual to cope. Is denial, even in circumstances less dramatic than the Treblinka example, truly a survival mechanism and should 'reality orientation' perhaps be attempted only with great care, for fear of doing more damage? Is the reality of some situations always conducive to mental health?

Projection is considered another primitive defence mechanism and occurs when an unacceptable impulse is repressed and turned or 'projected' outwards and attributed externally. Thus an individual with internal hostile impulses represses these and instead views others around them, external, as hostile. Projection is an inability to recognise hostility in oneself, instead attributing the characteristic to others. An old saying that 'a liar never believes anyone else' captures the essence of projection; an individual with a propensity to lie projects this onto others, thereby believing themselves to be honest and those around them to be liars.

Many interesting points have been raised in relation to Freud's defence mechanisms, mainly the question of whether these mechanisms are adaptive or maladaptive and of benefit to an individual's mental health. Freud believed that if the repressed thoughts and memories were brought to awareness, this would cure the mental illness afflicting the patient. This has not been supported (Brewin and Andrews, 2000, p.615); rather this process is seen as a step to recovery rather than a cure-all.

As one can see from Freud's theories, an emphasis is placed on explaining 'maladaptive behaviours'. In the following section on psychosexual theory we explore the concept of 'fixation', where an individual does not pass through the stage but instead becomes fixated at that point. Freud's psychosexual theory is arguably the most controversial of his theories; people tend to feel uncomfortable around the idea of children and sexuality, and indeed Erik Erikson distanced himself from this part of Freud's conceptualisation. It is important to remember that Freud is describing unconscious motivation here, not conscious.

Freud's psychosexual theory

Freud proposed a stage theory of development, suggesting that an individual must pass through one stage to reach the next stage of development. As we will see, Freud believed each stage could have a negative outcome and the individual could become 'fixated' or stuck at that stage.

Importantly, Freud, it could be argued, was one of the first lifespan developmentalists as he believed that early experiences could be responsible for behaviour or personality traits in later life. Freud stressed the importance of early experiences in determining the outcomes in later life for an individual.

The stages of psychosexual development

Freud described five stages we all pass through:

- oral (0–2 yrs)
- anal (2–3 yrs)
- phallic (3–6 yrs)
- latent (6–11 yrs)
- genital (11+ yrs).

Benson (2003, pp.53–5) takes us through the first three stages:

Oral stage:

The mouth is the prime source of pleasure, for survival: the baby instinctively sucks. Through oral satisfaction, the baby develops trust and an optimistic personality. Being stuck at this stage is described as 'oral fixation', e.g. if weaned too early, the personality may become pessimistic, aggressive and distrusting.

Anal stage:

The focus of pleasure shifts to the anus, helping the child become aware of its bowels and how to control them. By deciding itself, the child takes an important step of independence, developing confidence and a sense of when to 'give things up'. However, over-strictness about forcing a child to go to the toilet or about timing or cleanliness can cause personality problems.

Anal fixation – forcing a child to go may cause reluctance about giving away *anything*. The person may become a hoarder or miser. Conversely, over-concern about 'going regularly' may cause obsessive time-keeping or always being late.

Phallic stage:

Children become aware of their genitals and sexual differences. Consequently, development is different for boys and girls.

The Oedipus complex

Each boy unconsciously goes through a sequence of stages beginning with the development of a strong desire for his mother, noticing the bond between his parents (i.e. sleeping together), becoming jealous of his father and hating him, then becoming afraid of his father lest he discover his son's true feelings, which results in the final substage of fear of punishment – castration.

Latency stage

During this stage sexual urges remain repressed and children interact and play mostly with same-sex peers.

Genital stage

The final stage of psychosexual development begins at the start of puberty, when sexual urges are once again awakened. Adolescents direct their sexual urges onto opposite-sex peers, with the primary focus of pleasure in the genitals.

Criticisms of Freud's psychosexual theory

- Freud's theory is difficult to test and results from the few tests carried out have not been favourable.
- Some of the concepts Freud discusses are difficult to test as they cannot be observed.
- Freud's theory of 'penis envy' has been attacked by some feminists as sexist.
- Freud's observations were of adults; Freud did not conduct research of children in developing his theory of psychosexual development.

Albert Bandura (2001, p.19) suggests that psychoanalytic theory 'lacked predictive power and did not fare well in therapeutic effectiveness'.

It is very easy to criticise Freud in the current science-led culture; however, it is wrong to dismiss him out of hand. Many of us today are comfortable with the role of an unconscious in our conscious behaviour and motivations, and terms such as 'in denial' are in common usage. Freud has influenced the work of many, including Erikson and Bowlby. Freud still remains an important and influential figure within psychology today.

Erik Erikson (1902–1994)

Erik Erikson was born in Germany and became interested in psychology when he met Anna Freud, Sigmund Freud's daughter, who persuaded him to study child psychoanalysis in Vienna. While Erikson was influenced by Freud and accepted some of what he said, Erikson believed that Freud was incorrect in his proposition of psychosexual stages. Instead, Erikson proposed that individuals developed through *psychosocial* stages. Erikson moved to America and joined Harvard Medical School before moving on to Yale. Erikson's first book, *Childhood and Society*, reflected his interest in the role of society and culture on the development of the child. Erikson suggested that personality developed through the resolution of a series of eight major psychosocial stages occurring throughout an individual's life. Each stage involved a different 'crisis' or conflict between the 'self' (individual) and others, including the outside world, which could result in either a positive or a negative outcome. For example, in his first stage of 'Trust vs. Mistrust', if the infant is well cared for and its needs are met, it will develop trust (a positive outcome of this stage). However, if the infant is mistreated or abused, a negative outcome of 'mistrust' will result. Erikson was more positive than Freud as he believed that negative outcomes in a stage could be resolved at a later date.

Table 3.1: Erikson's eight psychosocial stages

Approximate age period	Stage	Psychosocial relationship
Birth to 1 year	**Trust vs. mistrust**	Trust in others and the world *or* suspicion and mistrust
1 to 2 years	**Autonomy vs. shame and doubt**	Sense of self-reliance *or* feelings of shame about own capability
3 to 5 years	**Initiative vs. guilt**	Ability to start activities *or* guilt about feelings
6 to 12 years	**Industry vs. inferiority**	Sense of confidence in ability to do things *or* feeling of inferiority based on reactions of others
12 to 20 years	**Identity vs. role confusion**	Sense of who you are *or* confusion as to who you are and role in life
20 to 40 years	**Intimacy vs. isolation**	Experience of love and formation of relationships *or* isolation, shallow relationships
40 to 65 years	**Generativity vs. stagnation**	Seeking to be productive *or* lack of growth and boredom
65 years onwards	**Integrity vs. despair**	Satisfaction with life *or* regret over missed opportunities

Erikson was one of the first theorists to see development in a lifespan context. His eight psychosocial stages are called 'The Eight Ages of Man' and cover the entire lifespan of the individual.

Trust vs. mistrust (0–1 year)
In the first year of life the infant is completely dependent on its caregivers. How well the infant's needs are met and how sensitive the parenting is will influence whether the infant develops trust or mistrust of the world.

Autonomy vs. shame and doubt (1–2 years)
Children begin to walk and assert their independence. As the term 'autonomy' suggests, children can come to believe in themselves and their abilities through the encouragement and support of their caregivers. If the child's efforts are ridiculed or belittled, the child will develop a feeling of shame and doubt in their abilities. Toilet training is seen as a key event which can influence the outcome of the stage.

Initiative vs. guilt (3–5 years)

As the child becomes older they exhibit increasing curiosity and interest, and they initiate play and question more. If this initiative is discouraged or they are held back, they will not develop self-initiative and instead will in turn hold back in later life.

Industry vs. inferiority (6–12 years)

During this time the child begins to attend school and interacts more with peers. If praised in their efforts, they develop a sense of industry and feel good about what they have achieved, which encourages the feeling that they can fulfil their goals. If they repeatedly fail or are not praised when they try, a sense of inferiority will develop.

Identity vs. role confusion (12–20 years)

This relates to the adolescent period of life when people are trying to establish their identity, their sense of who they are and their role in life. They are becoming more independent and their peers are increasingly important to them. If they can reconcile these issues, they will develop a feeling of identity; if not, role confusion will result.

Intimacy vs. isolation (20–40 years)

This period is marked by the desire to establish relationships with others. Successful completion leads to a sense of security and intimacy. Avoidance of intimacy or an inability to establish a secure relationship leads to feelings of isolation.

Generativity vs. stagnation (40–65 years)

During this period many people settle down in a relationship and begin having children. People also establish their careers. A sense of community and being part of a bigger picture become important. If a person does not achieve these objectives, the resulting feeling is one of stagnation.

Integrity vs. despair (65 years onwards)

In older age, people slow down and begin to reflect on their lives. If the individual feels they have had a successful life, a sense of integrity prevails. If the person believes their life to have been unproductive, a feeling of despair occurs.

Criticisms of psychosocial theory

According to Miller (2002, p.160), criticisms of Erikson's psychosocial theory include the following:

- Lack of systematicity – Erikson's theory is a loose connection of observations, empirical generalisations, and abstract theoretical claims. Consequently, it is difficult to state his claims in a way that can be tested or relate his empirical findings to the more abstract levels of the theory.
- Lack of specific mechanisms of development – Erikson did not explain in any detail how an individual moves from stage to stage or even how he resolves the crisis within a stage. He states what influences the movement (for example, physical maturation, parents, cultural beliefs, the extent to which earlier crises were resolved) but not specifically how the movement comes about. By what mechanisms does an infant learn to trust and when to mistrust?

Attachment theory

Attachment is a 'long-enduring, emotionally meaningful tie to a particular individual' (Schaffer, 1996). It is recognised as one of the most important concepts within psychology and as such has been heavily researched. Our ability to form secure and meaningful relationships not just to our parents or caregivers but also to others later in life is considered a touchstone for healthy and happy functioning. Difficulties in this realm can have immediate and long-term consequences for the individual. We will look at the following topics in relation to attachment theory:

1. Influences on attachment theory
   - ethology
   - psychoanalysis
2. John Bowlby and maternal deprivation
3. Mary Ainsworth and attachment classifications.

Development of attachment theory
Influences:

- ethology
- psychoanalysis.

Ethology
Ethology is the study of animal behaviour. Psychologists look to this area to gain insight into human behaviours.

- Imprinting: this term was coined by Konrad Lorenz and relates to the behaviour he observed in geese. When hatched they automatically 'attach' to the first moving object they encounter. Lorenz found that newly hatched geese attached to him even though he was not one of their species. Thus Lorenz believed that 'imprinting' was instinctual and could not be reversed.

- Harry Harlow's study of the effects of maternal deprivation on rhesus monkeys:

Harlow's monkey

This research involved removing newborn monkeys from their mothers and raising them in isolation without contact from others. The baby monkeys had access to two 'mothers' in their cage: one was made of wire mesh and had a bottle attached so the monkey could feed from it. The other was a 'cloth' figure covered in soft, tactile material but offered no opportunity for the monkey to feed. Harlow noted that when the baby monkeys were given the choice between a wire mesh figure with a feeding bottle or a figure covered in soft material, the monkeys chose to cling to the soft material rather than the other figure. Previously it was believed that the motivation for mammals to attach to a parent was for the purpose of feeding. However, Harlow's study indicated that monkeys sought 'comfort contact' and that social factors were as, if not more, important than feeding. Interestingly when the monkeys were re-introduced to the troupe they were frightened, exhibited anxious behaviours and had difficulty socialising with other monkeys. This suggested that their early experiences created difficulties for them later in their social relationships with others.

Psychoanalysis

- Mother–child relationship: Freud stressed the importance of the mother–child relationship. Further, many others working in psychoanalysis believed that early experiences could affect a person in later life.
- Object relations: A famous psychoanalyst, Melanie Klein, developed the 'object relations' approach which suggested that the 'loss' of an object could have a potentially negative effect (for example, to an infant an 'object' could be their mother; the loss of the mother perhaps through death or separation could in turn lead to negative outcomes for the child in later life).

John Bowlby

John Bowlby (1907–1990) originally devised the basic tenets of the theory of maternal deprivation. Bowlby was working in a home for children with behavioural problems. These children had disruptive relationships with their families and it struck Bowlby that these difficulties might hold the key to their emotional and behavioural disturbances. His time there prompted him to train as a child psychiatrist. Bowlby received training at the British Psychoanalytical Society (BPS). While there, Bowlby was supervised by a prominent psychoanalyst, Melanie Klein. Bowlby agreed with Klein's view that early experiences shaped an individual in later life. He also supported Klein's 'object relations' approach and the potentially negative effect of the loss of an 'object'. However, unlike Klein, Bowlby believed that *actual* family experiences were important and possibly the cause of emotional problems experienced by the children. Bowlby also came to believe that relationship problems between parent and child continued to be passed down through the generations; thus, in order to help the child, a practitioner should look at and help the parent. Bowlby was heavily influenced by the work of ethologists such as Konrad Lorenz and Harry Harlow (see above); this led Bowlby to believe that there was an instinctual aspect to the development of a bond between mother and child, and that there was a 'critical' period for its development. Further, Harlow's research suggested that feeding alone, or the satisfaction of hunger, was not necessarily the primary motivation for bonding, and that more social needs were at play. You will see how these beliefs came to shape Bowlby's attachment theory.

Bowlby's theory of maternal deprivation
Bowlby came to believe that if a child experienced a disruption in their relationship with their mother (through separation or death), this had a negative impact on the child. Bowlby believed that there was one fundamental attachment relationship and that was between mother and child; this is termed 'monotropism'. Further, he believed that a critical period existed between six months and three years where attachment must be maintained.

Criticisms of Bowlby
1. Monotropism – research indicates that infants form several important attachment relationships with figures other than their mother (such as father, grandparents and siblings).
2. Negative outcomes – Bowlby emphasised that if a child experienced difficulties in their attachment relationship, this could have disastrous outcomes in later life. Michael Rutter has rejected this bleak view. Rutter has pointed out that all children experience separation at some point (for example, going to school) and that we need to differentiate between different situations.
3. Feminists have attacked Bowlby's insistence that the mother must remain at home with the child to prevent the child's suffering in her absence. There have been suggestions that Bowlby's research coincided with the return home of male soldiers after World War II and the desire of the government to encourage

women to give up their jobs to the returning soldiers. By suggesting that children were being damaged by their mother's absence it was envisaged that women would not wish to work outside the home.

Mary Ainsworth

Mary Ainsworth joined Bowlby's research team when she came to Britain. Whereas Bowlby formulated ideas surrounding the nature of the attachment relationship, Ainsworth developed a way of testing the attachment relationship. Ainsworth conducted a huge number of 'naturalistic' observations in Uganda and in America, observing the behaviour of mothers and their infants. From these observations she developed a way of testing the quality of the attachment relationship through the 'strange situation'. In the 'strange situation' a mother and her child are placed in a room where their behaviour can be observed. The child should use the mother as a secure 'base' from which to explore. During the experiment, a 'stranger' will enter the room twice; once when the mother is present and a second time when the child has been left alone. The baby's reaction to the return of the mother is used to gauge what attachment pattern exists.

The reactions of the infants in this research formed the basis for the classification of attachment styles.

Attachment classifications

Type A – insecure/avoidant

Babies exhibited an avoidance of interactions with the mother on her return. The baby either completely ignores the mother or else displays avoidance behaviours such as turning away or avoiding eye contact. During separation the baby does not display distress or else the distress seems to be related to being left alone rather than the mother's absence.

Type B – secure

Babies classified as securely attached actively seek interaction and contact with the mother, especially during the reunion episode. If the baby shows distress during the separation episode, this is judged to be solely related to the absence of the mother.

Type C – ambivalent/resistant

These babies were extremely upset when the mother left. On reunion with the mother the baby seemed to want to be near her yet 'resisted' her efforts to comfort them. If the mother picked them up, they displayed a great deal of angry behaviours and tried to struggle free.

A fourth classification was added later:

Type D – disorganised

This category relates to babies who displayed 'disorganised' or disoriented patterns of behaviour that could not be classified under the other categories.

Behaviours that promote attachment

Bowlby believed 'parental sensitivity' was important for the development of attachment. Ainsworth *et al.* (1978, p.152) found that four scales were strongly linked to secure attachment:

- sensitivity
- acceptance
- co-operation
- accessibility.

Interestingly, De Wolff and Van Ijzendoorn (1997) found that 'playing' was an important factor in promoting attachment.

Just as certain behaviours can promote attachment, others can damage it or are more likely to elicit an insecure attachment pattern. Radke-Yarrow *et al.* (1985) examined patterns of attachment in two- and three-year-old children of depressed and 'normal' mothers. They found that the children of mothers with major depression were more likely to have an insecure attachment pattern (types A and C).

Internal working model

Bowlby believed that the child represents its relationship with its mother internally. It is thought that this model serves as a sort of template for future relationships. According to Smith *et al.* (2003), internal working models are 'described as cognitive structures embodying the memories of day-to-day interactions with the attachment figure. They may be "schemas" or "event scripts" that guide the child's interactions and the expectations and affective experiences associated with them' (p.98).

COGNITIVE THEORISTS

Cognitive development refers to the changes that occur in thinking, memory, problem solving and other cognitive mental abilities. One of the most famous and important theorists in the field of cognitive development is Jean Piaget and his work is still influential in areas of psychology, education and child development.

Jean Piaget (1896–1980)

Jean Piaget developed a four-stage theory to explain how young children acquire knowledge, based on a mass of empirical work.

Early years

Jean Piaget was born in Switzerland in 1896. After completing his Ph.D. he developed an interest in psychoanalysis and travelled to France to work in a boys' institution which had been founded by Alfred Binet. Binet is best known for his work in developing intelligence tests and Piaget worked on standardising these tests. It was through this work that Piaget came to the conclusion that young children think differently to adults. He noticed that many of the children were giving the same 'wrong' answer. Piaget began to understand that the children handle information differently to adults; as the child became older, their thinking continued to develop and change.

This work and these observations prompted him to develop a theory of cognitive development. Piaget's theory is a 'stage theory', meaning that the individual must pass through one stage before they can progress to the next. Piaget suggested that children pass through four stages of cognitive development spanning the period from infancy to adolescence. Interestingly Piaget was a forerunner of 'naturalistic observation'. This approach to collecting data relies on observing individuals in their natural environment, rather than in a laboratory. Piaget and his wife, Valentine, observed their three children from infancy and kept detailed journals noting their intellectual development.

Piaget can be daunting to understand, especially his terminology, but don't let that discourage you. Piaget tries to outline how he believes children organise the information that they receive in their daily lives. It is helpful to understand how Piaget believed learning occurs. Piaget used the term 'schemas' to describe 'internal frameworks' that the mind builds as it comes in contact with more and more information. (A schema is an internal framework that organises incoming information, thought and action.) The mind builds these structures to hold and make sense of incoming information. As the infant gathers more and more information, the schemas become more sophisticated.

Piaget believed that in order for learning to occur, the child must experience a sense of 'disequilibration'. This is when an experience occurs that does not fit their existing thinking: the child becomes dissatisfied with their original thinking and must adapt in order to process the new piece of information. This adaptation can be done in two ways: through assimilation or accommodation.

Assimilation is when the child fits incoming information or experience into an existing schema. For example, a young child who sees a fox for the first time might call it a 'doggie'. Here the child is trying to make sense of this new experience by applying an existing 'doggie' schema to the fox, which has four legs and a tail. This make sense as a dog also has four legs and a tail. Yet as we get older we come to understand that a fox and a dog are not the same and this might cause us to change our schema. This process is called **accommodation**. Accommodation is when an existing schema changes to incorporate new experiences.

Table 3.2: Piaget's theory of cognitive development

Age	Stage	Characteristics
0–2 years	Sensori-motor	The baby acquires knowledge about the world through movement and sensory information. The baby: • learns to differentiate itself from its environment • develops first schemas • achieves object permanence • experiences the emergence of symbolic thought • develops the capacity to form internal mental representations.
2–7 years	Pre-operational	Symbolic thinking emerges as the child uses symbols/images to represent objects and solve problems. The child: • begins to understand classification of objects • is egocentric • focuses on just one aspect of a task • believes inanimate objects have consciousness (animism) • engages in pretend play.
7–11 years	Concrete operational	The child understands concepts of mass, length, weight and volume. The child: • becomes less egocentric, taking more easily the perspectives of others (decentring) • may exhibit reversibility • can classify and order, as well as organise objects into series • is still tied to the immediate experience but within these limitations can perform logical mental operations.
12 years onwards	Formal operational	Abstract thinking marks this period as the individual is now able to manipulate ideas in their head. Inductive and deductive reasoning emerges, enabling the formulation and testing of hypotheses.

Adapted from Cowie *et al.*, 2003, p.336.

Sensori-motor stage (0–2 years)

'Sensori' represents the senses or sensation, such as taste, touch, smell, vision and hearing. 'Motor' is another term for movement. Thus the title gives us a clue as to how learning is accumulated during this period: through the senses and movement. During the sensori-motor period the child begins to know about the world they live in by acting directly upon it, through actions and sensory information.

Have you ever noticed how young babies are forever putting things in their mouth? This is because they are using their senses to explore the new world they inhabit. Also, as infants begin to crawl they usually head straight for the kitchen presses, much to the consternation of parents; again this reflects the child's attempts to use their new-found motor ability to explore their environment. The infant is hungry for new experiences and information that will form the basis of their developing schemas. By the end of this stage, infants will have acquired 'object permanence'. This is a very important concept and represents the understanding that objects continue to exist even when we can no longer see them. A simple test for object permanence is to allow the child to see a toy and then throw a blanket over it. If the child seeks the toy out it is an indication that they understand that the toy continues to exist even when they cannot see it. This ability comes towards the end of this stage. However, as you will see below, recent research has been critical of Piaget's assertion of the stage at which object permanence and, more particularly, mental representation occur. It is now claimed that these are acquired at an earlier age than Piaget suggested.

During the sensori-motor stage infants begins to differentiate themselves from the environment. Piaget divided the sensori-motor stage into six substages as follows:

1. Reflex activity occurs during the infant's first month of life and involves the practice of innate reflexes.
2. Primary circular reactions are typical of the following stage. 'Primary' refers to reflexes and motor responses, while 'circular' reflects the repeated aspect of the behaviour. At this period the infant still cannot differentiate itself from its environment. This changes with the onset of the third stage.
3. Secondary circular reactions: in this stage the infant 'is not limited to just repeating actions based on early reflexes, but having initiated new actions can repeat them if they are satisfying' (Smith et al., 2003, p.394). The infant begins to know that it is separate from its environment and experiments with this knowledge by attempting to manipulate its environment.
4/5. The fourth and fifth stages, co-ordination of secondary circular reactions (10–12 months) and tertiary circular reactions (12–18 months) signify the infant's growing abilities in problem solving. In the fourth stage the infant constructs goals to be accomplished and combines schemas towards this end. In the fifth stage the infant's problem-solving becomes more sophisticated through the process of trial and error.
6. Up to this point Piaget suggests that the infant has manipulated its environment directly in order to learn and to achieve goals; however, in the sixth stage, referred to as internal representation, mental representation has been achieved and the child is now able to represent the external world through symbols and ideas and manipulate these ideas as opposed to acting on the world directly.

Preoperational stage (2–7 years)

One of the most notable features of this stage is that the child is egocentric. Breaking the word up gives a clue as to its meaning: 'ego' can mean 'self' and 'centric' refers to the centre of things. So 'egocentric' seems to mean self-centred. However, when used in this context, we are referring to the fact that the child thinks that everyone else sees the world through the child's eyes and does not understand that other people might see or think about things differently, and this is reflected in the child's thinking.

Symbolic thinking develops as the child begins to acquire language (which is, of course, made up of symbols). The child can use this newly developed ability to enhance their thinking. The child can now use words and images (symbols) to represent objects; for example, when a toddler sees a dog they might exclaim 'woof woof'. The child uses that sound to represent a dog.

Pretend play is also enabled by symbolic thinking; for example, a stick is transformed into a sword. An interesting aspect of this stage is animism. For example, a parent may admonish a 'bold' table that a young child has just painfully collided with: children at this age ascribe consciousness to inanimate objects.

Concrete operational stage (7–11 years)

This is the third stage described in Piaget's theory of cognitive development. The main features of this stage are:

- conservation: the understanding that quantity, volume and length remain the same
- reversibility: the understanding that numbers or objects can be altered and then returned to their original state
- decentring: children become less egocentric.

Children learn through their interaction with concrete or 'real' objects. Further, a child can apply the learning strategies they have developed to real and immediate situations. However, the process of 'decentring', where the child becomes less egocentric, enables them to become more flexible in their thinking as they are now able to factor in other ways of looking or thinking about a situation. Another ability a child develops during this stage is to understand reversibility. This concept is best explained with an example: you have a ball of dough and you roll it into a long, cylindrical, snake-like object. Can you return it to its original state, and would it still be the same? Of course it would; we know this because we have embraced the concept of reversibility, which is the understanding that we can alter an object and then reverse the process returning the object to its original state. Reversibility is necessary for the acquisition of the next concept, conservation.

Ever had to deal with warring children complaining that one is getting more juice than another? You try to explain to them that even though the juice is in differently shaped glasses they still have the exact same amount of liquid in each, though it might not look like it. If they don't believe you, it is probably because they have not yet understood the concept of conservation. As adults we can factor in the shape and size of the glass and understand that the amount of liquid is the same in both glasses. During the concrete operational stage children begin to acquire this ability and apply it to number and weight as well as volume, as shown below. Piaget believed that the acquisition of conservation was an important developmental milestone.

Piaget's conservation studies

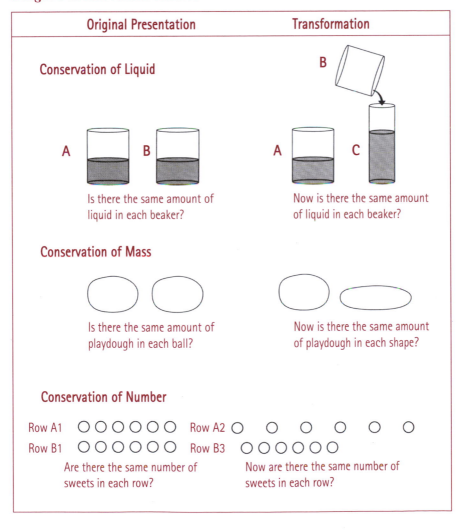

According to Smith *et al.* (2003), conservation is achieved at the following ages:
- Conservation of number: about five to six years of age
- Conservation of weight: seven or eight years of age
- Conservation of volume: between ten and eleven years of age.

Formal operational (12 years onwards)

This final stage is marked by the acquisition of abstract thinking as the individual is now able to manipulate ideas in their head. Up to this stage the child can only think about things that are 'real' or concrete. According to Piaget, they are unable to reason about make-believe problems or situations. They can now begin to think more logically and can consider hypotheses or explanations. Inductive and deductive reasoning emerge during this stage, enabling further formulation and testing of hypotheses.

Mental representation and criticism of Piaget's theory

Mental representations are cognitive representations of the world and include images, concepts and ideas. They form the basis for problem solving and thinking. Piaget believed that infants did not acquire mental representation until the end of the first stage of development, the sensori-motor period, which occurred between 12 and 18 months. Piaget proposed that evidence of object permanence, trial and error performance and deferred imitation confirmed that mental representation had been achieved. Object permanence relates to younger children's inability to recognise that an object still exists even when they can no longer see it. Piaget saw this as evidence that children did not have mental representation of the object. He conducted research where he would hide an object under a cloth: if the child had formed an internal representation of the object, then the child would recover the object. Piaget asserted that it was not until the final substage when the infant recognised that the object still existed, though out of sight, and recovered it, that mental representation had been achieved as the infant must have retained a memory and concept of the object.

Recent research has been critical of Piaget's account of mental representation, in particular the timing of it. Piaget posits that mental representation does not occur until the end of the sensori-motor stage, but recent research seems to suggest that Piaget underestimated the ability, and thus the age, that infants can acquire mental representation. His theory suggests that the infant goes from not having mental representation to acquiring it in a step-to-step process which does not occur in earlier substages. A stronger hypothesis is that the acquisition of mental representation is a gradual and consistent acquisition from birth. Research suggests that younger infants have demonstrated representation; researchers have proposed that babies of six weeks old have limited mental representation (Meltzoff, 1988). This adds strength to a theory that views the acquisition of mental representation as a gradual and cumulative process resulting in total achievement. Piaget observed the infant's reaching for an object in his empirical work as evidence of mental representation, but this reaching involved motor skills which may have been absent or immature in the younger infants, possibly explaining the apparent absence of mental representation. Piaget also did not devote much attention to the role of social learning or that an infant's acquisition of knowledge and abilities could be increased by external factors. Piaget's biological background is reflected in his findings and the rigid developmental stages he proposed. Neither did he have the more sophisticated tools of analysis and testing that we have now, such as the ability to track eye movements and physiological changes to unravel the mysteries of knowledge acquisition. Nonetheless, Piaget's theory endures as it does present a strong overall base and view of the development of children's thinking, though as with all theories it is subject to modification in light of new findings.

Criticisms of Piaget

In addition to criticism of Piaget's underestimation of children's abilities, Miller (2002, p.77) elaborates further criticisms of his theory:

- Inadequate support for the stage notion – the strongest attacks on Piaget's theory concern his notion of stages, the heart of the theory. Are there, in fact, broad stretches during the development that have characteristics that apply to all the psychological events during the period? Or does the notion of stages simply confuse and mislead by oversimplifying development and claiming more coherence among concepts than there actually is? A basic issue here is how stages are related to the child's actual intellectual functioning.
- Slighting of social and emotional aspects of development – despite the importance that Piaget assigned to the social and emotional realms, he paid relatively little attention to them in his theoretical or research activities. Moreover, he underestimated the role of sociohistorical influences. It has been said that Piaget's epistemic subject has no social class, sex, nationality, culture or personality.

Lev Vygotsky (1896–1934)

'Through others we become ourselves' (Vygotsky, 1978). This quote captures the essence of Vygotsky's conceptualisation of human development. Miller (2002, p.368) adds, 'in the Vygotskian-socio-cultural view, humans are embedded in a socio-cultural matrix and human behavior cannot be understood independently of this ever present matrix.' This approach emphasises the importance of the role of culture in the cognitive development of children.

Socio-cultural theory

Vygotsky was born in Russia in the same year as Piaget, yet it is only in recent years that his writings have come to the attention of the West. Vygotsky died at a young age and in the years preceding his death he had been under pressure from the government to modify his beliefs and teaching in line with the current orthodoxy. After his death his theories and ideas were repudiated by the Russian government and it is only for his students who kept his work alive that we, in the West, have come to know his work.

Vygotsky was a cognitive theorist, yet he is sometimes described as a socio-cultural theorist. This is because Vygotsky emphasised the role of others in the development of learning. Unlike Piaget, Vygotsky believed that social interactions were of particular influence in the learning of a child, as was their wider society, and it is this emphasis that has led to his being described as a socio-cultural theorist.

According to Fox and Riconscente (2008, p.383):

> Vygotsky views human psychological development as historically situated and culturally determined. As human beings we are born already immersed in an evolved society that uses conventional tools and signs. Development proceeds through the internalization of social interactions, with the fundamental social interaction being interaction through language. This internalization promotes increasing abstraction, which moves to the level of conscious abstractions or scientific concepts during the social institution of school instruction, in which culturally developed bodies of systematized knowledge are introduced. Metacognition and self-regulation, the awareness, knowledge, and control of thoughts and behavior, move along this same developmental path, in which change proceeds via qualitative transformations toward mature reflective awareness and deliberate control. This reflective awareness and deliberate control are exactly the internalization of language-based social interactions with others. The activity of language use is for Vygotsky essentially what it means for thought to be conscious, capable of self-direction, and capable of knowing itself in a systematic way.

Main points of Vygotsky's theory

- children learn from others (including other children)
- play is importance in the development of learning
- language plays a central role in mental development
- language and development build on each other
- development cannot be separated from its social context.

Importance of play

Like Piaget, Vygotsky emphasised the importance of play. Piaget emphasised the child as a solitary learner, in that when children play they discover new ideas for themselves. Vygotsky, on the other hand, believed that children learn through their interactions with others, who introduce them to new concepts and ideas.

Zone of proximal development

The zone of proximal development is '... the distance between the actual developmental level as determined by independent problem solving and the level of potential development as determined through problem solving under adult guidance or in collaboration with more capable peers' (Vygotsky, 1978, p.86).

The zone of proximal development represents the distance between what the child can actually achieve on their own and what they could achieve with the intervention or help of another. Vygotsky was interested in the role others could play as a 'scaffold', building a bridge to help the child reach their full potential development. For example, as an adult I started going to Irish classes as I was not as fluent in Irish as I wished to be. My tutor ('other') observed the level of Irish I did have and recognised what I could achieve with her help and so she devised a learning plan to enable me to reach my potential. The trick for the tutor was to make sure that it was challenging enough while ensuring it was not so far out of my capability that I could not do it, even with her help. As we've seen, Vygotsky felt that it was through interaction with others (teachers or peers) that children learn. This applies to an adult trying to brush up on their Irish as much as to a young child learning to tie their shoelaces.

Relationship between language and thought

Vygotsky believed that language represents an opportunity for social interaction and learning. Further, this shared experience that language brings is necessary for the development of cognitive ability. When children begin to talk, it opens a window into their minds and we can begin to understand their thought processes.

Cultural context

It is through the child's interaction with others that they learn the culture they are part of, including language and belief systems. Vygotsky's rejection of Freud is described because of the latter's continued embrace of physiological and universal explanations of behaviour instead of the cultural one that Vygotsky believed to be the best way of explaining behaviour. He also rejected the Piagetian approach that assumed social relations to be secondary to the child's biological nature. Vygotsky, on the other hand, viewed speech to be initially social, with egocentric speech developing after social speech. The strength of Vygotsky's conceptualisations lies in his emphasis on the socio-cutural context of development. Miller highlights the uniqueness, from a developmental perspective, of Vygotsky's weaving together insights from history, linguistics, art and literature into psychology. She (2002, p.409) outlines the following weaknesses of Vygotsky's socio-cultural theory:

- Vagueness of the notion of the zone of proximal development – knowing the width of children's zones does not provide an accurate picture of their learning ability, learning style or current level of development compared to other children of the same age, and degree of motivation.

- Difficulties of studying cultural-historical contexts – nearly all developmental psychologists would agree that it is important to examine the social, cultural, and historical contexts of development. ... The links between broad social-historical contexts and specific parent-child interactions, in particular, need to be worked out better.

This brings us to the end of the section on developmental theorists. Hopefully you have recognised the range and depth of knowledge that these theorists have attempted to explain. The common thread of these theorists is their emphasis on describing change over time. In the next section we explore behaviourism and learning. Unlike the developmentalists, behaviourists focus on behaviour and the underlying mechanisms for it.

BEHAVIOURISM AND LEARNING

What is learning? 'Learning is a process by which experience produces a relatively enduring change in an organism's behaviour or capabilities' (Passer, 2001, p.192).

Behaviourism is sometimes seen as the counterpoint to the psychoanalytic or Freudian approach. As the name suggests, behaviourism is interested in the science of behaviour, while Freud and his followers believed that human behaviour was the result of unconscious urges and drives of the unconscious. Behaviourists rejected this viewpoint, taking instead a far more pragmatic stance, positing that behaviour was observable and therefore measureable. Further, the motivation behind these behaviours could be explained and shaped without delving into the 'unconscious'.

The definition reflects an underlying precept of learning: the concept of adaptation. Ethologists (see Lorenz, p.44), when studying animal behaviour, consider not only how the behaviour increases the chance of survival but also how the environment shapes and influences behaviour.

Changes in our behaviour, feeling or emotions allow us to:

- use past experience to predict the future
- adapt to a rapidly changing environment.

As can be seen in the earlier section on 'attachment', this idea that the environment influences an individual's learning and behaviour holds critical importance to the area of social care. If we can understand how an individual learns behaviours, both positive and maladaptive, then potentially we have an opportunity to mould and support more 'adaptive' or 'positive' behaviours and also to eradicate or lessen maladaptive ones.

Founders of behaviourism

John B. Watson

Watson (1878–1958) is considered one of the founders of the behaviourist movement and is best known for his work on the acquisition of fear. Watson challenged the Freudian position that mental illness and phobias were the result of unconscious forces at work within the individual. Historically, psychology had been tied to the discipline of philosophy. Part of this approach included the use of 'introspection', of which Watson was critical, as emotions, feelings and the unconscious are not observable and therefore not measurable in any way. Watson favoured a more scientific approach to gain insight into the human condition. Initially he conducted experiments with animals, but he soon began working with humans. One of his best known experiments was his demonstration that conditioned emotional responses could be created.

'Little Albert' experiment

The experiment conducted by John B. Watson and Rosalie Raynor (1920) was premised on the idea that they could instil a fear (conditioned emotional response) of a stimulus in an organism (Little Albert). In the experiment, Albert, who was about nine months old, was first introduced to various items, including a white rat. Albert showed no fear of these items. At a later stage the researchers emitted a loud noise. Albert reacted by crying and was distressed. The researchers introduced the white rat to Albert who previously had shown no ill reaction to it, and as the child reached for the white rat the experimenters emitted the loud noise that had previously caused Albert to startle and cry. Albert reacted similarly again to the noise. This is the essence of the experiment; the twinning of the loud noise with a neutral stimulus (the white rat). Albert produced a fear response when the white rat was introduced to him, confirming that an emotional response can be conditioned. Further, when similar items to the white rat, such as a rabbit and the mask featured in the image above, were introduced to Albert, these items also provoked a fear response. This suggested that the fear response had been transferred or generalised to other stimuli that were similar to the initial stimulus that had conditioned the fear response. Watson and Raynor (1920, p.14), rejecting the Freudian explanation for phobic behaviour, suggest that, 'It is probable that many of the phobias in psychopathology are true conditioned emotional reactions either of the direct or the transferred type. … Emotional disturbances in adults cannot be traced back to sex alone. They must be retraced along at least three collateral lines – to conditioned and transferred responses set up in infancy and early youth.'

Edward Thorndike

Thorndike was another important and influential figure in the behaviourist movement. Thorndike's work with animal behaviour and the learning process led him to believe that behavioural responses to particular stimuli are established through a process of 'trial and error' rather than insight. As the animals did not 'learn' quickly but took many attempts, that is, by 'trial and error', Thorndike did not believe their actions to reflect 'insight' but rather a learned behaviour. Of course, this suggestion was not just a challenge to the Freudian perspective but also to a more cognitive explanation for actions and behaviour. In his experiments, the animal eliminated responses that had failed to open a door and increasingly became more likely to perform actions that worked. This process is known as 'instrumental learning' as the behaviour of the organism is 'instrumental' in causing particular outcomes.

Thorndike's 'law of effect' states 'that in a given situation, a response followed by a satisfying consequence will become more likely to occur and a response followed by an annoying consequence will become less likely to occur' (Passer, pp.202–3). Fundamentally, Thorndike's work suggests that behaviour is a function of its consequences.

Nevin (1999) comments that the stimulus–response (S–R) bond postulated by Thorndike's (1911) law of effect is not required in a functional account of behaviour in relation to its consequences. Moreover, the notion of a bond has been challenged by the findings of several experiments. Thorndike's law of effect links the selective effects of reinforcement to the strengthening of an S–R bond. Subsequent analyses suggest that these processes are separable, not that Thorndike was wrong to invoke the S–R bond as a way to capture what happens during learning. Nevin concedes that the strength of the bond is dependent on the level of satisfaction experienced, and this has been supported by recent research especially with respect to resistance to change.

The 'law of effect' was to prove influential in the development of Skinner's theory of operant conditioning.

Ivan Pavlov and classical conditioning

Pavlov's discovery of the principle of classical conditioning was, as is often the case, an accident. Pavlov had been studying digestion in dogs when he noticed that the dogs began to salivate upon hearing the footsteps of the researcher who was bringing their food. This observation set Pavlov on a new path of exploration. Pavlov was to demonstrate learning by association which has come to be popularly known as classical or 'Pavlovian' conditioning. Further this learning process contains an important adaptive function; it alerts the organism to stimuli that signal the impending arrival of an important event (Passer and Smith, 2001, p.196).

What is the relevance of his work for social care? Pavlov believed that if something like salivation could be conditioned then it might also be possible to apply the process to bodily processes that affect illness and mental disorders. Nowadays the principles of classical conditioning are applied in the treatment of phobias and in aversion therapies as discussed below.

Before, during and after conditioning

Before Conditioning

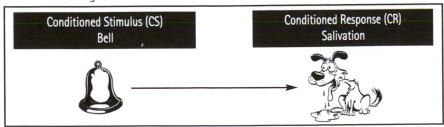

During Conditioning

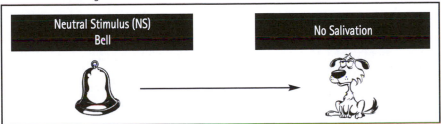

After Conditioning

The above diagram outlines the main aspect of Pavlov's theory.

In Pavlov's experiment, before conditioning, a neutral stimulus (the sound of the bell) provokes no response from the dog.

During conditioning, the neutral stimulus is twinned with a stimulus (food) that naturally causes a response, referred to as an 'unconditioned stimulus' (UCS). In response to the presence of the UCS (food, in this case), the animal salivates, which is a natural response to the food; this response is called an 'unconditioned response' (UCR). However, the aim of the experiment is for the dog to learn to associate the neutral stimulus (bell) with that of the food (UCS). If the experiment is successful, the dog, on hearing the now conditioned stimulus of the sound of the bell (CS), will respond by salivating (CR) even though there is no food (UCS) present.

This research demonstrated that response could be conditioned, even to neutral stimuli. The process during which the response is learned is referred to as 'acquisition'. More particularly, it relates to the repeated twinning of the conditioned stimulus (CS) with an unconditioned stimulus (UCS) in order to establish a strong conditioned response (CR). This emphasises that, generally speaking, there needs to be a repeated pairing of CS–UCS in order to elicit a strong response. However, Passer (Passer and Smith, 2001, p.196) comments that 'when a UCS is intense and/or traumatic, event conditioning may only require one CS–UCS pairing'. An example of a possible traumatic event can range from witnessing a car accident to being involved in one. Often people who are involved in serious car accidents find it difficult to be near cars; this is a conditioned response (CR) based on the pairing of the car (CS) with the accident (UCS). My mother, after a serious car accident, took nearly a year before she was able to overcome her fear and sit in the driver's seat again. This shows that once a conditioned response is initiated it can continue to persist for quite a period. This helps to explain the development of phobic behaviour.

Extinction and spontaneous recovery

A conditioned response eventually disappears if the conditioned stimulus is repeated without reinforcement. The decline of the response during repeated stimulation was referred to as 'extinction' by Pavlov.

Generalisation and discrimination: stimulus control studies

When the conditioned response (CR) transfers spontaneously from the initial conditioned stimuli (CS) to one which is similar yet different from it, this is referred to as 'generalisation'. Using an earlier example, if my mother after her accident involving a car (CS) had also developed a fear (CR) of buses or motorbikes, this would have represented a transfer from the original stimuli of the car to stimuli (buses and motorbikes) similar yet different from the CS.

Discrimination is the opposite of generalisation and happens when a conditioned response does not occur when there is a difference between the presented stimulus and the original conditioned stimulus. Using the example of Pavlov's dogs, if the dog heard a bell with a different tone and did not receive the unconditioned stimulus (food), the dog would eventually learn not to salivate to the second tone.

In his article, Windholz (1990) discusses how Pavlov believed he had found the root of neuroses during his experiments with animals. Pavlov was aware of Freud's well-documented case of Anna O., a woman suffering from neuroses. Pavlov believed that neurotic behaviour could be generated in laboratory settings and was not dependent on the unconscious machinations proposed by Freud and his followers. While experimenting with dogs, it was noted that the animals' behaviour became disorganised when discrimination became difficult. This became known as 'experimental neurosis'. Pavlov drew an analogy between the neurotic behaviour of the dogs and that of Anna O., concluding that he had demonstrated elements of neurosis in animals and humans alike within a laboratory setting.

Skinner and operant conditioning

'Operant conditioning is a type of learning in which behaviour is influenced by the consequences that follow it' (Skinner, 1938, p.14). Skinner's theory of operant conditioning was strongly influenced by Thorndike's law of effect, which states that behaviour is a function of its consequences. Operant behaviour means that an organism literally 'operates' on its environment in some way; it emits responses that produce certain consequences. Skinner believed that behaviour is shaped by its consequences and that those consequences can be positive or negative. A behaviour followed by a rewarding or favourable response is more likely to be repeated. Conversely an unfavourable or punishing response to a behaviour decreases the odds that the behaviour will be replicated. This process is a type of 'natural selection' that facilitates an organism's personal adaptation. Whereas classical conditioning associates two stimuli, operant conditioning instead associates a stimulus and a response. In experiments, the rate at which the rat pressed the lever depended not on any preceding stimuli (as with Watson and Pavlov) but on what followed the pressing of the lever. In contrast to Pavlov who had studied reflexes, the behaviour Skinner was observing was that operation on the environment was determined by its effects.

Skinner explains the Skinner box

In operant conditioning behaviour is also affected by its consequences, but the process is not trial-and-error learning. It can best be explained with an example: a hungry rat is placed in a semi-soundproof box. For several days pieces of food are occasionally delivered into a tray by an automatic dispenser. The rat soon goes to the tray immediately upon hearing the sound of the dispenser. A small horizontal section of a lever protruding from the wall has been resting in its lowest position, but it is now raised slightly so that when the rat touches it, it moves downward. In doing so it closes an electric circuit and operates the food dispenser. Immediately after eating the delivered food the rat begins to press the lever fairly rapidly. The behaviour has been strengthened or reinforced by a single consequence. The rat was not 'trying' to do anything when it first touched the lever and it did not learn from 'errors'.

A rat in a Skinner box

To a hungry rat, food is a natural reinforcer, but the reinforcer in this example is the sound of the food dispenser, which was conditioned as a reinforcer when it was repeatedly followed by the delivery of food before the lever was pressed. In fact, the sound of that one operation of the dispenser would have had an observable effect even though no food was delivered on that occasion, but when food no longer follows pressing the lever, the rat eventually stops pressing. The behaviour is said to have been extinguished. An operant can come under the control of a stimulus. If pressing the lever is reinforced when a light is on but not when it is off, responses continue to be made in the light but seldom, if at all, in the dark. The rat has formed a discrimination between light and dark. When one turns on the light, a response occurs, but that is not a reflex response. The lever can be pressed with different amounts of force, and if only strong responses are reinforced, the rat presses more and more forcefully. If only weak responses are reinforced, it eventually responds only very weakly. The process is called differentiation.

For more information: www.bfskinner.org.

Positive and negative reinforcement

As stated, reinforcers strengthen behaviour and can be positive or negative. A positive reinforcer reinforces when it is presented; a negative reinforcer reinforces when it is withdrawn. Negative reinforcement is not punishment. Reinforcers always strengthen behaviour; that is what 'reinforced' means. Punishment is used to suppress behaviour. It consists of removing a positive reinforcer or presenting a negative one. The punished person henceforth acts in ways which reduce the threat of punishment and which are incompatible with, and hence take the place of, the behaviour punished.

> ### The ABC of operant conditioning
> **Antecedents** (the stimulus conditions, such as the lever, the click of the food dispenser, a light that may go on when the lever is pressed)
> **Behaviours** (or operants, such as pressing the lever)
> **Consequences** (what happens as a result of the operant behaviour – reinforcement or punishment)
>
> *Source:* Gross, 2009, p.176

The main principles of operant conditioning are:

- reinforcement
- punishment
- extinction
- discrimination.

The application of behaviourism to improve the human condition

Skinner always wished the experimental work with animal behaviour to be translated into and applied to human affairs. Buskist reports that throughout his career and writings Skinner emphasised the importance and need for 'a thorough-going functional analysis of human behavior and human culture'. According to Skinner (Buskist, p.137): 'By turning from man qua man to external conditions of which man's behavior is a function, it has been possible to design better practices in the care of psychotics and retardates, in child care, in education (in both contingency management in the classroom and the design of instructional material), in incentive systems in industry, and in penal institutions.' Buskist points to the development of applied behaviour analysis as evidence of the call to arms and the successful application of behavioural technology to the analysis and modification of human behaviour.

From social learning to social cognitive theory

Bandura's theory represents the bridge between radical behaviourism and an attempt to ground it within a social context. Bandura (2006, p.55) felt it too narrow and prescriptive to ignore the role of social modelling. He states, 'I found this behavioristic theorizing discordant with the obvious social reality that much of what we learn is through the power of social modeling. I could not imagine a culture in which its language; mores; familial customs and practices; occupational competencies; and educational, religious, and political practices were gradually shaped in each new member by rewarding and punishing consequences of their trial-and-error performances.' This belief in the power of social learning was upheld in his study of hyper-aggressive boys living in advantaged areas considered not conducive to anti-social conduct. Bandura and his colleagues found that parental modelling of aggressive behaviours played a significant role in the familial transmission of aggression. This study led Bandura to attempt to study modelling through learning and social influence experimentally. Bandura was particularly interested in the role of violence on television in social learning. Bandura identified four major effects of exposure to televised violence. It can:

- teach novel aggressive styles of conduct
- weaken restraints over interpersonal aggression by legitimising, glamorising, and trivialising violent conduct
- desensitise and habituate viewers to human cruelty
- shape public images of reality.

The bobo doll experiment

The bobo doll laboratory experiments were conceived as part of his exploration into aggression. They were designed to clarify the processes governing observational learning. (See Chapter 9 for an account of this experiment.)

Drewes (2008, p.55) relates that Bandura considered aggressive behaviour, like other forms of social behaviour, to be under stimulus, reinforcement and cognitive control and that children learn what behaviours are appropriate and rewarding. Should they learn that aggressive behaviours are rewarding, they are then more likely to choose aggressive actions in response to conflict situations. (The relationship between learning and aggression is considered in greater depth in Chapter 9.)

Applied behavioural analysis is the application of behavioural principles to behaviours of social significance and is used as an approach in behaviour modification within the health and the social science arenas, particularly with autism. Behaviourism and its rigid and narrow approach to understanding behaviour is less popular within modern psychology as it ignores the complexity of the human condition. Learning and especially social learning, however, offer an interesting insight into the role and significance of 'other' in the behaviour of individuals.

Having examined behaviourism and learning, we will now look at the theories of humanism, which stand quite diametrically opposed to the theories of Freud and behaviourism.

HUMANISM

'The view that science is the only reliable path to knowledge is a naïve philosophical assumption which often goes unexamined. The makers of "normal science" are not the great discoverers who dared to take chances, but the majority of "normal scientists" who overstress caution and the art of not making mistakes. Science need not confine itself to a reductionist, atomistic view of the world in which man is dehumanized. Many nonscientists fear science for they see it as belittling the things they consider beautiful and valuable' (Maslow, 1965, p.219).

Maslow's quote is an apt introduction to the field of humanism that developed within psychology. While behaviourism rejected the introspective, untestable nature of the psychoanalytic Freudian tradition, humanism rejected what it saw as the reductionist approach to the understanding of human nature; an approach that humanism felt inherently debased the goodness and innate potential of the individual. Whereas both behaviourism and the psychoanalytic approach were deterministic, humanism proposed the idea of free will and an individual's choice in their actions.

Abraham Maslow and Carl Rogers were to epitomise this viewpoint and are influential figures in the field of humanistic psychology. Both men were interested in the concept of self-actualisation which, put at its most fundamental, equates with supreme self-expression. Though both are humanistic in their perspective, the direction and application of their work are seen in different fields: Maslow is often found in the field of motivation and Rogers is best known for his work within psychotherapy and its development.

What is humanism?

Maslow's quote captures the essence of the humanistic perspective on the development and nature of man. Humanism took a more positive viewpoint of human nature, grounded somewhat in the Renaissance tradition which celebrated the greatness and beauty of humankind. From the perspective of the history of Western thought, Davidson (2000, p.1) places humanism as a philosophy 'based on the belief that the human is irreducible to other forms of life, whether material or Divine. To the extent that humanistic psychology has its roots in the humanist tradition, it shares this conviction that the human cannot be understood except in its own terms.'

Humanism proposed that an individual's ultimate goal was towards growth and potential, that this in fact was humankind's instinct and that obstacles (personal and structural) blocked individuals from reaching their true potential. Maslow referred to this potential of 'self-actualisation' and produced a 'hierarchy of needs' to capture the journey towards that end goal. Rogers formulated human goodness, personal growth and potential in terms of psychotherapeutic approaches, such as congruence and genuineness.

According to Diaz-Laplante (2007, pp.59–60), 'Rogers held that human beings are inherently good and that movement away from goodness is a result of cultural or societal influences.'

Self-actualisation

Is self-actualisation a state of being or rather a developmental process? LeClerc *et al.* (1998, p.73) are clear that it is a developmental process, commenting, 'this aspect is clearly emphasized by Maslow in his definition of self-actualization as the "full use and exploitation of talents, capacities and potentialities"'(Maslow, 1970, p.150). This sets forth the idea of a continuous development of the individual's potential as a central aspect of self-actualisation. The same idea of a developmental process is present in Rogers' definition of self-actualisation as 'the inherent tendency of the organism to develop all its capacities in ways that serve to maintain or enhance the organism' (LeClerc, 1998, p.73).

Greening (2007), speaking of Bugental, a leading figure in the movement, outlines his major tenets of humanistic psychology or, as it was also known, the 'third force' in psychology:

Five basic postulates of humanistic psychology
1. Human beings, as human, supersede the sum of their parts. They cannot be reduced to components.
2. Human beings have their existence in a uniquely human context, as well as in a cosmic ecology.
3. Human beings are aware and aware of being aware—i.e. they are conscious. Human consciousness always includes an awareness of oneself in the context of other people.
4. Human beings have some choice and, with that, responsibility.
5. Human beings are intentional, aim at goals, are aware that they cause future events, and seek meaning, value, and creativity.

Bugental (1964) in his seminal article, 'Humanism psychology: A new perspective', states, 'I propose that the defining concept of man basic to the new humanistic movement in psychology is that man is the process that supersedes the sum of his part functions.' (p.564)

Maslow and Rogers: an introduction

Abraham Maslow
According to Pearson and Podeschi (1999), central to Maslow's work are four intertwining concepts: the idea of self, that we are capable of growth, responsible for what we become and capable of influencing social progress. The authors continue (1999, p.43):

> There is an inner core of the self-determining individual in which human freedom for Maslow is a combination of uncovering one's real self and deciding what one will become. This capacity for self-knowledge and willed self-renewal leads to growth (the self-actualizing process), moving the self from one state of consciousness to a more advanced state (e.g., basic needs of safety and belongingness to meta needs of wholeness and justice). For Maslow, knowledge of oneself is not only a path to better individual value choices, but self-actualization also leads to knowledge of universal human nature, for example, awareness of the synthesis of altruism and self-interest.

This fundamental belief framework forms the 'hierarchy of needs', a model for classifying human motives, which is arguably Maslow's most identifiable and well-known work. Maslow published his hierarchy of needs in a paper entitled 'A theory of human motivation' (1943).

The hierarchy ascends from basic physiological needs (food, drink, etc.) through to more complex psychological needs, such as security and esteem.

Maslow's hierarchy of needs

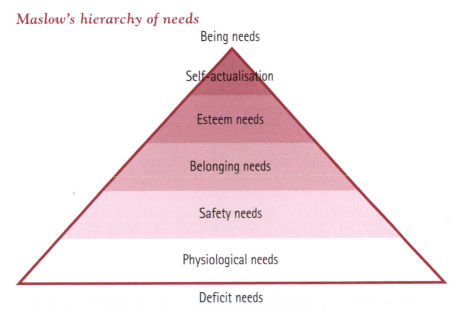

Source: Best et al., Hierarchy of Needs Addiction (2008, p.306)

The needs at one level must be at least partially satisfied before those at the next level become important determiners of action. When food or safety become difficult to obtain, higher needs are less relevant to the individual, whose attention is geared towards meeting the more basic needs they are lacking.

The hierarchy of needs and care planning in addiction services

Best et al. (2008) suggest that Maslow's hierarchical model of needs be considered as an exemplar in understanding the treatment and service provision of drug addiction. The authors quote Maslow (p.306) in terms of the most basic need of his hierarchy – physiological: 'If all other needs are unsatisfied, and the organism is then dominated by the physiological needs, all other needs may become simply non-existent or be pushed into the background. It is then fair to characterise the whole organism by saying simply that it is hungry, for consciousness is almost completely preempted by hunger.' Best et al. (2008, p.306) argue that the parallels between what Maslow is suggesting and drug-seeking 'are obvious with the basic physiological problems associated with drug deprivation, withdrawals, craving and anhedonia. At initial treatment presentation, it is therefore likely that other key issues are masked, and that only where equally pressing deprivations, most likely those caused by homelessness or significant mental or physical morbidities, are met will these arise as presenting needs.'

For the authors there are two major implications of the hierarchy of needs model for the delivery of treatment:

1. That lower-level interventions must precede higher-order ones.
2. That higher-order needs are unlikely to emerge in the initial contact stages.

Best *et al.* (2008) continue that this has fundamental implications in the area of care planning and review as part of the treatment process. Only as clients and workers manage the physiological needs (through prescribing, detoxification, etc.), 'can treatment start to look at issues of safety, then belonging, esteem and addressing more spiritual needs.'

In terms of the second implication of the model, what treatment workers do whilst managing the physical distress of addiction is paramount:

> The hierarchy of needs would suggest that any further gains in treatment are predicated on a care planning approach that is not 'addiction-specific' but is trans-disciplinary and grounded on the client's emerging pattern of needs. It would suggest that for many clients what is needed initially is case support rather than 'psychological change' and clients will be skeptical about the benefits of counselling if their needs are not compatible with the middle and higher-order levels of the pyramid. For many clients, the key tasks will be around benefits and housing, access to psychiatric services and GPs, and with little need for targeting lasting change in drug use until these issues have been addressed. (Best *et al.*, 2008, p.306)

Thus the thrust of this article on using the hierarchy of needs as a model for addiction treatment and care provision is that the basic physiological need must be fully resolved before any other 'higher' need is dealt with, and that the introduction of treatments to deal with more 'psychological' issues is likely to be unsuccessful unless physical needs have been fully met.

Here the direct relevance and relationship that exists between the discipline of psychology and social care practice is clear.

Carl Rogers

In Chapter 10 we will examine the contribution of Rogers to the development of psychotherapy, especially his pivotal role in recognising the influence of the client–therapist relationship. Here we will look at his work on personality and its development.

Rogers can be placed within the phenomenological approach to personality which places emphasis on the individual's subjective or private experience of the world. A focus on the 'here and now' and the individual's view of it is a fundamental tenet of this approach, differentiating it from the psychoanalytic approach, which delves into unconscious impulses.

The 'self' is a fundamentally important aspect of Rogers' theory of personality. The self is the 'I' or 'me' and includes awareness of 'what I am'; ideas, perceptions and values all form the structure of self. This perceived self is the referent for the individual's perception of the world and behaviour. Self-concept and self-esteem are related constructs that are informed by the individual's sense of self. Individuals with a strong, positive self-concept will view the world differently to a person with a weak or negative self-concept. Rogers contends that self-concept does not always reflect reality; a highly successful person may privately view themselves as a failure, for example. People use self-concept to evaluate experiences. Further, an individual's tendency is to behave in line with their self-image. Any feelings or experiences that are not consistent with this self-image are threatening and denied admittance to consciousness. This bears a resemblance to Freud's concept of repression. Anxiety develops, according to Rogers' theory, where the gap between self-image and feelings and experiences that are threatening to the self-image grows; in simple terms, a gulf exists between reality and self-concept. Atkinson *et al.* (1983, p.400) contend that, 'an individual whose image is incongruent with personal feelings and experiences must defend himself or herself against the truth because truth will result in anxiety. If the incongruence becomes too great, the defenses may break down, resulting in severe anxiety or other forms of emotional disturbance.' In contrast, the self-concept of a well-adjusted person is flexible and can change to integrate new experiences and ideas. The other 'self' that exists is the 'ideal self', which represents that person we wish to be. Should a significant gap exist between our 'ideal' self and 'real' self, this can result in an unhappy individual.

In Rogers' view the sense of self is the critical referent for self-evaluation. The contingencies for approval laid down by others – parents, teachers and other authority figures – inevitably play a significant role in self-esteem. Psychological dysfunction is often a result of having distorted or suppressed inner needs in an effort to satisfy the perceived standards of such dependency figures. From Rogers' perspective, continuing awareness of authentic inner desires is essential to healthy development and 'self-actualisation'.

Gross (2009, p.745) compares Maslow and Rogers in their shared positive evaluation of personal growth (self-actualisation), further commenting, 'While Maslow's theory is commonly referred to as a "psychology of being" (self-actualization is an end in itself and lies at the peak of his hierarchy of needs), Rogers' is a "psychology of becoming" (it's the process of becoming a "fully functioning person" that's of major importance and interest).'

Humanism: still a force to be reckoned with?

Elkins (2009, p.268) claims that the humanistic psychology of Maslow and Rogers has faded and that 'deterministic, mechanistic, and pathologizing models once again dominate clinical psychology—despite the fact that psychotherapy research clearly supports humanistic values and perspectives'.

Cain (2003) outlines the factors he believed are responsible for the non-advancement of humanistic psychology:

- a paucity of natural science research
- lack of publications in mainstream journals
- lack of effective organisation
- lack of political savvy
- a maverick attitude towards mainstream psychology
- having to contend with negative stereotypes.

Elkins (2009) identifies a lack of acknowledgment as a significant factor in the non-advancement of humanistic psychology. He claims that this has led to an erosion and undermining of the 'third force' perspective, especially in modern-day psychology. Elkins provides such an example in Seligman's positive psychology, which Elkins suggests is a reframing of humanistic psychology's long-standing emphasis upon the strengths and potentials of human beings. Elkins comments, 'Yet, when Seligman and Csikszentmihalyi (2000) edited the special issue of the *American Psychologist* . . . in which hundreds of references associated with this "new" approach were cited, only Viktor Frankl and Abraham Maslow made the list. Carl Rogers, the first psychologist to reject the pathology model and to develop a scientifically supported theory of psychotherapy that focused on the positive potentials of clients, did not appear in any of the reference lists!' (p.281)

Elkins provides a list of contributions which he feels humanistic psychology has made:

- The humanistic movement was primarily responsible for changing society's perception of psychotherapy from a 'medical treatment for mental illness' into a vehicle for personal growth and a source of support and guidance during difficult times
- Contemporary humanistic thought, which focuses on such postmodern perspectives as alternative epistemologies, the social construction of reality, and the relativity and limitations of abstract theoretical systems, is arguably more attuned to the postmodern age than is mainstream psychology, which often seems stuck in traditional perspectives that reflect modern era assumptions
- Humanistic scholars did groundbreaking work in the area of philosophy of research, writing about the limitations of the natural science model when applied to psychological phenomena and demonstrating the importance of phenomenological and other qualitative approaches in understanding human experience

- The humanistic movement was largely responsible for turning America into a 'therapeutic culture' and helping enlarge the field of psychology from a small guild of about 7,000 in 1950 into a profession of more than 90,000 today
- Rogers's Person-Centered Approach (PCA) has been the focus of hundreds of research studies that overwhelmingly have confirmed the effectiveness of his 'necessary and sufficient' conditions of therapy—empathy, congruence and unconditional positive regard
- By emphasizing the importance of the alliance, the relationship, the personality of the therapist, and so on in psychotherapy, humanistic psychologists anticipated contemporary meta-analytic studies that have convincingly demonstrated that therapeutic effectiveness is due primarily to contextual factors and not to modalities and techniques
- Humanistic psychology has had a significant impact on other fields, such as education, nursing, social work, organizational development and so on. (pp.282–4)

What of the role of humanistic psychology today?

Clearly, as we will see in Chapter 10 on counselling, the work of Rogers has been, and continues to be, hugely influential in psychotherapy and psychotherapeutic approaches to supporting individuals.

Diaz-Laplante (2007, p.58) outlines her belief that humanistic psychology offers the best model for intervention in modern-day society: 'Humanistic psychology provides a theoretical framework that invites us to develop models of intervention that engage individuals at all levels—intellectually, spiritually, physically, within the context of their community and intimate relationships, and across all dimensions of the life span.'

However, to demonstrate the application of humanistic psychology from another perspective, we can look at the link between positive psychology and humanistic psychology, and the role of positive psychology in the arena of social care work.

Positive psychology can be defined as 'a science of positive subjective experience, positive individual traits, and positive institutions which promises to improve quality of life and prevent the pathologies that arise when life is barren and meaningless' (Seligman and Csikszentmihalyi, 2000, p.5). The authors outline the field of positive psychology across the following levels:

> At the subjective level it is about valued subjective experiences: well-being, contentment, and satisfaction (in the past); hope and optimism (for the future); and flow and happiness (in the present).
>
> At the individual level, it is about positive individual traits: the capacity for love and vocation, courage, interpersonal skill, aesthetic sensibility, perseverance, forgiveness, originality, future mindedness, spirituality, high talent, and wisdom.

>At the group level, it is about the civic virtues and the institutions that move individuals toward better citizenship: responsibility, nurturance, altruism, civility, moderation, tolerance, and work ethic. (2000, p.5)

In studying those whose lives encapsulate positive and adaptive living, it is hoped to develop supports and promote those same traits, characteristics and behaviours in others towards the betterment of all. As already mentioned, positive psychology has its roots in the humanistic tradition (Seligman and Csikszentmihalyi, 2000; Robbins, 2008). Robbins (2008, p.98) directly links positive psychology to humanistic psychology, commenting 'that it was, in fact, Maslow (1987) who coined the phrase "positive psychology" (p.354) more than four decades prior to Seligman's use of the term for his own work and that of others. Not surprisingly, then, Peterson and Seligman (2004) credit Maslow as a pioneer in the study of character strengths and virtues, and they used Maslow's descriptions of the self-actualized individual as a means to identify and validate their taxomony of character strengths and virtues.'

Positive psychology and youth work

In Chapter 7 we will examine the construct of resilience which is part of the positive psychology paradigm; here we look at the role of positive psychology suggested by Larson (2000) in the development of youth activities to support and engender positive characteristics, such as initiative and agency within adolescents. Larson (2000, p.170) suggests that high rates of boredom, alienation and disconnection from meaningful challenge are not signs of psychopathology, at least not in most cases, but rather signs of a deficiency in positive development. The same might be said for many cases of problem behaviour, such as drug use, premature sexual involvement and minor delinquency; that they are more parsimoniously described, not as responses to family stress, emotional disturbance or maladaptive cognitions, but rather to the absence of engagement in a positive life trajectory.

Youth work is a central part of social care work. In developing his ideas Larson hopes to provide a framework for the development of youth activities that encourage and support the development of positive traits in adolescents. Larson (2000, p.178) suggests that during more structured youth activities, 'adolescents experience a unique combination of intrinsic motivation and concentration that is rarely present during their daily experiences in schoolwork and unstructured leisure. These two components of experience, I proposed, represent two critical elements of initiative, and when they occur in activities involving a temporal arc of action toward a goal, as is the case with many youth activities, all three elements for the experience and learning of initiative are in play.' Larson relates that these more structured activities towards a goal result in greater positive outcomes, including:

- diminished delinquency
- greater achievement
- increased self-control and self-efficacy.

Through their participation in the youth activities, the adolescents develop a greater sense of initiative and agency. Larson (2000, p.178) believes his research 'suggests processes of personal integration that may work in tandem with the sociological processes of social integration'.

ECOLOGICAL THEORY

Urie Bronfenbrenner (1917–2005)

This theory looks at a child's development within the context of the system of relationships that form his or her environment. You can see from his theoretical model that there are several systems that impact on the individual child's development. The really clever aspect of this approach is that it encompasses the immediate environment of the child (parents, siblings) to more distant influences at the outer circle (social welfare payments, for example).

Levels of ecosystems

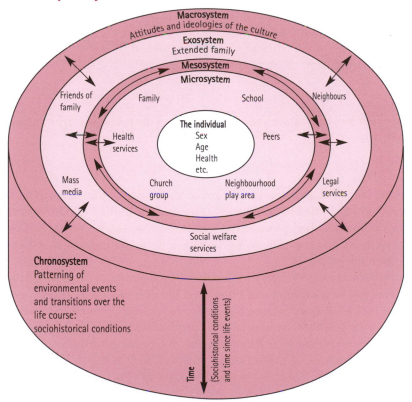

Microsystem

This circle takes in the immediate environment of the child and includes family, school/teacher, peers and neighbourhood. Thus anything that the child interacts with directly or has a relationship with can be included in this circle. Not only do these influences impact on the child, the child also impacts on its immediate environment; relationships at this level impact in two ways. Bronfenbrenner would call this a bi-directional influence.

Mesosystem

This can be a little trickier to understand. Basically, it refers to connections or relationships between different microsystems (for example, linkages between home and school). If a child has a difficult relationship with their parents, this can influence their interactions with peers (linkage between two microsystems, in this case parents and peers).

Exosystem

While the child does not have an active role or is not in immediate contact with it, this system can nonetheless affect what the child experiences in its immediate context. For example, work problems can affect the relationship between parents and also the child. If the father is promoted in work, this might mean he spends less time at home, leading to arguments with his wife and less time spent with his child. So the child is inadvertently impacted upon by the workplace of his father. The educational system, government agencies and mass media are influences that are seen in the exosystem.

Macrosystem

This system refers to the culture and belief patterns of the people/society in which the child lives.

Chronosystem

This relates to changing socio-historical circumstances. Put simply, each generation may have different experiences as time passes. In the 1950s in Ireland, a woman who married had to leave her job in the civil service. In the 2000s, women can marry and continue to work. This reflects the changes that have occurred with the passage of time.

Initially Bronfenbrenner's theory was a strongly ecological one, emphasising the effects of nurture or environmental influences. He later modified his theory to include the biological aspect of the child, reflecting the current view that both a child's biology and environment interact in the development of the child. This modified theory is referred to as Bronfenbrenner's bioecological theory. On the model in the diagram above you will see that aspects such as the child's sex, age and health are included in influencing development. So, given that nature continues on a given path, how does the world that surrounds the child help or hinder continued development? This is an important question for you to reflect on.

Glen H. Elder Jr. (1934–)

Life-course theory

Elder's theory represents another approach to conceptualising and understanding human development across the life course. Elder stresses the influence of social forces in shaping the life course and its developmental consequences. According to Elder, life-course theory represents a general change in how we think about and study human lives and development. Where Bronfenbrenner's ecological theory now encompasses the biological influence of the individual, Elder's life-course theory has evolved into an effective way to investigate the impact of social change on the developmental course of human lives. Instead of concentrating on individual case studies, Elder's attention focuses on multiple and interlocking pathways. Let's take a closer look at how Elder has constructed his theory.

Four themes are distinctive of life-course theory:

1. human lives in historical time and place
2. human agency and social constraints
3. the timing of lives
4. linked lives.

Human lives in historical time and place

Elder conducted research looking at the lives of boys who grew up during the Great Depression in America and those who grew up in Manchester, showing that they had very different life chances following their involvement in World War II. 'The California boys managed to escape the limitations of their deprived households by joining the armed forces and, after the war, using the benefits of the GI Bill for higher education' (2001, p.37). Here we can see how historical influences and place can affect the lives of individuals.

Human agency and social constraint

'Within the constraints of their world, people often plan and choose within options that become the building blocks of their evolving lives. . . . People of the same age do not march in concert across the major events of their life course; rather, they vary in pace and sequencing, and this variation has real consequences for people and society' (p.38). Having children, starting work or getting married (if at all) occur at different ages under differing circumstances that reflect the individual's personal life experiences and their interpretation of a given situation.

The timing of lives

Elder (2001, p.38) explains, 'social timing refers to the initiation of and departure from social roles, and to relevant age expectations and beliefs. The social meanings of age give structure to the life course through age norms and sanctions, social timetables for the occurrence and order of events, generalized age grades (such as childhood and adolescence), and age hierarchies in organizational settings (i.e., the age structure of firms).'

Linked lives

Most people's lives are intertwined with others, from their immediate family to more distantly placed work colleagues. Another interesting slant is the intergenerational aspect to this theme of linked lives. A failed marriage can impact on the children when, as adults, their life experience can be linked to the misfortunes of their parents; that is, they may be at increased risk of marital breakdown themselves. Elder comments 'each generation is bound to fateful decisions and events in the other's life course' (p.39).

Finally, another component of Elder's life-course theory is that of the cohort effect, which refers to 'one of the ways in which lives can be influenced by social change. History is experienced as a cohort effect when social change and culture differentiate the life patterns of successive cohorts' (p.37). What does this mean? Let's take the example of a child born with Down syndrome in Ireland in the present day. Compare and contrast their likely experience with that of a child born with Down syndrome in the 1940s.

Dr Louis Clifford: Survey of Learning Disability (1943)

The following is an extract from Griffin and Shevlin, *Responding to Special Educational Needs: An Irish Perspective* (2007). It highlights the attitudes and experience of those born with a disability in the 1940s:

> Having a disabled child, according to Clifford, was widely seen by parents of the time as a disgrace and a reflection on the family. The more affluent and socially superior the family, the more the condition was resented and abhorred. Families from lower socio-economic backgrounds were usually more philosophical about their misfortune. In his account, Dr Clifford records that disabled children were sometimes hidden away in top rooms and seldom taken out except at night. (p.39)

From this perspective, it would have been hard to imagine that children and adults would be participating in an event such as the Special Olympics in Ireland in 2003 (the global Special Olympics began in 1968); yet change does occur.

Does a child born with Down syndrome today face a different experience to a similar child born in the 1940s? If your answer is Yes, this represents the 'cohort effect' where the life experience of a generation differs to that of another due to social changes. It also demonstrates the power and influence that social change can produce. This is particularly important in areas where people experience prejudice, such as those with disabilities, as it demonstrates the power of social change and the difference it can make to the lives of individuals.

In focus: National Children's Office: The whole-child perspective

National Children's Strategy
The National Children's Strategy (2000) is a 10-year plan with a vision of: 'An Ireland where children are respected as young citizens with a valued contribution to make and a voice of their own; where all children are cherished and supported by family and the wider society; where they enjoy a fulfilling childhood and realise their potential.'

The three national goals of the strategy are:

Goal 1 – Children will have a voice in matters which affect them and their views will be given due weight in accordance with their age and maturity.

Goal 2 – Children's lives will be better understood; their lives will benefit from evaluation, research and information on their needs, rights and the effectiveness of services.

Goal 3 – Children will receive quality supports and services to promote all aspects of their development.

It includes a range of actions across such areas as giving children a voice so that their views are considered in relation to matters that affect them, eliminating child poverty, ensuring children have access to play and recreation facilities and improving research on children's lives in Ireland. The strategy provides the first comprehensive national policy document for the full range of statutory and non-statutory providers in the development of services for children and is underpinned by the United Nations Convention on the Rights of the Child.

The whole-child perspective
The strategy adopts a 'whole-child perspective', recognising the multidimensional nature of all aspects of children's lives. The recognition that all parts of children's lives are interlinked has, in turn, implications for public policy-making and the integration of services relating to children.

What is interesting about the whole-child perspective is that it takes an ecological approach in attempting to understand children's development. Bronfenbrenner, in his model, emphasises the importance of recognising that systems of influence exist in a child's life from immediate family to more distant influences such as government policy. In looking at the model of the whole-child perspective developed by the National Children's Office, we can see the many and varied influences they include in order to gain understanding of the child and the context of the child. So we can see here evidence of a theoretical approach being adopted by a government agency whose aim is to improve the lives of children.

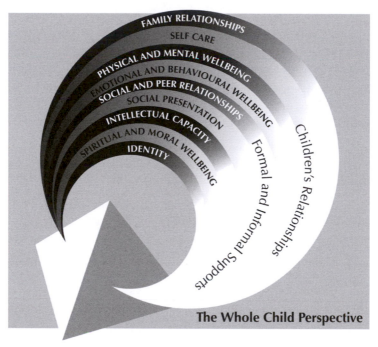

Source: www.dohc.ie/publications/pdf/choldstrat_report.pdf?direct=7.

This marks the end of our exploration of the different theoretical approaches that have been and are dominant in psychology at the moment. Obviously, newer models are continually being developed (narrative psychology and epigenetics, for example) and others exist that are relevant to specific domains of functioning such as the information-processing model in cognitive development. However, the purpose of this chapter has been to act as an introduction to some of the theories most relevant to the study and work of social care. In the following chapters we will consider more specific theories relating to specific age periods or to specific issues.

4

Psychology across the lifespan

This chapter examines human development across the lifespan from conception to the end of life. The lifespan is divided into five distinct stages: conception and prenatal development, childhood, adolescence, adulthood and old age. Developmental theories are examined within each stage, as well as age- or concept-specific theories (such as Elkind's theory of adolescent cognition). Throughout each section an emphasis is placed on Irish statistics, research and findings. 'In focus' sections are included where a particular topic is examined in greater detail.

DEVELOPMENT PSYCHOLOGY

According to Lerner (1998), a characteristic of modern psychological theories of development is that they are systematic rather than uni-factorial in their conceptions about the relevant influences and factors that affect development. Such newer conceptualisations have shied away from nature/nurture or individual/society dichotomies in an attempt to understand development across the lifespan using a more holistic and inclusive approach. This approach emphasises the causal role of various systems of influence that are based, for example, on historical-cultural differences, social strata and other characteristics of the developmental ecology. Put simply, models such as Bronfenbrenner and Lerner's (Chapter 3) hold a more rounded and modern approach to understanding human development. In this chapter we leave the more theoretical discussions alone and focus on the changes that occur throughout and across the lifespan.

CONCEPTION, PRENATAL DEVELOPMENT AND BIRTH

Often when people think of human development across the lifespan the starting point is birth. However, many of the foundations for development occur at the moment of conception. It is important to understand these processes and what is typical development, in order not just to support it but also to recognise when development deviates and becomes atypical. We will begin by exploring the processes that occur at conception and the possible impact they can have on a child's development after birth.

Fertilisation and conception

The menstrual cycle occurs in females of reproductive age. At the beginning of the cycle an egg (ovum) begins to develop in the ovary. This egg is released and travels down the fallopian tube. Fertilisation occurs when a woman's ovum or egg is penetrated or fertilised by a man's sperm. The fertilised egg is called a zygote. A continuous process of cell division then occurs until this mass of cells attaches itself to the mother's uterus approximately 10–14 days after fertilisation. The man's sperm and the woman's egg each contain hereditary information in the form of chromosomes.

Chromosomes and genes

A chromosome is a tightly coiled molecule of deoxyribonucleic acid (DNA) that consists of smaller segments called genes. A gene can be thought of as your body's instruction manual and genes affect how you look, your health and how your body works. The zygote contains 23 pairs of chromosomes: 23 single chromosomes from the sperm and 23 chromosomes from the egg (in total, 46 chromosomes: 23 pairs). Thus in the fertilised egg each pair of chromosomes contains one chromosome from each parent. Out of the 23 pairs of chromosomes, it is the final pair (the 23rd) that determine a person's sex.

- in males the 23rd pair consists of an X and Y chromosome
- in females the 23rd pair consists of two X chromosomes.

There are approximately 25,000 genes contained on the 46 chromosomes in each cell in a human body. This means that one chromosome contains thousands of genes. We inherit our genetic make-up from our parents through the transmission of their genes during conception.

- Our **genotype** is the sum total of our genetic make-up; the specific genetic make-up of the individual. Our genotype is present from conception and never changes.
- Our **phenotype** is the set of observable characteristics that are produced by that genetic endowment. Phenotypes can be affected by other genes and by the environment (such as climate, diet and lifestyle).

Many kinds of variation are influenced by both genetic and environmental factors. Though our genes govern what characteristics we inherit, our environment can affect *how* these inherited characteristics develop. For example, an individual may have inherited a tendency to be tall but a poor diet during childhood will cause poor growth.

Genetic conditions

Some genes are dominant and some are recessive. Consider the example of hair colour to understand the difference. Brown hair is regulated by a dominant gene, blond hair a recessive one. My father has brown hair and my mother has blond; I have brown hair yet my brother has blond: how is this so? If an individual has one brown-hair gene and one blond-hair gene, they will have brown hair, because the brown-hair gene is dominant and 'overpowers' the blond-hair gene. To have blond hair you must have two blond-hair genes. So my mother must have two blond-hair genes and has passed one blond-hair gene to my brother. My brown-haired father has one brown-hair gene and one blond-hair gene, and must have passed a blond-hair gene to my brother, as my blond-haired brother must have two blond-hair genes.

I always think of genetic inheritance as similar to the Lotto; you never know the mix of balls (numbers) you might end up with. So conception is literally a lottery!

Certain conditions and diseases are genetically inherited.

Recessive inheritance

If two parents are both carriers of a genetic condition with a recessive inheritance pattern, there is a one-in-four chance that each child will be affected. So on average, one-quarter of their children will be affected. There is also a one-in-two chance that each child will be an unaffected carrier, like the parents. Examples of genetic conditions that show a recessive pattern of inheritance are cystic fibrosis, sickle-cell disease, Tay-Sachs disease and phenylketonuria (PKU).

Inheritance pattern of cystic fibrosis

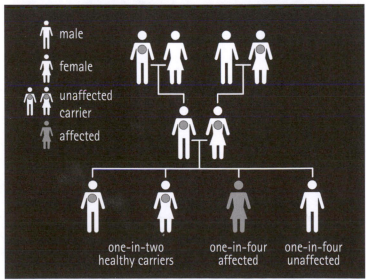

Dominant inheritance

If one of two parents is affected by a genetic condition with a dominant inheritance pattern, every child has a one-in-two chance of being affected. So on average, half their children will be affected, and half their children will not be affected and so will not pass on the condition. However, as chance determines inheritance, it is also possible that all or none of their children will be affected. An example of genetic conditions that show a dominant pattern of inheritance is Huntington's disease.

Inheritance pattern of Huntington's disease

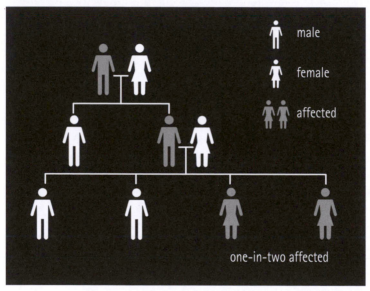

The major difference between dominant and recessive gene inheritance is as follows:

Recessive: For the child to inherit the condition, it must inherit two variant (affected) chromosomes; one from each parent. Thus a child has a 1:4 chance of inheriting the condition, a 1:2 chance of becoming a healthy carrier and a 1:4 chance of not inheriting the affected chromosome.

Dominant: One parent is affected whereas the other parent can be healthy. At conception, if the variant chromosome of the affected parent is transferred then the child will inherit the condition. It does not matter if the other parent's chromosome is healthy. Thus with dominant conditions such as Huntington's disease, the child has a 1:2 chance of inheriting the condition.

Chromosomal disorders

We have looked at gene-linked disorders including cystic fibrosis, PKU and Huntington's disease. These are different to chromosomal abnormalities such as Down syndrome. Both occur at conception but whereas the gene-linked conditions are inherited, chromosomal conditions generally occur through the presence of an extra chromosome. If you recall, each cell has 23 pairs of chromosomes. In Down syndrome an extra copy of chromosome 21 is present. Sometimes you will find Down syndrome referred to as 'trisomy 21', the 'tri-' referring to the three chromosomes present instead of two. Down syndrome is examined in Chapter 5. Other chromosomal syndromes include Patau syndrome (trisomy 13) and Edwards syndrome (trisomy 18). Sex-linked chromosome abnormalities can also occur, such as Fragile X syndrome.

Phenylketonuria

Earlier in the section on conception we encountered a genetically inherited condition called phenylketonuria (PKU). This is a condition that, if diagnosed, can be treated and controlled. However, if undetected this condition can lead to severe mental retardation, as amino acids build up, causing brain damage in the child. It can be treated with a modified diet that excludes the specific amino acid concerned, thus preventing it from accumulating in the child's system. Within the first few days of life a pin prick is made on an infant's heel and blood is extracted and analysed, which allows for a diagnosis to be made. According to the *National PKU News* (Fall 2001), since testing began in Ireland an incidence rate of 1 in 4,500 has been seen, which they note is far greater than the incidence rate of 1 in 12,000 seen in America. They report that currently 611 individuals with PKU (334 males and 277 females) attend the National Centre for Metabolic Disorders at the Children's Hospital in Temple Street, Dublin.

Prenatal development

Prenatal development consists of three stages:

1. the germinal stage
2. the embryonic stage
3. the foetal stage.

The germinal stage – approximately the first two weeks of development: when a woman's egg (ovum) is fertilised by a man's sperm, the fertilised egg is called a zygote. Once fertilised, a process of continual cell division begins. Approximately 10 to 14 days after conception the zygote, which now contains a mass of cells, attaches itself to the mother's uterus.

The embryonic stage – end of the second week to the eighth week: the cell mass is now called an embryo. The placenta and umbilical cord begin to develop during this stage and the bodily organs and systems begin to form. By week eight the heart is beating and the brain is forming. Facial features such as eyes become discernible.

The foetal stage – from the ninth week until birth: the embryo is now referred to as a foetus. At 24 weeks the eyes open. At 28 weeks the foetus attains the age of viability, meaning that it is likely to survive outside the womb in the event of premature birth (Hetherington and Parke, 1999).

Critical periods in human development

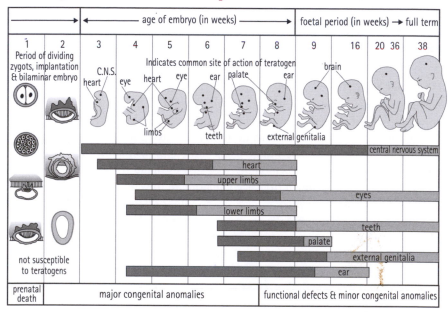

Source: Boyd and Bee, 2005, p.65.

Hazards during prenatal development

As we saw earlier, chromosomal and genetic disorders affect the foetus at the moment of conception. Other external factors can affect and influence the foetus's development in the womb. Diet and nutrition can be an influence: if a pregnant mother is not getting the required calories needed, the foetus is more likely to have a low birth weight, compared to pregnant women who gain 26 or more pounds. Factors such as age and emotional stress have been implicated in prenatal development as well as HIV/AIDS and Rubella. Some external influences called teratogens can cause birth defects. The timing of exposure and dose of a teratogen can make a difference in outcome. Take the example of thalidomide, a drug available in chemists for use in easing morning sickness, which was recommended to pregnant women in the later 1950s. As the pregnant women who had taken the drug began to give birth it became apparent that their babies had been affected by the drug. The infants were born with missing or shortened arms and legs. In the table above you will notice periods where different parts of the body are more vulnerable to teratogenic exposure. These women were taking thalidomide for morning sickness, which can occur early in pregnancy; just the time when the limbs of the foetus are vulnerable.

As we examine different teratogens, bear in mind that timing, dose and duration of exposure all interact in determining outcomes. Another factor can be genetic vulnerability, which we will explore below in the section on foetal alcohol syndrome disorder.

Some teratogens and their effects

Drugs
Smoking during pregnancy increases the risk of miscarriage, premature birth and low birth weight.

Alcohol: see below.

Marijuana and heroin: According to Boyd and Bee (2005, p.67), 'The infants of twice-weekly marijuana smokers suffer from tremors and sleep problems. They seem to have little interest in their surroundings for up to 2 weeks after birth; . . . both heroin and methadone . . . can cause miscarriage, premature labour, and early death.' They continue that 60 to 80 per cent of babies born to heroin- or methadone-addicted mothers are addicted themselves and suffer withdrawal symptoms such as making high-pitched cries and having convulsions.

Low-birth-weight babies
- Low birth weight: less than 5½ pounds (2,500 grams) at birth
- Very low weight: less than 3 pounds (1,360 grams) at birth
- Extremely low weight: under 2 pounds (907 grams) at birth.

Preterm babies
- Born before 38 weeks' gestation
- Most preterm babies are low-weight.

Small-for-date infants
- Birth weight is below normal when the length of pregnancy is considered
- Weigh less than 90 per cent of the average weight of all babies of the same gestational age.

Cigarette smoking is the leading cause of low birth weight (LBW) in infants (Unicef, 2004). Adolescents who give birth when their bodies have not fully developed are at risk of having LBW babies. In Chapter 7 low birth weight and social inequality is examined. Low birth weight and preterm are not the only potential consequences of using harmful substances during pregnancy. In the following section Michele Savage of Foetal Alcohol Spectrum Disorders Ireland (www.fasd.ie) gives us an insight into Foetal Alcohol Syndrome and its implications for those in social care.

Foetal Alcohol Spectrum Disorders (FASD) – much more than a syndrome

Alcohol and pregnancy

Alcohol is a drug, a poison, a carcinogen and a mutagen, but it is also a physical and a neuropsychiatric teratogen which can and does interfere with the normal development of the embryo or foetus at any stage in pregnancy, causing more harm than any of the other so-called 'recreational' drugs.

Table 4.1: Agents affecting foetal development

Affecting agent	alcohol	marijuana	cocaine	heroin	tobacco
Low birth weight	✗	–	✗	✗	✗
Impaired growth	✗	–	–	–	–
Facial malformation	✗	–	–	–	–
Small head size	✗	–	–	–	–
Intellectual and developmental delays	✗	✗	–	–	–
Hyperactivity and inattention	✗	✗	–	✗	✗
Sleeping problems	✗	✗	✗	✗	✗
Poor feeding	✗	–	✗	–	–
Excessive crying	✗	✗	✗	✗	–
Higher risk for sudden infant death syndrome	–	–	–	✗	✗
Organ damage, birth defects	✗	–	–	–	–
Respiratory problems	✗	–	–	✗	✗

Source: US Department of Health and Human Services, 1994 (Day et al., 1994)

Alcohol vs. other drugs

'Of all the substances of abuse including cocaine, heroin, and marijuana, alcohol produces by far the most serious neurobehavioral effects in the fetus resulting in life-long permanent disorders of memory function, impulse control and judgment' (Stratton *et al.*, 1996).

How does prenatal exposure to alcohol affect a foetus?

Alcohol crosses the placenta undiluted, and within minutes, the level of alcohol in the foetus's blood reaches maternal levels. Alcohol interferes with the normal development of cells and causes unnecessary cell death. As the foetus is still at an early stage of development, it is ill-equipped to process the alcohol. The effects are:

- 1st trimester: major morphological anomalies
- 2nd trimester: spontaneous abortion
- 3rd trimester: decreased foetal growth.

The central nervous system (CNS) develops throughout the entire nine months, and the biggest period of brain growth begins at the start of the third trimester, and continues until a child is about two years old.

There is no proven safe time, no proven safe amount and no proven safe type of alcohol to consume in pregnancy. One does not have to be alcohol-dependent to have a child with a foetal alcohol condition, although binge-drinking is particularly risky.

Other factors which determine outcomes are: maternal age, health (including that of the liver), and nutrition. Although FASD is associated with all social classes, Anderson and Baumberg (2007) state that the very poorest women may not be able to afford alcohol.

Ireland's Chief Medical Officer (CMO) has stated that:

- Alcohol consumption by pregnant women in Ireland poses a risk to unborn babies.
- There is no known safe level of alcohol consumption during pregnancy.
- Alcohol offers no benefits to pregnancy outcomes.
- It is in the child's best interests for a pregnant woman not to drink alcohol during pregnancy.

The CMO is now providing unambiguous advice in relation to alcohol consumption and pregnancy:

> Given the harmful drinking patterns in Ireland and the propensity to 'binge drink', there is a substantial risk of neurological damage to the

foetus resulting in Foetal Alcohol Spectrum Disorders (FASD). Alcohol offers no benefits to pregnancy outcomes. Therefore, it is in the child's best interest for a pregnant woman not to drink alcohol during pregnancy.

Source: www.dohc.ie

Classification and nomenclature

Damage arising from prenatal alcohol exposure was previously classified as either Foetal Alcohol Syndrome (FAS) or Foetal Alcohol Effects (FAE). In 2004 new terminology reflecting the range and scope of outcomes was agreed:

> Fetal Alcohol Spectrum Disorders (FASD) is an umbrella term describing the range of effects that can occur in an individual whose mother drank alcohol during pregnancy. These effects may include physical, mental, behavioral, and/or learning disabilities with possible lifelong implications.
> The term FASD is not intended for use as a clinical diagnosis.

Source: Consensus statement, NOFAS 2004 Summit of Experts: www.eed.state.ak.us/tls/fasd/pdf/ConsesusStatement.pdf

The conditions on the Foetal Alcohol Spectrum are:

- Foetal Alcohol Syndrome (maternal consumption confirmed)
- Foetal Alcohol Syndrome (maternal consumption unconfirmed)
- Partial Foetal Alcohol Syndrome
- Alcohol-Related Neurodevelopmental Disorder
- Alcohol-Related Birth Defects

Diagnostic criteria for all conditions are detailed in Stratton *et al.*, 1996, pp.76–7.

Foetal Alcohol Syndrome (FAS)

Even though prenatal alcohol exposure is the most common cause of non-genetic disability, 75 per cent of people with Foetal Alcohol Syndrome (FAS) have an IQ within the 'normal' range. FAS that presents with distinctive dysmorphic features (that is, a characteristic pattern of facial anomalies such as short eye openings, a thin upper lip, low nasal bridge, flattened philtrum and a flat midface), can be identified earliest and most easily. However FAS is the rarest of the conditions, occurring in only 10 to 15 per cent of those affected.

The face of Foetal Alcohol Syndrome

As the child grows older the specific dysmorphic facial features will become less evident.

Alcohol-related neurodevelopmental disorder (ARND)

Eighty-five to ninety per cent of those affected do not have dysmorphic features, though they may have some congenital defects (alcohol-related birth defects). As such, they are far harder to diagnose, given that their difficulties with

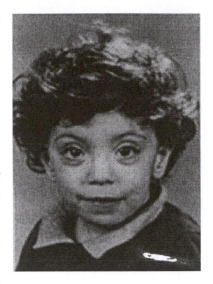

behaviour and educational and social functioning can be masked by hyperactivity and attention deficit, and/or autistic-type symptoms.

For a diagnosis of ARND, there must be evidence of at least one of the following central nervous system neurodevelopmental abnormalities:

- decreased cranial size at birth
- structural brain abnormalities such as microcephaly, partial or complete agenesis of the corpus callosum, cerebella hypoplasia
- neurological hard or soft signs (as age-appropriate), such as impaired fine motor skills, neuro-sensory hearing loss, poor tandem gait, poor hand-eye co-ordination, sensory integration issues.

Alcohol-related birth defects (ARBD)

Alcohol is associated with all congenital anomalies. Birth defects are not always linked back to their aetiology.

Prevalence of Foetal Alcohol Spectrum Disorders (FASDs)

There is no official data on the prevalence of Foetal Alcohol Spectrum Disorders, which are under-recognised and therefore under-reported worldwide. We can only make a rough estimate by drawing from US statistics, where 22 per cent of pregnant women self-report as drinking alcohol, and about 1 per cent of the population has a foetal alcohol condition. There is cause for concern in countries such as Ireland where in one subset of years in retrospective research, the Coombe Women's Hospital Study of Alcohol, Smoking and Illicit Drug Use, 1988–2005, 79 per cent of pregnant women self-reported as drinking alcohol. Given that different questions were asked in another period within the report's remit of different years, the overall average was that 66 per cent of women said they drank while pregnant.

If we apply the rates of Foetal Alcohol Syndrome reported by the Substance Abuse and Mental Health Services Agency, Center for Disease Control in the United States (SAMHSA 2005),* to the 2002 Irish birth rates (Central Statistics Office, 2002), we can estimate that 1 per cent, that is 605 of the 60,503 babies born in Ireland in 2002, could have FASD. The incidence may be higher due to the high rate of binge drinking among young women in Ireland.

* SAMHSA 2005, cited in Ryan and Ní Chionnaith, *On the Spectrum* (2005, p.4)

Benefits of a diagnosis

To diagnose is not to 'label', but to ascertain and acknowledge that a child's challenges arise from brain damage caused by prenatal exposure. There is increasing evidence that this damage can occur at low-dose levels. No two children with a condition on the foetal alcohol spectrum are exactly alike, either behaviourally or physically.

Diagnosis means that children will be better understood at home, in school and in the community; their difficulties arise from 'can't', not 'won't'. Those with Foetal Alcohol Syndrome are arguably the luckiest in that their condition is most easily recognised and they are more likely to receive early intervention.

People with Alcohol-Related Neurodevelopmental Disorder (ARND) are less likely to have their condition ascertained, therefore co-occurring behavioural, social and learning characteristics, most of which will only manifest later on, may be wrongly attributed to bad or inconsistent parenting. Symptoms of ARND include:

- attention problems or hyperactivity (Morse, 1991; Nanson and Hiscock, 1990)
- academic problems, including specific deficits in mathematics and memory skills (Streissguth et al., 1993)
- very specific language deficits (Abkarian, 1992)
- problems with adaptive functioning that grow more significant with age (Lemoine and Lemoine, 1992; Streissguth and Randels, 1989)
- behavioural challenges, including impulsivity
- co-morbid psychiatric conditions
- social or relationship challenges, including difficulty making and/or keeping friendships

- sensory impairments such as vision or hearing
- sensory integration challenges, meaning that children can be overwhelmed or, conversely, under-stimulated by noise (sudden individual and/or continuous background sounds), by smells, visual stimuli, and by things which touch them or which they themselves touch
- sensory processing challenges, meaning that affected children may not be able to deal with (modulate) how they process sensory intake without intervention of a sensory integration specialist.

It is vital that these challenges and their aetiology are not only recognised early, but that they are treated and managed with the understanding that difficulties arise from brain damage as opposed to an unwillingness to behave or learn, so that the likelihood of the occurrence of what Streissguth *et al.* term the secondary disabilities of foetal alcohol is minimised. Their longitudinal study of babies diagnosed at birth as having FAS showed that even though the children had been raised in nurturing and consistent homes, by the time the children were 12 years old, the following problems had emerged:

- mental health problems from six years old   90 per cent
- disrupted school careers   60 per cent
- trouble with the law   50 per cent
- being confined in secure settings
  (including mental health ones)   60 per cent
- inappropriate sexual behaviour   60 per cent
- addiction problems   30 per cent
- at risk of abuse   70 per cent
- problems with getting and keeping a job   80 per cent
- dependent living situations   80 per cent

Source: Streissguth *et al.*, 1997

These outcomes happened despite early diagnosis and being raised in nurturing homes. It must be noted that these children were born in the US in the 1970s, when FASD-specific multi-disciplinary intervention services were not available. Protective factors against such outcomes include:

- living in a stable and nurturing home for more than 72 per cent of one's life
- being diagnosed before six years of age
- never having experienced violence against oneself
- staying in each living situation for more than 2.8 years
- experiencing a good quality home (more than 10 out of 12 or more good qualities) from age 8–12 years old

- being eligible for learning disability services
- having a diagnosis of FAS rather than ARND and/or ARBD
- having basic needs met for at least 13 per cent of life.

How to access diagnosis in Ireland

FAS is being recognised in Ireland, but partial FAS (pFAS), ARND and ARBD are harder to ascertain. Attention deficit (including hyperactivity) and autistic-type behaviours, either alone or as co-morbid conditions, are associated with organic brain damage arising from prenatal exposure to alcohol.

Although a FASD specialist consultant psychiatrist has been in place in Belfast since 2007, and in Dublin since late 2009, Ireland still does not have a multi-disciplinary FASD clinic, to assess and address current and future sensory integration, speech and language, pervasive development disorder, physiotherapy, psychology (both educational, currently WISC IV, and social-adaptive-behavioural, currently Bailey's for Infants, or Vineland II for children, teenagers and adults), occupational therapy, and psychiatric needs of affected babies, children, young people and adults.

To conclude

Foetal alcohol conditions affect everyone – perhaps not in the immediate or extended family, but in neighbourhood and school communities and at service-provision level, whether on a statutory or a charity basis. Services cost money, which impacts on tax-payers, that is, the public in general.

Given the primary disabilities of physical anomalies along with the secondary disabilities outlined by Streissguth *et al.*, and that an unpublished small study found that 75 per cent of children coming into care came from alcohol-troubled families, it is highly likely that social care workers will work with infants, children, young people and adults who have one or more of the avoidable lifelong foetal alcohol conditions.

That concludes our brief introduction to prenatal development. Hopefully you can see the importance of early development for later development and the need to support best outcomes where possible. The notion of support is an integral part of social care work and we will look at the Community Mothers Programme as an example of such a support initiative aimed at supporting and encouraging young mothers.

CHILDHOOD

Infancy and the first two years of life

The first two years of life are a time of immense development and growth. This is very obvious in the realm of physical development where an infant will within a year generally be able to crawl, stand and begin to walk. Within a lifespan perspective it can be argued that these years are particularly significant for future functioning in later life. Within a nature–nurture context, we will look at the role and impact of 'nurture' (environment) on a child's development.

In Chapter 2 we examined the development of the brain across the lifespan. To recap, the brain at birth weighs 25 per cent of its eventual adult weight; by the child's second birthday the brain will have increased to 75 per cent of its adult weight. Thus this period in the child's life represents a period of marked growth. It is therefore imperative that this development is supported and the child suitably stimulated to ensure the best outcomes possible. Brain development and functioning is inextricably tied to cognitive ability. In Chapter 3 we discussed what is meant by cognitive development and theories related to it. Here we briefly recap Piaget's theory of cognitive development within a specific age period or stage; please see Chapter 3 for a more detailed account of his theory.

Cognitive development

Piaget's sensori-motor stage (0–2 years)

Features of this stage include:

- object permanence
- causality
- representational ability
- imitation.

The sensori-motor stage represents the first stage of Piaget's cognitive theory. During this stage we witness the use of the senses and movement by the infant to learn about its world and to construct knowledge of it.

As they develop, infants realise that they can make things happen; they bang spoons and throw objects from their high chair. This also highlights that the infant sees itself as separate from its environment and is developing a sense of agency about its actions, in other words, that it is the 'agent' or initiator of its actions. Another aspect to this is causality, when the child begins to recognise a causal relationship that exists; for example, 'If I shake this rattle it will make a noise.'

Object permanence

Object permanence refers to the understanding that objects continue to exist even when we can no longer see them. Its acquisition towards the end of this stage is considered an important milestone in cognitive development. Related to object permanence is the concept of representational ability. This involves the ability to make a mental representation of an object; that is, to be able to represent it mentally or within your mind. This allows the child to manipulate the object, which can lead to the further acquisition of problem-solving skills. A good way to understand representational ability or mental representation is to imagine you're driving to college or work and you get stuck in a traffic jam. If you know the area you can mentally represent a map of it and start figuring out a new way to get to your destination. You map out your new route in your mind before you commit to it. The ability to map the area in your mind reflects a representational ability. Piaget believed this ability developed between 18 and 24 months of age.

Imitation

Imitation is the reproduction of an expression or behaviour. Piaget proposed that imitation was achieved at roughly nine months of age and that deferred imitation occurred later, again after the acquisition of mental representation.

Meltzoff and Moore (1977) found that babies could, within a few weeks of life, imitate or reproduce a facial expression made by an adult, such as sticking a tongue out. Some have argued that this is merely a reflex; however Meltzoff and Moore believe it reflects a biologically based capacity to imitate. Meltzoff (1988) also found evidence of what he believes to be a nine-month-old's capacity for deferred imitation. This means that the infant reproduces a gesture after a certain amount of time has lapsed, for example, the following day. This is noteworthy when we consider that Piaget did not believe that children acquired 'object permanence' until the end of the second year. In order to have object permanence the child must be able to make a mental representation of the object so that they know the object continues to exist even though they can no longer see it. Yet in order to imitate a facial expression these very young infants must already possess these abilities to some degree. Not only does Meltzoff and Moore's research demonstrate that imitation is acquired earlier than Piaget proposed, it would also suggest that infants acquire concepts such as object permanence and mental representation earlier than proposed by Piaget.

Piaget's pre-operational stage (2–7 years)

One of the most notable features of this stage is that the child is egocentric: they believe that everyone else sees the world through their eyes and do not understand that other people might see or think about things differently; and this is reflected in their thinking.

Symbolic thinking develops as the child begins to acquire language, which they can use to enhance their thinking. The child now can use words and images (symbols) to represent objects. By the end of this stage, features such as animism (where the child ascribes consciousness to an inanimate object) begin to fade.

Piaget discussed pretend play as another feature of this stage where, for example, a stick is transformed into a sword. Piaget believed that play and imitation were important activities in the developing child. While he saw play's primary function for children as one of enjoyment, he felt that imitation reflected the child's attempt to master or copy some new movement or action from another. Piaget proposed that while play involved a process of assimilation by the child, imitation was a product of accommodation in their construction of knowledge.

Piaget conceived that the development of play was broken into three parts; the second stage, termed 'play stage', was witnessed during the pre-operational period between the ages of three and six years old. This stage is dominated by the child's egocentrism and, as such, the child engages in mainly solitary play as they are generally too egocentric to play co-operatively with others, although parallel play does occur. In the pre-operational stage, symbolic thinking is emerging and this is reflected through the symbolic use of objects and actions during pretend play. Thus a cardboard box becomes a boat, for example.

Piaget's concrete operational stage (7–11 years)

Children learn through concrete or 'real' objects. Piaget believed that the acquisition of conservation was an important developmental milestone (see the illustration on p.53). There are several types of conservation (length, volume, mass and weight). An example is the understanding that two differently shaped glasses contain the same amount of juice. Reversibility – the ability to mentally undo an action – is reached at the conclusion of this phase and is needed to enable the child to grasp conservation. Decentring is achieved when the child becomes less egocentric in their thinking and able to take the perspective of others.

Vygotsky

Vygotsky was a cognitive theorist who also emphasised the importance of play. Vygotsky believed that play allowed the child the opportunity to interact with other children, which in turn increased the potential for learning to occur. Another aspect of play according to Vygotsky is that language is used in the interaction between peers, through negotiation of rules for games and discussions around role playing. Vygotsky emphasised that language and development build upon each other.

Theory of mind

'Theory of mind' is the understanding that others see and understand things differently than you do. This ability is vital in the arena of social relationships; it enables us to predict the behaviour of others and have insight into their actions. Piaget suggested that children do not develop this ability until the age of six or seven; however, subsequent research has demonstrated that children typically acquire theory of mind earlier than this. The 'Sally Ann doll test' can be used to assess if theory of mind is present.

The Sally Anne doll test

Imagine a young child watching a puppet show with two dolls named Sally and Ann. Sally decides to go for a walk but before she leaves she places her marble in her basket. After Sally leaves, Ann removes the marble from the basket and places it in her box. When Sally returns where will she look for her marble?

If the child replies that Sally will look for the marble in Ann's box (where Ann hid it) then the child does not yet possess theory of mind. To demonstrate theory of mind the child has to be able to appreciate that Sally has her own beliefs about the world which can differ from the child's own. A deficit in theory of mind has been implicated in autism (see Chapter 5). As you can see, theory of mind is important in the social sphere of our lives where the ability to understand other people's state of mind is essential. The social sphere is imperative for healthy functioning through the lifespan. In the following section we will recap the major theorists in this area from Chapter 3. We will look also at more specific theories (such as maternal bonding and object relations theory) and issues such as parenting and its implications for development.

Socio-emotional development

Freud's oral stage (0–2 years)

As we saw in Chapter 3, Freud considered the mouth as the prime source of pleasure and believed that feeding and, more particularly, the weaning period should be handled with care. He advised against weaning a baby too early or indulging the infant and weaning too late, as either could result in the infant's becoming 'fixated' at the oral stage. This could have negative consequences in later life, including swearing, smoking, biting of nails, overeating and so on. You will notice that all these behaviours are related to the area of the mouth. Freud advised that through oral satisfaction, the baby develops trust and an optimistic personality. If the child experiences oral dissatisfaction, then the personality may become pessimistic, aggressive and distrusting.

Freud's psychosexual theory: anal and phallic stages

Anal stage (2–3 years)

The focus of pleasure shifts to the anus, helping the child become aware of its bowels and how to control them. By deciding itself, the child takes an important step of independence, developing confidence and a sense of when to 'give things up'. However, over-strictness can cause personality problems such as anal fixation – a child forced 'to go' may develop a reluctance about giving away *anything* and may become a hoarder or miser. Conversely over-concern about 'going regularly' may cause obsessive timekeeping or always being late.

Phallic stage (3–6 years)

Children become aware of their genitals and sexual differences. This stage is where the paths of males and females begin to diverge as the realisation of their differences becomes apparent to them.

The Oedipus complex

Each boy unconsciously goes through a sequence of stages beginning with the development of a strong desire for his mother, noticing the bond between his parents, becoming jealous of his father and hating him, then becoming afraid lest his father discover his son's true feelings, resulting in fear of punishment – castration.

Historically the other major theorist in the area of social and emotional development is Erikson.

Erikson

Trust vs. mistrust (0–1 year)

In the first year of life the infant is completely dependent on its caregivers. How well the infant's needs are met and how sensitive the parenting is decides whether the infant develops trust or mistrust of the world.

Autonomy vs. shame and doubt (1–2 years)

Children begin to walk and assert their independence. Children can come to believe in themselves and their abilities through the encouragement and support of their caregivers. If the child's efforts are ridiculed, the child will develop a feeling of shame and doubt. Toilet training is seen as one of the key events which can influence the outcome of this stage.

Initiative vs. guilt (3–5 years)

As the child becomes older they exhibit increasing curiosity and interest, they initiate play and question more. The main aim of this stage is to acquire a sense of purpose. If this is discouraged or they are held back, they will not develop self-initiative and instead will hold back in later life.

Attachment

Before looking at maternal bonding and object-relation theories it is useful to ground these theories against attachment, which is defined as 'a long-enduring, emotionally meaningful tie to a particular individual' (Schaffer, 1996, p.127). This very early relationship we form with another acts as a template for our later relationships in life. Thus it is of critical importance that attachment is supported and nurtured, especially at the early stages. It is reflective of the importance of this early relationship that many intervention programmes involve parenting as a significant element, reflecting the recognition that secure attachment is generally associated with better outcomes later in life (see Chapter 3 for in-depth discussion on attachment). (We will examine adult attachment styles and their implications below.) Somewhat similar to the concept of attachment is that of maternal bonding theory and both share an emphasis in the mother–child relationship.

Maternal bonding theory

Herbert (2006, p.54) comments that the 1970s were a stark 'critical period' for bonding, where it was proposed that during the first hours after birth the mother should engage in bonding with her baby through tactile, visual and olfactory stimulation. It was suggested that interruption of this bonding (for example, where the baby is removed to intensive care) could have negative long-term effects on the mother–child relationship. Thankfully this stark belief is no longer popular, but maternal bonding still holds interest in many quarters. Studies have found no evidence that disruption of 'close contact' between mother and child has any impact on their relationship or mothering effectiveness.

Early attachment theory and maternal bonding theory both emphasise the importance of the mother–child relationship in a child's development. Bowlby outlines the deleterious effects of that relationship, as discussed in Chapter 3. Another conceptualisation of loss is that of object relations, as developed by Melanie Klein. Klein was a famous psychoanalyst, and in developing object relations theory she suggested that the 'loss' of an object could have a potentially negative effect (for example, to an infant an 'object' could be their mother; the loss of the mother through perhaps death or separation could lead to negative outcomes for the child in later life).

Object relations theory continues the study of psychological development and contributes its own special lens with which to look into a person's inner world. The focus of object relations theory is not on the forces of libido and aggression nor on the adaptive functions of the ego. Rather, it is on the complex relationship of self to other. Object relations theory explores the process whereby people come to experience themselves as separate and independent from others, while at the same time needing profound attachment to others. Klein (1952) summarised the core tenet of this theory: 'there is no instinctual urge, no anxiety situation, no mental process which does not involve objects, external or internal; in other words, object relations are at the centre of emotional life' (p.53).

It is interesting that Klein emphasises the notion of the individual experiencing themself as other and separate from others. The development of a sense of self has also been considered from perspectives other than the psychoanalytic perspective.

The development of 'self'

The development of a sense of self is a quality that marks us as unique individually, and possibly even as a species. In terms of the development of self-awareness, it is believed that by:

- 18 months old – children learn to recognise themselves
- one year old – children begin to express their emotional states.

It is then that they must make the distinction between self and other. Rochat (2001) charts the development of self-knowledge in infants from implicit self-knowledge towards explicit self-knowledge.

Implicit self-knowledge

There are two types of implicit self-knowledge. The first is perceptual in origin and relates to the development of knowledge about our own body through self-exploration and action on objects. The second is social and refers to the development of specific knowledge through our interactions and reciprocation with others.

The development of a sense of self can be witnessed through our use of language. Rochat (2001) contends that the use of 'me' refers to the early stage of implicit self-knowledge, while the use of 'I' is accomplished at the explicit stage of self-knowledge, or when self-concept is formed. Regardless of how one conceptualises the development of a sense of self, it is an integral part of the development of an individual. Personality is a concept used to describe characteristics that form the core sense of who a person is. There have been many approaches to conceptualising personality, which we will examine next.

Personality and temperament

Before considering what personality is and the theories that attempt to explain it, it is valuable to define and consider 'temperament' and how it differs from personality. Put simply, temperament is considered more a biological predisposition than the construct of personality. Temperament is a biologically based propensity for individuals to react emotionally and behaviourally to events in a certain way.

What kind of temperament did you have as a baby? Were you a happy or easygoing baby or did you frequently throw tantrums? Temperament is believed to contribute towards the development of personality. With regard to infancy, theorists have tended to focus on whether an infant's temperament impacts on the parent–child interaction. Another area of interest is whether temperament is stable across a person's lifespan and if childhood temperament predicts adult outcomes.

Personality

I was drawn to studying psychology as I've always been interested in why we are the way we are. Many explanations are offered: the nature versus nurture argument; those who believe we are creatures of biology and others who hold the role of the social world as paramount. Personality fundamentally examines our uniqueness; the characteristics and behaviours that make us uniquely ourselves. Passer (2001) relates that the concept of personality rests on the observation that people appear to behave somewhat consistently over time and across different situations. From this consistency 'comes the notion of personality traits that characterise individuals' customary ways of responding to their world' (p.542).
Definition: Personality is the distinctive and relatively enduring way of thinking, feeling and acting that characterises a person's responses to life situations.

We have already met some of the theorists who have developed theories of personality. In Chapter 3 we examined Freud's theory of personality, which consisted of the id, ego and superego. In the same chapter humanism was considered, especially relevant being Carl Rogers' 'self' approach, which encompasses the need for positive regard and self-esteem (see Chapter 10 for more on his theory). In this section we will focus on trait and biological approaches to the conceptualisation of personality. These include:

- Cattell's sixteen personality factors
- the five-factor model.

Cattell's sixteen personality factors

Cattell can be thought of as a trait theorist; this means he focused on ways to describe the basic classes of behaviour that define personality, to devise ways of measuring individual differences in personality traits, and to use these measures to understand and predict a person's behaviour.

Revelle (2009, p.256) recounts that Cattell believed that 'it is possible to divide traits into those that reflect abilities, those that are dynamic, and those that are stable temperaments. Ability traits are all positively correlated and are sensitive to differences in task difficulty. ... Dynamic traits may be measured as responses to cues for reward and punishment, and temperamental traits were what was left over when the other two are removed.' Cattell recognises the interplay between ability (what one can do) and temperamental traits (what one normally does). As you can see from the table below, people are asked to rate themselves in line with the sixteen personality factors listed.

Table 4.2: Cattell's sixteen factors of personality

	1	2	3	4	5	6	7	8	
reserved									outgoing
less intelligent									more intelligent
affected by feelings									emotionally stable
submissive									dominant
serious									happy-go-lucky
expedient									conscientious
timid									venturesome
tough-minded									sensitive
trusting									suspicious
practical									imaginative
forthright									shrewd
self-assured									apprehensive
conservative									experimenting
group dependent									self-sufficient
uncontrolled									controlled
relaxed									tense

The sixteen personality factors questionnaire (16PF) can be used for individuals, and also to profile groups of people (for example, the personality traits of Olympic athletes). It can be used in vocational, counselling and educational settings.

The five-factor model (FFM)

This model also belongs to the trait approach to understanding personality. Not everyone agreed with Cattell's 16 factors believing that this number could be reduced to only five 'higher-order' factors as shown in the table below.

When ratings for large numbers of behaviours or characteristics are analysed, it is found that five factors often emerge. This was noticed as long ago as the early 1930s, but it wasn't until the 1980s that a number of researchers began to reach a consensus: that you could capture most of the broad-level variations in behaviour or the characteristics of human beings using the 'big five' factors.

Costa and McCrae (2005, p.81) add that, 'in the past 20 years, the FFM has become the dominant model of personality trait structure, assessed by a variety of measures (De Raad and Perugini, 2002) that include both self-report and observer rating versions. A large body of research has established the universality of the structure (Rolland, 2002) and the heritability (Bouchard and Loehlin, 2001) and long-term stability (Roberts and DelVecchio, 2000) of the factors.'

Table 4.3: The five-factor model

Dimension	High scorers are . . .	Low scorers are . . .
Extroversion	Outgoing, enthusiastic and active; you seek novelty and excitement.	Aloof, quiet and independent; you are cautious and enjoy time alone.
Neuroticism	Prone to stress, worry and negative emotions.	Emotionally stable but can take unnecessary risks.
Conscientiousness	Organised, self-directed and successful, but controlling.	Spontaneous, careless, can be prone to addiction.
Agreeableness	Trusting, empathetic and compliant, you are slow to anger.	Unco-operative and hostile, find it hard to empathise with others.
Openness	Creative, imaginative, eccentric and open to new experiences.	Practical, conventional, sceptical and rational.

The role of parenting in development

The role of parenting is perhaps considered one of the most crucial influences in development not just in childhood but also for later life. The emphasis on and plethora of parenting research, support and interventions reflects the primacy attached to this activity. Gilligan (1995, p.71), reflecting on parenting interventions, suggests that 'To be effective, family support must be responsive and accessible: above all, it must connect with the family who need the support when they need it. ... Family support must be offered and available on terms that make sense within the lived reality of its target users. In practice this will mean emphasising a low key, local, non-clinical, unfussy, user friendly approach.' Before we look at interventions aimed at supporting parenting, we will examine one of the best known theories regarding parenting – Baumrind's parenting styles, as well as research into parenting and finally a parenting intervention in Ireland designed to support families at risk.

Diana Baumrind's parenting styles

Attachment is an important aspect in the study of the relationship between parent and child. Research has also been carried out into parenting style and the differences that appear to exist (some parents adopt a strict approach while others do not). Diana Baumrind (1966), in her paper 'Effects of authoritative parental control on child behaviour', suggests the following three styles of parenting:

Permissive

- Parents tend to be relaxed about discipline, avoid exercise of control.
- Parents make few demands upon the child regarding household chores or orderly behaviour.
- Parents sees themselves not as active agents shaping the child but as a resource for the child to use.
- Parents do not encourage the child to obey externally defined standards.

Authoritarian

- Parents value obedience, child in its place.
- When disagreement exists between parents and child, parents favour a punitive approach.
- Parents believe the child should accept the word of the parents, do not believe in verbal give and take or discussions.

Authoritative

- Parents encourage verbal give and take.
- Parents willing to share reasoning behind their decision-making with the child and are open to adapting.
- Parents set standards for future behaviour.
- Parents praise and affirm the child's qualities.

Implicit in this and other research on parenting styles is that different parenting styles can lead to different outcomes for the child. Dekovic and Janssens (1992) found that children of authoritative parents tended to be more popular, while children of authoritarian parents were less so.

Studies by Zahn-Waxler *et al.* (1979, 1994) propose that parental type is closely associated with children's prosocial behaviour. These instrumental types are:

- **Provision of clear rules and principles:** which maintains that if a parent explains a rule of behaviour the child is more likely to exhibit prosocial behaviour; for example, explaining to a child why it should not bite another is more likely to elicit a positive response than merely telling them not to do it.
- **Attributing prosocial qualities to the child:** suggests if a child is told that it is kind and so on then the child is more likely to internalise these characteristics as part of their own perceived personality.
- **Modelling by parent:** this is believed to be one of the most vital functions of parents and is almost common sense.
- **Empathic care-giving to the child:** if parents are warm and responsive towards the child then the likelihood increases of the child displaying the same tendencies.

Parenting and family environment

The family environment and relationship, as witnessed with Eron's findings (Eron *et al.*, 1971), play an influential role in the development of aggressiveness. Several types of parenting have been associated with increased levels of aggression in children.

Olweus' (1980) types of parenting style

Dan Olweus (cited in Schaffer, 1996, p.287) identified several parenting styles, which he proposed were implicated in children's aggression:

- **Rejection by parents:** suggests that adolescent boys whose mothers are indifferent or fully reject them behave more aggressively. The mother's indifference is reflected in a lack of interest in the youth's attempt to develop self-control, and a lack of praise.
- **Parental permissiveness:** When a parent does not set limits of behaviour and maintain them the boy feels he can behave as he wishes with apparent parental approval. Olweus found a strong relationship between a high incidence of aggression and a high degree of laxness on the mother's part.
- **Parental modelling of aggression:** Children imitate and learn behaviours from their parents, including aggression. Aggression has been traced across three generations (Eron study).

We have seen in many guises the essential importance of the parent–child relationship in promoting positive development. We will now look at an intervention whose aim is to support parents within the community. Hopefully this will highlight the interconnectedness and relevance of the world of theory and research with that of real-life interventions.

In focus: Community interventions supporting parents

Community Mothers Programme

According to the Irish College of Psychiatrists (2005, p.17) there is a clear and documented relationship between mental well-being and early experiences, especially in the realm of attachment relationships. Further, 'Interventions specifically targeting this age group [0–5 years] can have preventative/protective value and have been shown to be successful (e.g. the Community Mothers Programme and programmes for the prevention of antisocial behaviour in childhood and adolescence).'

The Community Mothers Programme (CMP) is an example of Bronfenbrenner's ecological approach in practice. Bronfenbrenner suggested that the individual is influenced by their environment, from their immediate family right up to government policy. The Community Mothers Programme is a community-based programme funded by the Health Service Executive (HSE), that seeks to support new mothers who are perceived to be vulnerable. Experienced mothers from the community are given training and visit these new mothers offering them guidance. Thus we can see how Bronfenbrenner's approach, recognising many different sources of influence in the child's life, can be put into operation in the form of a practical support programme. Let's take a closer look at a piece written by the Director of the Community Mothers Programme, Brenda Molloy.

Mothers helping mothers

'A unique programme in which experienced mothers help other first-time mothers, mainly in disadvantaged areas, has proven to be a great success,' writes Brenda Molloy.*

Today's pressures mean that all parents, and particularly those who live in areas of social stress and disadvantage, need support if they are to promote the health and development of their children, their families and the next generation.

It is now accepted that there is a link between childhood experiences and adult outcomes. Failure to provide good quality support in the early years of child-rearing means that a much higher level of resources may need to be invested by the health, social and education services in later years in order to address and overcome the many problems that may arise as a result.

In addition to professional services, families need support networks to promote a sense of belonging and connection to the community.

The Community Mothers Programme, run by the HSE, has evolved since 1980, first using public health nurses as visitors to families with newborn babies, and then training experienced mothers from the local community to visit families to provide necessary support. Programmes like the CMP can provide a source of support to the family and help in building social networks.

The CMP is a support programme for first-time and some second-time parents of children from birth to 24 months who live in mainly disadvantaged areas. This includes lone parents, teenage parents, Travellers, asylum-seekers and refugees.

The CMP evolved from a UK-based child development programme. Following pilot phases, the programme was formally launched in the former Eastern Health Board in 1988. Today it is delivered to nearly 1,200 parents each year in the HSE Dublin/North East, and Dublin/Mid-Leinster regions.

The programme aims to support and aid the development of parenting skills, and enhance parents' confidence and self-esteem. It is delivered by non-professional volunteer mothers known as 'community mothers', who are recruited, trained and supported by family development nurses.

A key element in recruiting community mothers is that they reflect the ethos of the community they intend to visit. Each full-time family development nurse works with a team of 18–20 community mothers and supports 100–120 families at any one time.

The community mothers visit parents once a month in their own homes, providing empathy and information in a non-directive way to foster parenting skills and parental self-esteem. They use a clear and flexible set of strategies and focus on healthcare, nutrition and overall child development.

The community mothers are all experienced mothers who work on a voluntary basis. They are given nominal expenses for each visit. They typically spend upwards of 13 hours each month on their visits to between 5 and 15 families.

Community mothers' motivation is to help their community with the knowledge and experience each has gained through child-rearing. Participation in the programme helps to increase their feelings of self-worth as they see parents developing an understanding of child development and they find themselves gaining status in their own community.

A recent study also showed that volunteering in the programme contributed to lifelong learning. At the same time, the parents are empowered to believe in their own capabilities and skills for parenting without becoming dependent on professionals.

The monthly visit to the family is the main focus of the programme. The issues discussed at each visit are tailored to the particular needs of the family. The approach is supportive of the parents' own ideas and recognises the parents' desire to do what is best for their child.

The main focus of the community mother's visit is to encourage new parents, both mothers and fathers, to set themselves targets for achievement during the month before the next visit, and to facilitate the development of the child, both physically and mentally. This is done by drawing out the parent's own potential rather than by giving advice and direction. The community mother uses illustrated information sheets to show both effective ways of achieving childrearing goals.

The information sheets provide an easy, non-threatening and relevant way of raising difficult issues and discussing them, and they are also easily understood because of their direct style. The philosophy of the programme is simple yet profound. The parent is acknowledged as the expert with their own child and the programme works to support the parents to help them achieve their own goals for their child's development.

The family development nurse is available to the community mother to discuss problems and developments in relation to the programme. Once a month, the family development nurse meets with the community mother to discuss the families being visited. The community mothers also meet as a group, along with the family development nurse each month for support and ongoing training. Additional supports in the form of breastfeeding support groups and parent and toddler groups have evolved over the years. They are facilitated by community mothers and they support an additional 600 parents each year. In 1990 the programme was evaluated and was found to have significant beneficial effects for mothers and children.

Children in the programme scored better in terms of immunisation, cognitive stimulation and nutrition, and their mothers scored better in terms of nutrition and self-esteem than those not in the programme.

At that time the programme was only aimed at first-time parents during the first 12 months of the child's life; parents received a maximum of 12 visits, usually one a month lasting approximately one hour.

Further evaluation was conducted seven years later, when the children were aged eight. A major finding was the persistence of superior parenting skills among the programme families. Children whose mothers were in the CMP were more likely to have better nutritional intake, read books and to visit the library regularly.

Mothers in the programme had higher levels of self-esteem. They were also more likely to oppose smacking, to have developed strategies to help them and their children to deal with conflict, to enjoy participating in their children's games, eat appropriate foods, and to express positive feelings about motherhood.

The benefits extended to subsequent children who were more likely to have completed their primary and MMR immunisation and to be breastfed. The results are positive as they show that just 12 contact hours in the first year of a child's life can make a difference.

The CMP programme empowers the women who deliver it as well as the parents who receive it. It is helping some 2,000 children a year to reach their full potential.

*Brenda Molloy is Director of the Community Mothers Programme, HSE Dublin/ North East and Dublin/Mid-Leinster

Source: www.irishhealth.com

The Springboard initiative

The Springboard Family Support pilot projects for children at risk is the first major family support initiative of its kind in Ireland. It was established by the Department of Health and Children in 1998 with approval from the Cabinet Committee on Social Inclusion. Initially 14 projects were established throughout the country aimed at supporting vulnerable families. An important part of the work of Springboard during the pilot phase was in fully evaluating the services provided and the outcomes for families. This evaluation report fills a gap in Irish-based research on what works in intensive family support services. According to the Department of Health and Children (DoHC), the intention of the initiative is to provide a valuable framework for how child and family difficulties should be tackled at local community level, and a baseline for quality service provision in supporting troubled families.

Source: www.dohc.ie

Further interventions designed to support families and children can be found in Appendix 1.

Table 4.4: An evaluation of the Naas Child and Family Project

Project ethos:	• Ability of project staff to translate the ethos of the project, which clearly values and respects individuals and families, into a practice which places them centre stage. • Commitment to the empowerment of families particularly evident in individual/family work. • Evidence of ability to provide services to the community in the community. • Ability to respond to immediate and local need, identifying gaps in service provision, listening to the local community and planning their services accordingly. • Highly accessible, visible and transparent service. • Provision of a flexible and responsive service.
Project practice:	• Team commitment to the development and provision of a high quality service reflected in the work to date on policies and procedures, and the commitment to the need for ongoing attention in this area. • Ability to reach families other services have failed to engage with. • Clear examples of interventions and strategies that work, effecting real change and improving the quality of life for the families engaged with. • Provision of a wide range of relevant, appropriate, diverse and innovative services. • Provision of a range of both referred and open access activities and interventions. • High availability of staff to families, referrers, and other professionals for support, consultation and advice. • Provision of non-stigmatising, non-threatening service which is perceived to be user-friendly. • Ability to work intensively, over time, with families. • Ability to pace intensity of the intervention in response to the individual needs of each family.

Project staff:	• Clear structure for the provision of staff support and supervision. • Stable staff complement with only one personnel change in two years. • Evidence of mutual support structure among staff members. • Evidence of diverse and specialised skill base, with stated commitment to continue to build on this. • Team commitment to training and skill building. • High quality of report writing and recording practice with a commitment to updating these practices.
Project partnerships:	• Stated commitment to collaborative practice involving evidence of co-working, and involving outside agencies/professionals in the direct provision of an initiative or service. • Clear inter-agency and inter-professional focus apparent, with progress recorded regarding links with schools and social work departments in particular. • Commitment to working in partnership with families with structures in place to support this. • Partnership approach evident at management level, with structures developed for SWAHB, KYS and NC&PP collaboration and co-operation. • Commitment to updating other services and agencies with regular project presentations given.
Project focus:	• Clear commitment to engaging 'hard to reach' families, with priority given to 'at risk' cases.

Source: Holt *et al.*, 2002, p.78

As can be seen from the pieces on Springboard and the Community Mothers Programme, emphasis has clearly been placed on supporting families to effect positive outcomes for children. Adolescence can hold particular risks for many reasons; certainly the physiological changes teenagers experience can make it more difficult for them to weather the 'storm', as Stanley Hall described the period of adolescence. As we learned in Chapter 2, the brain undergoes major changes which have been implicated in risky behaviours. If family, school or peer difficulties are added to this potentially volatile period the consequences can be dire, ranging from eating disorders to suicide (see below).

ADOLESCENCE

Adolescence, which comes from the Latin *adolescere* meaning 'to grow up', is seen as a unique transitionary period between childhood and adulthood encompassing not just physical but also social, emotional and cognitive changes. Puberty refers to the commencement and maturation of biological, physical and sexual characteristics and is generally considered in most cultures to signify the change or transition from childhood to adulthood. Puberty refers to the physical and sexual changes that are experienced during this period. Adolescence encompasses the behavioural, social and emotional aspects of this transition and is influenced by physical and social/cultural factors.

The World Health Organization defines adolescence as the second decade of life, from 10 to 20 years of age. Yet adolescence is not merely chronological age; it is also socially constructed, which means that some societies have different ideas about what 'adolescence' means. In some cultures puberty marks the child's coming of age and ability to take on 'adult' roles. Girls may marry or begin childbearing far earlier than we would be accustomed to in the West.

There is a difference in the age that males and females start their growth spurt:

- Girls: approximately 10 years of age
- Boys: approximately 12 years of age.

So as we can see, girls begin their development approximately two years earlier than boys. It is worth noting that these ages indicate just the beginning of biological changes and not necessarily the associated secondary sexual characteristics associated with adolescence.

Sexual maturation

One of the most obvious characteristics associated with adolescence is the changing appearance of the teenager. Pubertal timing refers to the commencement of puberty and its associated physical and sexual changes. More noticeable changes in girls are the development of breasts and in boys the appearance of facial hair, for instance. Differentiation is made between primary and secondary sexual characteristics.

Primary sexual characteristics

These are the changes and development that directly involve the sex organs.

Girls – menarche: this refers to the start of menstruation (periods) in girls. The average age of puberty for Irish girls (menarche) is 13.5 years, within a range of 10.9 to 16.1 years of age (Malina *et al.*, 2004, p.314). The average age of menarche in the US is 12.8 years of age.

Boys – spermarche: This term was coined to mark the sexual maturation of boys, when males become capable of reproduction. 'Spermarche' refers to the first time a boy ejaculates. As this is a private event it is difficult to determine an age for this event or to conduct useful research.

Differences in timing of puberty

While puberty encompasses changes in males and females, we will examine the onset of menarche to examine influences on the timing of puberty.

Factors involved in the timing of puberty include hereditary factors and nutrition. There is a trend for younger menarche, with societal (secular) influences being implicated.

Early pubertal timing in girls and absent fathers

Research in the field of pubertal timing has found that a number of different factors affect the start of puberty. Physical influences include weight, nutrition and exercise. For example, high levels of exercise in female dancers have been found to delay pubertal maturation. While physical factors may make intuitive sense to us, some other factors might appear more puzzling. Ellis (2000) relates perhaps one of the most fascinating pieces of research to emerge regarding pubertal timing: that a relationship exists between early puberty in girls and the absence of fathers in their lives. Ellis cites Belsky *et al.* (1991), who found that a family environment with an absent biological father and maternal depression related to early pubertal timing in girls. I stress biological father because they found that girls who had stepfathers present in their lives were also more likely to begin puberty early.

Belsky, Steinberg and Draper have proposed an 'evolutionary' explanation for early pubertal timing. Evolutionary psychology attempts to explain human behaviours by claiming that the motivation for these behaviours is found in how we have evolved or adapted to our environment. The main focus of evolution is the reproduction of the organism. So the aim of all human behaviour is seen in terms of survival and reproduction. With this in mind, the evolutionary explanation of early pubertal timing rests on the notion that a girl whose biological father is absent is more 'vulnerable', has fewer resources and less protection and, as such, it makes evolutionary sense for such a girl to be able to reproduce earlier than females whose biological fathers are present and caring for them.

Effect of pubertal timing

We looked at how factors such as father absence have been implicated in the early start of menarche in girls, but what are the effects of early and late pubertal maturation on females and males? This has been a popular source of research and findings suggest a number of outcomes. Brooks-Gunn *et al.* (1985) suggested that adolescents who are 'off-time' (early or late maturation) with their peers, experience more stress and as such are more susceptible to adjustment problems in adolescence. A second explanation offered is that early developers, especially females, face more social pressure. If they mature earlier they will face the attention of male sexual interest earlier, and the physical development of their body does not match that of their brain and cognitive development, so they have less advanced 'thinking' skills with which to handle the increased attention that their early maturation attracts. As such teenagers look older there can be a tendency for them to be viewed as more socially and cognitively developed than they actually are. It is also suggested that in developing earlier these adolescents miss the opportunity to complete the normal development tasks of middle childhood as they fast forward past this stage.

Early maturation

Boys: early maturation appears to be associated with more positive outcomes, particularly in terms of social development; they enjoy prestige.

Girls: in contrast, girls face more problems, including an increased likelihood of negative moods and behaviours. Brooks-Gunn et al. (1985) reported negative body image.

Early maturers are more vulnerable to engaging in risk-taking behaviours, including smoking, drinking and sexual activity at an earlier age (Magnusson et al., 1985).

Late maturation

Boys: may demonstrate lower achievement (Dubas et al., 1991), lower self-esteem and happiness (Crockett and Petersen, 1987).

Girls: higher achievement in girls was evident in research conducted by Dubas et al. (1991).

In focus: Eating disorders

Eating disorder as a psychopathological condition is often associated with adolescence. Eating disorders, while they manifest themselves in the physical domain (weight loss and disturbed eating patterns), are seen as a psychological disorder. Examining them offers us a bridge between the physical and psychological domains of functioning.

Anorexia nervosa

Anorexia nervosa, from the Greek meaning 'loss of appetite', is an eating disorder that inflicts self-starvation on millions of people each year. Further, this disorder allows adolescents to gain control by limiting food intake. Anorexics often obsess about thinness, need attention, lack individuality and deny sexuality. It affects females 15 times more than it affects males. It usually begins during adolescence or in early adulthood, but hardly ever occurs in women past the age of 25. The disorder affects one teenager in every two hundred among adolescents aged between 16 and 18.

The criteria for anorexia nervosa given by the most recent diagnostic system includes intense fear of becoming obese which does not diminish with the progression of weight loss; disturbance of body image, feeling 'fat' even when emaciated; refusal to maintain body weight over a minimal weight for age and height; weight loss of 25 per cent of original body weight or 25 per cent below the expected weight based on standard growth charts; and no known physical illness that would account for the weight loss (Field and Domangue, 1987, p.31).

Bulimia

Bulimia is a Greek word meaning 'ox' and 'hunger' because the sufferer eats like a hungry ox. A bulimic eats in unrestrained eating sprees. One major characteristic of bulimia is binge eating, in which the sufferer can consume between 10,000 to 20,000 calories. These binge-eating episodes are usually followed by purging. Purging is accomplished by one of the following methods: vomiting, laxatives, diuretics, enemas, compulsive exercising, weight-reducing drugs, or intermittent periods of strict dieting.

Bulimia can be associated with anorexia nervosa. In the past it was actually considered to be a part of the disorder. Most anorexics develop bulimia in the course of their illness. Unlike anorexia, bulimia affects 3 to 7 per cent of women aged between 15 and 35. Bulimia is defined as a syndrome in which gorging on food alternates with purging by forced vomiting, fasting or laxatives (Field and Domangue, 1987, p.32). The effects on people who suffer from this include guilt, depression and disgust with oneself. Bulimics know that their eating habits are unhealthy but fear not being able to stop eating voluntarily.

What are the similarities between bulimia and anorexia?

Both disorders carry an obsession with weight and body image, and both are usually found in white, middle/upper-class females. These females usually have the characteristics of being perfectionists, high achievers, often academically or vocationally successful, and have a great need to please others.

The mortality rate for eating disorders is higher than for any other psychiatric disorder and studies suggest that the rate has been increasing over the last 20 years.

Mental attributes of teenagers with eating disorders

It is important for people to understand that adolescents suffering from eating disorders, both male and female, may not appear to be underweight. Weight is only a physical sign of an eating disorder, when in fact the adolescent is likely to be suffering from a deeper emotional conflict that needs to be resolved. Eating disorders are only addictions to a behaviour and the obsession with food is only a symptom of deeper problems, such as low self-esteem, depression, poor self-image and self-hate. Hilde Bruch, a pre-eminent psychiatrist, describes the relentless pursuit of thinness as an effort to mask underlying problems (Bruch *et al.*, 1988). The following are some of the mental characteristics of adolescent males and females suffering from eating disorders.

Perfectionism: Many adolescents suffering from eating disorders are perfectionists and high achievers. They strive to reach perfection in every aspect of their lives. They are eager to please and in the process lose their true selves. When they feel they have failed to reach perfection they often unrealistically blame themselves for their failure and attempt to punish themselves. Punishment often occurs in the form of starvation for anorexics and purging for bulimics.

Low self-esteem: Feelings of inadequacy are common among teenagers suffering from eating disorders. They have a poor self-image and perception of themselves. They irrationally believe they are fat regardless of how thin they become. They experience a sense of inner emptiness, uncertainty and helplessness, and a lack of self-confidence and self-trust (Bruch *et al.*, 1988). Often they are afraid of being judged by others or thought of as stupid. They feel confident if they are losing weight but suffer from feelings of worthlessness and guilt if they are not (Pipher, 1994). It is also common for them to believe they do not deserve good things or to be happy.

Depression: Mood swings, feelings of hopelessness, anxiety, isolation and loneliness are common to sufferers of eating disorders. Bulimics experience a loss of control that leads to depression, whereas anorexics experience depression as a result of gaining weight (Schlundt and Johnson, 1990).

Obsession: These adolescents deal with an intense obsession and pre-occupation with food, calories, fat content, and with their weight. Weight becomes their most important and self-defining attribute. Eating disorders are considered addictions in which starvation, bingeing and purging are the addictive behaviors and food is the narcotic (Pipher, 1994).

Guilt: Adolescents with eating disorders often feel guilty because they do not think they have met the expectations of others. They are striving for the perfect body and for a sense of control but in the process they start to feel guilty about their habit (Pipher, 1994). Lying becomes essential.

Treatment principles

According to the Irish College of Psychiatrists' report *A Better Future Now* (p.78), treatment principles for eating disorders are as follows:

- The treatment of anorexic patients must be based on a comprehensive and detailed assessment of their mental and physical status.
- A decision is then made as to whether treatment in an in-patient or outpatient setting is more appropriate.
- The increase in clinical cases has affected admission rates not only to psychiatric units but also to paediatric medical wards.

- It is clear that a severely emaciated patient will require intensive medical treatment; it can be extremely difficult to provide the necessary psychotherapeutic milieu in such an environment.
- In-patient treatment in a specialist unit offers the attraction of a wealth of accumulated experience in treating these disorders; however, patients with eating disorders can be effectively treated in a unit that treats a range of psychiatric disorders.
- Working with the parents is an integral part of any intervention programme.
- Out-patient programmes are increasingly considered as a treatment option; these involve specialist teams, who may work jointly with community teams.

Cognitive development

With the increasing activity seen in the brain, one would expect an increase in the cognitive abilities of the adolescent. This growth spurt brings many changes in the way young adults think, such as a better ability to handle more information and an improved ability to devise mental strategies to help them remember and organise information. The growth of the frontal lobe results in greater ability in higher reasoning and thinking. According to Kolb, the growth in the frontal lobe corresponds with Piaget's formal operational stage of thinking, the main features of which are abstract, inductive and deductive thinking.

Piaget's formal operational stage (age 12 onwards)

The main characteristic of this stage is the growing ability to think in abstract terms and the use of deductive logic. Up to this stage the child can only think about things that are 'real' or concrete. According to Piaget they are unable to reason about make-believe problems or situations. Concepts such as justice, ethics or love are abstract terms; you can't touch them or see them. As the adolescent develops abstract thinking they also begin to think more logically; they are able to consider hypotheses (educated guesses or explanations) and test them. Think of algebra and theorems in school. Shaffer (1999) reports that 12-year-old children, when asked where they'd put a 'third eye', provide more creative answers than younger children at the concrete level. One answer at this higher level was from a child who would put a third eye on their hand so they could use it to see around corners. Reflective of their growing cognitive abilities is that they can think about their own thoughts. The ability to think abstractly gives us great freedom in our thinking as we are no longer confined to the world of 'real' objects, concepts or ideas.

Is Piaget's abstract thinking related to other areas?

Neurological – there is increased growth in the prefrontal cortex which is responsible for higher reasoning and thought.

Moral – Kohlberg and Piaget believed that the ability to reason morally at higher and more complex levels came in the early teens.

Self – teenagers can now think about who they are, their different selves and their possible and future selves, which involves the use of abstract thinking.

Do your own research: Ask children and teenagers of varying ages where they would put a third eye and why? Note their answers and justifications and see if age differences exist.

David Elkind's theory of 'adolescent egocentrism'

In her teens, my younger sister routinely refused to leave the house because her make-up wasn't right or because she had a spot. I took great pleasure in pointing out that she wasn't that important and who would be looking at her to notice her face anyway! Sound familiar? If it doesn't, count your blessings, but if it rings true, David Elkind has an explanation for this behaviour: the 'imaginary audience', which is the belief that others are as concerned about the teenager's thoughts and behaviour, that others are as interested in them as they are themselves. It is quite literally the idea that they have an audience watching them. Now in my thirties I care far less what others think of me than I did when I was younger. Yet adolescents do care, very much so, and they assume that everyone else is as interested in them as they are. This is why a pimple on the nose turns into a major crisis as the teenager believes everyone will notice, everyone will be looking at them. This increased self-consciousness in adolescents is referred to as 'adolescent egocentrism' by Elkind. Indeed, it's hard not to feel sorry for the hapless adolescent going about their daily business in the belief that everyone is watching them.

While the imaginary audience forms one part of the social thinking that characterises 'adolescent egocentrism', another aspect of it is called the 'personal fable'. The 'personal fable' refers to the adolescent's belief that their experiences are unique; further, it feeds into a belief that they are not subject to the rules that govern the rest of the world, which contributes to a sense of invincibility. This belief has been implicated in some of the risk-taking behaviours seen in adolescence. Thus a teenager might take drugs with the belief that they won't become addicted, that it won't happen to *them*. While the belief in the 'imaginary audience' is strongest in early teenage years, it declines as the individual moves into later adolescence. The 'personal fable', on the other hand, can persist into early adulthood.

Socio-emotional development

David Elkind describes how adolescent behaviours can be explained by their unique style of thinking. Elkind proposes that the 'personal fable' is responsible for the teenager's belief in their own invincibility and this leads to risk-taking behaviours. Erikson, who is a socio-emotional theorist, suggests a different explanation. If you recall from Chapter 2, each of Erikson's stages can have either a negative or a positive outcome. The negative outcome, according to Erikson, for the teenager is 'role confusion', and it is this that is responsible for risky behaviours. Let's take a closer look.

Erikson's fifth stage: Identity vs. role confusion

As teenagers make the transition from childhood to adulthood, they face questions of 'who' they are and their future role in life. Erikson's fifth stage reflects this. The major developmental 'crisis' to be resolved is that of 'identity'. Adolescence, at least in the West, is synonymous with angst about 'Who am I?' and 'What is my role in life?' and those who successfully navigate this period develop their identity. Erikson referred to a 'psychological moratorium', meaning the gap between childhood and adulthood where the teenager explores different roles. By the end of the stage the adolescent will have successfully emerged with a sense of who they are. However, some will be unable to resolve the challenge of emerging identity. According to Erikson, they suffer from 'role confusion', resulting in either isolation or a willingness to take on the identity of others.

Identity is influenced by how the adolescent sees themself and is also based on their relationships with others and how they perceive others to see them. The concept of identity and self-concept is examined in more depth below. For Erikson, the development of self and identity is a major developmental milestone for the teenager to accomplish. Those who do not resolve this stage face 'role confusion', which leaves the person unsure of who they are and where their lives are going. Role confusion has been linked to risk-taking behaviours.

As noted by Erikson, identity is the major development 'crisis' to be resolved in the transition from childhood to adulthood. Other theories have been put forward to explain how identity emerges. We're going to examine identity and also the related concepts of self-concept and self-esteem. Let's look at another approach to understanding how adolescents characterise self-concept.

Definition of identity

Identity is the stable, consistent and reliable sense of who one is and what one stands for in the world. It integrates one's meaning to oneself and one's meaning to others; it provides a match between what one regards as central to oneself and how one is viewed by significant others in one's life.

Identity is not a unitary concept; it can have many aspects:

- religious identity
- sexual identity
- career identity
- cultural or ethnic identity.

Who I am in the classroom can be quite different to who I am at home with my son or out with friends; I am Irish, a woman, mother, teacher, friend, daughter and sister.

How do you see yourself? List some of your roles and identities.

James Marcia: Identity statuses and development

Building on the work of Erikson, Marcia suggested that identity involves the adoption of ideals and values, sexual orientation and work possibilities. Having considered the possibilities, the young person at the end of adolescence must make commitments about what to become and what to believe. Marcia used an interview technique to assess identity status. Unlike Erikson, whose theory is a stage-based one, Marcia formulated the idea of status, which allowed for a more fluid conception of identity formation.

Identity statuses

- moratorium (in crisis, no commitment)
- achievement (have had crisis and commitment)
- foreclosure (no crisis and commitment)
- diffusion (might have had crisis, no commitment).

Marcia's identity statuses

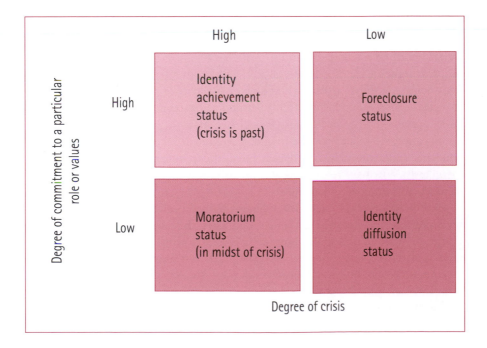

Moratorium

This is marked by intense crisis as the teenager searches out the possibilities, considering different roles in their search for identity. No commitment has been made yet.

Identity diffusion

The main characteristic of this stage is that the teenager is not in 'crisis', actively considering the possibilities; further, they are avoiding making a commitment. The stereotypical difficult teenager watching television and refusing to talk might be said to be in this state.

Identity foreclosure

This teenager might seem like the perfect adolescent who dutifully doesn't question or rebel. This teenager has made a commitment to an identity without going through the crisis and exploring alternatives. Instead, they have accepted a parental or culturally defined commitment. Erikson would believe that the teenager had not tackled the challenges of this period and instead relied on identification with others rather than carving out their own identity.

Identity achievement

The adolescent has come through the 'crisis' and a commitment has been made to ideological, occupational and other goals. They have established a sense of self, of their identity.

Self-concept and self-esteem

Another term for identity is self-concept, which can refer to all aspects of the self. We compare ourselves to others and how we evaluate or judge aspects of ourselves is called self-esteem. Harter (1990) defined self-esteem as 'how much a person likes, accepts, and respects himself [sic] overall as a person' (p. 255). During adolescence, self-esteem can be fragile; if you recall Elkind's imaginary audience you can understand that teenagers have the potential to judge themselves mercilessly. Why have researchers who are interested in identity development paid so much attention to adolescence?

In the section on physical development we examined the changes that occur with puberty and how these changes can alter the teenager's self-conception. Piaget maintained that adolescents are now able to think at far higher levels; this increased ability allows them to appreciate fully just how significant the changes are. They also can imagine themselves in the future or in different roles with the acquisition of abstract thinking. This feeds into a greater self-consciousness. Earlier in the chapter we saw that low self-esteem has been implicated in eating disorders.

The area of self-esteem has been extensively researched. A relationship exists between low self-esteem and low life satisfaction, loneliness, anxiety, resentment, irritability and depression (Rosenberg, 1985). High self-esteem was found amongst teenagers who saw themselves as close to their parents (Blyth and Traeger, 1988). As we have seen so far, the area of adolescent development is one fraught with difficulties and dependent on an array of different factors which influence outcomes. The following is a list of major life transitions from infancy to adolescence, identified by Carr (2003).

Adjustment to major life transitions

Problems of infancy and early childhood
- Sleep problems
- Toileting problems
- Learning and communication difficulties
- Autism and pervasive developmental disorders

Problems of middle childhood
- Conduct problems
- Attention and overactivity problems
- Fear and anxiety problems
- Repetition problems
- Somatic problems

Problems in adolescence
- Drug abuse
- Mood problems
- Anorexia and bulimia nervosa
- Schizophrenia

Child abuse
- Physical abuse
- Emotional abuse and neglect
- Sexual abuse

Adjustment to major life transitions
- Foster care
- Separation and divorce
- Grief and bereavement

Antisocial and criminal activities
Difficulties with children and adolescents participating in antisocial and criminal activities is a serious issue. Conduct disorder (see Chapter 7) is categorised as a

middle-childhood transition. It should be recognised that when dealing with young people, a different approach should be taken by law enforcement, which reflects and includes the complexity of their developmental stage. The **Garda Special Projects** aim to establish a positive system for diverting young people from offending through developing an infrastructure for development towards a locally based youth crime prevention programme. The following evaluation of Garda Special Projects uncovers changes in the behaviour of participants and their explanation for these changes.

Reported changes in behaviour and lifestyle of the participants

- Participants across the five Project sites studied in-depth indicated that they made changes in behaviour, attitude and lifestyle.
- The participants reported decreases in their offending and unacceptable behaviours as a result of their involvement with the Project.
- Positive changes and learning outcomes were also reported by them including:
  - development and acquisition of personal skills and abilities;
  - changes in lifestyles, outlook and socialising patterns.

To what features of the Projects do the participants attribute these changes? Interviews with 51 Project participants suggest the following key explanations for personal change from their own understanding:

- Positive relationships with Project staff – for the young people, the Projects have facilitated the creation of positive, trusting and supportive relationships with adults;
- Awareness of boundaries and rules – participants believe that they have to abide by rules or codes of behaviour in order to stay involved in the Project. This is more effective in structured groups where there is an apparent pre-condition of compliance to codes of behaviour, both inside and outside the Project. Conversely, this is less effective in activities of a casual or 'drop-in' nature or other unstructured Project actions where the same pre-condition is not enforced.
- Creation of positive alternatives by the Project – all the young people reported positively about their experiences of the Project in that they perceived that the Projects were providing them with alternative leisure, creative and developmental opportunities.

These mechanisms in turn contribute to a sense of attachment and commitment to the Projects. The majority of young people reported having an input into programme content, which further reinforces their commitment to the Project and their adherence to codes of behaviour. The latter is especially true where there is a sense that the participant has had a direct input into the formulation of agreed boundaries.

Finding a clear focus

While the results of the evaluation are very positive, the clear lesson arising from the findings presented above is that GSPs need to be focused. The young people have identified three clear outputs that make the Projects work:

- that they have established sound and positive relationships with youth work staff;
- that they are made aware of boundaries both outside and within the Project itself;
- that the Project affords them alternatives in terms of lifestyles, development opportunities and leisure.

It is clear that good practice in youth diversion projects must mobilise interventions to guarantee these three outputs. From our research, it appears that structured and focused interventions are more likely to have a greater impact particularly where there is a clear commitment assured from participants to working within agreed behavioural boundaries.

Source: www.tcd.ie

For those who work with young people, especially those who have offended or are at risk of offending or participating in antisocial behaviour, the findings of the Garda Special Projects evaluation are noteworthy. Many strands can be identified as influential; one such factor is positive relationships with staff. In Chapter 10 we consider interpersonal skills and the qualities needed to effect positive and supportive influence in the lives of others. Another factor identified is the importance of leisure activities. At a community level this is an issue we can try to work on. Leisure in the lives of young people has been consistently identified as important. The Office of the Minister for Children and Youth Affairs commissioned research which lead to *Teenspace: The National Recreation Policy for Young People*, which was published in September 2007 and provides a strategic framework for the promotion of positive recreational opportunities aimed principally at young people aged 12 to 18. The policy adopts an evidence-based approach and makes proposals to address issues that emerged from a public consultation process to give all interested parties, including young people, a chance to have a say in the development of the policy. Information on the policy and its implementation through, for example, youth cafes can be viewed at www.omc.gov.ie.

That concludes the section covering infancy up to adolescence; we are now going to explore the ignored area of adulthood. Historically, childhood and adolescence have been heavily researched in an attempt to understand development, and to plan and support positive development. In more recent times the issue of old age (see below) has begun to be developed in terms of research, policy and practice, highlighting the growing recognition of the paucity of knowledge that exists regarding older people. However, adulthood has still not received recognition as an important area that deserves consideration; hopefully that will change in the near future. In the meantime we will take a quick journey through this developmental period.

ADULTHOOD

Compared to childhood and adolescence, the period of adulthood has not received the same degree of attention or study. Different sources will use different parameters for the definition of adulthood, but the following are what I believe to be the most universal. This section is divided into three subsections:

- Early adulthood: age 20–40
- Middle adulthood: age 40–65
- Late adulthood: age 65 onwards.

Early and middle adulthood will be amalgamated, and we will explore theories relevant to this period including Levinson's season of man and Schaie's cognitive theory. Late adulthood or old age will be dealt with separately, reflecting the increasing research and policy being devoted to this area, such as TILDA (The Irish Longitudinal Study on Ageing) and Professor Robertson's work on the brain and ageing, which was mentioned in Chapter 2. Cognitive and socio-emotional domains will be looked at, but first a general introduction to ageing and related concepts is necessary.

Ageing

Many theories of ageing exist, but first the distinction needs to be made between primary and secondary aging:

- Primary ageing refers to the gradual age-related changes that we have no control over, reflecting the biological aspects of aging which affect everyone. Changes include greying hair and deterioration in hearing and vision.
- Secondary ageing is more individual in that it is influenced by lifestyle and environmental factors such as lack of exercise, smoking, alcohol consumption and obesity. Disease is a factor in secondary ageing.

Theories of ageing
Damage-based theories suggest that ageing results from a continuous process of damage which accumulates throughout the entire lifespan. This approach argues that ageing is predominantly a result of interactions with the environment.

Programmed theories of ageing suggest that ageing is not a result of random processes but rather that ageing is predetermined and occurs on a fixed schedule.

Signs of senescence

Senescence is the deterioration of bodily functions that accompanies ageing in a living organism. Some signs of ageing include:

- an overall decrease in energy
- the tendency to become easily tired
- changes to skin such as wrinkles, brown spots on the skin and loss of skin elasticity
- greying and thinning of hair
- a loss or decrease in vision and hearing
- slower reaction times.

Early and middle adulthood

Though this period of adulthood has not been as well researched as other stages, some theories do exist in regard to cognitive and social/emotional development. We will consider cognitive theories first, looking at Schaie's theory and that of post-formal thought.

Cognitive development

Schaie's theory of cognitive development

K. Warner Schaie (2000) offers a theory of cognitive development across the lifespan beginning with 'acquisition' and moving towards the end of life with 'legacy creating'. We will examine each stage of his theory within its age specificity:

Early adulthood

- **Acquisition** (childhood and adolescence): This involves the acquisition of mental structures, information and skills in order to gain understanding of the world.
- **Achieving** (late teens to early twenties): Young adults use their knowledge to pursue a career, choose a lifestyle and solve personal dilemmas.
- **Responsibility** (middle adulthood): Individuals use their abilities to solve problems related to their responsibilities to others; for example, family members.
- **Executive** (middle adulthood): This stage reflects a concern for the welfare of the broader social system. Individuals deal with complex relationships on multiple levels.
- **Reorganisation** (end of middle adulthood to the beginning of late adulthood): This stage is marked by retirement. Cognitive tasks involve the reorganisation of life around new interests and pursuits.
- **Reintegrative** (late adulthood): Older adults look back over their lives, to make sense of life. The older person learns to be selective in using more limited energies.

- **Legacy-creating** (advanced old age): This is the final stage of Schaie's theory and represents attempts by the older person to insure that some part of them will continue after they are gone; that they leave a legacy. Activities such as making a will or funeral arrangements will be engaged in.

As can be seen with Schaie's theory, it is a stage-based one concentrating on developmental changes across the span of adulthood into old age. The strength of this theory is its specificity. The next theoretical exposition is a development on Piaget's formal operational stage and is sometimes labelled as the 'fifth stage'. This postformal stage considers that rather than the mere acquisition of mental structures the individual is now able to apply this new level of thinking to problem solving and reasoning. 'Postformal thought' incorporates the ability to recognise that the correct answer to a problem requires reflective thinking and may vary from situation to situation. Adolescents tend to think in a dualistic manner, such as right or wrong; adults recognise that shades of grey exist and that each situation or problem is unique.

Both theories emphasise qualitative differences in how adults think and process information compared to earlier years. Certainly Piaget's formal operational stage is erroneous if one considers it the final point in the acquisition and development of adult cognitive capabilities.

We are going to move on to socio-emotional development beginning, as always, with Erikson and a recap of his theory; and then a theory specific to adulthood is considered: Levinson's stages of man, which breaks adulthood into tight parameters in consideration of the social changes that occur during adulthood.

Socio-emotional development

Erikson's isolation vs. intimacy (20–30 years)
In this stage Erikson proposes a positive outcome: intimacy, and a negative one: isolation. Intimacy relates to forming an intimate or love relationship and committing to it. Erikson suggested that isolation reflected an individual's hesitation to form a relationship, possibly due to a fear of losing identity or else self-absorption.

Erikson's generativity vs. stagnation
Generativity comes from 'to generate' and Erikson envisaged this stage as offering the opportunity to the individual to reach out to others and guide the younger generation. This can be seen particularly in child-rearing but also in more civic-minded activities such as coaching or community involvement. Here the focus lies beyond the self, to others. If this does not occur, the individual is faced with feelings of stagnation where they place their needs above challenge and sacrifice. They are self-indulgent, displaying little interest in work productivity or involvement with younger people.

Levinson's seasons of man

Daniel Levinson (1986) devised a theory that extends over the entire lifespan but pays particular attention to the 'nature' of adult development. Central to his theory is the idea of four 'seasonal cycles': pre-adulthood, early adulthood, middle adulthood and late adulthood. The scheme was initially based on interviews with 40 men, but Levinson later interviewed women and found they proceeded through the same eras (life cycles) in a similar manner to men. Levinson did however find that women's lives are more closely linked to the family cycle.

Underlying Levinson's theory are several important concepts:

- A **life structure** refers to the underlying pattern of an individual's life at a given time and is shaped by their social and physical environment, primarily family and work, although other factors such as religion and economic status are often important.
- A **life cycle** relates to the underlying order spanning adult life, consisting of a sequence of eras. The move from one era to another is not smooth; there are cross-era periods of transition which last for about five years.

Levinson's seasons of man

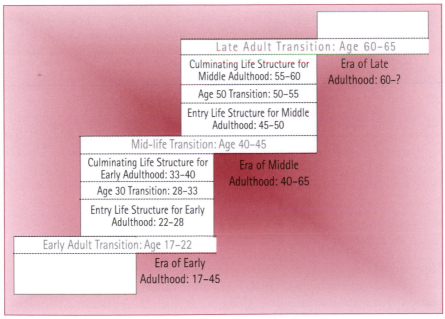

As you can see from the image, according to Levinson (1986, p.7), nine developmental periods exist. We are going to examine the ones pertaining to early adulthood (20–40). You will notice that the 'mid-life transition' stage, which covers the shift from early to middle adulthood, has been included. The section on middle adulthood will begin with that stage for the sake of clarity.

The stages for early adulthood are:

- The **Early adult transition** (17–22) is a developmental bridge between pre-adulthood and early adulthood.
- The **Entry life structure for early adulthood** (22–28) is the time for building and maintaining an initial mode of adult living.
- The **Age 30 transition** (28–33) is an opportunity to reappraise and modify the entry structure and to create the basis for the next life structure.
- The **Culminating life structure for early adulthood** (33–40) is the vehicle for completing this era and realising our youthful ambitions.
- The **Midlife transition** (40–45) is another of the great cross-era shifts, serving both to terminate early adulthood and to initiate middle adulthood.
- The **Entry life structure for middle adulthood** (45–50), like its counterpart above, provides an initial basis for life in a new era.
- The **Age 50 transition** (50–55) offers a mid-era opportunity for modifying and perhaps improving the entry life structure.
- The **Culminating life structure for middle adulthood** (55–60) is the framework in which we conclude this era.
- The **Late adult transition** (55–60) is a boundary period between middle and late adulthood, separating and linking the two eras.
- The **Late adult transition** (55–60) is a period that lasts approximately five years while the individual makes the transition between middle and late adulthood. The transition to late adulthood marks an opportunity to reflect upon successes and failures and enjoy the rest of life.

As we can see, starting careers and families mark the beginning of early adulthood. Around age 30 an evaluation occurs and people begin to settle down and also work towards career advancement. Another transition begins at age 40 with the realisation that not all the ambitions and goals that were set will be achieved. I have included Levinson's final stage here for ease though it falls in the section that deals with late adulthood, otherwise termed 'old age', which we will now deal with.

Late adulthood

Late adulthood, marking the period from 65 years onwards, has historically been a neglected area in psychology. This is beginning to change with more interest and research being given to this area. There can be little doubt that the increasing longevity we are experiencing in the West is forcing us to reconsider this period of development. In Ireland a longitudinal study researching the lives of older people (TILDA) has been launched. Its stated aim is to gather information from a nationally representative survey which will become the foundation for policy formation and implementation to enable successful ageing in Ireland. The study will provide an accurate picture of the needs and contributions of older people. To begin with, let us consider the physical, cognitive and emotional issues connected with older age.

Physical changes

Some of the following changes are witnessed during old age. Individual variation must be taken into account as lifestyle and other factors can determine the rate of ageing and the magnitude of its effects.

- Loss of brain weight increases after 60 years of age.
- Neurons (nerve cells) are lost in visual, hearing and motor areas of the brain.
- Vision and hearing become increasingly impaired.
- Heart rate slows, as does blood flow.
- Sleep patterns change, less sleep is needed.
- Appearance of skin continues to change, age spots develop.
- There is a loss of weight and height after 60.
- Muscle strength declines, there is less flexibility.

Ageing in Ireland

The following statistics on people aged 65 and over in Ireland were gathered by the Central Statistics Office in 2006:

- In line with the increasing overall population, the number of persons aged 65 and over increased by 54,000 people between 1996 and 2006.
- In 2006, Ireland had the lowest proportion of its population aged 65 and over among EU countries at 11.0%, this compared to an EU 27 average of 16.8%.
- There is a projected upward trend in the 65 and over dependency ratios for both Ireland and the EU from 2006 to 2026. This dependency ratio is expected to increase from 16.4% to 25.1% for Ireland, and increase from 25.2% to 36.6% for the EU 25.
- The age-specific death rate for males aged 65 and over has decreased from around 77 per 1,000 in 1980 to 51 in 2005. The corresponding decrease for females was from 60 to 44 per 1,000, indicating a significant narrowing between both rates.
- In 2006, 29.5% of persons aged 65 and over indicated they had a disability compared to 9.3% of all persons. The proportion of persons with a disability increased with age, particularly for the older age groups. The disability rate varied from 18.7% for the 65–69 age group to 58.6% for the 85 and over age group.
- The proportion of women aged 65 and over living alone in Ireland (31.7%) was the eighth lowest of EU countries, but the rate for men at 20.6% was the fourth highest.

- In 2005, around 20% of persons aged 65 and over were at risk of poverty, which was substantially lower than the 2004 rate of 27.1%. This decrease was due mainly to an increase in the old age pension in 2005.

Source: CSO, *Ageing in Ireland*, 2007, p.10.

Think about it! 'There is a projected upward trend in the 65 and over dependency ratios for both Ireland and the EU from 2006 to 2026.' The CSO reports that the number of over-65s in Ireland will continue to grow in comparison to the rest of the population. What implications does this increasing 'dependency ratio' pose for government policy?

Cognitive development

Paul Baltes' dual-process model

Paul Baltes (1939–2006) was a leading researcher in the field of ageing and has contributed enormously to our understanding of this area. Baltes proposed a dual-process model of cognitive functioning. The dual-process model attempts to measure what aspects of intelligence are likely to improve or deteriorate with age. Papalia *et al.* (2005, p.654) relate that in his model,

> mechanics of intelligence are the brain's neurophysiological 'hardware': information-processing and problem-solving function independent of any particular content. This dimension, like fluid intelligence, often declines with age. Pragmatics of intelligence are culture-based 'software': practical thinking, application of accumulated knowledge and skills, specialized expertise, professional productivity, and wisdom. This domain, which may continue to develop until very late adulthood, is similar to, but broader than, crystallized intelligence and includes information and know-how garnered from education, work, and life experience.

Socio-emotional development

Erikson's integrity vs. despair

This is the final stage of Erikson's theory of psychosocial development. It is characterised by the features of integrity and despair. The former represents the positive outcome and is associated with a feeling of satisfaction with one's life and achievements. The individual feels content and at peace, reflecting, according to Erikson, psychosocial maturity on their part. However, if the outcome of this stage is despair, then the individual believes that they have made many mistakes in their life and that it is too late to correct them. They are unhappy looking back over their life and experience despair as they feel it is now too late to change things. This despair manifests itself in bitterness and anger. An individual in 'despair' may not be accepting of death.

Ageism and cohort effect

In Chapter 2 we examined the theory of Glen H. Elder Jr, which referred to the 'cohort effect' where lives can be influenced by social change. We compared the lives of people with disabilities born in the 1940s to those born today in order to elaborate on what is meant by a 'cohort effect'. It was clear that the lives of those born with a disability in Ireland today are better than those from generations ago, though of course there is still some way to go before parity is achieved.

If we apply the cohort effect to older people, do you think their lives are better or worse than they were several generations ago? It is certain that today people live longer lives and generally have access to better healthcare services in old age. However, in social terms, is the old custom of respecting your elders in as much evidence as it was many years ago? Many cultures have great respect for their older generation, for their wisdom and life experience. Yet in the West it appears that we have started to devalue older people. The current campaigns against ageism would seem to indicate that negative attitudes exist towards older people. What do you think? Have attitudes towards older people changed in the last 50 years? If so, why?

Research on the experiences of Irish elderly

Horkan and Woods (1986) undertook research examining the lives of elderly people and their experiences and highlight some of the issues facing them. Their report is entitled *Perspective of Some Elderly People on Life in Suburban Dublin* and explores the social changes and difficulties experienced by elderly people. Through interviews with the elderly participants, four themes were identified:

- 'Life has changed'
- 'Life can be lonely and isolated'
- 'Life can be dangerous'
- 'Life can be difficult'

The goal of the research was to highlight the issues facing older people and heighten public awareness of the problems they face. They argue that if older people are to continue living in the community we must take more notice of the issues facing them.

For more information: www.ncaop.ie

The importance of identifying issues affecting older people is paramount when attempting to meet these needs through service provision. The following piece examines a study which attempted to do just that.

Community profile of supports and services for older people in Galway City

Research objectives

This study is concerned with establishing a community profile of the needs of older people in Galway City, with a particular emphasis on those experiencing disadvantage.

This study was undertaken to determine the needs of older people in Galway City.

Background to the study

Galway City Partnership commissioned this research in March 2008. The study seeks to establish a community profile of the needs of older people in Galway City, especially those experiencing disadvantage. The research combined primary and secondary techniques. This report is based on a series of interviews, consultation forums, a questionnaire survey, observations and documentary analyses.

Profile of older people in Galway City

There are 11,600 people aged over 55 in Galway City, which represents 16 per cent of the overall population of the city. There are 6,386 females and 5,214 males. The Rockbarton, Renmore and Lough Atalia communities have the highest percentage of older people.

Services and supports

Nineteen services are working specifically to support older people in Galway City and at least 37 organisations provide services to older people as part of their overall service. The range of organisations reflects the diversity of older people's needs and interests. Most referrals to organisations come through professional health services, particularly the Public Health Nurse Service.

Issues for older people

- The stretched and under-resourced services, particularly some of the health/social care services, are not supporting this stage of life change in a positive, empowering manner.
- The lack of primary care teams in the community is seen by many service providers as a problem, as is the lack of co-ordination and liaison between services.
- Different parts of the city present different needs for older people.
- Loneliness and isolation are highlighted as key issues for older people.

Service providers feel that older people could be more active, more involved in the community, more self-reliant, but the 'for the elderly' label stops people from getting involved.

- The lack of societal connections in the community, and the fact that support structures are breaking down, were recurring themes.
- An increasing number of older people present with addiction problems and associated conditions such as depression and other mental health issues.
- Key gaps in services include the lack of day centres, respite for carers, information centres, out-of-hours service, sheltered housing and advocacy.
- The home help service is not meeting the practical needs of older people.
- Elder abuse is becoming increasingly common.

Recommendation 1: Support infrastructure

- Day care centres with a full suite of services (showers, food, etc.) and supports (counselling, advice services, etc.), including transport, should be strategically developed in areas throughout the city.
- The feasibility of establishing lunch clubs similar to those established by COPE in the Imperial Hotel should be examined in other parts of the city, where demand or population numbers do not allow for the establishment of day care centres.
- The City Council should meet with community and voluntary groups in the city to begin establishing sheltered housing schemes throughout the city.
- An older people's resource centre and a dementia-specific respite centre should be developed in conjunction with older people, carers, state agencies and community and voluntary organisations.
- The HSE should develop a call centre for older people where they can have their queries dealt with effectively and sensitively and be directed to the most appropriate service within the HSE.

Recommendation 2: Raising awareness

- An awareness-raising campaign on the dangers of addiction and on sources of support should be aimed at older people.
- The work of Care and Repair and Westside Age Inclusion should be highlighted in the local media to inform service users and providers.
- A safety and crime-prevention campaign should be developed to raise awareness among older people in the city on how to stay safe in their homes and communities.
- Local media, both radio and newspapers, should develop an older people's advice and information slot every four to six weeks, to ensure that older people hear about rights, entitlement, social and community events, etc.

Recommendation 3: Building supports
- Visitation programmes such as Galway Contact and Care Service (Care and Repair) should be expanded and structured accordingly with adequate staff, resources and volunteers.
- A phone link service should be established in the city to check in on older people living alone and to remind them of appointments.
- An advocacy service for older people should be developed to help them find information, make informed decisions, support those decisions and tell families and services what they want.
- A local study should be carried out with older people and organisations supporting visitation programmes, to ascertain the levels and causes of and solutions to loneliness, isolation and lack of social contact in Galway City.
- The HSE should review their home help service and evaluate its effectiveness and the level of customer satisfaction.

Recommendation 4: Representation
- All service providers should meet annually to exchange information on activities and issues, and to seek joint projects for collaboration.
- Galway City Partnership, in conjunction with community and voluntary groups, should build capacity, train in policy making, and lobby communities of older people around the city before the local council elections in 2009, with the specific aim of achieving sheltered housing schemes in Galway City.
- A local action plan should be developed by older people's service providers and communities, to help address some of the issues raised in this report.

Source: www.icsg.ie

This piece highlights the complex nature of meeting needs of older people. In Chapter 8 the subject of elder abuse is addressed.

Ethical dilemmas in old age care
Moody (2005, p.583) presents the following case study to capture the ethical dilemmas faced in old age care:

Sylvia Senex, aged 80, suffers from disabling arthritis and has been living at home with her daughter for the past six years. During this period the mother's memory problems have gotten worse and her care has become burdensome. Mrs Senex was given tests three years ago suggesting dementia but was never told the results. Her daughter has informed her mother that she has a 'neurological problem' and told her what to expect in the future but she has refused to use the word 'Alzheimer's'. She says that her mother would react badly to that word and her brother, despite doubts, defers to his sister as primary caregiver. Mrs Senex has recently started receiving home care services, but the home care agency is disturbed by the fact that she has been kept in the dark about her diagnosis. What should the agency do?

This case illustrates a series of features that are common in cases of old age care that pose ethical dilemmas:

- Dependency. We are confronted here with a chronic, not acute, health problem: indeed, there is more than one problem with the result that activities of daily living are limited and freedom of action is diminished.
- Shared responsibility. Caregiving is provided by a family member but there is some prospect of formal care with tasks shared between formal and informal sectors, raising questions of accountability.
- Diminished mental capacity. There is some indication of diminished mental capacity, posing questions about the patient's ability to render informed consent concerning major life decisions.
- Trajectory of decline. The condition of the patient, if she does in fact have Alzheimer's, is likely to deteriorate further, raising the prospect of later difficult decisions – such as whether Mrs Senex might belong in a nursing home.

This case study and the accompanying ethical dilemmas identified by Moody clearly illustrate the difficulties faced when making decisions regarding the care of the elderly. Using the case study, consider whether you believe Mrs Senex's daughter is right in withholding the information from her mother. Is the agency correct to have concerns regarding the withholding of information from the mother? What are your concerns and what dilemmas do you feel this case study raises?

Finally, there is some good news on the horizon; Professor Robertson of Trinity College Dublin has presented the following initiative to attempt to prevent dementia and general cognitive impairment.

Neuroenhancement for Inequalities in Elder Lives: Preventing dementia

Led by Professor Ian Robertson, Neuroenhancement for Inequalities in Elder Lives (NIEL) aims to develop an internationally-replicable, technology-linked approach to the prevention of dementia and elder cognitive impairment by enhancing cognitive function.

NIEL's goals for 2012 are:

- establishment of a series of research trials to identify methods for enhancing brain function in socially disadvantaged elderly people at high risk for dementia

- development of technologies and methods for delivering optimal brain stimulation methods
- development of the arrangements for engaging at-risk elderly people in an educational-preventive context.

Seed funding of €2.5m received from the Atlantic Philanthropies will leverage considerable funding from other sources to take the programme to scale.

Source: www.tcd.ie

Hopefully you will have gained from this chapter a greater understanding of how seemingly unrelated influences conspire in a holistic manner to shape how we develop. The choices we make in our 20s can shape the lives we have in our 60s. We need to grasp the impact of societal attitudes and change on the lives of people as they age. Ageism is a real problem with huge consequences for individual lives, yet we have seen that societal attitudes can be challenged and changed for the better. We all have our part to play.

5

Disabilities

DEFINITIONS OF DISABILITY

Defining disability is contentious, as is the use of language in this context. Language can play a pivotal role in people's perception and treatment of others. For example, for many years terms such as 'handicap' and 'retardation' were used in discussing disability, but implicit in the meanings of those words, intentional or otherwise, are negative connotations. 'Retardation' means to 'make slow or late', and one of the meanings of 'handicap' is 'a thing that makes progress or success difficult'. In 2007 the American Association of Mental Retardation changed its name to the 'American Association of Intellectual and Developmental Disabilities' (AAIDD) in recognition of the progression away from terminology that contributes to disabling people. 'This new name is an idea whose time has come,' says Doreen Croser, Executive Director of AAIDD. 'Individuals with disabilities and family members do not like the term "mental retardation" and their advocacy is encouraging political and social change at national, state, and local levels. Our members demanded that we keep up with times and they voted for this name change' (www.aamr.org).

The National Disability Authority (NDA) is an invaluable resource for disability issues in Ireland. The following extract is, I believe, the clearest definition of disability and includes the definition from the Disability Act 2005:

> There are many definitions of 'disability' and the issue of a definition has proven to be one of the most contentious issues facing the delegates of the United Nations committee on a Comprehensive and Integral International Convention on Protection and Promotion of the Rights and Dignity of Persons with Disabilities. In 2006 the following definition was proposed as a 'working proposal':
>
> 'Disability results from the interaction between persons with impairments, conditions, or illnesses and the environmental and attitudinal barriers they face. Such impairments, conditions, or illnesses may be permanent, temporary, intermittent, or imputed, and those that are physical, sensory, psychosocial, neurological, medical or intellectual.'

The International Classification of Functioning Disability and Health (ICF) provided the following definition of disability:

'Disability is a decrement in functioning at the body, individual or societal level that arises when an individual with a health condition encounters barriers in the environment.'

Either of the two above definitions clearly express the essential structure of the concept of disability as a result of an interaction between features of an individual with a health condition and features of the physical, individual and societal environment. It clearly recognises the 3 dimensions of disability (body, individual and societal levels) to increase inclusiveness and to be applicable to the full range and diversity of disability experience at the same time. It further ensures inclusiveness and the complete coverage of all relevant disability rights issues, by defining disability as to apply to a person with impairment alone, or an activity limitation alone, or a participation restriction alone.

The Disability Act (Government of Ireland, 2005) defines disability as 'a substantial restriction in the capacity of the person to carry on a profession, business or occupation in the Irish State or to participate in social or cultural life in the Irish State by reason of an enduring physical, sensory, mental health or intellectual impairment' (p.6). The definition of disability contains the concept 'substantial restriction' and this is seen as a restriction which (a) is permanent or likely to be permanent, results in a significant difficulty in communication, learning or mobility or in significantly disordered cognitive processes, and (b) gives rise to the need for services to be provided continually to the person whether or not a child or, if the person is a child, to the need for services to be provided early in life to ameliorate the disability (Government of Ireland, 2005).

Impairment
The definition covers physical and mental impairments. These include:

- physical impairments affecting the senses, such as sight and hearing
- mental impairments, including learning disabilities and mental illness (if it is recognised by a respected body of medical opinion).

Substantial
For an effect to be substantial, it must be more than minor. The following are examples that are likely to be considered substantial:

- inability to see moving traffic clearly enough to cross a road safely
- inability to turn taps or knobs
- inability to remember and relay a simple message correctly.

Long-term

Long-term effects are those that

- have lasted at least 12 months, or
- are likely to last at least 12 months, or
- are likely to last for the rest of the life of the person affected.

Long-term effects include those which are likely to recur. For example, an effect is considered long-term if it is likely both to recur, and to do so at least once beyond the 12-month period following the first occurrence.

Day-to-day activities

Day-to-day activities are normal activities carried out by most people on a regular basis, and must involve one of the following broad categories:

- mobility – moving from place to place
- manual dexterity – for example, use of the hands
- physical co-ordination
- continence
- the ability to lift, carry or move ordinary objects
- speech, hearing or eyesight
- memory, or ability to concentrate, learn or understand
- being able to recognise physical danger.

Source: www.nda.ie

A *Strategy for Equality*, a report of the Commission on the Status of People with Disabilities (1996, p.11), further outlines that impairment in and of itself does not cause a disadvantage to the individual, rather the societal response does:

> A given level of impairment or degree of restriction does not necessarily lead to disadvantage: it is the societal response (in terms of attitudes and expectations as well as the services and facilities made available) which has an important impact on the extent to which impairment or disability lead to disadvantage. The impairment may be caused by physical, mental, intellectual, emotional or sensory factors. The fact, for example, that many public buildings are inaccessible to people with mobility impairment is not something which is caused by the impairment. It is perfectly possible to construct buildings which are readily accessible to people who use wheelchairs or have other types of mobility impairment. Inaccessible buildings are caused by society's decision, whether informed or uninformed, to build structures in such a way that they will not be accessible to some people.

The growing recognition of the role of environmental and societal factors can be witnessed in the models of disability that currently exist, so let's take a look at both the medical and social models of disability.

MODELS OF DISABILITY

In terms of support for those with disabilities, according to the British Institute of Learning Disabilities, there has been a move away from the medical model to a social model based on inclusion and integration. Historically, disability has been viewed from a medical-model approach that views the difficulties faced by a person with disability to be the result of their individual impairment.

The social model challenges this view, advocating that it is structural and societal obstacles that limit a person with a disability, not the disability itself. For example, if a building is inaccessible to a wheelchair user because it has no ramp, the medical model would view the inability of the wheelchair user to access the building as a result of their disability. The social model would instead suggest that it is not the physical impairment of the individual that limits their access to the building, but that the fault lies in a society that builds inaccessible buildings.

The medical model is still dominant, not just within the arena of disability but also in mental illness. Thus, for those with a disability, attempting to live within the medical-model paradigm, life can be a constant struggle, and yet this can be a double-edged sword as the diagnosis or 'labelling' of the medical model opens access to services. As practitioners, the model of disability that we adopt will influence our practice. This has further consequences in terms of discrimination and our ability to advocate for change.

CAUSES OF DISABILITY

Genetic, chromosomal and acquired disabilities

Chapter 4 explored the development of a human being from conception, and the genetic, chromosomal and environmental aspects affecting the development of the foetus. To recap, both chromosomal and genetic disabilities occur at conception, but whereas the gene-linked conditions are inherited, chromosomal conditions generally occur through the presence of an extra chromosome. Each cell has 23 pairs of chromosomes. In Down syndrome an extra copy of chromosome 21 is present. Sometimes you will find Down syndrome referred to as 'trisomy 21', the 'tri' referring to the three chromosomes present instead of two.

Disabilities can also be caused by environmental factors or can be acquired at birth or during the life course of an individual. In Chapter 4 we examined environmental factors in utero which are described as teratogens, such as alcohol or maternal illness. A teratogen is an external influence that can cause birth defects. The timing of exposure and dose of a teratogen can make a difference in outcome.

Lack of oxygen (hypoxia) during pregnancy or at birth can cause disability if the brain is starved of oxygen and becomes damaged. The extent of the disability is dependent on the level of oxygen starvation. Lack of oxygen is one of the causes of cerebral palsy (see below).

Finally, a disability can be acquired by an individual who was born without a disability through accident or illness. For example, a car accident may leave a person paralysed, resulting in a physical disability. Acquired brain injury is covered in Chapter 2.

Categories of disability

1. physical disability
2. sensory disability
3. intellectual/learning disability
4. pervasive developmental disorder
5. specific learning disability.

PREVALENCE OF DISABILITIES IN IRELAND

According to O'Donovan and Doyle (2009), the 2006 Census figures show that persons with disabilities represent 9.3 per cent of the total population. Of those with disability, 35.1 per cent are aged 65 years or over (CSO, 2007). The recent National Disability Survey provides estimates of disability at 18.5 per cent with 30.0 per cent of this group aged 65 years or over (CSO, 2008, cited in O'Donovan and Doyle, 2009). The difference in disability estimates is due to the expanded definition of disability used in the National Disability Survey. However, according to the National Disability Authority, there exists only a partial picture of the prevalence of disability in Ireland. This contrasts poorly with other countries, which maintain a statistical database. The lack of a coherent and comprehensive picture of disability in this country has implications for policy and practice – for how can policy respond if an accurate picture, not just of numbers but of needs that accompany disability, does not exist? Further interventions aimed at meeting needs and facilitating full participation by those with disability is not and cannot be properly assessed. The Commission on the Status of People with Disabilities, in its 1996 Report, placed considerable emphasis on the 'silence of relevant official statistics' and in particular on the fact that no comprehensive statistics are available on the prevalence of disability among adults and children in Ireland. However, the Census collected information in 2002 through the inclusion of two questions related to disability, the first on whether the person was affected by a long-lasting limiting condition, and the second about difficulty in doing certain activities due to a physical, mental or emotional condition lasting six months or more. Results indicate that 8.3 per cent of all respondents are classified as having a disability in terms of the specific questions asked in the Census. Though it is recognised as a step forward, the Census information is general; in comparison a specially designed in-depth instrument dedicated to disability has been called for. As it stands, little information about the social and environmental context in which disability is experienced is available.

PHYSICAL DISABILITIES

Definition: Kirk *et al.* (2000, p.485), suggest that in defining physical disability two categories can be considered; physical disability and health impairment. A physical disability is defined as 'a condition that interferes with a person's ability to use his or her body'. This highlights that most physical disabilities involve difficulties with skeletal, muscular or nervous systems. A health impairment is defined as 'a condition that requires ongoing medical attention'. The categorisation of health impairment as a disability is interesting as opinion is sometimes divided as to whether cancer, for example, and its effects on a person's ability to interact fully, is 'disabling' in comparison to someone born with a physical disability. Is the inclusion of asthma within the definition of physical disability, in terms of its physical impact on the individual and consequent inability to fully participate in one or more of life's activities, a correct one? What do you think? Regardless, there is a recognition that any physical condition that limits or impacts on a person can possibly be considered a disability.

Health impairments can include conditions such as asthma, cystic fibrosis, heart defects and cancer. Having one of these conditions is not in itself automatically considered a physical disability; it is their potential impact that elevates them to such a classification.

Causes of physical disabilities

- congenital disabilities
- acquired disabilities.

Congenital disabilities means that the disability is present at birth (it may or may not have been present earlier *in utero* but it must be present at birth, though the condition might sometimes show itself soon after birth). Congenital disabilities can span from mild to severe and include cerebral palsy, epilepsy, neural tube disorders (spina bifida) and muscular dystrophy, to name just a few.

Acquired disabilities are physical impairments that develop, usually through an accident or illness, after a period of typical development.

Prevalence

The National Physical and Sensory Disability Database Committee (NPSDDC) was set up in 1998 by the Department of Health and Children (DoHC) with the task of developing a national database that would collect information on the specialised health and social service needs of people with physical or sensory disability. Implementation of the NPSDD on a nationwide basis began in 2002.

O'Donovan and Doyle (2009) report that within the National Intellectual Disability Database (NIDD), the top three diagnostic categories within each age group are as follows:

- 16–24 years: cerebral palsy, cystic fibrosis, congenital deafness
- 25–44 years: multiple sclerosis, cerebral palsy, head injury
- 45–65 years: multiple sclerosis, diabetes 1, stroke/hemiplegia.

Table 5.1: The main diagnosis of conditions leading to physical impairment in young adulthood

Condition	Incidence per live births	Survival rate/Life expectancy	Prevalence in young adulthood
Cerebral palsy	2 per 1000	90% to adulthood; normal life expectancy for those minimally affected, reduced if epilepsy and severe disability present	2 per 1,000
Spina bifida	2–4 per 1000. Influenced by antenatal screening programme	60% to age 21; severely affected may not survive infancy. Survivors susceptible to renal impairment and pressure area damage. Prognosis depends on level of lesion	2 per 100,000
Duchenne muscular dystrophy	1 per 3,000 males	To 20 years, although long-term ventilator support may increase to 30 years	
Cystic fibrosis	1 per 2,500 Caucasians	50% to age 20 25% alive at age 30	About 1 per 9,000
Juvenile idiopathic arthritis	About 3.5 per 100,000	Almost normal life expectancy	2–3 per 10,000
Traumatic brain injury	N/A	Normal life expectancy, except in cases with severe disability or epilepsy	Not known
Spinal cord injury	N/A	Approaching normal life expectancy in paraplegia, reduced in tetraplegia, 30.2 years mean life expectancy	30 cases per million persons at risk; these survival rates correspond to prevalence rates ranging from 486 to 969 per million persons

Modified from a table in Chamberlain and Kent with permission of Minerva Medica, Editor of *Eur Med Phys* (now *Eur J Phys Rehabil Med*).

CEREBRAL PALSY

Cerebral palsy (CP) is defined by Enable Ireland as a physical condition affecting the part of the brain which controls movement and posture. This is why people with cerebral palsy cannot control their muscles very well. They may move jerkily or hold themselves awkwardly. Cerebral palsy can be caused by a number of things, such as an illness during pregnancy, lack of oxygen as a result of complications during birth or a serious accident or illness after birth. The degree of severity ranges widely. Some children are only mildly affected, taking only a little longer than others to sit up and walk, etc. People with a moderate degree of cerebral palsy may require a wheelchair or walking aid for mobility. Some people are affected very severely and can do very little for themselves physically.

Causes of cerebral palsy

Cerebral palsy is caused by damage to, or failure in the development of, the part of the brain that controls movement. This happens before birth, during birth or during early childhood before the brain's growth has reached a certain level of maturity.

SPARCLE (a study of participation of children with cerebral palsy living in Europe) relates that:

- CP is the commonest cause of significant motor impairment, occurring in 1 in 500 births or 10,000 new cases a year in the EU prior to recent enlargement.
- Children with CP often have impairments of learning, hearing, vision, communication and epilepsy in addition to their motor ones and so are representative of the wider population of disabled children.
- Children with CP are a group with relatively stable impairment where Participation and QoL will be influenced by social and educational environmental factors as well as by medical interventions.
- Adults with CP are disadvantaged in social relationships and employment . . . and children are disadvantaged in education, social relationships and employment prospects.

For more information: www.enableireland.ie

SENSORY DISABILITIES

Sensory disabilities include any impairment to the senses, the most common being visual or hearing impairment. There are degrees of impairment from mild to complete or profound loss. Sensory disability is often an invisible disability; unlike a physical or chromosomal disability (such as Down syndrome) that is apparent to others, an invisible or 'hidden' disability is not obvious to others.

Visual disability

According to the National Council for the Blind of Ireland (NCBI), most people with sight loss can see something. They further elaborate that a minority of blind people can distinguish light but nothing else, others have reduced central vision, while some have no side vision. Some people see everything as a vague blur; others see a patchwork of blanks.

There are a number of different eye conditions that can cause types of sight loss. Some people are born with no vision or significantly reduced vision. Others lose vision due to accidents or ageing. The effect of the sight loss varies widely, depending on the condition, its progress and the person's managing skills.

The NCBI outline the following guidelines for meeting and greeting people with visual impairment:

- Greet a person by saying your name, as he or she may not recognise your voice. Do not ask or expect them to guess who you are, even if they know you.
- Talk directly to the person rather than through a third party. It's easier if you know the person with sight loss by name – say his or her name when you are speaking to them. If you don't know their name, don't be afraid to ask, as well as giving your own name.
- In a group situation, introduce the other people present. Address the person with sight loss by name when directing conversation to them in a group situation.
- If someone joins or leaves the group, tell the person with sight loss that this has happened.
- Before giving assistance, always ask the person first if they would like assistance, and if they do, ask what assistance is needed. Do not assume what assistance the person needs.
- If a person with sight loss says that he or she would like to be guided, offer your elbow. Keep your arm by your side and the person with sight loss can walk a little behind you, holding your arm just above the elbow.
- When assisting, it is helpful to give commentary on what is around the person, for example, 'the chair is to your right'.
- If you've been talking to a person with sight loss, tell him or her when you are leaving, so that they are not left talking to themselves.
- If you have been guiding a blind person and have to leave them, bring them to some reference point that they can feel, like a wall, table or chair. To be left in open space can be disorientating for a person with no vision.

The person is the expert on what assistance they require. Always ask the person what kind of assistance they need, if any. Only they will know what works best for them and not everyone who has a visual impairment will require the same adaptations.

NCBI also provides a network of community resource workers who provide a range of services to those with a visual impairment, such as:

- peer counselling
- day activity centres
- early learning centre
- employment support
- mobility training.

More information about the work of the National Council of the Blind, including practical information for those working with individuals with visual impairment, can be found at www.ncbi.ie.

INTELLECTUAL DISABILITIES

History and theories of intelligence

Francis Galton, a cousin of Darwin, was the first person to attempt to examine the construct of intelligence and to measure it. Alfred Binet had more success and formulated the first intelligence test called the 'Binet-Simon' test, which tests general knowledge that one would expect a child to know. The test was graded in difficulty according to the child's age. The scoring of the test produced a number referred to as the child's mental age. The test was in French and was translated for use in America and became known as the Stanford-Binet test, and is still in use today. The test has been adapted to use the following formula which calculates Intelligence Quotient (IQ) as the sum of (Mental Age/Chronological Age) x 100.

No matter what the child's chronological age, if the mental age matches the chronological age, then the IQ will equal 100. An IQ of 100 thus indicates a child of average intellectual development. If the mental age is above the chronological age (a more gifted than average child), then the IQ is above 100. If the mental age is below the chronological age, then the IQ is below 100, indicating a possible intellectual disability.

Wechsler tests are used to assess not only intellectual disabilities but also specific learning disabilities (such as dyslexia). These tests consist of the WISC (Wechsler Intelligence Scale for Children) and the WAIS (Wechsler Adult Intelligence Scale). The Wechsler tests moved away from an emphasis on verbal skills to a more varied construct, looking at many elements of 'intelligence' including numerical, processing speed, working memory and perceptual reasoning.

Criticisms of IQ
Berger (1986, in Herbert, 2006, p.387) outlines two reasons for the negative ethos surrounding the measurement of IQ:

- First, there is now a well-documented historical and contemporary association between IQ testing and allegations of discrimination – racial, educational, or otherwise.

- Second, philosophers, many psychologists – especially those in the developmental and cognitive fields – as well as others are, to say the least, sceptical if not dismissive of the way IQ tests are paraded as devices that can generate a measure that in turn encompasses something as remarkable, complex, and subtle as human intelligence.

The issue of racism and IQ is a long-standing one. Richard J. Herrnstein and Charles Murray's *The Bell Curve* (1994) was effectively an apologia or justification for racist attitudes towards black people as it alleged that white people were intellectually superior to black people. The Irish have not escaped the gaze of IQ, with Eysenck, a leading figure in the field of intelligence testing and in psychology, purporting that Irish people have low IQ scores compared to other nationalities in Europe. These 'findings' merely confirm the inherent weaknesses of intelligence testing.

Other approaches to conceptualising intelligence

Multiple intelligences

Howard Gardner's (1983) theory of multiple intelligences states that 'An intelligence is the ability to solve problems, or to create products, that are valued within one or more cultural settings.' More recently he has adapted his definition of intelligence to include psychological and biological elements: 'Intelligence is a bio-psychological potential to process information that can be activated in a cultural setting to solve problems or create products that are of value in a culture.'

Howard Gardner conceived of seven types of intelligence in his book *Frames of Mind* (1983). Gardner suggested that intelligence is not necessarily one unitary concept but rather that there are different types of intelligence that exist independently of one another but interact with each other. Each of us has different strengths and these represent our unique mix of different types of intelligence.

The seven types of intelligence first identified by Gardner include:

- linguistic – reading, writing, talking and listening
- logical-mathematical – numbers, scientific thinking
- bodily/kinesthetic – use of one's body, sport and dance
- musical – singing, playing and composing
- interpersonal – ability to understand and relate to others
- intrapersonal – self-understanding
- spatial – used in navigation, and parking your car!

Gardner added that:

- Naturalistic intelligence is the ability to recognise and categorise objects in nature (plants and animals).

- Existential intelligence is the capacity to ask questions regarding the meaning of life.

Gardner's theory has been heavily criticised by those who claim that it lacks scientific rigour and that some of his intelligences are not within the cognitive domain, such as inter- and intrapersonal intelligences. Gardner has countered that criticism of his multiple intelligence approach represents a fear of moving away from measuring intelligence through the use of traditional standardised tests towards his less quantifiable approach in conceptualising intelligence.

Theory of fluid and crystallised intelligence

Raymond Cattell and John L. Horn (1967) together produced a new understanding of the course of intellectual development across the lifespan. Their theory proposed that general intelligence is not a unitary factor but instead a grouping of approximately 100 abilities working together. These numerous abilities are separated into two strands or abilities, fluid and crystallised, that have quite different developmental pathways across the lifespan.

Fluid intelligence drives the individual's ability to think and act quickly and to solve problems. Fluid intelligence is grounded in physiological efficiency, and is thus relatively independent of education or cultural influences (Cattell and Horn, 1967). Many studies have demonstrated that fluid intelligence peaks in early adulthood and then declines, gradually at first and then more rapidly as old age sets in after about 70 years of age.

Crystallised intelligence stems from learning and cultural influences, and is reflected in tests of knowledge and general information and also a wide variety of acquired skills (Cattell and Horn, 1967). Personality factors, motivation and educational and cultural opportunity are central to its development. Crystallised abilities continue to improve as individuals age. Crystallised intelligence can be thought of as wisdom which the individual accumulates as they progress through life.

Sternberg's triarchic theory of successful intelligence

Robert J. Sternberg (1949) argues that intelligent behaviour derives from a balance between analytical, creative and practical abilities. Intelligent behaviour is reflected in optimal adaptation to your environment or particular sociocultural context (Sternberg, 1988).

- **Analytical abilities** enable the individual to evaluate, analyse, compare and contrast information.
- **Creative abilities** generate invention, discovery and other creative endeavours.
- **Practical abilities** tie everything together by allowing individuals to apply what they have learned in the appropriate setting.

To be successful in life, the individual must make the best use of their analytical, creative and practical strengths, while at the same time compensating for weaknesses in any of these areas. For example, a person with highly developed analytical and practical abilities, but with less well-developed creative abilities, might choose to work in a field that values technical expertise but does not require a great deal of imaginative thinking. Thus, a central feature of the triarchic theory of successful intelligence is adaptability – both within the individual and within their sociocultural context (Cianciolo and Sternberg, 2004).

What is an intellectual/learning disability?

It should be noted that intellectual disabilities receive more attention than other categories of disability in this chapter. This is because a lot of care-practice students will work with people with intellectual disabilities at some point, so it is important to understand the complexity of intellectual disabilities, which are not a homogenous group. Finally, note that the terms intellectual disability and learning disability are used interchangeably.

The American Association on Intellectual and Developmental Disability defines intellectual disability as:

> a disability characterized by significant limitations both in intellectual functioning and in adaptive behavior, which covers many everyday social and practical skills. This disability originates before the age of 18.
>
> Intellectual functioning—also called intelligence—refers to general mental capacity, such as learning, reasoning, problem solving, and so on.
>
> One criterion to measure intellectual functioning is an IQ test. Generally, an IQ test score of around 70 or as high as 75 indicates a limitation in intellectual functioning.
>
> Standardized tests can also determine limitations in adaptive behavior, which comprises three skill types:
> - Conceptual skills—language and literacy; money, time, and number concepts; and self-direction.
> - Social skills—interpersonal skills, social responsibility, self-esteem, gullibility, naïveté (i.e., wariness), social problem solving, and the ability to follow rules/obey laws and to avoid being victimized.
> - Practical skills—activities of daily living (personal care), occupational skills, healthcare, travel/transportation, schedules/routines, safety, use of money, use of the telephone.

Source: www.aamr.org

The assessment and classification of learning or intellectual disabilities (these terms are used interchangeably) has been based historically upon the assessment of IQ (Intelligence Quotient). Though more recent developments have encouraged practitioners to consider additional factors, such as the community environment typical of the individual's peers and culture, the main focus in diagnosing a learning disability remains the evaluation of IQ.

Classification of intellectual impairment

As we have seen, the construct of intelligence is not without controversy; however, it remains an integral part of the assessment of intellectual disabilities. Using IQ as a measure, intellectual disabilities are classified as follows:

- 50–70: mild learning disability
- 35–50: moderate learning disability
- 20–35: severe learning disability
- below 20: profound learning disability

Source: British Institute of Learning Disability

These classifications represent different levels of impairment in cognitive functioning.

IQ and learning disability

The British Institute of Learning Disability (BILD) outline the following difficulties of using IQ as a measurement of an individual's intellectual disability: firstly there are problems with using IQ alone. Measurements can vary during a person's growth and development. Secondly, many of us have individual strengths and abilities which do not show up well in IQ tests. It is important to take into account also the degree of social functioning and adaptation.

Effects of congenital and acquired disability

A distinction needs to be made at this stage between an intellectual disability existing at birth and one which is acquired. In the case of the former, from a developmental perspective, the individual's life is affected by the learning disability from day one, in terms of their own development and in access to education, societal attitudes, etc. In the case of an acquired brain injury, the intellectual disability is not present at birth but is 'acquired' at a later date in the person's development, most commonly through an accident. Thus the impact of a learning disability on the development of an individual is not always the same.

Causes of learning disability

The causes of learning disabilities are mainly classified into environmental factors, genetic factors and chromosomal abnormalities. A number of genetic and chromosomal disabilities were examined in Chapter 4. Environmental factors (teratogens), maternal illness and anoxia (lack of oxygen) at birth can be causes of learning disability, as already mentioned.

The British Institute of Learning Disabilities suggests that, for about 50 per cent of people who have a mild learning disability, no cause has been identified. A number of environmental and genetic factors are thought to be significant, although clearly diagnosed genetic causes have been found in only 5 per cent of people in this category. Higher rates in some social classes suggest that factors such as large families, overcrowding and poverty are important. Research increasingly points also to organic causes, such as exposure to alcohol and other toxins, hypoxia and other problems at the time of birth, and some chromosomal abnormalities. In people with severe or profound learning disabilities, chromosomal abnormalities cause about 40 per cent of cases. Genetic factors account for 15 per cent, prenatal and perinatal problems 10 per cent, and postnatal issues a further 10 per cent. Cases which are of unknown cause are fewer, but still high at around 25 per cent.

This highlights the role of environmental factors in the causation and development of learning disabilities. As we will see again in Chapter 6, factors such as poverty and housing conditions continue to affect life outcomes and development. Of course, there is the hope that these factors can be improved; however, in the context of Bronfenbrenner's ecological approach, state policy, response and more particularly resources, or lack of them, it becomes clear that such environmental problems are not going to be eradicated even though they carry such a high human cost.

The example of Down syndrome below demonstrates the importance of considering the individual within a broad ecological context and recognising the influence of apparently 'non-psychological' factors upon an individual's psychological well-being and development.

In Focus: Down syndrome

Down syndrome is the most common of the chromosomal disorders. In Ireland one baby in 600 is estimated to be born with Down syndrome. Physical characteristics associated with Down syndrome include a downward sloping skinfold at the inner eye corners, flat appearance of the face, protruding tongue and low muscle tone (which means in babies that their head and neck need extra support). Down syndrome is accompanied by developmental delay: IQ can range from low to severe learning disability.

'Share the journey' is the motto of Down Syndrome Ireland. Their mission statement states: 'People experience many great things and also face many challenges throughout their lives. People with Down syndrome are no different, but may need a little extra help and support along the way. Down Syndrome Ireland's goal is to help people with Down syndrome make their own futures as bright and independent as possible by providing them with education, support and friendship every step of the way.' It is very important that people with disabilities are seen as individuals first, who happen to have a disability.

Compare and contrast

Down syndrome Ireland states that 'the quality of life of people with Down syndrome has improved immensely in the last thirty years. Just like the rest of us, they now enjoy longer life expectancy and can live happy, fulfilling and active lives as part of the community.'

What do you think was the experience of a child born with Down syndrome in the 1940s? Do you think their experience would be different to a child with Down syndrome born in Ireland today?

Mild intellectual disability

The following is an extract from a paper produced by the Psychological Society of Ireland which outlines issues affecting people with mild intellectual disability (MID), including their increased vulnerability to the following risks:

- Poverty and homelessness
- Physical ill health
- Injury and violence
- Psychological disorders
- Victimisation and maltreatment
- Lowered life satisfaction
- Child removal, foster care
- Judicial system failures
- Women are at even greater physical and mental health risk, and
- Women have lowered life satisfaction.

Persisting with exclusively mainstream services, without adaptation for people with mild intellectual disability, perpetuates the risks that such people face in life.

Pervasiveness of MID

There are two identifiable 'groupings' of people with mild intellectual disability. One group is comprised of individuals who have been formally diagnosed as having a learning disability, perhaps having come from a special school background or having received special support in a mainstream school and/or receiving services from a learning disability service. There is another, much broader group of people who have not been formally diagnosed but who nonetheless have high levels of impairment and who present with various personal and social problems.

Some of the difficulties experienced by both groups include at least some of the following:

- Vagueness about basic facts;
- Illiteracy;

- Problems managing money;
- Overwhelmed by routine demands;
- Difficulty in new situations;
- Poor independent living skills;
- Difficulty understanding consequences of actions;
- Difficulty sustaining relationships;
- Difficulty recognising own needs;
- Being influenced or led in an exploitative way; and acting out in response to frustration.

These difficulties are long-term and lifelong. The demands of ordinary life (i.e. social, educational, domestic, safety, communication) create ongoing threats to people with mild intellectual disability.

Mild intellectual disability: implications for service providers

The needs and issues of adults with MID affect a range of agencies and services including the Gardaí, the judicial system, Adult Mental Health Services, child protection services, vocational training and social welfare. Anecdotal clinical evidence suggests that professionals in mainstream agencies with responsibility for providing services to this population do not have sufficient experience or understanding of the issues and have difficulties and challenges with people with MID. In relation to children with mild intellectual disability who are in statutory care, there are additional implications for when they leave care, i.e. post 18. The usual 'aftercare' is a transition phase between 18 and 21 years and this is insufficient and inadequate to assist young people with mild intellectual disability to move toward independent adulthood. Specialised, ongoing, adult support services need to be made available to these young people when they leave care. Child protection and welfare issues are also further complicated when children have parents who have an intellectual disability, which is not an uncommon event.

Source: www.psihq.ie

Intellectual disability and mental health

The Mental Health Commission acknowledges certain factors impacting on the delivery of mental health services to people with intellectual disabilities:

- Pathways to access mental health services are often unclear.
- People with intellectual disabilities are more likely to have additional and often more complex health needs.
- People with intellectual disabilities are more likely to have communication difficulties.
- There is currently no capacity legislation in Ireland and adults with intellectual disabilities have been identified as 'vulnerable adults' in relation to consent and capacity issues. (Mental Health Commission, 2009, p.12)

Pervasive developmental disorders

Autism

Autism is part of a spectrum of pervasive development disorders. The very basic criteria for autism is a qualitative impairment in reciprocal social interaction, in verbal and non-verbal communication and in imaginative activity. Individuals with autism can have mild to severe symptoms.

Autism was first described by Hans Asperger and Leo Kanner in the 1940s, independently of one another. Kanner and Asperger chose to use the term 'autistic' to reflect one of the main characteristics often witnessed, that is, a withdrawal from others. *Autos* denotes 'self' in Greek, and Frith (1996, p.7) comments that 'this narrowing could be described as a withdrawal from the fabric of social life into the self'.

In the 1950s when the disorder was first recognised, its causation was believed to be poor parenting; there were no special schools and education was not considered an important element in the treatment of autism. This changed as a result of research findings which shone a new light of understanding and enquiry upon this disorder, influencing attitudes towards its causation and treatment.

Prevalence in Ireland

According to the Irish College of Psychiatrists (2005, p.55), the estimated prevalence of this disorder is 60 in every 10,000 children and in Ireland it is estimated that there are approximately 5,330 children and adolescents (under the age of 16 years) with autism spectrum disorder. Further, 'it may coexist with intellectual disability or other disorders of development and can occur with other physical or psychological disorders. It is estimated that 40–60% of those diagnosed with autism spectrum disorder have intellectual disability.' It appears to affect males more than females; the male:female ratio for autism is 3 or 4:1. According to the ICD-10 and the DSM IV (the diagnostic manuals used by psychologists):

- Autism is classified as part of the pervasive developmental disorders.
- It affects males predominantly and individuals with autism display marked abnormalities in their capacity for reciprocal social interaction, in language and communication and in the development of symbolic play.
- With respect to the communicative abilities, a person with autism takes a literal meaning from what is said, so if it was said that Mary had a hard neck, rather than believing Mary to be brazen the individual would believe Mary to literally have a hard neck.
- They also display repetitive behaviours and activities of play (Carr, 2003).
- Individuals with autism also exhibit an apparent inability to empathise with others.

A spectrum of disorders exists and ranges from classic autism to high-functioning autism, which is often termed Asperger's syndrome. 'Asperger's syndrome, like autism, is characterised by abnormalities in reciprocal interactions and restricted, repetitive patterns of activities and interests. However, it differs from autism in so far as no delay in language development or intellectual development occurs. Often people with Asperger's syndrome have outstanding memories for facts or figures.' (Carr, 2003)

Cognitive theory of mind in autism

Research conducted with children of normal development, with autism and with Down syndrome has found that both groups of children without autism did well on the 'Sally and Ann' exercise (see Chapter 4) that tests the existence of theory of mind; but the children with autism performed poorly. An example of this lack of theory of mind was a story related by Margaret Dewey (Frith, 1996, p.182) of an autistic boy who was sent to the kitchen to get himself a drink of milk. His father came in to find the child pouring the carton of milk down the drain. The father started shouting at his son to stop, which the child did, and began crying but made no attempt to explain why he had done it. It later transpired that the child believed the milk to have gone off and was doing what he had witnessed his parents do with bad milk; pour it down the drain. The child did not defend his action when told to stop, exactly what one would expect from a child who does not realise that someone else does not necessarily have the same knowledge as himself. Thus being shouted out was a shocking turn of events that made no sense to him at all.

Biological causes

Biological research suggests a neuro-developmental aspect to autism and holds genetics as instrumental in its origins. Oliver Sacks, in his book *The Man Who Mistook His Wife for a Hat,* describes the autistic artist José, who had developed apparently normally until a childhood illness caused swelling to the brain that caused irreparable damage. José displayed many autistic characteristics and this could suggest that in some cases neurological damage can be held accountable. Recent developments and research in neurology claim to have found that some autistic people have shorter brain stems than individuals with normal development.

There also exists the relatively recent association between the MMR vaccine and autism, which remains unproven.

Genetic factor

Initially the possibility of a genetic factor in autism was disregarded as early studies suggested that the likelihood of having more than one autistic child in a family was relatively low at 2 per cent. However, more recent studies have increased the incidence rate to 4 per 10,000 base rate in the general population, which is considered quite high. Subsequent twin studies confirm a very strong genetic component, and it is now accepted that the inheritance of autism exceeds 90 per cent (Rutter *et al.*, 1997).

Treatment

While there is no cure for autism (Cohen and Volkmar, 1997), treatments do exist. These tend to follow a behaviour-modification approach; for example, the Lovaas method is popular, particularly for targeting challenging behaviours.

The Treatment and Education of Autistic and Communication-related Handicapped Children (TEACCH) approach emphasises an intensive structured educative programme that aims to make the world intelligible to the autistic child by acknowledging deficits and building on the strengths of the child. The provision of a structured environment seems to be desirable, according to the findings of Rutter and Bartak (1973).

Rutter (1998) maintains that both clinical and experimental studies have shown the importance of basic cognitive deficits in the disorder and this has led to a focus on educational and behavioural approaches to treatment, and systematic evaluations show their efficacy. They now constitute the mainstay of treatment and all over the world special schools and classes for autistic children have been developed.

In Ireland, the Irish College of Psychiatrists, in their position statement *A Better Future Now* (2005), highlight the need for quick diagnosis and provision of service. They identify the following gaps in the service provision for autism:

- specialist autism services have developed in an uneven manner
- specialist out-patient sector teams do not have resources to carry out initial assessments or to offer appropriate long-term interventions. (p.56)

People with autism face many obstacles to participating in society, from educational to social. Certainly the lack of educational facilities and funding for such services is well documented.

We will now look at a very different type of condition that can affect children's ability to participate fully in class and in society.

Specific learning disability – ADHD

The main features of attention deficit hyperactivity disorder (ADHD), according to the American Psychiatric Association, include hyperactivity, impulsiveness and an inability to sustain attention or concentration. These symptoms occur at levels that cause significant distress and impairment and are far more severe than typically found in children of similar ages and developmental levels. More common in boys than in girls, this disorder often develops before age seven, but is usually diagnosed between ages eight and ten. Children with ADHD:

- have difficulty finishing any activity that requires concentration
- don't seem to listen to anything said to them
- are excessively active – running or climbing at inappropriate times, squirming in or jumping out of their seats
- are very easily distracted
- talk incessantly, often blurting out responses before questions are finished
- have serious difficulty waiting their turn in games or groups
- may have specific learning disabilities.

Rutter (1998) relates that ADHD was initially conceived to be the result of some type of 'minimal brain dysfunction' resulting in the hyperactive symptomology that is associated with this condition. However, this more 'medicalised' view was discredited by research findings that established that most children with ADHD did not have apparent brain dysfunction. These findings heralded a new conception of the cause of ADHD, leading to a shift in focus of researchers along the flowing lines:

1. One set of investigative approaches sought to determine whether hyperkinetic (hyperactivity or frenetic activity) disorder differed meaningfully from other syndromes of disruptive behaviour involving oppositional or conduct problems. The findings showed that it did, although they also suggested that the syndrome was probably not as common as the prevailing diagnostic practice in North America would lead one to believe.
2. A second set of studies concentrated on investigations of cognitive and attentional deficits. The findings have been consistent in showing their presence, but the precise nature of the deficits remains somewhat elusive.
3. A third research approach has concerned evaluation of the efficacy of drug treatment, especially the use of stimulants. The findings have been very consistent in showing major short-term benefits, although there is more uncertainty regarding long-term gains. Also, it has seemed that, in the longer term (a necessary perspective with a chronic disorder), it is advantageous to combine medication with psychological interventions. Initially it had appeared that the drug response was diagnosis-specific, but it is now clear that that is not so.

In more recent times, two other research perspectives have come on the scene:

4. Fourth, there is growing evidence that there is a strong genetic component and that this applies to hyperactivity well beyond the range of the relatively narrow diagnostic concept as used in the UK and much of the rest of Europe.
5. Fifth, epidemiological and longitudinal studies have shown the importance of hyperactivity (dealt with as a behaviour rather than a diagnosis) as a risk factor for conduct disturbance. It remains uncertain, however, whether this antisocial progression requires, in addition to hyperactivity, the presence of psychosocial adversity.

Most clinicians now recognise the validity of the diagnostic concept of hyperkinetic disorder; the benefits that follow the use of stimulant medication are generally accepted; and the need to combine drug treatment with psychological approaches is becoming widely appreciated.

Dyslexia is another specific learning disability (SLD) which presents in people with typical IQs but who experience difficulty processing words as symbols; this should not be confused with literacy problems which are not a result of processing difficulties. Dyslexia is a developmental condition that is lifelong whereas literacy issues are the product of environmental factors.

We have now considered the many types of disabilities, their aetiology and characteristics. This final piece deals with the issue of challenging behaviours and how best it can be addressed. Eleanor Fitzmaurice's chapter on 'Challenging behaviour in applied social care' (2009) offers a more in-depth exploration of this topic.

Practice: Working with challenging behaviour

Herbert (2006, p.325) reports that 'prevalence data suggest that the presence of *challenging behaviours* (notably attention-seeking, overactivity, temper tantrums, aggression, screaming, wandering, destructiveness and self-injury, night-walking and settling difficulties) is high. Such children may have as many as seven or eight behaviours problems on average.' He further reports that those with intellectual disabilities are at much greater risk of developing psychopathology than those without an intellectual disability.

The following are examples of some factors that may contribute to problem behaviours:

- physical illness
- discomfort or pain
- side effects of medication
- psychological distress
- incompatibility between the person and their carers, other residents or environment.

Fitzmaurice (2009, pp.205–9) outlines the following 10 key characteristics that are found in models designed to address the management of challenging behaviours:

1. An ethos of respect for all members of the service community, including management, team leaders, staff and clients
2. Endorsement and support of the behavior management system by management
3. Effective risk assessment procedures
4. An individualized approach to understanding and relating to clients with challenging behavior

5. Self-awareness of staff
6. Clear incident and response plans and reporting procedures
7. Staff training
8. An effective and relevant behavior management approach
9. A team approach
10. Debriefing.

With respect to point 8, Fitzmaurice (2009, p.208) elaborates that it is essential that practitioners are able to:

- Identify the stages of a client's gradual build-up (or 'escalation') to a crisis
- Quickly make use of individual and team responses that will assist the client to de-escalate
- Use verbal and sometimes non-verbal interventions to manage behavior that is in danger of becoming out of control
- Use debriefing techniques appropriate to the client's level of understanding and self-awareness and to the needs of practitioners
- Document the incident honestly, thoroughly, dispassionately and fairly.

The TCI (Therapeutic Crisis Intervention), developed by Cornell University, is an approach to behaviour management that is used in residential care facilities under the aegis of the HSE.

See http://rccp.cornell.edu

The Convention on the Rights of Persons with Disabilities

The general principles of the Convention on the Rights of Persons with Disabilities (Mental Health Commission, 2009) can be used as a guide with regard to attitudes and interaction with people with disabilities. We have seen the wide spectrum of disabilities and the variety of factors and causes associated with each of the disabilities considered. It is fundamentally important to remember that it is environmental and social factors that can cause the disadvantage, prejudice and discrimination to those with disabilities. Attitudes can be changed and environmental factors modified to ensure an inclusive society for all.

Convention on the Rights of Persons with Disabilities: Article 3 – General principles
The principles of the present Convention shall be:
a. Respect for inherent dignity, individual autonomy including the freedom to make one's own choices, and independence of persons;
b. Non-discrimination;

c. Full and effective participation and inclusion in society;
d. Respect for difference and acceptance of persons with disabilities as part of human diversity and humanity;
e. Equality of opportunity;
f. Accessibility;
g. Equality between men and women;
h. Respect for the evolving capacities of children with disabilities and respect for the right of children with disabilities to preserve their identities.

6
Psychopathology

INTRODUCTION: WHAT IS MENTAL HEALTH?

The World Health Organization has proposed the following definition of mental health: 'a state of well-being in which the individual realizes his or her own abilities, can cope with the normal stresses of life, can work productively and fruitfully, and is able to make a contribution to his or her community'.

Jahoda (1958) elaborated on this by separating mental health into three domains. First, mental health involves 'self-realization', meaning that individuals are allowed to fully exploit their potential. Second, mental health includes 'a sense of mastery' by the individual over their environment and, third, positive mental health means 'autonomy'; that is, having the ability to identify, confront and solve problems.

It has been suggested that Jahoda's conceptualisation of mental health is heavily influenced by Western cultural ideas of individualism and therefore not applicable to other cultures which are more collectivist in orientation. The definition of mental health is therefore clearly influenced by the culture that defines it and has different meanings depending on setting, culture and socioeconomic and political influences.

The medical model approach to mental health

Wyatt and Livson (1994, p.120) suggest that there are two general models of mental illness to which most mental health practitioner and theoreticians subscribe: the medical and the psychosocial models:

> The medical model conceptualizes a patient's maladaptive psychological, emotional, and interpersonal experiences primarily in terms of organic, biochemical, or physiological aetiology, leading its adherents to advocate biochemical or physical methods of treatment. Psychotherapy and social therapies are then viewed as adjuncts to medical interventions. The psychosocial model, by contrast, conceptualizes emotional disturbances as primarily the consequence of social, psychological, interpersonal, cultural,

and ethical conflicts. Within this framework, psychotherapy and social interventions are deemed the primary modes for helping clients resolve their conflicts; psychotropic medications may or may not be used as adjuncts to the psychotherapeutic process.

Beecher (2009, p.10) defines the medical model further, suggesting two approaches to its conceptualisation. The first theme is a causal or aetiological model (also known as the biomedical model), which defines mental illness as a disorder of the brain or nervous system and which is amenable to pharmacological or physical treatment. The second theme is referred to as a 'practice oriented (help or treatment) model which focuses on the identification of a problem through diagnosis and then the prescribing of treatment to ameliorate or eradicate the problem'.

Criticisms of a medical-model approach stem from its limited scope in considering the person's external environment, and claim that it is too problem-focused. A further criticism of the medical model is that it can result in the individual with a mental illness being seen only as the illness. In other words, practitioners see only the disorder and not the person. McLean (1990, cited in Beecher, 2009, p.10) concluded that the view of mental illness as a 'disease of the brain' perpetuates this depersonalisation of the individual with mental illness and their family.

The bio-psychosocial model

This model provides a framework for the understanding of the biological model of the mind and applying it to various psychological disorders. A biological approach to understanding mental disorders focuses on the physiological aspect of the person (including genes, brain, cells, etc.); the psychological approach meanwhile focuses on preceding mental states. With this approach, different psychological models (psychodynamic and cognitive-behavioural, for example) are considered in the search for understanding. Finally, the social approach considers patterns of maladaptive stress and social interactions in the causation and maintenance of mental disorders. Rutter elaborates on the different mechanisms at play within the bio-psychosocial approach. The vulnerability-stress approach is also examined below.

The recovery model

The profession-centred debate regarding which model of mental health a team adopts distracts teams from the advantages of embracing a recovery model of mental health. Such a model fits with an affirming, aspirational and solution-focused approach based on integrating models. Rather than asking whether 'a single dominant model or theory of mental distress' or 'a babble of multiple theoretical perspectives' will be effective, this model recognises the need to 'develop a tight bundle of relevant responses congruent' with those of the service user. Moving beyond the one-model-fits-all approach to a service-user-centred approach recognises that this bundle will vary from service user to service user (p.18).

See: www.mhcirl.ie

The anti-psychiatry movement

Laing expounded his political views in *The Politics of Experience*, where he regards madness as the product of a struggle between the repressive society and the individual who is seeking to escape its repression. The main purpose of psychiatry is to medicalise defiance and persecute the non-obedient in order to teach its citizens how to conform to society's norms.

Szasz's contribution to the anti-psychiatric movement was made in his famous and notorious book, *The Myth of Mental Illness*, which described mental illness as a metaphorical illness, because 'the mind (whatever that is) is not an organ or part of the body. Hence it cannot be diseased in the same sense as the body can'. Szasz drew attention to psychiatric prejudice and the role of values in psychiatric decision-making.

Goffman (1961), a sociologist, articulated the impact of psychiatric labelling on the mentally ill in his influential book, *Asylums*. Goffman's theory of labelling and mental illness is examined in more depth in Chapter 9. An idea allied to Goffman's concept of psychiatric labelling is how language can shape our perception of a given thing, person or construct. This realisation is reflected in the change of language in recent years when discussing aspects of mental health. 'Therapy' has largely replaced 'treatment' and the 'patient' is commonly referred to as a 'client'. Indeed, one aspect of Laing's political argument was his contempt for psychiatric literature, which he referred to as a vocabulary of denigration. Nasser (1995, p.746) believes the ultimate success of the anti-psychiatry movement lies 'in the shift of focus from large mental institutions to the provision of care in the community'.

Hopefully, reading about the anti-psychiatry movement will challenge you to consider how you think about the term and concept of 'mental illness' and, more specifically, who determines what is mental illness and who is affected by it. It is important to always challenge the orthodoxy and maintain an open mind. It is only in recent history that homosexuality was classified as a mental illness and, in Ireland, unmarried mothers deemed mentally and morally defective. Bearing this in mind we are going to examine the current classifications of mental illness beginning with the different approaches considered in understanding mental illness.

APPROACHES TO UNDERSTANDING MENTAL ILLNESS

Bio-psychosocial approach

Rutter (1989)

Biological pathways

- **Genetics:** for example, a possible genetic component in the link between conduct disorder in childhood and personality disorder in adulthood.
- **Biology:** for example, the purported link between pregnancy and birth complications and schizophrenia in adult life.

Psychological pathways

- **Cognition:** children raised in high-risk environments are less likely to develop later psychiatric disorders when they have a higher IQ or greater scholastic attainment.
- **Social skills:** some evidence for this view of the importance of early childrearing comes from the work of Tizard and Hodges.
- **Self-esteem/self-efficacy:** low self-esteem may leave the individual vulnerable to later psychiatric disorders. High self-esteem/self-efficacy may serve as a protection against future problems.
- **Habits, cognitive sets, coping styles:** for example, inability to cope with stress may result in increased difficulty in coping throughout childhood and adulthood.

Environmental pathways

- **Linked experiences:** many life experiences are inter-linked. For example, children who spend their early years in institutional settings are less likely to have access to a supportive extended family when they themselves become parents.
- **Shaping environments:** individuals may shape their adult environments through decisions made in childhood. For example, there is the link between education in childhood and occupation in adulthood.

Vulnerability-stress model

The origins of this model lie in Beck's diathesis stress model of depression, and Sameroff's transactional model of development. The model posits that individual psychopathology is triggered and develops in response to underlying vulnerabilities within the person and external stressors. It is the interaction of these two elements (nature–nurture) that creates and maintains individual competencies over time. There has been some criticism of this approach; it has been suggested that the field of stressors has not been given the same attention as that of vulnerabilities. Also, scant regard has been given to the potential for vulnerabilities to generate new stressors in an individual's life, and for stressors to introduce or worsen vulnerabilities.

1. How do vulnerabilities change with age? It seems unlikely that most would be static or immutable.
2. Are there sensitive or critical periods for vulnerabilities to be impacted by stressors?
3. Are there matches between specific vulnerabilities and specific stressors that make particular psychopathologies more likely to develop?
4. How do early caregiver–infant relationships develop into 'internal' vulnerabilities and 'external' stressors later in childhood?
5. Are biological, emotional, cognitive and social-cognitive vulnerabilities just different faces of a common, core susceptibility to psychopathology, or are they meaningfully distinct?
6. What are the roles of resilience and protective factors in the development of well-being? Is the good mental health of children and youth supported by anything other than the absence of vulnerability and stress?
7. Do any of these models pertain to the majority of the world's children and youth, who live outside the generally privileged conditions of most families in North America and western Europe? Culture provides context and meaning to stress, vulnerability, and psychopathology. For hundreds of millions of children in developing countries, stress means living in conditions of war, poverty, hunger, malnutrition, overcrowding, homelessness, and lack of education and health care. When we look beyond our own borders, what do we know about the development of psychopathology?

Early warning signs of mental illness

What are the signs and symptoms to be concerned about? If several of the following occur, a serious condition may be developing:

- Recent social withdrawal and loss of interest in others. An unusual drop in functioning, especially at school or work, such as quitting sports, failing in school or difficulty performing familiar tasks.
- Problems with concentration, memory or logical thought and speech that are hard to explain.
- Loss of initiative or desire to participate in any activity; apathy.
- A vague feeling of being disconnected from oneself or one's surroundings; a sense of unreality.
- Fear or suspiciousness of others or a strong nervous feeling.
- Dramatic sleep and appetite changes or deterioration in personal hygiene.
- Rapid or dramatic shifts in feelings or 'mood swings'.

Source: www.healthyminds.org

CHILDHOOD MENTAL ILLNESS

Depression (childhood)

As many as 1 in 10 children between the ages of 6 and 12 experiences persistent feelings of sadness – the hallmark of depression. Since children may not be able to express or understand many of the core symptoms that would indicate depression in adults, it is important to be aware of some key behaviours – in addition to changes in eating or sleeping patterns – that may signal depression in children.

The Royal College of Psychiatrists lists the following symptoms of depression experienced by children and teenagers:

- Being moody and irritable – easily upset, 'ratty' or tearful.
- Becoming withdrawn – avoiding friends, family and regular activities.
- Feeling guilty or bad, being self-critical and self-blaming – hating yourself.
- Feeling unhappy, miserable and lonely a lot of the time.
- Feeling hopeless and wanting to die.
- Finding it difficult to concentrate.
- Not looking after your personal appearance.
- Changes in sleep pattern: sleeping too little or too much.
- Tiredness and lack of energy.
- Frequent minor health problems, such as headaches or stomach-aches.

Depression is increasingly becoming recognised as an issue that is affecting more and more children. Depression is a disorder that affects both children and adults. Attention Deficit Hyperactivity Disorder (ADHD) is an issue mainly associated with children, but it can continue to affect adults also. In Chapter 5 ADHD is described in depth. The main features of this disorder include hyperactivity, impulsiveness and an inability to sustain attention or concentration. It is arguable that it is in recent times that ADHD has been accepted as a condition; historically, there has been a reluctance to accept and acknowledge the existence of certain psychiatric disorders in childhood. The following disorders start in childhood but can follow into adulthood as antisocial personality disorders.

Conduct disorder

Children with conduct disorder exhibit behaviour that shows a persistent disregard for the norms and rules of society. Conduct disorder is one of the most frequently seen mental disorders in adolescents. Because the symptoms are closely tied to socially unacceptable or violent behaviour, many people confuse this illness with either juvenile delinquency or the turmoil of the teen years. Children who have demonstrated at least three of the following behaviours over six months should be evaluated for possible conduct disorder:

- stealing
- constantly lying
- deliberately setting fires
- skipping school
- breaking into homes, offices or cars
- deliberately destroying others' property
- displaying physical cruelty to animals or humans
- forcing others into sexual activity
- often starting fights
- using weapons in fights.

Source: American Psychiatric Association

Oppositional defiant disorder

According to Hartman (2007), 'Oppositional Defiant Disorder is, in my book, a red flag. It is an indication that there is something else going on. I have never. . . seen a kid that meets criteria for ODD and did not meet criteria for some other diagnosis. It is as if the oppositional and defiant behavior is a coping strategy for dealing with other issues or a poorly functional reaction to other issues that are not being dealt with.' Carr (2003) remarks that a distinction can be made between oppositional defiant disorder (ODD) and conduct disorder, with the former reflecting a less pervasive disturbance than the latter and possibly being a developmental precursor of conduct disorder. In other words, oppositional defiant disorder is a less severe form of, and can be a precursor to, conduct disorder. It represents a child or teenager acting in a deliberately hostile fashion. Another possible distinction is that ODD is sometimes directed within the home whereas the progression to conduct disorders includes a continuation of hostility outside of the home.

Rutter (1998, p.807) outlines the four main advances he suggests have been made with respect to conduct disorders:

Developmental continuities and discontinuities
- Greater awareness of the extent to which conduct disorders have their origins in the preschool years.
- Realisation of the high frequency with which there is a progression to personality disorders in adult life.
- Evidence has accumulated on the reality of important changes for the better in adult life if there is a sufficiently major change in the relevant life circumstances.

Sharpening of diagnostic concepts
- Recognition that oppositional defiance disorder in early childhood often leads to conduct disorders in later childhood.

- Importantly, the differentiation between 'life-persistent' and 'adolescence-limited' antisocial problems.

Recognition of the importance of risk factors associated with individual characteristics

- Temperamental features
- Reading and other cognitive difficulties
- Genetic factors.

Advances in approaches to treatment

- Attention has been paid to the cognitive processing of experiences, to social problem-solving, to patterns of family interaction, and to the need to focus on schools as well as families.

Treatments

- Psychoeducation
- Monitoring antisocial and prosocial behavioural targets
- Behavioural parent training with a focus on reward training and time out
- Family-based communication and problem-solving training
- Home-school liaison meetings and tuition
- Child-based social problem-solving skills training
- Parent counselling for managing personal or marital difficulties
- Treatment foster-care placement where families are extremely disorganized
- Interprofessional and interagency co-ordination meetings.

(Carr, 2003, p.348)

Carr and Byrne (2000) report that prevalence rates for psychological disorders in Irish children range from between 10 to 17 per cent with approximately 13 per cent of this figure accounted for by conduct disorders. Further studies of referrals to the Department of Child and Family Psychiatry at the Mater Hospital identified subtypes of conduct disorders as follows (Carr and Byrne, 2000, p.84):

1. Unsocialized aggression, characterized by family dysfunction
2. The second group exhibited a variety of conduct problems in association with emotional difficulties such as anxiety or depressed mood and this group was also characterized by family dysfunction.

Rutter (1998) concedes that conduct disorders remain a challenge and that therapeutic outcomes remain modest rather than hugely significant. He recognises the difficulties in engaging families in treatment. Other initiatives that can support young offenders include the Special Garda Projects (see Chapter 4).

Autism is part of the pervasive development disorders spectrum and the basic criteria for autism are qualitative impairment in reciprocal social interaction, in verbal and non-verbal communication and in imaginative activity (see Chapter 5).

ADULT MENTAL ILLNESS

Anxiety disorders

Anxiety is an emotion characterised by feelings of tension, worried thoughts and physical changes such as increased blood pressure. People with anxiety disorders usually have recurring intrusive thoughts or concerns. They may avoid certain situations out of worry. They may also have physical symptoms such as sweating, trembling, dizziness or a rapid heartbeat. Anxiety disorders differ from normal feelings of nervousness. Untreated anxiety disorders can push people into avoiding situations that trigger or worsen their symptoms. People with anxiety disorders are likely to suffer from depression, and they may also abuse alcohol and other drugs in an effort to gain relief from their symptoms. Job performance, school work and personal relationships can also suffer.

Types of anxiety disorders
- panic disorder
- generalised anxiety disorder phobias
- post-traumatic stress disorder
- obsessive-compulsive disorder.

Anxiety disorders are the most common of the 'emotional' disorders. Post-traumatic stress disorder (PTSD, see Chapter 8) is a psychiatric disorder that can occur in people who have experienced or witnessed life-threatening events, including serious accidents or violent personal assaults such as rape. People who suffer from PTSD often relive the experience through flashbacks or nightmares, have difficulty sleeping and feel detached or estranged.

Schizophrenia

Schizophrenia is a psychotic disorder that involves severe disturbances in speech, thinking, perception, emotion and behaviour. The National Institute of Mental Health (NIMH) states that schizophrenia is 'the most chronic and disabling of the severe mental illnesses' (2001, p.1). The term 'schizophrenia' was introduced in 1911 by Eugen Bleuler and, in Latin, means 'split mind'. Bleuler was attempting to capture how psychological functions appear to be split or disconnected in schizophrenics compared to normal people whose functions are quite unified. Whereas depression is considered to be a disorder of mood, schizophrenia is suggested as a disorder of thought. As you will see, there can be a variety in the symptoms of schizophrenia which has led to the premise that schizophrenia constitutes a group of disorders, not unlike other chronic illnesses. Symptoms usually first appear in early adulthood. Men often experience symptoms in their early 20s and women typically first show signs of the disease in their late 20s and early 30s.

Features of schizophrenia

Carr (2003) amalgamated the following features of schizophrenia based on ICD 10 and DSM IV (diagnostic manual) descriptions. The following features are present in schizophrenia and are considered to be clinical features of the disorder:

- **Perception:** individuals may experience auditory hallucinations; their ability to focus on important information or stimuli to the exclusion of other stimuli becomes impaired.
- **Thought/cognitive:** the thought process becomes disordered and delusions may occur. Logical trains of thought become difficult to form or follow.
- **Emotion/affect:** anxiety and depression may occur during the prodromal stage and inappropriate and flattened affect may also be present.
- **Behaviour:** during the prodromal period sleep patterns can be affected and behaviour can be impulsive and compulsive. During psychotic episodes negativism, catatonia (impairment of movement) and mutism can occur.

Clearly there is a significant diversity in the symptoms presented in schizophrenia. This is reflected in the classification system devised for schizophrenia and also in the aetiological factors that are believed to contribute to the disorder. This diversity has implications for the course and treatment of schizophrenia. Both diagnostic manuals, DSM IV and ICD 10, focus on the symptomology of schizophrenia in classifying the illness into four categories or subtypes: paranoid, catatonic, hebephrenic and undifferentiated:

- **Paranoid:** where delusions dominate, a diagnosis of paranoid schizophrenia is given. Two categories of delusions exist: delusions of persecution (in which people believe that others mean to harm them), and delusions of grandeur (in which they believe they are enormously important).
- **Catatonic:** identified by unusual psychomotor features or psychomotor abnormalities. Those with this form of schizophrenia may alternate between extremes of excitability and stupor and they may adopt peculiar postures for long periods.
- **Hebephrenic** (ICD 10)/**Disorganised** (DSM IV): characterised by flat or inappropriate affect and a disorganisation of speech and behaviour.
- **Undifferentiated:** finally, where none of the previous three classifications are fully applicable a classification of undifferentiated schizophrenia is made.

Psychotic episodes can last from between one month to one year and are usually preceded by a prodromal (early onset) period of several weeks.

Type I schizophrenia is characterised by a predominance of positive symptoms such as delusions, hallucinations and disordered speech and thinking. These symptoms are called positive because they represent pathological extremes of normal processes.

Type II schizophrenia features negative symptoms – an absence of normal reactions, such as lack of emotional expression, loss of motivation and an absence of normal speech.

Many factors have been studied in examining the causes of schizophrenia. It is believed that a number of biological and environmental factors play a role in the onset and course of the disorder. It is still unclear as to which factors produce the illness.

There is a genetic vulnerability for this disorder, but while this can contribute towards the illness it does not necessarily cause it. Rather, it would appear that many factors interact to cause schizophrenia; family or environmental stress, possibly drug taking, with the genetic vulnerability being the strongest predisposing force. Studies have shown that identical twins have a higher concordance rate than fraternal twins and that adopted children whose biological parent is schizophrenic have a higher rate of concordance than if the adopted parent suffers the illness. Thus although the origin of schizophrenia has not been identified, scientists know that there is some hereditary basis or genetic predisposition for the disease, as it runs in families.

Factors in schizophrenia

Biological factors

Dopamine hypothesis

This approach suggests a dysfunction of the mesolymbic dopaminergic system. Pharmacological treatments of schizophrenia have centred on neuroleptic medication which prohibits dopamine activity in people. However, these drugs tend to impact only on schizophrenics showing positive effects rather than negative effects. Further, it has been suggested that the effect on behaviour does not alleviate immediately even though the drug immediately affects dopamine levels. According to Carr, 25 per cent of schizophrenics do not respond to anti-psychotic drugs. If the dopamine hypothesis was the cause of schizophrenia, one would expect all sufferers to benefit immediately from drugs reducing dopamine levels. Finally, an interesting point has been raised as to whether dopamine levels are *caused by* the schizophrenia rather than causing the illness.

Neurodevelopmental hypothesis

There is growing support for the neurodevelopmental hypothesis that argues that prenatal neurological insults and prenatal intrauterine environment, such as maternal flu virus, may be responsible for schizophrenia (Murray and Lewis, 1987, cited in Carr, 2003). This could tie in with the structural abnormalities found in scans of the brains of schizophrenics.

Cognitive factors

Some cognitive theorists maintain that schizophrenia is due to a defective attentional mechanism, which normally filters out irrelevant stimuli, resulting in an overload of internal and external stimuli, thus explaining the schizophrenic's feeling of being overwhelmed by disconnected thoughts. Other cognitive theories include the cognitive bias theory and the prodromal hypothesis.

Family dynamics

It would appear that schizophrenics from families that exhibit high levels of expressed emotion are more likely to relapse compared to those from families with lower levels. In videotapes of the behaviour of schizophrenics in the former group, where families were more likely to make negative comments, the schizophrenics engaged in four times as many strange and disruptive behaviours than did the schizophrenics in families with lower expressed levels of emotion.

Sociocultural factors

Evidence suggests that schizophrenia appears to be of higher prevalence in poorer or lower socio-economic populations. However, does poverty cause schizophrenia, or vice versa? The social causation hypothesis maintains that people who live in poorer urban settings experience more stresses and this leaves them vulnerable to developing schizophrenia. On the opposite side is the social drift hypothesis that posits that schizophrenic people find it increasingly difficult to maintain professional and personal lives and begin to drift into poorer economic conditions and live in increasingly low-cost urban environments.

The World Health Organization study of schizophrenia has concluded that it is quite culture-free insofar as there is prevalence of the disease across the globe (Jablensky et al., 1992). What does appear to be culturally relevant is the recovery rate, which is higher in the developing world than in America and Canada. Possible explanations are the stronger community ties and social support demonstrated towards the schizophrenic patient found in these countries.

What is certainly not in doubt is that schizophrenia remains a complex illness and that no one factor has yet conclusively been identified as a cause. An integrative approach has been promoted which aims to include and amalgamate the many strands thus linked to schizophrenia into a larger biological and psychosocial framework (Zublin and Ludwig, 1983; Nuechterlin and Dawson, 1984, cited in Carr, 2003).

Is split personality (dissociative identity disorder) the same as schizophrenia?

As stated, confusion stems from Bleuler's description of a 'split' in schizophrenia; he was referring to the disconnected nature of processes such as thought and language. Multiple personality disorder, or as it is more commonly referred to, dissociative identity disorder (DID), should not be confused with schizophrenia. Many differences exist: epidemiology, treatment and even professional recognition of the disorder itself. Since the film *The Three Faces of Eve* and the book *Sybil* have raised the profile of this disorder, the numbers of those claiming to be affected has increased significantly. Critics also point to high-profile criminals who have attempted to blame their crimes on this disorder. With DID an individual can have other separate and distinct personalities, as well as the 'host' personality, within the one body and with no or limited knowledge of the other personalities.

Theories have been suggested to explain this phenomenon but a diathesis-stress model has been generally accepted (Maldonado *et al.*, 1998). High levels of abuse and trauma in childhood while the individual's personality is developing and at a fragile point have been held responsible. As a coping mechanism the child might dissociate themselves from the reality of the trauma they are experiencing. Some create new identities in an attempt to distance themselves from the trauma; this dissociation brings a degree of relief and in doing so reinforces the dissociation. As the child reaches adulthood, rather than the alternate personality being integrated into a unified personality they remain separate, acting as a protection against further suffering. Frank Putnam in his study of 100 diagnosed DID cases found that 97 reported high levels of physical and sexual abuse. Treatments for schizophrenia are very different to approaches used in the treatment of DID.

It can be difficult to imagine what life might be like for someone with schizophrenia. An illustrative example of the descent into psychosis by the artist Louis Wain, who has schizophrenia, can be found in the online resources available with this book.

Treatment of schizophrenia

There is no cure for schizophrenia, but treatments are available to reduce the intensity and frequency of the symptoms. Medication and psychosocial treatments can help some people with schizophrenia to lead highly productive and rewarding lives, while for others the illness continues to cause impairments in function despite treatment and family support.

A variety of antipsychotic medications are effective in reducing the psychotic symptoms present in the acute phase of the illness, and they also help reduce the potential for future acute episodes. Before treatment can begin, however, a psychiatrist should conduct a thorough medical examination to rule out substance abuse or other medical illnesses whose symptoms mimic schizophrenia.

People with schizophrenia abuse drugs more often than the general population. Substance abuse complicates the diagnosis of schizophrenia and also reduces the effectiveness of treatment for schizophrenia. If a patient shows signs of addiction, treatment for substance abuse should be pursued along with other treatments.

Recovery and rehabilitation

When the symptoms of schizophrenia are controlled, therapy can help people learn social skills, cope with stress, identify early warning signs of relapse, and prolong periods of remission. Many people with the disease, following treatment, can reach their full potential by managing the illness. Because schizophrenia typically strikes in early adulthood, individuals with the disorder need rehabilitation to help develop life-management skills, complete vocational or educational training and hold a job. For example, supported employment programmes have been established to help persons with schizophrenia achieve self-sufficiency. These programmes provide people with severe mental illness with jobs in competitive, real-world settings.

Many people living with schizophrenia receive emotional and material support from their family. Therefore, it is important that families be provided with education and assistance in managing their ill relative's disease. Such assistance has been shown to help prevent relapses and improve the overall mental health of the family members as well as the person with schizophrenia.

People with schizophrenia may receive rehabilitation services on an individual basis, in the community, or in a hospital or clinic. When living alone or with family is not an option, supportive housing is often available and includes halfway and group houses as well as monitored co-operative apartments.

Source: www.healthyminds.org

Early warning signs of schizophrenia

Changes in mood such as moodiness, depression, inability to cry, excessive crying, laughing for no particular reason or inability to laugh.

Sensory changes such as hearing voices, unusual sensitivity to noise or light.

Changes in activity such as becoming extremely active or inactive, sleeping excessively or hardly at all.

Changes in social behaviour such as avoiding social situations, dropping out of activities, refusing to go out, allowing relationships to deteriorate, saying irrational or inappropriate things, using peculiar words or making meaningless statements.

Changes in relations with family such as constantly arguing, never phoning home, phoning home at strange times of the night.

Changes at school or work such as problems in concentrating, declining academic performance.

Changes in behaviour such as strange postures, prolonged staring, extreme religious beliefs, using illegal drugs.

Changes in appearance such as wearing bizarre clothes, poor personal hygiene.

Source: Schizophrenia Ireland, 2005, p.16.

Mood disorders

Depression

Along with anxiety disorders, mood disorders are the most frequently experienced psychological disorder. Depression is a disorder where, clearly, the individual's mood is affected. Those affected by depression often suffer from very low moods and feelings of helplessness. The DSM (diagnostic manual) classification of mood disorders includes bipolar disorder, major (unipolar) depression disorder, dysthymia (a less intense form of depression that has less dramatic effects on personal and occupational functioning), seasonal affective disorder and post-partum depression. It is important to recognise that there is a difference between having a 'bad day' or having feelings of 'low mood', and clinical depression. Also, there are different forms of depression, the main ones being bipolar depression (referred to in the past as manic depression) and unipolar depression.

Depression and sadness are different

In life most of us will experience sadness through the death or loss of a loved one or some trauma or stressor such as divorce or losing a job. It is normal to experience sadness surrounding such events; however, with time, the sadness should begin to ease. There lies the main difference between depression and sadness; sadness usually has a trigger or event that causes it, and it does ease with time. Depression, on the other hand, does not lessen with time, continuing for months, if not years. There is not always a clear trigger or event that has precipitated the onset of depression. Depression is a more severe and intense experience and can have a very disabling effect upon an individual's life, leaving some unable to function in their lives.

Symptoms of depression can include:

- depressed mood; lack of interest in, and pleasure from, almost all activities
- decreased appetite leading to weight loss
- insomnia or hypersomnia, psychomotor agitation or retardation
- lack of energy
- feelings of worthlessness and guilt
- inability to think clearly or concentrate effectively, indecisiveness
- thoughts of death, suicidal thoughts.

Blatt and Zuroff (1992, p.158) outline that investigators from several different theoretical positions have identified two major types of experience that can result in depression:

- disruptions of gratifying interpersonal relationships (for example, object loss)
- disruptions of an effective and essentially positive sense of self.

Whereas Beck (1983), for example, describes differences between patients primarily in terms of current cognitive distortions, Bowlby (1980) discusses differences in terms of the attachment patterns formed in the patient's childhood.

Factors in mood disorders

Biological
- Genetic – studies of twins and adoption studies seem to suggest a genetic basis or predisposition to mood disorders. Bipolar depression appears to have a stronger genetic component.
- Neurochemical – brain chemistry has been examined in an effort to understand the causes of depression with underactivity of certain neurotransmitters appearing to play a role. Abnormalities in two chemicals in the brain, serotonin and norepinephrine, might contribute to symptoms of depression, including anxiety, irritability and fatigue.

Psychological
1. **Personality-based vulnerability:** this is a theory that was advocated by psychoanalysts Freud and Abraham, who believed that early losses or rejection created a vulnerability, triggering an underlying rage or grief process that left the individual susceptible to depression in later life.

    Blatt's attachment and autonomy theory also focuses on early child–parent relationships which engender vulnerability to developing depression in later life, in response to two distinct stressors:

    - loss of attachment relationships may precipitate depression in those who experienced neglecting or overindulgent parenting
    - loss of autonomy may precipitate depression in those whose parents were punitive or critical.
2. **Humanistic:** Martin Seligman posits that the 'me' generation which propounds individuality and self-control has contributed to the rapid increase in depression witnessed since the 1960s.
3. **Cognitive:** Aaron Beck has put forward the 'depressive cognitive triad' to explain the negative thinking patterns that appear with depression. The triad consists of negative thoughts about oneself, the world and the future. This approach highlights the depressed individual's focus on their 'failures' and

inability to take any credit for their positive actions – 'depressive attributional pattern'. These negative schemas, developed in early life, lead to negative automatic thoughts and cognitive distortions which maintain a depressed mood. Negative schemas have their roots in loss experience in early childhood, including:

- loss of parents or family members through death, illness or separation
- loss of positive parental care through parental rejection, criticism, severe punishment, over-protection, neglect or abuse
- loss of personal health
- loss or lack of positive peer relationships through bullying or exclusion from peer group.

4. **Family systems** (Carr p.636): this approach focuses on the structure and functioning of the family as being involved in the development of depression. It is posited that maladaptive functioning prevents the child from completing age-appropriate developmental tasks. Further disruption in the family structure though bereavement, parental discord, divorce and abuse can lead to depression. Finally, in adolescence, family enmeshment and related parent–child conflict over individuation may be associated with depression.

What is noteworthy of the personality and cognitive approaches to understanding depression is the emphasis placed on early experiences in the formulation and precipitation of vulnerability to the development of depression later in life. This emphasis fits within a developmental approach to the understanding of human development.

Seligman's theory of learned helplessness

As with Skinner's experiment, Seligman was experimenting with dogs and their behaviour. However, during the course of his experiments he noticed a phenomenon that led him to develop the theory of learned helplessness. Seligman demonstrated that following a series of uncontrollable, stressful events dogs fail to respond on simple tasks. Seligman proposed a learned helplessness hypothesis: that uncontrollable events produce an individual who perceives that response is useless and whose motivation to respond is weakened. The phenomenon of learned helplessness bears much in common with depression in humans. The theory was reformulated (Abramson *et al.*, 1978) in order to take account of explanatory style – that is, the way people explain negative events to themselves. People who have a pessimistic explanatory style explain negative events as stable, global and internal. Such people are hypothesised to be more predisposed to depression than people with an optimistic explanatory style, who explain negative events as unstable, specific and external.

The reformulated learned helplessness model (Abramson *et al.*, 1978) bears a striking similarity to the negative cognitive triad in Beck's cognitive theory of depression (Beck *et al.*, 1979).

Table 6.1: Learned helplessness model/cognitive theory of depression

Abramson, Seligman and Teasdale (1978)	Beck, Rush, Shaw and Emery (1979)
Internal attributions	Negative thoughts about the *self*
Global attributions	Negative thoughts about the *world*
Stable attributions	Negative thoughts about the *future*

However one formulates the aetiology and factors involved in depression, it is clear that it has a major impact on people's lives. The following short account of research highlights the prevalence of mental illness in prisons. An interesting question to consider is whether those suffering from mental illness are at higher risk of being incarcerated or whether the experience of being imprisoned causes or contributes to mental illness; what do you think?

Prison and mental illness

Kelly (2007, p.374) found strong evidence of a high prevalence of mental illness in prisons: one systematic review of 62 studies from 12 countries found that 3.7 per cent of male prisoners and 4 per cent of female prisoners had psychosis, while 10 per cent of male prisoners and 12 per cent of female prisoners had major depression. In Ireland the six-month prevalence of psychosis in life-sentenced male prisoners is 7.1 per cent.

Suicide

Suicide is often allied to depression. There is a growing recognition of the increasing numbers taking their own lives, especially in the young male category. *Definition:* Suicide is defined as the wilful taking of one's own life.

Some facts:

- The World Health Organization (WHO) estimates that 500,000 people worldwide commit suicide annually; about 1.4 every minute.
- In the US, suicide rates among 15 and 24 year olds have tripled since 1960.
- Women make about three times as many suicide attempts as men, but men are three times more likely to actually kill themselves. These differences may be due to
  — a higher incidence of depression in women
  — men's choice of more lethal methods, such as shooting themselves or jumping off buildings.
- The rate for both genders is higher among those who have been divorced or widowed.

- Women who commit suicide have a relatively greater tendency to be motivated by failures in love relationships, whereas men have a greater tendency to be motivated by failure in their occupations.
- A history of sexual or physical abuse significantly increases the likelihood of later suicide attempts (Garnefski and Arends, 1998).
- Depression is one of the strongest predictors of suicide; approximately 15 per cent of clinically depressed individuals kill themselves.

Motives for suicide

There appear to be two fundamental motivations for suicide:

1. the desire to end one's life
2. the desire to manipulate and coerce other people into doing what the suicidal person wants.

In one study, 56 per cent of suicide attempts were classified as having been motivated by the desire to die (Beck, 1976). Parasuicide is an attempt that does not end in death; often seen as a cry for help or an attempt to coerce people to meet one's need.

Suicide: An Irish perspective

Prevalence

- Ireland ranks fifth highest in the EU for rates of youth suicide (14–24 year olds), and although the precise rates of mental health problems for young people can be difficult to calculate, it is estimated that the prevalence of mental health difficulties for children and young people can be up to 20 per cent at any one time.
- For every woman who commits suicide approximately four to five men will.
- Figures for 2003 showed that there were 12.5 suicide deaths per 100,000 of the population in Ireland, compared to 8.5 such deaths in Northern Ireland. Comparative figures for the UK in the same year were: England 9.9 deaths; Wales 12 deaths; Scotland 15.7 deaths per 100,000 – the highest rate in these islands.
- Derek Chambers, research and resource officer of Ireland's National Suicide Review Group, pointed out that among people in their 20s or early 30s the suicide rate was higher, at 15.7 deaths per 100,000. He said that while almost one in four suicide victims was reported by a doctor or psychiatrist to have a history of alcohol abuse, a US expert on suicide prevention claims that 90 per cent of people who took their own lives had 'diagnosable mental or substance-abuse disorders, or both' (Irish Times, 26 August 2005, p.7).

National Suicide Research Foundation: Young Men's Study

From a sociological perspective:

A sense of community (social integration) and shared values (social regulation) can influence the behaviour and actions of individuals. In this context, the social changes that have occurred in Ireland in recent years merit investigation in terms of their impact on men's sense of personal worth and belonging in our modern society. Previous research has speculated that sociocultural changes in Western societies in recent years have adversely affected men more than women and that a gender difference has emerged in terms of how 'the self is seen or construed'.

Furthermore, increased individualism may be contributing to a greater sense of isolation for young men as women tend to remain more socially connected and to view the self as interdependent with others whereas men are more likely to view the self as separate.

Psychologically:

The individual's perceived sense of control is also important in determining how problems are dealt with and challenges in life are met. By clarifying young men's existing sense of control, realistic and meaningful health promotion strategies may be identified.

Anomy:

A concept that has been applied to the understanding of changes in suicide rates is the concept of anomy. Anomy describes the unbalancing of social forces that affect individual action. It implies an upsetting of the balance or normality in a previously accepted way of life. It is based on the notion that society usually exercises control over individual behaviour and desire through social rules and norms, and when these rules and norms break down, individual behaviour is no longer regulated by society. At an individual level it can be described as a personal feeling of not being part of, or responsible to, society. Underlying the notion of anomy is the belief that human desire is basically infinite; human beings will always want more unless society controls desires through the existence of everyday shared values and institutionalised rules or laws. Without a sense of accepted social values, individual behaviour or desire may not be controlled or regulated and the level of so called deviant or unacceptable behaviour, including suicide, increases.

At an individual level:

Changes in personal circumstances can lead to uncertainty or can upset the normal way of life. For example, by winning a large sum of money an individual may be forced to question values and desires that were previously taken for granted as new opportunities present themselves. Similarly, negative events such as job loss or divorce can upset the balance or equilibrium that previously governed an individual's way of life.

Anomy is also related to the values and expectations in a society and the means to achieve these expectations. When there is a discrepancy between expectations and means to achieve them, then the level of anomy increases. For example, in Irish society home ownership is something that is valued and is associated with independence and passage into adulthood. However, the means to achieve home ownership are not readily available to the majority of young people attempting to make the transition from adolescence to adulthood. The resulting situation may be that an individual is achieving societal expectations on some levels, e.g. in terms of career, but not on other levels, such as home ownership.

While anomy contributes to our overall understanding of suicide as a social problem, as a symptom of social transition, it may be difficult to apply to the understanding of individual deaths by suicide.

Sources of information

National Suicide Research Foundation	www.nsrf.org
Department of Health	www.doh.ie
Health Research Board (good link to drug section)	www.hrb.ie

Useful contacts

Aware run a Helpline Counselling Service for people with depression and their families, 24 hours a day, seven days a week:
Aware Helpline: 1890 303 302 72
Aware, Lower Leeson Street, Dublin 2
Tel: 01-6617211
Email: aware@iol.ie
Website: www.aware.ie

The Samaritans provide confidential 24-hour emotional support for people experiencing feelings of distress or despair, including those which may lead to suicide.
The Samaritans Helpline: 1850 609090
The Samaritans, 112 Marlborough Street, Dublin 1
Tel: 01 8727700
Email: jo@samaritans.org
Website: www.samaritans.org

Personality disorders

There are 10 disorders classified within the umbrella term of personality disorders. These are divided into three clusters:

Cluster A: odd or eccentric (paranoid, schizoid, schizotypal)
Cluster B: dramatic, emotional or erratic (histrionic, narcissistic, antisocial, borderline)
Cluster C: anxious and fearful (obsessive-compulsive, avoidant and dependent)

Each personality disorder is described in Appendix 2.

As you read through the descriptions of each type, you may well recognise some aspects of your own personality. This doesn't necessarily mean that you have a personality disorder. Some of these characteristics may even be helpful in some areas of your life. However, if you do have a personality disorder, these aspects of your personality will be quite extreme. They may spoil your life, and often the lives of those around you.

How common are personality disorders?
- About 40–70 per cent of people on a psychiatric ward will have a personality disorder.
- About 30–40 per cent of psychiatric patients being treated in the community by a psychiatric service will have a personality disorder.
- Around 10–30 per cent of patients who see their general practitioner (GP) will have a personality disorder.

Antisocial personality disorder
Antisocial personality disorder is a condition that affects a person's thoughts, emotions and behaviour in a way that is disruptive to, and may be harmful to, other people. People with this personality disorder exhibit traits of impulsivity, anger and associated behaviours, including irresponsibility, recklessness and deceitfulness. They have often grown up in fractured families in which parental conflict is typical and parenting is harsh and inconsistent. Antisocial personality disorder is not usually diagnosed before the age of 18 but characteristics of the disorder can be recognised in younger people as conduct problems. Early treatment of children (aged 5–11 years) and young people (aged 12–17 years) with conduct problems may help to prevent antisocial personality disorder from developing later.

The UK National Institute for Clinical Excellence (NICE) have produced guidelines for those who work with people with antisocial personality disorders. The guidelines aim to outline how healthcare professionals can manage and prevent this particular disorder.

- Staff working with people with antisocial personality disorder should recognise that a positive and rewarding approach is more likely to be successful than a punitive approach in engaging and retaining people in treatment.

- Cognitive problem-solving skills training should be considered for children aged eight years and older with conduct problems.
- For people with antisocial personality disorder with a history of offending behaviour who are in community and institutional care, consider offering group-based cognitive and behavioural interventions (for example, programmes such as 'reasoning and rehabilitation') focused on reducing offending and other antisocial behaviour.

Source: www.nice.org.uk

Predictors of compliance with psychological interventions offered in the community

The authors of this research (Ayuso-Mateos *et al.*, 2007) examined psychological interventions within the community for those experiencing depression. The research considered whether certain factors were more indicative of whether a person would complete an intervention designed to ameliorate and treat their depression. The authors' main finding was the important role of social support as a predictor of compliance with a psychological treatment. They suggest that programmes are designed to engage depressed individuals from the community in brief psychological therapies; we should have in mind that the programme must reach people who might be socially isolated and do not attend any social or health service. Campaigns which aim to reduce the burden of depression in the community should use alternative ways to reach these individuals, as well as the traditional ones. Secondly, the factors that predict attendance at psychological therapy sessions are different from those that predict completion of treatment once it has been started. Again, social support is important, but also we should bear in mind that men and subjects who do not show a disability are more likely to abandon treatment. Men might be less likely to try verbal therapy than women, and might question its usefulness.

SUMMARY

Hopefully, at the end of this chapter, you will appreciate the complexity of psychopathologies that exist, from their aetiology to their characteristics. The anti-psychiatry movement demonstrates the social element of classifying and determining what is considered a mental illness. It could perhaps be argued that nowadays there is a tendency to 'pathologise' normal behaviours as problematic; for example, feelings of sadness and grief are surely 'normal' reactions to the loss of a loved one. When do we decide when this reaction is no longer normal and needs an intervention? Regardless, it is clear that people with mental health issues are excluded and isolated from society through many avenues, including attitudes towards mental illness. This is an opportunity to reflect on your attitude to mental illness and consider whether it creates barriers for those who suffer it.

7

Health and well-being

The relationship between physical and psychological well-being is well documented. You should also be able to see the relationships that exist within an individual's environment, immediate and distant, and how these can influence their development. Bronfenbrenner's ecological model (Chapter 2) shows that in order to gain a greater understanding of how we develop, we must look at the different influences on an individual and how they interact to shape the developmental pathway. Bronfenbrenner modified his theory to include the biological aspects of an individual's make-up, understanding this to be necessary to gain a fuller picture of the individual's development. Factors such as food poverty, low income and other social variations contribute to health outcomes and point to the diverse influences on health that exist within Irish society.

WHAT ARE HEALTH AND WELL-BEING?

The World Health Organization's Ottawa Charter of Health Promotion provides the most widely cited definition of health promotion (WHO, 1986, p.40). It places emphasis on the idea that the promotion of health is a process that requires broad participation:

> Health promotion is the process of enabling people to increase control over, and to improve, their health. To reach a state of complete physical, mental and social well-being, an individual or group must be able to identify and to realize aspirations, to satisfy needs, and to change or cope with the environment. Health is, therefore, seen as a resource for everyday life, not the objective of living. Health is a positive concept emphasizing social and personal resources, as well as physical capacities. Therefore, health promotion is not just the responsibility of the health sector, but goes beyond healthy life-styles to well-being.

This definition covers wide territory indeed, including as it does environmental as well as individual factors in the range of resources that define health. The obvious implication is that the promotion of health must focus on both the individual and the environment. This calls for the involvement of a much broader array of interventions and factors than does the traditional medical model approach. Indeed, many of the determinants of health are beyond the control of the health care system.

Social determinants of health

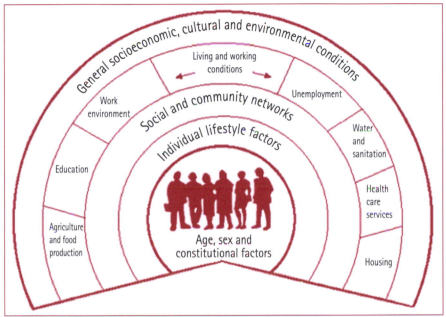

As the diagram illustrates, factors that influence health are varied and involve an interplay. You can see from the layout of the diagram that it is modelled on the ecological approach proposed by Bronfenbrenner. This locates health within a complex nesting of contexts that must be considered. We will explore some of these factors to illustrate their impact on health and well-being, such as the impact of socio-economic status (SES) on mental health. First we need to establish how 'mental health' is defined.

What is mental health?

Jahoda (1958) constructed a definition of 'mental health' by separating it into three parts:

- First, mental health involves 'self-realisation' in that individuals are allowed to fully exploit their potential.
- Second, mental health includes 'a sense of mastery' by the individual over their environment.
- Third, positive mental health means 'autonomy', in that individuals have the ability to identify, confront and solve problems.

Mental health: a cultural construct?

One of the major criticisms levelled at the area of psychology is that a lot of the research is on Western populations and grounded in Western thought, making the findings not as applicable to other groups or cultures (for example, African or Asian). If a lot of psychology is based on, for example, American research, constructs and values, are these findings valid for those whose values and constructs differ? In terms of mental health, some have argued that definitions of mental health (such as Jahoda's above) are culturally biased and influenced by the North American culture that favours individualism, and so not reflective of many other cultures, where the group may be as important as the individual.

Thus the definition of mental health is clearly influenced by the culture that defines it and has different meanings depending on setting, culture and socioeconomic and political influences, which are examined below:

- biomedical model: illness, disease, prevention and treatment
- politico-economic model: how health is related to living conditions
- quality-of-life model: looking at all dimensions of health, including relationships.

INFLUENCES ON HEALTH AND WELL-BEING

Historically, different groups of people have examined the concept of health in a narrow and specific way. For example, the medical profession has tended to use a 'biomedical' model that concentrates on illness and disease, and how these can be prevented or treated. On the other hand politicians have introduced a 'politico-economic' model that sees health and ill health as the outcomes of particular living conditions. A broader model is the 'quality-of-life' model that focuses on how our prospects of a happy, useful and fulfilled life are influenced by our state of health and well-being.

As illustrated in the diagram above, health is not just influenced by biological or physiological considerations; social factors also play their part in affecting an individual's health and well-being. The relationship between socio-economic status (SES) and poor mental health is a well-documented one. The relationship between social inequality and physical health is illuminated in the following account of the impact of social inequality on birth weight of newborns.

Low birth weight and social inequality

A report entitled *Unequal at Birth* was published by the Institute for Public Health in Ireland. The authors, McAvoy *et al.* (2006), outline that social inequalities exist in the incidence of low birth weight babies. In the report the indicator used for low birth weight babies was a weight less than 2,500 grams (5½ pounds).

Some of their findings are presented below:

In 2000, 55,166 births were notified to the National Perinatal Reporting System (NPRS) in the Republic of Ireland. The average birthweight of babies born in that year was 3,491 grams. There were an estimated 2,703 low birthweight babies recorded in 2000, representing 4.9% of all births. Between 1991 and 2000 the proportion of low birthweight babies has increased by 15.1%. ... It is not possible to conclude whether this increase observed in the proportion of low birthweight babies born is significant, representing a true increase, or whether it could be attributed to improvements in the NPRS data collection system since 1998 (p.20).

... Certain women are especially vulnerable to poverty and social exclusion and are therefore likely to suffer health inequalities in relation to their pregnancy and their babies. These groups were identified and include teenage mothers, lone parents, disabled women, Travellers, refugees and asylum seekers, other ethnic minority women, women prisoners and homeless women (p.28).

... From observational studies conducted in Ireland and from previous annual reports of Ireland's National Perinatal Reporting System, it is evident that women in lower socioeconomic groupings are more likely to experience a teenage pregnancy and, as young mothers (aged 19 years or less), they are more likely to deliver a low birthweight baby. Teenage pregnancies are associated with prematurity and the preterm delivery rate of teenagers far exceeded matched controls of women aged 20–24 years in one Irish maternity hospital (Connolly et al.,1998).

Almost 90 per cent of attendees at a Dublin Adolescent Antenatal Booking Clinic were recorded as being in the lowest socio-economic group and most had poor educational attainment. Eighty-seven per cent of these mothers had left school. Eighty per cent of them had not sat the Leaving Certificate with another 10 per cent reporting never sitting a state examination. A quarter of these women were over twenty weeks pregnant at first presentation to health services with over two-thirds saying they were afraid to attend hospital earlier (Fitzpatrick et al., 1997). It is also well recognised that pregnant schoolgirls are more likely to live in areas with poor housing, overcrowding and high unemployment rates (p.23).

Psychosocial factors that affect health and well-being

Everyone recognises the importance of psychosocial and environmental problems in the pathogenesis, course and treatment of many, if not all, mental disorders. The problem is that there has not been any wide agreement as to which aspects of the psychosocial context should be included in the diagnostic system. DSM IV, the Diagnostic Statistical Manual (4th edition) (American Psychiatry Association, 2000), is a manual that psychologists use in classifying and determining psychopathologies. In DSM IV a method for the listing of psychosocial and environmental problems was introduced that may have an impact on diagnosis and or management. Examples include death in the family, discrimination, problems at work, inadequate resources and homelessness. Below is a list of the different issues considered by DSM as relevant in the manifestation and management of psychological difficulties.

- Problems with primary support group, for example, death of a family member; health problems in the family; disruption of the family by separation, divorce or estrangement; removal from the home; remarriage of a parent; sexual or physical abuse; parental overprotection; neglect of child; inadequate discipline; discord with siblings; birth of a sibling.
- Problems related to the social environment, for example, death or loss of a friend; inadequate social support; living alone; difficulty with acculturation; discrimination; adjustment to life-cycle transition (such as retirement).
- Educational problems, for example, illiteracy; academic problems; discord with teachers or classmates; inadequate school environment.
- Occupational problems, for example, unemployment; threat of job loss; stressful work schedule; difficult work conditions; job dissatisfaction; job change; discord with boss or co-workers.
- Housing problems, for example, homelessness; inadequate housing; unsafe neighbourhood; discord with neighbours or landlord.
- Economic problems, for example, extreme poverty; inadequate finances; insufficient welfare support.
- Problems with access to health care services, for example, inadequate health care services; transportation to health care facilities unavailable; inadequate health insurance.
- Problems related to interaction with the legal system/crime, for example, arrest, incarceration; litigation; victim of crime.
- Other psychosocial and environmental problems, for example, exposure to disasters; war or other hostilities; discord with nonfamily caregivers, such as counsellors, social worker, or physician; unavailability of social services.

As you can see, the list of factors is comprehensive. Consider which you think play the greatest role in contributing toward mental health difficulties. It is important to note that many, if not all, of these factors are ones that can be changed. It is frustrating to consider that most of the factors are preventable and yet through a lack of resources being made available to care and health services these preventable issues are allowed to impact on people's well-being.

There are many approaches that attempt to improve mental health functioning. We are going to look first at mental health promotion in the prevention of mental disorders. We will then consider practical guidelines aimed at promoting health in young people.

Mental health promotion and the prevention of mental disorders

Although mental health promotion and the prevention of mental disorders have overlapping and related properties, they are derived from different conceptual principles and frameworks.

Mental health promotion focuses on positive mental health and, in the main, on the building of competences, resources and strengths; whereas the prevention of mental disorders concerns itself primarily with specific disorders and aims to reduce the incidence, prevalence or seriousness of targeted problems. Mental health promotion is not primarily about the prevention of mental disorders but is a desirable activity in itself and has a major contribution to make to promoting personal and social development. It can also assist in the prevention of a whole range of behaviour-related diseases; for example, by preventing smoking and therefore lung cancer, or reducing unprotected sex and consequently teenage pregnancies and AIDS.

Six key principles for promoting health in young people

So how can we as practitioners encourage health and well-being with those we work with? The National Children's Bureau (NCB) has developed a training manual (2006, pp.43–4) for those working with clients in supported housing. Though the principles are devised for young people, they can be related to other groups also. The NCB have devised six key principles for engaging young people to promote their health and well-being:

1. Address the whole community

The involvement of everyone in the project will motivate the young people. Foster a sense of community and the idea that 'we all take care of each other'. The more genuine and comprehensive this is, the more effective it will be. Could the project brand itself as a health-promoting project? You could include a review of policies to make sure every policy is a healthy policy. You could identify obstacles to the adoption of healthy policies and ways of removing them. Health cannot be separated from the ethos, values and other goals of the project, and health promotion works best through community action. Can your health goals be integrated into other initiatives? Are there consistent and supportive practices that underpin the work?

2. Give maximum opportunities for participation

Everyone has valuable knowledge and experience, so involve young people (and all staff) at every stage, e.g. in activities such as a health audit, menu planning and décor. Young people learn best about responsibility through participation in decision-making, so make sure they have good information and that decision-making meetings are held at times when they can attend them. Learning to handle choice will help them to have more control over their health, so we should not simply tell young people what to do, or give them information, but also give them opportunities to develop skills of assertiveness and self-reflection so they can deal with the issues affecting their lives.

3. Be clear about confidentiality

There needs to be a clear understanding between all parties that anything divulged within the activities will remain private, unless it poses a significant risk to someone's safety that cannot be ignored. Make sure that confidentiality is available on health issues in particular. This may give you a better opportunity to provide early intervention. You must also be sensitive and respect cultural needs. If you are involving other agencies in delivering this project, make sure that your confidentiality policies work across all professional boundaries.

4. Enjoyment equals engagement

The young people will engage much better if they perceive the work as exciting and fun. This can be done by using strong motivators like food, events, trips, websites and games. Find ways to help them perceive health as something that will help them to earn more money, have better leisure opportunities and enjoy better relationships, and conversely that work, leisure and good relationships are themselves a source of health. Enjoyment will only take place if there is a sense that the young people (and the staff) are not being judged on unhealthy habits, but encouraged in ones which will give them real benefits.

5. Make sure the programme is seen as relevant

The young people need to be able to see a good reason for participating. There will be challenges to stop doing things that they find it hard to stop, or do things that require discipline. They will only do this if they recognise the end product as being something they really want. All the information given must be checked to ensure it is meaningful, relevant to the needs of the young people and up to date.

6. Be creative

The wider the range of methods and activities you can use to assist learning, the more opportunities everyone will have to learn. Where it is at all practicable, encourage new ideas and approaches. Leaflets are only one way to give information: consider getting a drama group to come in for a performance on one of the health issues, or looking for relevant DVDs or getting the young people to make their own information video. Use the talents of your young people and be sensitive to how they learn best.

As we have seen, a relationship exists between social inequality and environmental factors that impact on physical and mental health and well-being. Policy in this country is reflecting a growing realisation of the necessity to encourage healthy living behaviours so as to support mental and physical wellness. In this section we are going to consider research and policy that has been designed to address these very issues.

Irish health research policy

Appreciating the need for current research to gain insight into the health behaviours of people in Ireland, major initiatives have been launched to gather data and build a picture of the health of the nation. This in turn, it is hoped, will guide policy and inform practice to improve the lives of individuals in this country. Several initiatives were launched, including the National Longitudinal Study of Children in Ireland and TILDA, both of which are long-term studies (see Chapter 11 for an explanation of longitudinal research). The first to be briefly addressed below is the National Health Promotion Strategy (2000–2005), which was launched in 2000 by the Department of Health and Children. The strategy aims to improve the health and well-being of the nation and outlines the intended areas for policy development and intervention. Though this is an older piece of policy, it is worthy of consideration as it illuminates the areas identified by the State as relevant to the well-being of the nation. We will then look at HBSC (Health Behaviour in School Children), which surveys Irish children every four years to obtain data regarding their health and lifestyle behaviours; and SLAN (Survey of Lifestyle, Attitudes and Nutrition), which conducts similar surveys of the adult Irish population.

The National Health Promotion Strategy 2000–2005

This strategy was launched with the aim of improving the health and well-being of the nation. The purpose of this new health promotion strategy was to set out a broad policy framework within which action could be carried out at an appropriate level to advance its strategic aims and objectives. (See www.dohc.ie)

In defining the health promotion strategy, it became clear that data were needed to ascertain trends and to identify the health behaviours of Irish people. HBSC and SLAN were implemented to meet these needs.

Health Behaviour in School-aged Children (HBSC)

The Health Behaviour in School-aged Children (HBSC) survey is part of an international research initiative examining health-related behaviours in children and adolescents. According to HBSC Ireland, the population of young people (up to 19 years) in the Republic of Ireland is 1,140,616, representing 29 per cent of the population, which is higher than the European average.

The researchers carry out the surveys every four years in an effort to identify trends and gather information about the well-being of Irish children. This research will inform those involved in policy making, enabling them to put in practice strategies to improve the well-being of children in this country. Further, this research enables us to gauge our levels of general well-being in comparison to the other European countries participating in the HBSC research initiative. The principal researcher/investigator is the Centre for Health Promotion Studies, University College Galway. In 2002, HBSC Ireland surveyed 8,424 Irish children (age categories 10–11, 12–14 and 15–16) from randomly selected schools throughout the country. They repeated the survey in 2006 and again in 2010. Some of the findings of the 2006 survey (the 2010 findings are not yet available) are examined below.

For more information: www.nuigalway.ie/hbsc and www.hbsc.org

Key findings from HBSC Ireland 2006

Smoking
Smoking is a leading cause of premature illness and death in developed countries. HBSC Ireland has found that 19 per cent of children report that they currently smoke. Current smoking refers to children who report they smoke at least monthly. Those who smoke report feeling less healthy and less happy about their lives compared to non-smokers.

Drunkenness
A greater number of young people are starting to drink at a younger age, and a higher percentage are regular drinkers by 18 years, with many abusing alcohol. HBSC Ireland has found that 31 per cent of children have had so much alcohol that they were really drunk. Children who have been drunk are less likely to have excellent health and to be happy with their lives.

Dieting
HBSC Ireland has fond that 13 per cent of children report that they are currently on a diet or doing something to lose weight. This behaviour is of concern among older girls in particular; 24 per cent of 15–17-year-old girls reported that they are currently dieting. The researchers found that children who report being on a diet also reported feeling less likely to find it easy to talk to their parents and less likely to have excellent health or feel happy.

Exercise
Physical activity is associated with good social, emotional and physical health, and increasing levels of physical activity, both moderate and vigorous, are recommended. HBSC Ireland has found that 47 per cent of children report that they exercise four or more times a week outside of school hours; enough to get out

of breath or sweat. Children who exercise four or more times a week are less likely to feel pressured by school work and are more likely to report excellent health and feel happy.

Food poverty

When a person cannot obtain an adequate and nutritious diet they are said to be experiencing food poverty. Food poverty tends to affect those from socially disadvantaged groups. HBSC Ireland has found that 16 per cent of Irish children report that they go to school or to bed hungry because there is not enough food at home. Children who report going hungry are less likely to report excellent health and feeling happy while they are more likely to report frequent physical and emotional symptoms.

Health perceptions

Self-reported measures of health can indicate an emotional aspect of adolescent well-being. HBSC Ireland has found that 28 per cent of Irish children report excellent health. Children who report having excellent health are more likely to be from a higher social class.

Survey of Lifestyle, Attitudes and Nutrition (SLAN)

SLAN, a parallel survey to the HBSC, examines the health and lifestyle of Irish adults from 18 upwards. SLAN examines topics across age categories (18–34, 35–54 and 55 onwards) and gender. Educational status and social class are also categorised, thus giving a fuller picture of the relationship between these variables or factors.

In building a base of knowledge, it is envisaged that these findings will allow for trends to be identified and for the implementation of policy to meet health needs. The 2007 survey marks the third national survey of lifestyle, attitudes and nutrition in Ireland.

Key findings from SLAN 2007

Smoking

Forty-eight per cent of respondents had smoked at some point in their lives, with 29 per cent reporting being current smokers (31 per cent men and 27 per cent women). Younger people were more likely to smoke (35 per cent of those aged 18–29 years), as were those in lower social class groups. SLAN found that rates of smoking have decreased since 1998 across men and women, all ages and all social class groups. Rates were 33 per cent in 1998, 27 per cent in 2002 and 29 per cent in 2007.

Body weight and weight management

- More than one-third of respondents (36 per cent) reported themselves as being overweight and 14 per cent reported being obese, according to the body mass index (BMI). Men were more likely to report being overweight (43 per cent) or obese (16 per cent) than women (28 per cent overweight and 13 per cent obese).

- Overall, the percentage of respondents who reported themselves (self-reported) as being overweight has increased, from 31 per cent in 1998 to 33 per cent in 2002 to 36 per cent in 2007. Obesity levels have remained steady since 2002: 11 per cent (1998), 15 per cent (2002) and 14 per cent (2007).

- Independently measured height and weight data were collected for a sub-sample of respondents and were compared to the self-reported measurements. The sub-sample consisted of 967 adults aged 18–44 and 1,207 adults aged 45 years and over. Similar to other international studies, BMI figures derived from self-reported data underestimated the true prevalence of overweight and obesity, particularly among older respondents. Combining the sub-sample of measured BMI data for the under-45 and over-45 age groups, 1 per cent of all respondents were underweight (1 per cent men and 1 per cent women), 35 per cent had BMIs within the healthy range (30 per cent men and 40 per cent women), 39 per cent were overweight (45 per cent men and 33 per cent women) and 25 per cent were obese (24 per cent men and 26 per cent women).

- One in ten respondents (10 per cent) was advised by a health professional to manage their weight in the previous year. Almost half (43 per cent) were actively trying to do this. Most were trying to lose weight (67 per cent), while 3 per cent were trying to gain weight. Similar percentages were reducing fat intake (80 per cent) and taking exercise (79 per cent), while over two-thirds (68 per cent) were eating fewer calories in order to maintain or lose weight.

Alcohol and use of illicit drugs

- Most men (85 per cent) and women (77 per cent) drank alcohol on some occasions. One-quarter (28 per cent) reported excessive drinking (that is, having six or more standard drinks on one occasion) in the last year. This was more common in younger respondents and those in lower social class groups.

- Comparisons with previous surveys were made, again with caution because of the changed survey methods (from self-report postal questionnaire in 1998 and 2002, to personal interview in 2007). Of those respondents who had had an alcoholic drink within the previous year, the average number of alcoholic drinks consumed in an average week across the three surveys decreased from 11 drinks (1998) to nine (2002) to seven (2007).

- The percentage of drivers who reported driving a car after consuming two or more standard drinks in the past year had also decreased from 2002 (16 per cent) to 2007 (12 per cent).

- There was a decrease in the percentage of respondents who reported consuming six or more standard drinks at least once a week, from 45 per cent (2002) to 28 per cent (2007). The percentages consuming over the recommended weekly alcohol limit (21 or more units for men and 14 or more units for women) also decreased over the course of the three surveys, from 15 per cent (1998) to 13 per cent (2002) to 8 per cent (2007).

• Across five categories of illicit drugs assessed, only marijuana was used by more than 1 in 100 respondents in 2007 (5 per cent reported using marijuana in the previous year). Use of all five categories of drug was similar or lower in 2007 than in 1998.

As can be seen, both the HBSC and SLAN findings indicate a nation with unhealthy lifestyles and habits. There is a growing recognition of the impact of physical well-being upon psychological functioning.

For more information: www.slan06.ie

We are going to look next at the emerging field of 'positive psychology', whose aim is to support and encourage positive psychological behaviours and functioning.

POSITIVE PSYCHOLOGY

Within the field of psychology there is an emphasis on examining abnormal feelings, emotions and behaviours; in other words, focusing on psychopathology. Positive psychology is a new movement which grew as a reaction against this emphasis on psychological dysfunction within psychology. As the name suggests, its focus is on examining healthy and well-adapted individuals in order to understand the factors that contribute to their good functioning. In other words, positive psychology is the scientific pursuit of optimal human functioning and the building of a field focusing on human strength and virtue. It opens the door to understanding prevention and health promotion (Seligman, 1992). Within this field lie many new concepts, one of which is resilience.

Resilience

Resilience may be defined as 'unusually good adaptation in the face of severe stress' (Beardslee, 1999, p.267) and has been applied to a wide spectrum of domains, from psychology to social work to education (Masten, 2001). Within the domain of psychology, resilience has been explored in issues ranging from psychopathology, child development, elderly populations and individuals with disabilities.

Masten (2001) relates that interest in resilience has its roots in work done in the 1970s examining children at risk of psychopathology. It reflected the move towards a strengths-based approach, rather than the traditional deficit model that underpinned much theory and applied research previously. Resilience has an applicatory nature in policy and practice, potentially informing interventions that aim to prevent problem behaviours and psychopathology, and further to offer opportunities to strengthen those identified as vulnerable (Rutter, 1987).

Definition

Reflecting its broad appeal and applications, definitions of resilience are wide and diverse as are the approaches to its theoretical exposition. Masten (2001) offers the following definition: 'resilience refers to a class of phenomenon characterized by good outcomes in spite of serious threats to adaptation or development' (p.228). Carr (2004) mirrors the emphasis on lack of psychopathology in the definition he proposes: 'the capacity to withstand exceptional stresses and demands without developing stress-related problems' (p.300).

Theoretical approaches

Having considered the definition of resilience, it is necessary to explore some of the approaches to understanding the concept. Luthar and Zigler (1991), in their review of research into resilience, outlined two central aspects associated with this construct: stress and competence. Risk, threat or stressors have been used interchangeably to refer to the class of phenomenon considered to increase the likelihood of negative or maladaptive outcomes. Adverse life events have long been considered predictive of poorer outcomes among adults and youth evidenced by a plethora of empirical research (Tiet *et al.*, 1998). Beardslee (1989, p.267) comments that there have been four approaches to the study of resilience: (1) longitudinal studies of children considered at risk due to economic factors, minority status and other variables; (2) epidemiological studies that focus on populations considered disadvantaged; (3) studies that investigate responses to specific stressful circumstances, for example medical illness; and (4) studies that have explored the experiences of being raised in a home with an affectively disordered parent.

Werner (1993, p.510) succinctly judges that 'the concepts of resilience and protective factors are the positive counterparts to the constructs of vulnerability (which denotes an individual's susceptibility to a negative outcome) and risk factors (which denote biological or psychosocial hazards that increase the likelihood of a negative development outcome)'. Garmezy (1983) outlines three categories of factors that appear to offer protective value: personality factors, family cohesion and the availability of support systems external to the child or individual.

Rutter (1999) remarks that several methodological considerations need to be taken into account when studying resilience. The issue of how to assess which criteria constitute a markedly increased risk for the development of psychopathology needs to be addressed when examining resistance to stress. Rutter makes a distinction between risk factors and risk mechanisms.

Waller (2001) contends that very few research studies have attempted to gauge resilience from a more ecological perspective, charting the presence and interaction of variables across many levels between individual and social systems (for example, societies, communities or organisations) and further points out that human development does not occur in a vacuum (p.290). Methodological issues must be taken into account when generalising findings from vulnerable samples to the wider population.

As you can see, the concept of resilience is a complex one, especially in methodological and theoretical terms. Yet this concept is not a purely theoretical one; it has a 'practice' element which can be seen in research by Robbie Gilligan, who examines 'resilience, roles and relationships for children in long term care'.

Resilience and long-term care

Gilligan (2008, p.46) argues that 'work and recreation settings may be sources of resilience-enhancing experiences for young people in care and young care-leavers. Recreation and work may offer opportunities to develop a precious sense of mastery in certain spheres of activity and to broaden social networks. They may also help to cultivate a set of social roles that may enhance health and well-being for the young person.' This piece of research examines this theme through a specific focus on the needs of young people in long-term care.

Gilligan reports that the research indicates that the range and strength of relationships young people can access can be strengthened through participation in recreational activity. Further, it can improve their educational attainment and achievement. Gilligan (pp.41–2) quotes a number of examples given by social workers and carers that attest to the benefits of participation:

Participation in recreational activity may widen and strengthen the range of relationships the young person can access in their social network (McGee *et al.*, 2006 [as cited in Gilligan, 2008]). It may also increase educational attainment and achievement (Mahoney *et al.*, 2005 [as cited in Gilligan, 2008]). Among the other advantages that may flow from participation in recreational activities is that they may often serve as a pathway for the young person to work opportunities. The following are drawn from examples contributed to the author by social workers and carers:

- the encouragement of talent at art in a young person in care led to their securing a place in art college
- learning the flute, an activity that was sustained by the foster carer and long-term social worker, led on to a career as a music teacher for a young person in care
- a girl in care who loved disco dancing put her talents to use by hiring a local hall once per week to teach disco-dancing classes
- an interest in horses led to a successful bid by an under-age girl in care to work as a live-in stable hand
- a teenage boy in foster care in the countryside who helped a neighbour with farm horses later put his love and knowledge of horses to use in securing a place as an apprentice jockey
- a boy in foster care who was a very competent swimmer went on to get summer work as a lifeguard (despite a mild learning disability), and
- a boy introduced to rugby by his foster mother went on to play rugby professionally.

These examples illustrate the potential that participation in recreational activity can afford children in long-term care to gain life-enhancing competencies and skills. Gilligan (pp.47–8) emphasises the role carers and social workers can play in strengthening participation and creating opportunities for children to build successful lives.

Carers, social workers and other professionals may have important parts to play in helping young people to tap into those resources and particularly into the opportunities for supportive roles and relationships in work and recreation settings.

Carers may be able to assist in:

- cultivating positive expectations in the young person, something that may be very important in relation to issues such as future educational participation and attainment
- cultivating planning on the part of the young person
- identifying interests and talents
- identifying and helping the young person to utilise options and opportunities in the arenas of recreation and work
- serving as a role model or identifying other role models appropriate for the purpose
- supporting initial connections and sustaining ongoing engagement in a recreational or work-related activity
- encouraging a role for other supportive adults in the young person's life.

Social workers may be able to assist by:

- giving due attention to the potential of recreational and work-related experiences in the lives of young people in care
- helping to nurture such interests in young people in care
- providing training and support to carers in that regard
- ensuring briefing of new carers to maximise chances of preserving connections to recreational interests for the young person across care settings
- appreciating how gender may lead to different experiences and opportunities for support and resilience for young people in care
- appreciating the power of positive role models for young people in care and, for example, the specific (and under-recognised) contribution, in this regard, that male foster carers may be able to make
- recognising the value of continuity in care placements and relationships into young adulthood and the need to avoid premature rupturing of viable placements at what may be both a psychologically vulnerable developmental stage and, effectively, an arbitrary administrative cut-off point in a young person's care career.

These guidelines not only highlight the relationship between recreational participation for young people in long-term care and its potential for building resilience and encouraging life-enhancing skills, they also show the pivotal role carers and social workers can play in shaping and supporting the lives of these children. It also emphasises that sometimes it is the 'little' things such as encouraging a child in a sport or recreational activity that can be vital to the overall development of the child. We sometimes think that intervention must involve professionals or therapy and so on, whereas simply encouraging the child in an activity can prove to be highly effective.

We are now going to consider an issue that affects well-being negatively, that of addiction.

ALCOHOLISM AND DRUG ADDICTION

What is addiction?

Addiction, or dependence, is defined as 'a cluster of three of more symptoms listed below occurring at any time in the same 12-month period' (American Psychiatric Association [APA], 1994, p.176).

Those symptoms are:

1. tolerance, or needing more and more of a substance to achieve the same effect
2. withdrawal, which involves unpleasant symptoms when the body is deprived of the substance, resulting in more frequent use to alleviate the negative symptoms
3. taking the substance for a longer period of time or in larger amounts than originally intended
4. unsuccessful desire to minimise use of the substance
5. much time spent to obtain, use or recover from the effects of the substance
6. social, occupational or recreational activities are missed because of substance abuse
7. substance use is continued despite knowledge of causing a problem.

If neither tolerance nor withdrawal are present, then at least three of the remaining symptoms must be present (APA).

Did you know?

- One in 15 children will become alcoholic in their lifetime because of genetic predisposition (Weber and McCormick, 1992).
- Children from alcoholic families are four to six times more likely to become alcoholic than children raised in non-alcoholic homes (Weber and McCormick, 1992).
- By their mid-20s, nearly 80 per cent of young adults have used an illicit drug.

Types of drug abuse

- Habitual and chronic polydrug abuse
- Experimental or recreational drugs abuse.

Carr (2003, p.590) remarks that seven categories of possible explanation for drug abuse exist:

> **First**, biological theories of drug abuse focus on specific genetic factors; on temperamental attributes that are known to be strongly genetically determined; and on the role of physiological mechanisms in the development of tolerance, dependence and withdrawal.
>
> **Second**, intrapsychic deficit theories point to the importance of personal psychological vulnerabilities in the development of drug-using behaviour patterns.
>
> **Third**, cognitive-behavioural theories underlie the significance of certain learning processes in the genesis of drug problems.
>
> **Fourth**, family systems theories emphasise the importance of parental drug-using behaviour, parenting style and family organisation patterns in the aetiology and maintenance of drug abuse.
>
> **Fifth**, the role of societal factors such as social disadvantage, neighbourhood norms concerning drug use and abuse, and drug availability are the central concerns of sociological theories of drug abuse.
>
> **Sixth**, multiple-risk factor theories highlight the roles of factors at biological, psychological and social levels in the aetiology of drug abuse.
>
> **Finally**, change-process theories offer explanations for how recovery and relapse occur.

Prevalence of drug use: 2006 National Report to EMCDDA
In Ireland each year a report is compiled and presented to the European Monitoring Centre for Drugs and Drug Addiction (EMCDDA). Below are some of the findings of the report regarding the prevalence of drug use in Ireland:

- The results of the general population survey 2002/2003 indicate that one in five (18.5%) adults reported using an illegal drug in their lifetime. For young adults (aged 15–34 years) this rose to one in four (26.0%) people. Twice as many men as women reported the use of an illegal drug during the last month or the last year.
- The majority of those who have tried any illicit drug have used cannabis (marijuana or hashish). The lifetime prevalence rates for cannabis use are thus similar to those for use of any illicit drug and reflect the same trend. Lifetime use of inhalants dropped slightly between 1999 (22%) and 2003 (18%) but remains high. The average for the 35 ESPAD countries in 2003 was 10%.

- The results of a national survey of third-level students were published in April 2005. Cannabis was the most common illicit drug used by students, with over one-third (37%) reporting that they had used it in the past 12 months. Ecstasy was the second most used illicit drug, followed by cocaine, magic mushrooms and amphetamines. For all drugs, the levels of use were higher among students than among those of a similar age group (15–24 years) in the general population. The use of solvents (inhalants) was particularly high.

For more information: www.ndc.hrb.ie

Can addiction be treated?
There are several successful treatments for addiction. It goes without saying that the earlier the addiction is treated, the easier it will be to control. Some of the most effective treatments for addiction are 12-step programmes such as Alcoholics Anonymous (Weber and McCormick, 1992). Other treatments include individual and family therapy, group therapy, educational programmes and self-esteem-building and anger-management workshops.

Drug abuse and its impact on interpersonal adjustment
According to Carr (2003, p.589) drug abuse impacts on interpersonal relationships. He outlines its possible ramifications:

> Within the family, drug abuse often leads to conflict. Individuals that abuse drugs within a peer-group situation may become deeply involved in a drug-oriented subculture and break ties with peers who do not abuse drugs. Some develop a solitary drug-using pattern and become more and more socially isolated as their drug using progresses. ... Within the wider community, drug-related antisocial behaviour such as aggression, theft and selling drugs may bring youngsters into contact with the juvenile justice system. ... Drug-related health problems and drug dependency may bring them into contact with the health service.

It is clear that addiction affects not just the individual who is addicted but also has ramifications for those around them, especially their families.

Social and psychological needs of children of drug-using parents

Trinity College Dublin Children's Research Centre
Children in this study experienced exposure to parental opiate use in different ways. Half had been prenatally exposed to opiates, according to parents. All had experienced the effects indirectly, however, either through changes evident in parental behaviour and/or through separation from and loss of parents.

Many had been exposed at an early age to the legal system, having experienced their parent being incarcerated and in some cases witnessing the arrest and visiting a parent in prison. The majority of the children had experienced separations from parents, due to parental incarceration, hospitalisation and/or inability to provide care.

Few of the children showed evidence of social-emotional problems relating to parental drug use, with only one child having received treatment for psychological or behavioural problems.

Impact on children's school progress

The majority of children were experiencing difficulties at school. These problems were related to poor attendance, concentration difficulties, poor work completion and low levels of parental involvement with their education.

Parental concerns about drug use and parenting

Drug-using parents had three primary areas of concern about the impact of their problem drug use on their parenting. The first was that preoccupation with acquiring drugs distracted them from giving adequate attention to their children. The second concern was that their drug use affected their social interactions with their children, making them irritable and short-tempered. The third area of concern was that their involvement with drugs created an atmosphere of secrecy in the home and distrustful relationships between parents and children.

Key-worker concerns about drug use and parenting

Key workers also had three primary areas of concern about the ability of drug-using parents to provide adequate caregiving to their children. First, they were concerned that some drug-using parents appeared to be unable to provide consistently good quality caregiving to their children. Second, there were concerns that some drug-using parents may have neglected the physical needs of their children. Third, they were concerned that some children may have witnessed drug-use and drug paraphernalia in their homes. It appeared that parents who were receiving treatment for their problem drug use were less likely to experience such parenting difficulties. There were a number of parents about whom no concerns were raised, and whose competence as parents was emphasised.

Implications for children's development

Children in this study appeared to be exposed to a number of difficulties arising from their parents' use of opiates. These included higher levels of separation from and loss of parents and lessened parental involvement in their lives, in some cases raising concerns of neglect. They also appeared to experience a good deal of tension in the home and to be subject to harsh discipline in some cases. Furthermore, they were exposed, to varying degrees, to the lifestyle associated with opiate dependence, including drug-taking activity and crime. What are the implications of these findings for children's development?

First, separation from and loss of parents was a particular problem in the lives of the 10 children studied. Other research has found that disruptions to parental care, especially early disruption of maternal care, is linked to children themselves having long-term difficulties in parenting their own children. It has also been linked with depression, and in the shorter term, with problems with peer relationships.

Low levels of involvement by parents who are present in the home, such as low levels of supervision and monitoring and infrequent communication with children, have been linked to a range of problem behaviours in children, and especially to fighting, non-compliance and delinquency. They have also been linked with depression, irritability and somatic problems in some children. In its extreme form, low parental involvement implies neglect of children's basic physical care, which has serious health as well as psychological implications.

Low levels of parental involvement in children's schooling, such as poor attendance at school functions, has been found to have negative implications for children's performance at school and with poor school attendance by children, also leading to their falling behind at school. Children in the present study appear to be experiencing similar problems associated with their parents' low levels of involvement in their education.

Low levels of emotional involvement by parents, or a lack of closeness and supportiveness, also appears to have negative implications for children's well-being. It has been identified as a factor in delinquency in adolescents. Supportive parenting, on the other hand, in the form of affection, nurturance and interest shown towards children, is associated with positive attributes in children, such as greater self-esteem, life satisfaction, and both social and cognitive competence.

In spite of these potentially negative implications for children, it should be noted that the problems listed above were not experienced to the same degree by all families. Furthermore, there was evidence that families coped differently when such problems did arise, depending on a number of circumstances, including the duration and extent of the drug problem, the type of services available to parents, and the degree of social support from the community and from family members. In addition, individual children appeared to cope differently with problems in the home associated with parental drug use, showing different levels of resilience. It would be incorrect, therefore, to assume that all children are at risk for the range of problems described here.

These findings highlight the interesting role of resilience in determining the individual outcomes of the children who participated in this study. Also demonstrated is the complex nature of the developmental outcomes and how difficult it can be to extricate the different factors at play and their impact on individuals. The study did outline policy implications from their findings, showing that research informs policy informs practice. The policy recommendations regarding services and interventions they suggest include:

- make recommendations on appropriate interventions to counteract the negative social and psychological effects on children
- make recommendations on appropriate steps to be taken to prevent children of drug users from becoming drug users themselves.

Source: www.tcd.ie

For information on the role of family support services in drug prevention, see the National Advisory Committee on Drugs: www.nacd.ie.

SUMMARY

This chapter attempts to explore the complex relationships that exist in creating and supporting physical and mental well-being. Throughout the chapter we have seen the interplay between physical and psychological health. The impact of social and environmental factors on physical and mental outcomes was highlighted in examining social inequality and socio-economic status. The new and emerging field of positive psychology and its focus on understanding the factors that enable individuals to overcome adversity marks a departure from psychology's emphasis on studying psychopathology. In continuing the study of positive psychology we will hopefully discover ways to support healthy and happy functioning.

8

Abuse and trauma

Ireland has experienced the continuing revelations of a shocking history of abuse, perpetrated on an institutional scale, by those who were considered to be in positions of trust. Collusions by government departments and others in the cover-up have been documented and the scale of the abuse has been horrific. Clearly I'm referring to the scandal of clerical and institutional abuse that is continuing to come to light. Later in this chapter we will examine the findings of Professor Carr's research into the effects of institutional abuse upon those who were its victims. The scope of this book is a psychological one; however, I would encourage all to read the many reports that have been published (Ryan, Murphy) to fully grasp the extent of the abuse that occurred but also the factors at play that supported its continuance. Though psychology is concerned with the study of the individual and their development, as you have seen from the ecological approach, one has to understand an individual's ecology (including the society a person lives within, its mores and history) to fully understand the individual and their life experiences. Further in the chapter we will examine 'Ireland' as a risk factor for abuse.

The emphasis of this chapter is on child abuse, reflecting the volume of work devoted to this area and the fact that in the area of protection and social services most resources tend to be devoted to this 'at risk' group. However, recent developments have included the study of elder abuse. This can involve the physical and emotional abuse seen in child abuse, though there is less sexual abuse than with children. Financial abuse is also encountered by the 'at risk' elder group. Those with disabilities are also considered an 'at risk' group. The existence of sibling abuse and the fact that women sexually abuse has gained increasing recognition. In Ireland the recent case of a mother in the West who sexually abused her son illustrated not only the occurrence of females who sexually abuse, but also the shortcomings in legislation governing this area, no doubt a reflection of the taboo around female perpetrators of sexual abuse.

DEFINING ABUSE

First let us define what is meant by abuse, before looking at specific categories of abuse: neglect, emotional, physical and sexual abuse. The first distinction that should be made is that of 'intentionality'.

Neglect and abuse: an issue of intentionality?

It can be controversial to draw a line between abuse and neglect as both can have devastating effects. Intentionality can offer an (albeit simplistic) approach to differentiating between abuse and neglect. Whereas abuse is intentional on the part of the abuser, with neglect, according to Carr (2003, p.782), there is 'a passive ignoring of the child's needs'. These include:

- physical needs for feeding, clothing and shelter
- safety needs for protection
- emotional needs for nurturance and a secure base
- intellectual needs for stimulation, social interaction and conversation
- the need for age-appropriate limit-setting and discipline
- the need for age-appropriate opportunities for autonomy and independence.

Typically, parents who neglect their children do not do so intentionally. Rather, neglect arises through parents' lack of awareness of their children's needs. Though neglect is not intentional if you agree with the above definition, it is still a form of abuse and its effects are as significant as other forms of abuse.

What is child abuse?

The World Health Organization defines child abuse as follows:

> Child maltreatment, sometimes referred to as child abuse and neglect, includes all forms of physical and emotional ill-treatment, sexual abuse, neglect, and exploitation that results in actual or potential harm to the child's health, development or dignity. Within this broad definition, five subtypes can be distinguished – physical abuse; sexual abuse; neglect and negligent treatment; emotional abuse; and exploitation.
>
> *Source:* WHO, 2010

Factors influencing risks to children

Before we consider the individual groups at risk of abuse, it is useful to examine the risk factors at play in neglect and abuse, or 'maltreatment' as it tends to be referred to in North America. Though the following information deals with factors relating to children, it is applicable to other groups vulnerable to abuse.

Ecological approach to the aetiology of maltreatment

Before we consider factors contributing to neglect and abuse, it is important to bear in mind that 'contribute to' is not the same as 'cause'; it merely reflects that a relationship exists between two variables. Usually when we look at most phenomena, causation involves a complex interaction of differing contributing factors.

Thomas *et al.* (2003) take an ecological approach to conceptualising the factors that can contribute to child abuse and maltreatment, delineating the origins of abuse into four strands:

1. the child
2. the family
3. the community
4. the society.

The child

To be very clear, in no way is it suggested that the child is responsible for the abuse or neglect that they suffer. When we examine factors involved in the increased vulnerability of a child to abuse, what we are doing is looking for any factors that make it more likely for a child to be victimised and abused. Certain factors have been found to be more prevalent in cases of abuse, including:

- disability
- age
- gender
- premature or low birth weight
- developmental delay or frequent illness.

Though children are not responsible for the abuse inflicted upon them, certain child characteristics have been found to increase the risk or potential for maltreatment. Children with disabilities or mental retardation, for example, are significantly more likely to be abused (Crosse *et al.*, 1993; Schilling and Schinke, 1984). Evidence also suggests that age and gender are predictive of maltreatment risk. Younger children are more likely to be neglected, while the risk for sexual abuse increases with age (Mraovick and Wilson, 1999). Female children and adolescents are significantly more likely than males to suffer sexual abuse.

The family

Thomas *et al.* (2003) outline the following family characteristics that are linked to child neglect and abuse:

- substance abuse
- domestic violence
- lack of parenting skills.

Families where substance abuse is an issue have been found to be at higher risk of abuse, with the authors suggesting that substance abuse is present in 40 to 80 per cent of families in which children are victims of abuse. Domestic violence and lack of parenting or communication skills also increase the risks of maltreatment of children.

The community

Factors related to the community and the larger society also are linked with child maltreatment. Poverty, for example, has been linked with maltreatment, particularly neglect, in each of the national incidence studies (Sedlak and Broadhurst, 1996), and has been associated with child neglect by Black (2000) and found to be a strong predictor of substantiated child maltreatment by Lee and Goerge (1999). Bishop and Leadbeater (1999) found that abusive mothers reported fewer friends in their social support networks, less contact with friends and lower ratings of quality support received from friends.

Violence and unemployment are other community-level variables that have been found to be associated with child maltreatment.

The society

Perhaps the least understood and studied factors in child maltreatment are those at a societal level. Ecological theories postulate that factors such as the narrow legal definitions of child maltreatment, the social acceptance of violence (as evidenced by video games, television and films and music lyrics), and political or religious views that value non-interference in families above all may be associated with child maltreatment (Tzeng et al., 1991).

Researchers, practitioners and policy-makers are now increasingly thinking about protective factors in children and families that can reduce risks, build family capacity and foster resilience. In 1987 case studies of three victims of child maltreatment began to shed light on the dynamics of survival in high-risk settings. Resilience in maltreated children was found to be related to personal characteristics that included a child's ability to recognise danger and adapt, distance oneself from intense feelings, create relationships that are crucial for support and project oneself into a time and place in the future in which the perpetrator is no longer present (Mrazek and Mrazek, 1987).

Society as a factor in abuse is an important consideration as it is open to change; modes of thinking or prejudice that increase the likelihood of abuse and neglect can be challenged. Ireland has a shocking history of abuse as referred to above; this surely leads to the question of whether Irish society, and, more specifically, 'Irish culture', is a factor in the levels of abuse that have been witnessed here. We might like to feel that those times are behind us, but I don't believe we have shaken off certain thinking and prejudices that lend themselves to abusive practices. A recent court case in Killarney, where over a dozen men, including a priest, lined up to shake the hand of a man convicted of sexual assault – in front of the victim – demonstrates, I believe, that we still have much left to do.

The following extract from 'Ireland and Rape Crises' (McKay, 2007, p.94), illustrates attitudes that have existed in Ireland and the roles culture and society play in abuse. In her article, Susan McKay offers insights into attitudes in Ireland towards the area of abuse including domestic violence and rape. She offers the following as an example of Irish cultural values and their role in the perpetuation of such abuse: 'In 1969 the legendary Irish agony aunt, Angela MacNamara, had warned in the *Sunday Press* that it is the nature of a man to be the aggressor – the one who initiates and that if a girl allowed a man to fondle and embrace her . . . she cannot blame him if his nature propels him in passion to seek the ultimate closeness of sexual intercourse.' McKay offers another shocking example: Dr Percy Patton who in the 1970s and 1980s carried out most of the medical examinations of women who had alleged rape to the Gardaí. He declared (*Irish Review*, 2007, p.94), 'the fear of parental rebuke and the fear of pregnancy are the two outstanding reasons why so many willing partners, later on reflection, decide to report their case as one of rape'. Finally, McKay reveals that some medical textbooks suggested to trainee doctors that 10 of 12 rape allegations were false and that the doctor needed to single out 'the chaste from the wanton, . . . the shy and bewildered from the brazen and affectedly hurt'. It is clear from these examples alone that Irish culture was one that was hostile to allegations of rape and was certainly a society where abuse or violence within the home was not discussed. The Magdalene laundries are another example. (Here is a link to interviews with women who participated in a documentary on the 'launderies' and whose personal experiences were to form the basis for the documentary, *Sex in a Cold Climate*: http://www.youtube.com/watch?v=OJs-4cncGmk.)

Thus, a combination of individual, relational, community and societal factors contribute to the risk of child maltreatment. Although children are not responsible for the harm inflicted upon them, certain individual characteristics have been found to increase their risk of being maltreated. Risk factors are contributing factors – not direct causes.

Examples of risk factors

- disabilities or mental retardation in children that may increase caregiver burden
- social isolation of families
- parents' lack of understanding of children's needs and child development
- parents' history of domestic abuse
- poverty and other socioeconomic disadvantages, such as unemployment
- family disorganisation, dissolution and violence, including intimate partner violence
- lack of family cohesion
- substance abuse in the family
- young, single, non-biological parents
- poor parent-child relationships and negative interactions
- parental thoughts and emotions supporting maltreatment behaviours
- parental stress and distress, including depression or other mental health conditions
- community violence.

Protective factors are the opposite of risk factors and may lessen the risk of child maltreatment. Protective factors exist at individual, relational, community and societal levels.

Examples of protective factors
- supportive family environment
- nurturing parenting skills
- stable family relationships
- household rules and monitoring of the child
- parental employment
- adequate housing
- access to health care and social services
- caring adults outside the family who can serve as role models or mentors
- communities that support parents and take responsibility for preventing abuse (Thomas *et al.*, 2003).

TYPES OF ABUSE

Emotional abuse

According to Carr (2003, p.785), emotional abuse 'involves intentionally carrying out some of the following actions with respect to the child:

- frequent punishments for minor misdemeanours
- frequent punishments for positive behaviours such as smiling, playing or solving problems
- frequent criticism, ridicule, humiliation and threats
- frequent rejection, discouragement of attachment and exclusion from family life
- frequent blocking of the development of appropriate peer relationships
- frequent corruption through parents involving the child in drug use, prostitution or theft
- frequent attitudinal corruption through encouraging prejudicial hatred of specific groups of people (on the basis of race, gender, religious beliefs, etc.).'

Physical abuse

Carr (2003, p.751) suggests that 'Physical abuse refers to deliberately inflicted injury or deliberate attempts to poison a child. … Physical abuse is usually intrafamilial and may occur alone or in conjunction with sexual abuse, neglect or emotional abuse. Many studies have found a high level of co-morbidity for physical abuse and neglect.'

Sexual abuse

Children

Carr (2003, p.806) states, 'Child sexual abuse (CSA) refers to the use of a child for sexual gratification. Sexual abuse actions may vary in intrusiveness (from viewing or exposure to penetration) and frequency (from a single episode to frequent and chronic abuse). A distinction is made between intrafamilial sexual abuse, the most common form of which is father-daughter incest, and extrafamilial sexual abuse, where the abuser resides outside the family home.'

The Sexual Abuse and Violence in Ireland (SAVI) report: A picture of abuse in Ireland

Sexual assault as a child

Most sexual abuse in childhood and adolescence occurs in the earlier years of childhood with 67% of abused girls and 62% of the abused boys experiencing abuse by age 12, i.e. before or during their primary-school years.

A higher proportion of girls than boys were abused by age 8 years (29 versus 19%). For many girls and boys (over 40%), abuse was not a once-off event. Many also reported repeated abuse as children which continued over long periods; 58% of girls and 42% of boys abused more than once experienced sexual abuse in childhood that continued for longer than a year.

Perpetrators

In a simple overview, five types of perpetrator each accounted for approximately one-fifth of abuse: family members, neighbours, authority figures, friends/acquaintances and strangers.

- Perpetrators who were authority figures were reported by 22% of men and 16% of women.
- Neighbours were identified as the perpetrators for 19% of men and 21% of women.
- Strangers were identified by 19% of men and 23% of women.
- Across all perpetrator groups, a much greater proportion of the perpetrators of abuse in childhood were known by the abused child than unknown.

The SAVI Report is a comprehensive overview of sexual violence in Ireland and can be downloaded in its entirety from: www.drcc.ie.

Statistics on child protection (Barnardos)
- There were 195 incidents of child abuse reported in 2004; this increased to 303 in 2006 and rose again to 566 in 2007 according to headline crime statistics.
- As of June 2007, there were 5,477 children in care; of these 4,731 children were in foster care and another 423 in residential care. This is an increase on 2004, when there were 5,060 children in care with 4,243 (84%) in foster care and 442 (9%) in residential care.
- Neglect of the child was the most frequent reason (27%) that children were taken into care followed by (23%) parents unable to cope/family difficulties regarding accommodation or finance.
- One in three women and one in four men reported some level of sexual abuse in childhood.
- 25% of perpetrators of sexual abuse were another child or adolescent (17 years old or younger).

Source: www.barnardos.ie

Percentage of reported cases that went to initial assessment for child welfare and protection concerns, by type of concern (2006)

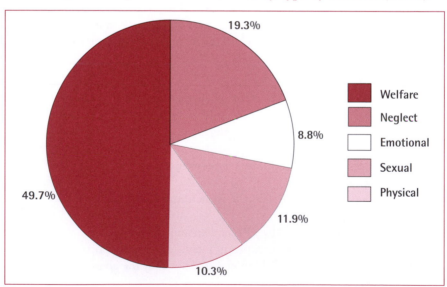

Source: www.omc.gov.ie

AT-RISK GROUPS

We will now look at groups other than children who are considered 'at risk' of abuse and neglect. Growing awareness of the prevalence and occurrence of elder abuse has led to increased activity in terms of research and policy in this area. This form of abuse is complex and involves issues such as the social construction of old age as a problem, the increasing demographic of an ageing population and the policy implications that come with this. It reflects also the changing family patterns that are now seen. In the past, people would have cared for the older members of their families; however, with the splintering of families, dislocation and so on, increasingly the care of the elderly is entrusted to the State. In the Health Service Executive (HSE) document *Open Your Eyes*, it is suggested that mostly the abuse is not intentional but is a reflection of carer stress or ignorance, highlighting the important role that agencies can play in supporting carers. Relationships of dependency can increase vulnerability to abuse and neglect. This can be found in familial situations but also in institutional contexts such as nursing homes. Instances of abuse have been recorded in Leas Cross and St Mary's Nursing Home in Dublin. Statistics and prevalence can be difficult to gauge as older people can feel a sense of shame or unwillingness to reveal that they are being abused. Firstly, how is elder abuse defined?

Elder abuse

The National Centre for the Protection of Older People (www.ncpop.ie) offer a definition of elder abuse from the 2002 Report of the HSE Working Group on Elder Abuse, *Protecting Our Future*:

> a single or repeated act or lack of appropriate action occurring within any relationship where there is an expectation of trust which causes harm or distress to an older person or violates their human and civil rights.

Abuse may be categorised under physical abuse, sexual abuse, financial/material abuse, neglect (by omission or commission) and discriminatory abuse. Elder abuse and neglect are being increasingly identified as international social problems in a growing older population. International studies estimate the prevalence of abuse in the community at between 1 and 5 per cent of the population aged 65 years and older; however, these figures are regarded as an underestimate.

According to the Health Service Executive (2002, p.27), patterns of abuse and abusing vary and reflect different circumstances:

- long-term abuse, in the context of an ongoing family relationship, such as domestic violence or sexual abuse between spouses or generations
- opportunistic abuse, such as theft occurring because money has been left around

- situational abuse, which arises because pressures have built up and/or because of the difficult or challenging behaviour of the older person
- neglect of a person's needs because those around him or her are not able to be responsible for their care; for example if the carer has difficulties because of debt, alcohol or mental health problems
- institutional abuse, which may be because of poor care standards, lack of positive responses to complex needs, rigid routines, inadequate staffing and an insufficient knowledge base within the service
- unacceptable 'treatments' or 'programmes', which include sanctions or punishment, such as the withholding of food and drink, seclusion, the unnecessary and unauthorised use of control and restraint, or the over- or under-use of medication
- racist and discriminatory practice by staff, including ageism, racism and other discriminatory practices, which may be attributable to the lack of appropriate guidance
- inability to get access to key services such as health care, dentistry, prostheses
- misappropriation of benefits and/or use of the person's money by other members of the household or by care staff
- fraud or intimidation in connection with wills, property or other assets.

The National Centre for the Protection of Older People (NCPOP) refer to the findings of a landmark American study, the National Elder Abuse Incidence Study, whose aim was to establish the numbers of older people suffering abuse or neglect. The following is a summary of their findings:

- An incidence rate of 1.6% was found.
- Family members were the most common perpetrators of elder abuse.
- The incidence of abuse and/or neglect increased with increasing age and was more common in women and in elders who were unable to care for themselves.
- The findings of the study supported the validity of the iceberg theory of elder abuse, which argues that the identified cases represent only a partial and incomplete picture of prevalence or incidence of elder abuse; that while the most visible types of abuse and neglect may be reported, a large number of incidents go unidentified and unreported.
- The study identified social isolation as a factor which may both hinder the detection and increase the risk of abuse and neglect.
- Educating health professionals and caregivers in how to recognise and report the signs and symptoms of elder abuse and neglect was identified by the report as paramount.

Daichman (2005, p.326) relates risk factors identified by the World Health Organization through elders' focus groups:

- being old
- being ill
- living alone
- isolation
- family history of mistreatment
- lack of a social network
- lack of information about available resources
- poor contact with peers
- inter-generational conflict.

What is significant from these findings is the social element, be it isolation or dependency on others; a familial history of mistreatment is also common, which highlights the complexity and inter-generational nature of abuse and violence within families.

What are the effects of elder abuse?

Daichman (2005, p.327) refers to seminal research which examined the effects of elder abuse on health: 'when they compared mortality rates of the non-abused and the abused, they found that, by the thirteenth year following the study's initiation, 40% of the non-reported (i.e. non-abused, non-neglected) group were still alive and only 9% of the physically abused or neglected elders. After controlling for all the possible factors that might affect mortality (e.g. age, gender, income, functional status, cognitive status, diagnosis, social supports, etc.) and finding no significant relationships, the researchers speculated that mistreatment causes extreme interpersonal stress that may confer an additional death risk.' These findings reflect the consequences of abuse, which is not just psychological, as is often thought, but also has physical implications, such as stress and distress.

Elder abuse is now known to be more widespread than previously thought. The Health Service Executive has published two documents of particular importance in this area: the Report of the Working Group on Elder Abuse – *Protecting Our Future* (2002) (www.dohc.ie); and *Open Your Eyes* (2008) (www.hse.ie).

Abuse of people with disabilities

People with disabilities are a group that has been identified as vulnerable to abuse and neglect. The National Disability Authority (NDA) issued a briefing paper on the abuse of people with disabilities, which offers the following advice:

> People with disabilities may have a higher vulnerability to abuse because of social circumstances linked to their impairment. For example, children or adults with disabilities may be exposed to higher risks in services if there are not appropriate safeguards in place. They may be more isolated from friends and family, which renders them more vulnerable to abuse. People with

disabilities may feel disempowered from making complaints, may find it more difficult to communicate, or to be taken seriously if they do complain. So they may be easier for abusers to victimise.

Additional risks can be faced by people with disabilities because of:

- care and stress at home between partners and generations
- dependency on relationships with powerful professionals
- the nature and culture of institutional settings
- predatory abusers who target and groom vulnerable people
- discrimination
- public harassment and hate crime.

Groups requiring particular attention are those with extensive or complex health care needs; those who cannot advocate for themselves; those with impairments which are expressed through challenging behaviour or other stigmatising conditions; those who are involved in the criminal justice system; those placed in institutions; and those from disadvantaged communities (Brown, NDA seminar presentation, 14 September 2006).

The significant barriers to people with disabilities accessing support and redress include:

- being unable to name and identify abuse due to a lack of experience, awareness and knowledge
- past experience of care or medical practices that undermined or transgressed personal boundaries and bodily integrity
- disempowerment and low self-esteem
- isolation (including physical, communication, social)
- having one's credibility questioned, particularly persons with intellectual and mental health disabilities
- the capacity of staff with whom they are in contact to detect and respond to abuse
- the capacity of the justice system and other redress mechanisms to provide an accessible system to deal with complaints from people with disabilities
- the absence of a system of independent advocacy particularly in closed environments
- negative attitudes
- failure of staff to identify where abuse is occurring within intimate relationships
- fear of consequences of disclosure, including retaliation, rejection or being moved from home or service environment. These fears are likely to be particularly significant if the person is reliant on the abuser for the activities of daily living.

Source: www.nda.ie

Institutional abuse

The issue of institutional abuse and the psychological adjustment of adult survivors of institutional abuse were the subject of a research project commissioned by the Commission to Inquire into Child Abuse (CICA):

> In 2005 and 2006, 247 adult survivors of institutional abuse in industrial and reformatory schools recruited through CICA were interviewed. Other witnesses to the Commission who reported institutional abuse in other institutions and out-of-home care settings were not included in this study. There were approximately equal numbers of men and women who were about 60 years of age, and who had entered institutions run by nuns or religious brothers due to family adversity or petty criminality.
>
> Participants had spent, on average, about five years living with their families before entering institutions and about 10 years living in institutions. More than 90 per cent had experienced institutional physical and emotional child abuse and about half, institutional child sexual abuse. Just over a third of those who had memories of having lived with their families reported family-based child abuse or neglect.
>
> All participants had experienced one or more significant life problems with mental health problems, unemployment and substance use being the most common. More than four-fifths of participants had an insecure adult attachment style, indicative of having problems making and maintaining satisfying intimate relationships.
>
> About four-fifths of participants at some point in their life had had a psychological disorder, including anxiety, mood, substance use and personality disorders. The overall rates of psychological disorders among survivors of institutional living, for most disorders, were double those found in normal community populations in Europe and North America.
>
> Participants with multiple co-morbid psychological disorders had experienced more institutional abuse and showed poorer adult psychological adjustment than those with fewer disorders. Those with no diagnoses were the best adjusted as adults. Subgroups selected by specific diagnosis showed an intermediate level of adult psychological adjustment between these extremes.
>
> In the analysis of groups of participants who had spent different amounts of time in institutions and entered under different circumstances, the most poorly adjusted as adults were not those who had spent longest living in institutions (more than 12 years), but rather, those who had spent less time in institutions (under 11 years), entered institutions through the courts and reported institutional sexual abuse, in addition to physical abuse within their families.
>
> The psychological processes of traumatization and re-enactment of abuse on self and others were associated with multiple difficulties in adult life and a history of institutional abuse, but not family-based child abuse.

Source: http://childabusecommission.ie

PREVENTING ABUSE

The initiative described below is evidence-based and aims to improve the lives of children and also prevent abuse. This initiative offers a multi-faceted approach to intervening and supporting families and communities.

In focus: Prevention of abuse

The Pathway to the Prevention of Child Abuse and Neglect: A community approach to the prevention of abuse and neglect

The Pathway to the Prevention of Child Abuse and Neglect (Schorr and Marchand, 2007) is an initiative that aims to collect findings from research, practice, theory and policy about what it takes to improve the lives of children and families, particularly those living in 'tough' neighbourhoods. Rather than viewing the prevention of abuse as the responsibility of a sole agency, this initiative adopts a community-led approach in the prevention of abuse. For the effective prevention of abuse, strategies include multiple actions at the individual, family and community levels to reduce risk factors and strengthen protective factors. According to Schorr and Marchand, (2007, pp.1–5), communities can prevent child abuse and neglect by working effectively toward the following six goals and respective 'action areas' suggested to meet those goals:

Children and youth
- **Children and youth are nurtured, safe and engaged**
  - Action area 1.A: Early detection of health and developmental concerns
  - Action area 1.B: High-quality childcare settings and schools support social and cognitive development
  - Action area 1.C: Opportunities for youth to engage in civic and community life

Families
- **Families are strong and connected**
  - Action area 2.A: Help and support to parents to improve their parenting skills and their understanding of how they can contribute to their children's success
  - Action area 2.B: Social networks and services attuned to child development and connected to specialty care
  - Action area 2.C: Supports and services help parents to meet basic needs and decrease stress

- **Identified families access services and supports**
  - Action area 3.A: Community-based services are structured to respond to 'screened-out' families
  - Action area 3.B: Staff who encounter families are trained in screening and referrals
  - Action area 3.C: Adequate capacity to provide services exists, based on information systems that track family needs and progress
- **Families free from substance abuse and mental illness**
  - Action area 4.A: High-quality, accessible, family-centred treatment services for substance abuse and mental illness
  - Action area 4.B: Co-ordination among public systems that encounter families struggling with addiction, mental illness, and domestic violence

Communities

- **Communities are caring and responsive**
  - Action area 5.A: Sustainable networks of services and supports contribute to child protection
  - Action area 5.B: Systems of care stay connected to families over time and assist with challenges as needed
  - Action area 5.C: Neighborhoods are safe, stable, and supportive
- **Vulnerable communities have capacity to respond**
  - Action area 6.A: Services and supports target populations in communities with concentrated risk factors
  - Action area 6.B: Promising community-based organisations achieve geographic saturation with interventions and supports that respond to an array of needs.

Schorr and Marchand, (2007, pp.6–7) outline the following rationale or reasons for the goals outlined and the action areas proposed to combat abuse and neglect:

1. Children who have been neglected or abused are more likely to suffer from a variety of other problems, including attention deficit disorders, depression, conduct problems, reduced cognitive development, language deficits, reduced emotional stability and poor self-regulation, poor problem-solving skills, an inability to cope with or adapt to new or stressful situations, and shortfalls in physical health. All of these are important factors in school readiness and school success.
2. Prompt and effective responses to abuse, neglect, and other crises can ameliorate or protect against many negative effects. The fields of child abuse prevention, family strengthening and support, early care and education, public health and others have all recognized the importance of a coordinated approach

to reaching families and staying connected over time for the purpose of preventing child abuse and avoiding the long-terms costs of child maltreatment. Treatment is more effective and recurrences less likely the earlier treatment begins.

3. Over the years, child maltreatment researchers and practitioners have explicitly recognized that most maltreatment results from a complex web of factors related to a person's personality, family history, and community context. Ecological theory, with its acknowledgement that individual, familial, community, and societal factors interact to increase or decrease the likelihood of child maltreatment, now represents the most commonly accepted theory of maltreatment.

4. Depression, attachment difficulties, and post-traumatic stress—prevalent among mothers living in poverty—undermine mothers' development of empathy, sensitivity, and responsiveness to their children, often leading to poorer developmental outcomes. Children who have clinically depressed parents or parents reporting signs of depression are at risk for a variety of negative outcomes, including health, cognitive, and socio-emotional problems; behavioral problems and poorer performance on math and reading assessments; and poor emotional adjustment as they age. Their parents have poorer parenting skills and fewer cognitive, stimulating, and supportive interactions with their children.

5. Programs that connect low-income, high-risk families to responsive and supportive networks, services, and institutions help to prevent child abuse and neglect because they identify early warning signs and link children and parents with the help they need. Traditional child welfare approaches to maltreatment focus largely on physical injury, the relative risk of recurrent harm, and questions of child custody, with a strong criminal justice orientation. When viewed through a child development lens, however, the abuse or neglect of young children should be evaluated and treated as a matter of child health and development within the context of a family relationship crisis.

6. Families are an integral and critical component of interventions that aim to improve academic and social outcomes for children and youth. Family strengthening programs make a deliberate and sustained effort to ensure that parents have the necessary opportunities, relationships, networks, and supports to raise their children successfully. This approach has a positive impact on family environment, parent-child relationships, parenting, family involvement and, as part of a larger comprehensive intervention, can improve child outcomes.

7. The regular referral of suspected cases of child abuse or neglect from the child welfare system to the early intervention system would ensure that developmental and behavioral needs are assessed and treated. Child abuse prevention strategies that emphasize both the developmental needs of children and the importance of community-based supports for families show how we can

close the gap between science and practice for our most vulnerable young children.

Source: www.cssp.org

Dealing with a disclosure of abuse

The following are the Office of the Minister for Children and Youth Affairs (OMCYA) guidelines on dealing with a disclosure of abuse:

> The Office of the Minister for Children and Youth Affairs values and encourages the full participation of children and young people in many aspects of our work and we strive to ensure that the experience of the child/young person in our work is a happy and productive one. In the event of a child/young person disclosing an incident of abuse it is essential that this is dealt with sensitively and professionally by the staff member/volunteer involved. The following are guidelines to support the worker/volunteer in this:

- React calmly;
- Listen carefully and attentively; take the young person seriously;
- Reassure the young person that they have taken the right action in talking to you;
- Do not promise to keep anything secret;
- Ask questions for clarification only. Do not ask leading questions;
- Check back with the child/young person that what you have heard is correct and understood;
- Do not express any opinions about the alleged abuser;
- Record the conversation as soon as possible, in as much detail as possible. Sign and date the record;
- Ensure that the child/young person understands the procedures which will follow;
- Pass the information to the Child Protection Officer, do not attempt to deal with the problem alone;
- Treat the information confidentially.

Source: www.omc.gov.ie

Our Duty to Care: The Principles of Good Practice for the Protection of Children and Young People is aimed at community and voluntary organisations of any size or type that provide services for children. It offers guidance on the promotion of child welfare and the development of safe practices in work with children. It also gives information on how to recognise signs of child abuse and the correct steps to take within organisations if it is suspected, witnessed or disclosed. The process of reporting suspected or actual child abuse to the health board is described step by step, and guidance is given on how to handle sensitive areas. *Our Duty to Care* offers a practical guide to those who work with children by outlining a number of fundamental principles of good practice, highlighting the key elements of each one and discussing the issues raised. The guide should be read in conjunction with *Children First – National Guidelines for the Protection and Welfare of Children* (Department of Health and Children, 1999).

Our Duty to Care is available from www.omc.gov.ie

Children First is available from www.dohc.ie

Child protection

Margaret Prangnell lectures in Childcare at Inchicore College of Further Education and is also an independent trainer (CHMT). She is on Barnardos' training panel and regularly provides child protection training workshops. Here Margaret outlines key issues to be aware of, illustrated by case studies.

> The following information will only provide the reader with an overview of factors to consider when working directly with children and young people. It is essential that the reader undertakes formal child protection training to enable them to meet the requirements placed upon them by legislation.
>
> Even the experts have difficulty at times deciding conclusively if a child is being abused. Remember, once you become involved in a child abuse situation do not expect to feel good about it. It is a situation that is likely to lead to great upset in the lives of a few and possibly many people who will be affected directly and indirectly. However, this must not lead you to avoid taking action if it is needed.

Principle of paramountcy

In our work with children/young people we should always be guided by this principle which requires that: **the welfare of the child should be the paramount consideration.** (Department of Health and Children, 1999)

There is no absolute list of signs and symptoms of abuse in the four different categories. Usually, but not always, we build up a picture of indicators which lead us to come to a conclusion that a child is likely to be at risk. Accurate record keeping is vital as you may not remember accurately something you observed in a child some time ago. By referring to written records the professionals involved will be able to build a picture from the history as well as what is evident today. Sometimes the abuse may be acute and immediately evident, such as in physical abuse where the child is seriously injured.

Neglect:
Physical indicators
- constant hunger
- exposed to danger
- lack of supervision
- inadequate/inappropriate clothing
- poor hygiene
- untreated illnesses

Behavioural indicators
- tiredness, listlessness
- lack of peer relationships
- low self esteem
- compulsive stealing/begging

Physical abuse:
Physical indicators
- scratches
- bite marks or welts
- bruises in places difficult to mark, e.g. behind ears, groin
- burns, especially cigarette burns
- untreated injuries

Behavioural indicators
- self-mutilation tendencies
- chronic runaway
- aggressive or withdrawn
- fear of returning home
- undue fear of adults
- fearful watchfulness

Sexual abuse:
Physical indicators
- soreness, bleeding in genital areas
- itching in genital area
- stained or bloody underwear
- stomach pains or headaches
- pain on urination
- difficulty in walking or sitting
- bruises in inner thighs or buttocks
- anorexia/bulimia

Behavioural indicators
- chronic depression
- inappropriate language, sexual knowledge for age group
- making sexual advances to adults or other children
- low self-esteem
- afraid of the dark
- wariness of being approached by anyone
- substance/drug abuse

Emotional abuse:
Physical indicators
- sudden speech disorder
- wetting and soiling
- signs of mutilation
- attention-seeking behaviour
- frequent vomiting

Behavioural indicators
- rocking, thumb sucking
- fear of change
- chronic runaway
- poor peer relationships

As mentioned above, there is no absolute definitive list so if in doubt seek professional advice.

Examples of reasonable grounds for concern:
- a child or young person disclosing to you that they are being abused
- a statement from a person who witnessed abuse of a child or young person
- an illness, injury or behaviour consistent with abuse
- consistent signs of neglect over a period of time
- child in an unsafe situation

What should you do if you suspect abuse?
- react calmly
- listen carefully and attentively
- reassure the person if they are disclosing something to you
- do not make any promises regarding secrecy
- pass the information to the designated child protection officer who, in turn, will report to the statutory authorities for advice and possible investigation
- treat the information with absolute confidentiality

Confidentiality is about managing sensitive information in a professional and purposeful way. The sharing of information must be on a 'need to know basis' only.

Case study 1 (youth worker)

You have met with a young person (14 years old) you have been supporting for the last month. She has never looked well but today she appeared to be very tired, withdrawn and when you asked her was she OK she said no.

You asked her was there anything you could do to help. She then disclosed the following information.

> My mother's brother who used to live abroad has come to live with us. At first he was all right and I really liked him. He spent time with me and even took me shopping for new clothes. He did not mind that it took me ages to pick things out and kept telling me how great I looked. He made me feel good and important. No one else does.
>
> Then he started putting his arm around me which was OK, after all he is my uncle.
>
> Last night my mum and dad went out and it was just us two left at home. We were watching television together when he put his arm around me. Then he started to kiss my neck. I told him to stop but he would not. . . . [She alleged he then went on to rape her].

There should be no doubt in your mind that there is a strong possibility of abuse here or, if the allegation is untrue, that this young person has serious issues which she will need help to deal with.

Questions for you

1. How should you react to this girl?
2. What should you say?
3. How should you say it? What language should you use?
4. What should you do?

Answers

1. Be calm and in control.
2. Tell her that you take what she is saying seriously. Do not tell her that you will not tell anyone. Remember this girl may already be a victim of abuse and your breaking a promise will be yet another form of abuse.
3. Use simple clear language. Tell her that you are not qualified to help her and will need to involve someone reliable and very experienced who can.
4. Do not ask any questions. You are not trained to do so and will only complicate the situation.

Case study 2 (pre-school setting)

Recently a three-and-a-half-year-old girl started in the crèche. Her parents have told you that she is going through a tantrum phase at present but did not make anything of it. The mum collects the little girl and the dad drops her off in the morning. She has settled in with you very well and is happy and contented. She has now been coming to you every day for three weeks. For the last three mornings she has had a tantrum as soon as the dad says he is going. The first morning he was patient and caring towards her. Yesterday and today he was shouting at her to stop and today he told her if she did not stop they would not come back for her; he then slapped her on the bottom. He was in a rage. You told him to go, that you would look after her. Then he just stormed out of the house.

Questions for you

1. What should you do immediately?
2. Is this an abuse case?
3. Should you report it to your designated child protection officer/designated person?
4. What should you say to the parents?

Answers

1. Calm the little girl and reassure her that everything is fine.
2. No, based on the evidence given in the case study there are no reasonable grounds to suspect that this is an abuse case. However, if the father's behaviour is repeated you would need to assess the impact on the little girl's development.
3. Report to your line manager as the behaviour of the father is totally inappropriate and must be addressed to ensure it does not happen again.
4. The parents must be invited to a meeting as soon as possible to discuss what took place, the effect the father's behaviour will have on the child and how the staff could support father/family in dealing with the little girl's tantrums. Do not be judgemental about the father; you never know what is going on in people's lives and the support of caring staff could make a great difference to the lives of all members of this family.

Case study 3 (home setting)

You are on work placement in the community. You and your supervisor visit a one-year-old child in his home to undertake a developmental assessment. The mother is required to undress the child and you notice bruising on his back, legs and inside his upper arms. When weighed the little boy is underweight and does not meet his physical development milestones. He appears to be pale and tired and not interested in you or your supervisor.

Questions for you
1. Do you suspect possible abuse?
2. Consult the indicators given earlier in the chapter. How many possible indicators can you tick?
3. Does this help you to decide that there is suspected abuse?
4. What should you do now?

Margaret Prangnell's guidelines draw attention to the delicacy of child protection in practice. The case studies should have given you food for thought as to how best to deal with a disclosure of abuse. Physical and behavioural indicators of abuse are outlined as is the importance of the principle of paramountcy.

TRAUMA

As well as the aetiology and factors associated with abuse, it is important to consider the effects that abuse can have upon an individual. One such effect is post-traumatic stress disorder (PTSD). The history of PTSD is interesting. It was first seen as a syndrome in American soldiers returning from the Vietnam War. Initially there was scepticism regarding the existence of a cluster of behaviours which were triggered by a traumatic event. There was also a reluctance on the part of the American administration to recognise that these soldiers had suffered psychological anguish through participation in the war. Now, of course, it is a recognised syndrome. The range of traumas that can trigger it has been widened to include not just war, but also rape, and any event where an individual's ability to recover is affected. Of course, it is important to realise that we all experience events that are upsetting and to be depressed and saddened by them is quite normal. PTSD is different in that the person continues to be affected by it for a length of time.

Post-traumatic stress disorder

Post-traumatic stress disorder (PTSD) is a psychiatric disorder that can occur in people who have experienced or witnessed life-threatening events, such as natural disasters, serious accidents, terrorist incidents, war or violent personal assaults such as rape. People who suffer from PTSD often relive the experience as flashbacks or nightmares, have difficulty sleeping and feel detached or estranged. The history of PSTD is an interesting insight into how we categorise mental health. The disorder is a relatively recent addition to the Diagnostic and Statistical Manual (DSM), following the development of psychiatric difficulties in Vietnam veterans.

Four major symptoms commonly occur in this anxiety disorder:

- The person experiences severe symptoms of anxiety, arousal and distress that were not present before the trauma.
- The person relives the trauma recurrently in flashbacks, dreams and fantasy. This happens when sudden, vivid memories, accompanied by painful emotions, take over the person's attention. Flashbacks may be so strong that individuals feel as though they are actually reliving the traumatic experience or seeing it unfold before their eyes or in nightmares.
- The person becomes numb to the world and avoids stimuli that remind them of the trauma.
- After events where others have been killed, the person may experience extreme guilt about surviving the catastrophe when others did not.

PTSD usually appears within three months of the trauma, but sometimes later. Some will try to self-medicate with alcohol or drugs to dull or ease the pain and trauma.

Treatment

Cognitive behaviour therapy focuses on correcting the painful and intrusive patterns of behaviour and thought, by teaching people with PTSD relaxation techniques and examining (and challenging) the mental processes that are causing the problem.

Psychodynamic psychotherapy focuses on helping the individual examine personal values and how behaviour and experience during the traumatic event affected them.

Exposure therapy uses careful, repeated, detailed imagining of the trauma (exposure) or progressive exposures to symptom 'triggers' in a safe, controlled context to help the survivor face and gain control of the fear and distress that was overwhelming during the trauma. In some cases, trauma memories can be confronted all at once (flooding). For others, it is preferable to work up to the most severe trauma gradually or by taking the trauma one piece at a time (desensitisation).

Meaning and trauma

The aim of this section is to illustrate in depth the many aspects that can be considered in how a person makes sense or 'meaning' from the trauma they have suffered, to enable you to gain an appreciation of the mechanisms that create meaning; the meaning an individual who has suffered a trauma possibly creates; and finally perhaps to reflect and challenge any assumptions you may hold regarding this area.

Definition of schema

Fiske and Taylor (1984) define a schema as a 'cognitive structure that represents organized knowledge about a given concept or type of stimulus' (p.140).

- Fiske and Taylor further maintain that schemas tend to be resistant to change and people are more likely to modify incoming information to fit the existing schema rather than modify the schema in response to new and challenging information. Compared to Piaget's type of schema, the schemas referred to here are of a higher order and form the essence of how we view ourselves, others and the world around us.
- Janoff-Bulman (1992, p.5) refers to these schemas as 'global' theories or assumptions that people hold about themselves and their world. These schemas, or conceptual systems, guide and inform our actions and perceptions. Further, we operate on the basis of these assumptions without even being aware or conscious of them' (Janoff-Bulman and Frantz, 1997, p.97).

When incoming information so greatly challenges an individual's existing conceptual system or 'assumptive world' that it cannot be 'assimilated' or 'accommodated', the potential for trauma exists, as this information continues to be stored in active consciousness.

Janoff-Bulman eloquently explains how this occurs: 'Traumatic life events force survivors to confront questions of meaning in their lives. These questions are posed with an intensity and immediacy that reflect the overwhelming power of meaning-related concerns in the aftermath of extreme negative events. Survivors are struck by the extent to which meaning, in its many guises, had typically been assumed and taken for granted in their lives. Now their traumatic experience compels them to re-examine these earlier, easy assumptions.' (p. 12).

Meaning defined

Meaning can be broadly defined in various ways to include purpose, intent, order, interpretation and significance. Within the fundamental assumptions framework are three core assumptions:

- the world is benevolent
- the world is meaningful
- the self has worth.

What happens when trauma occurs?

Victims of trauma are plagued by a double dose of fear and anxiety as both their internal and external worlds are assaulted.

Internally, they experience the disintegration of basic assumptions, which had provided psychological stability and coherence in a complex world. The survivor's inner world is now a state of dramatic upheaval, and is no longer able to provide a trustworthy road map for negotiating daily life.

As a result, the external world is now perceived as frightening. Survivors realise all too vividly the possibility of their own annihilation. They can no longer assume that their own self-worth and precautionary behaviours will protect them, for randomness and arbitrariness now characterise the workings of the universe. Old certainties and securities are gone. They are intensely aware that bad things can happen to them. The world no longer makes sense, and this realisation is devastating. As Ernest Becker writes in *The Denial of Death* (p.63), it is terrifying 'to see the world as it really is. ... It makes routine, automatic, secure, self confident activity impossible. ... It places a trembling animal at the mercy of the entire cosmos and the problem of the meaning of it'.

The self is good

One of the three core assumptions outlined by Janoff-Bulman is that the self is good. When a traumatic event occurs, this can prompt an individual to question this: 'If I was a good person surely this would not have happened to me?' Further, others may reinforce this view thus increasing the distress of the victim.

The expression 'Belief in a Just World' (BJW) was coined by Lerner in 1965, and refers to the belief that good things happen to good people and conversely bad things happen to bad people; that is, you get what you deserve. Lerner and Miller captured the essence of the 'Belief in a Just World' theory as follows:

> Individuals have a need to believe that they live in a world where people generally get what they deserve. The belief that the world is just enables the individual to confront his physical and social environment as though they are stable and orderly. Without such a belief it would be difficult for the individual to commit himself to the pursuit of long-range goals or even to the socially regulated behaviour of day to day life. Since the belief that the world is just serves such an important adaptive function for the individual, people are very reluctant to give up this belief, and they can be greatly troubled if they encounter evidence that suggests that the world is not really just or orderly after all' (pp.1030–31, in Furnham, 2003, p.796).

It has been found that BJW is cross-culturally generalisable and stable across the lifespan. Belief in a Just World is seen as a bedrock in many religions, for example; thus the cultural values of a society impact both on the victim and those around them. If a society has a high BJW, this can increase the distress of trauma victims, as their fundamental assumptions are even more greatly challenged; and the negative reaction of others towards the victim increases, again further increasing the victim's suffering.

'Creeping determinism', also known as 'hindsight bias', is a phenomenon identified by psychologist Baruch Fischhoff, where once people know the outcome of events they overestimate the likelihood of that outcome. Victimisation demonstrates that, contrary to 'Belief in a Just World', bad things do happen to people who don't 'deserve' them, therefore, by default, 'it could happen to us, too'. So we search for any reasoning that explains why a traumatic event happens and in blaming the victims we can rest easily in our just, benevolent world.

Within a cultural context Wasco claims that these assumptions are not necessarily transferable to ethnic minority and other marginalised groups, especially in the United States. Wasco (2003) claims that 'these theories operate on the assumption that all nontraumatised people believe that the world is basically a safe, just, and predictable place and that trauma disrupts victims' assumptions about themselves, others, and the world' (p.313). Wasco includes working-class people, immigrant and refugee peoples, women and children exposed to violence and abuse as individuals who never had an opportunity to establish Janoff-Bulman's three core assumptions.

Pathology of the self
Pathology of the self is considered by many trauma experts to be the central negative reaction in trauma victims (Aarts and Op Den Velde, 1996, p.371). Pathology of the self refers to a shattering of the self in trauma victims.

When shattering occurs it can form a split into so-called 'good' and 'bad' self representations. Focus of treatment is towards the reintegration of the self and a restoration of the sense of self in trauma survivors.

Search for meaning
Ochberg (1995) refers to the search for meaning in relation to post-traumatic therapy. The principles underpinning this therapy include the view that 'every individual has a unique pathway to recovery after traumatic stress' (p.246). This principle highlights the interesting and relatively unique position held by post-traumatic stress disorder within psychopathology, where the symptomology is the main focus of investigation and treatment.

Ochberg (p.261) describes the 'individualised search for meaning' in the wake of shattered assumptions and offers Viktor Frankl, a famous Viennese psychiatrist, as an example of such an individual.

Janoff-Bulman and Frantz (1997), when discussing survivors of trauma, recognise the role of 'secondary control' over future victimisation, that is, the idea that they can cope with whatever comes their way. Secondary control can be framed another way as a belief in one's own personal strength, and this can help alleviate the apparent meaninglessness of the world following the shattering of an individual's 'assumptive world'. Also, with the increased sense of vulnerability and senselessness can spring forth a heightened appreciation of life and meaning in even the most banal and mundane experiences, and especially with respect to family and friends.

SUMMARY

This chapter has outlined the causes and factors implicated in different types of abuse, and those groups who are at particular risk, such as older people. We have also looked at the Pathway to the Prevention of Child Abuse and Neglect, an initiative that aims to improve the lives of children and families. Margaret Prangnell outlined the more practical elements of child protection; what to do with a disclosure of abuse. Finally, we looked at post-traumatic stress disorder and how people who have suffered trauma attempt to make meaning from their experiences. Important policy and guidelines in the area of child welfare were referred to and I would strongly suggest that you make yourself aware of them. Though the legal aspect of child protection is not within the remit of this book, I would recommend Geoffrey Shannon's *Report of the Special Rapporteur on Child Protection* (2007), which is a comprehensive critique of the law in this area and especially the deficits relating to it: www.omc.gov.ie.

9

Social psychology

Man is biologically predestined to construct and to inhabit a world with others.
    – Berger and Luckmann, *The Social Construction of Reality*, 1967

INTRODUCTION

Definition of social psychology

The field of social psychology studies how other people influence our behaviour (social influence), how we think about and perceive our social world (social thinking and social perception) and how we behave toward other people (social relations). In Philip Zimbardo's APA presidential address, he reflected on the capacity of social-psychological knowledge to offer a more positive contribution to social welfare and social life (Zimbardo, 2004, pp.339–51).

Pancer (1997) argues that social psychology within psychology (as opposed to sociology) has become increasingly asocial, focusing specifically on mainstream social psychology in North America, which continues to dominate the field despite efforts to devise alternatives. This is in contrast to the 'reform-oriented aspirations' of social psychology's pioneers, such as Lewin, who wished to make the discipline socially useful. Pancer concludes that modern social psychology has adopted approaches that do little to advance human welfare. He claims that this is in part due to the influence of the 'cognitive revolution' which is increasingly dominant. Pancer advocates for a 'redirected, critical social psychology' which can help to elucidate why people acquiesce to conditions of oppression and teach us to collaborate with others.

Social psychology thus has the potential for applications in the field of 'care practice' if we envision Pancer's clarion call. Certainly social phenomena, such as prejudice and discrimination, must be of concern to those who work in the field of care practice. Later in this chapter we will consider prejudice from a social psychology perspective; this perhaps is a good time for you to reflect on what prejudices you hold and whether these belief systems affect your treatment of others (particularly in care settings) in the form of discrimination.

Some figures in social psychology

Gordon Allport was one of the founders of social psychology. He wrote the seminal *Handbook of Social Psychology* (1954) and in it defined social psychology as 'an attempt to understand and explain how the thought, feeling, and behavior of individuals are influenced by the actual, imagined, or implied presence of other human beings' (p.5).

Kurt Lewin was an early leader of group dynamic research and is regarded by many as the founder of modern social psychology. Lewin's equation, $B = f(P,E)$, stipulates that behaviour is a function of the person and environment, and he advocated 'action research', applying this equation and scientific methods to address social problems such as prejudice and group conflict.

Social constructionism

Differences between constuctivism and constructionism

Perhaps the simplest way of distinguishing constructionism from constructivism is by defining the former as a sociological description of knowledge, and the latter as a psychological description of knowledge. That is to say, while constructivism deals with knowledge formation in the head, constructionism deals with knowledge formation outside the head, between participants in social relationship. Constructivism can include theorists such as Piaget and Vygotsky, for example.

Hruby recognises Gergen as one of the leading and most influential figures in the postmodern approach to social constructionism. According to Hruby (2001, p.54), Gergen defines social construction using the following four themes:

1. Understanding of the world is not derived by observation but by linguistic, cultural and historical contingencies.
2. 'Understanding is not automatically driven by the forces of nature, but is the result of an active, cooperative enterprise of persons in relationship' (1985, p.263).
3. 'The degree to which a given form of understanding prevails . . . is not fundamentally dependent on the empirical validity of the perspective in question, but on the vicissitudes of social processes (e.g., communication, negotiation, conflict, rhetoric)' (1985, p.268).
4. Negotiated understandings are a form of social action and as such are integrated with all other human activities; an idea with profound implications for the analysis of the metaphors and assessments used in psychology, and more generally in social science.

Social constructionism emphasises how contextual, linguistic and relational factors combine to determine the kinds of human beings that people will become and how their views of the world will develop. Knowledge is negotiated between people within a given context and time frame. Thus all knowledge and even personhood itself is fleeting. Psychological constructs such as personality are viewed very differently than in the social-constructionist approach, which sees 'personality' as a socially constructed idea rather than something inherently intrapsychic. Many would use the term 'identity' rather than 'self' or 'personality', emphasising the idea that we each have multiple selves which are situated within the boundaries of culture, context and language.

Social constructionism proposes that reality is socially negotiated. This leads to questions such as 'what is mental illness?', 'what is disability?', 'what is woman?'; fundamentally, every construct or concept is informed or constructed by social knowledge. We saw in Chapter 5 that Irish people were, at one time, said to have a low IQ compared to other nationalities in Europe. This belief was created by others and accepted as such. Of course, the difficulty is that 'intelligence' is also a construct; what is perceived as 'intelligence' in the West would be different in another part of the world. Who decides what 'intelligence' is, anyway? And yet we all are influenced and create constructions in almost every facet of our lives. This also explains how we can challenge such social constructions; for example, of disability. Fifty years ago the view of disability was different to the one we have now, capturing the idea that it is fleeting and culturally situated.

Symbolic interactionism

Symbolic interaction can best be understood as a framework whose general proposition holds that self reflects society and organises social behaviour. Further, society can be viewed as a web of communication or 'symbolic interaction', conducted through meanings developed in a person's interdependent activity. Society is created and recreated as individuals interact. Both society and individual derives from interaction: each presupposes the other.

Three assumptions characterise this perspective:

1. Adequate accounts of behaviour must reflect the perspectives of the actors engaged in that behaviour and cannot rest on the perspective of observers alone.
2. Priority is assigned to social interaction with respect to the emergence of both social organisation and the individual: 'In the beginning there is society.' This assumption differentiates symbolic interactionism from social psychological approaches used by psychologists giving priority to the individual.
3. The self, people's reflexive responses to themselves, links societal processes to social interactions and behaviours.

Goffman and symbolic interactionism

Slattery (2003) points to differences between symbolic interactionism (SI) and the work of Erving Goffman. Whereas SI tries to examine how people create or negotiate their self-images, Goffman focuses on how society forces people to present a certain image of themselves. As such, we are forced to switch back and forth between many complicated roles. Goffman seeks to explore and explain social action in respect of its meaning for others rather than focusing on the causal aspects. It is the relationship between social order, social interaction and the self – the interrelationship between society at large and everyday social intercourse – that is important to Goffman, whose interest lies in elucidating a more sociological account of the individual in an effort to analyse the distinction between the self as a character and the self as social actor, maintaining an image of self in various situations.

In Goffman's interpretations, the self is multifaceted, putting on whatever social mask is needed for different situations. Goffman's work on labelling highlighted not just the way people react to being labelled but also how the process of labelling can create 'abnormal behaviours'. His seminal work, *Asylums*, highlights this phenomenon; in being labelled or, more negatively, stigmatised as 'insane' or 'sick', the individual's self-image began to change, leaving them feeling abnormal and reducing the likelihood of their recovery and their ability to recover. The result was that the individual adopted a new self-image and personality that kept them insulated from 'normal' society; for example, patients in mental health facilities or homeless people in a refuge. The labelling had a self-fulfilling prophecy where the stigmatised person became the image created for them by the label; thus, if labelled as deviant and antisocial, the person would eventually adopt such a persona. This finding had serious implications for those who work with patients and clients, especially in the social care arena.

Goffman's work on asylums was one of the first sociological examinations of the social situation of mental patients, the hospital world as subjectively experienced by the patient. His ideas were based on the use of the 'total institution model' and were not just confined to mental hospitals. Prisons, concentration camps, monasteries, orphanages and military organisations were also considered institutions. As Weinstein (1982, p.268) relates; 'total institutions are places of residence and work where a large number of individuals are cut off from the wider society for a period of time. There is a fundamental split between a large managed group (inmates) and a small supervisory staff. Human needs are handled in a bureaucratic and impersonal way. The social distance between the inmates and staff is great, and each group tends to be hostile toward the other.' Weinstein relays Goffman's description of the 'inmate world' of the total institution. Upon entering the establishment, processes are set in motion to destroy the inmate's old self and create a new self. The person is dispossessed from normal social roles, stripped of their usual identities. The inmate undergoes a mortification of self via physical and social abuse. Contacts with outside persons are limited and inmates cannot prevent their visitors from seeing them in humiliating circumstances.

As a social care practitioner, do you feel that the residential placements you have worked in resemble Goffman's description of the 'total institution'? Do any similarities exist? What steps can be taken to minimise the potential of residential care settings such as nursing homes coming to resemble the 'total institution' described by Goffman?

'Like a Prison!'

Homeless women's narratives of surviving shelter

De Ward and Moe (2010) examine how the bureaucracy and institutionalisation within a homeless shelter fit various tenets of Goffman's (1961) 'total institution', particularly with regard to systematic deterioration of personhood and loss of autonomy. Women's experiences as shelter residents are then explored via a typology of survival strategies: submission, adaptation and resistance.

> Upon entering the shelter, however, their familial leadership roles were usurped by staff authority. Subsequently, both mothers and their children were subjected to the rules and discipline of the shelter.
>
> Prior research on homeless women's shelter experiences substantiates these elements of the total institution. For example, Stark (1994) cites the loss of respect experienced by parents from their children within shelter institutions. More specifically, Breese and Feltey (1996) found that the privacy, freedom and control women had within their homes, and lives in general, were drastically compromised upon entering a shelter. Becoming homeless and accepting space within a shelter institution were equated with forsaking the 'privileges' that housed people take for granted. So while shelters are distinct from institutions, such as prisons and some mental health hospitals, wherein people are confined against their will and are not free to leave, there is an element of coercion within them. While women were free to leave, this 'freedom' was mitigated by the consequences of living homeless on the streets or otherwise without secure access to shelter, food and clothing. To put oneself, and in many instances one's children, in such perilous circumstances is not a realistic 'choice' per se. The safety of the shelter, regardless of its bureaucratic nature, becomes the most pragmatic and reasonable means of survival. (pp.121–2)

SOCIAL INFLUENCE

- social norms
- conformity
- obedience.

Social norms

Definition: Social norms are the shared expectations about how people should think, feel and behave, and they are the cement that binds social systems together.

Some norms are formal laws, others are unspoken. Either way, they exert a huge influence upon our daily lives.

A social role consists of a set of norms that characterise how people in a given social position ought to behave. The roles of 'garda', 'doctor' and 'spouse' carry different sets of behaviour expectations.

Norms and roles can influence behaviour so strongly that they compel a person to act uncharacteristically. The 'guards' in the Stanford Prison study were well-adjusted students, yet norms related to the role of 'guard' and to concepts of crime and punishment seemed to override their values, leading to dehumanising treatment of the prisoners.

Social roles – Stanford Prison experiment

The Stanford Prison experiment aimed to examine social roles in order to research the power of the immediate social situation in individuals' behaviour. Philip Zimbardo designed a mock prison in the basement of Stanford University and placed an advertisement looking for volunteers to participate in his research. Twenty-four male volunteers were selected: 12 guards and 12 prisoners. These volunteers were judged to be emotionally stable and with no prior history of criminal behaviour. Zimbardo told the 'wardens' that they were allowed to run the prison as they saw fit; there was only one rule: that there was to be no physical punishment. The wardens were dressed in military-style clothing and mirrored sunglasses to limit eye contact, and were given wooden batons. Those volunteers assigned to 'prisoner' role were told to stay at home and wait to be called. Then their homes were raided and they were arrested by real policemen (the local police force had agreed to co-operate with the research); they were finger-printed and stripped. They were then transported to the 'prison' where they were to spend the next two weeks during the experiment. The prisoners were dressed in smock-like clothing and given identity numbers rather than their names and were supplied with a basic mattress and plain food. As you can see, great efforts were made to make the experiment as lifelike as possible. What happened next was quite shocking, as Zimbardo and Haney (1998, p.709) recount:

> Otherwise emotionally strong college students who were randomly assigned to be mock-prisoners suffered acute psychological trauma and breakdowns. Some of the students begged to be released from the intense pains of less than a week of merely simulated imprisonment, whereas others adapted by becoming blindly obedient to the unjust authority of the guards. The guards, too – who also had been carefully chosen on the basis of their normal-average scores on a variety of personality measures, quickly internalized their

randomly assigned role. Many of these seemingly gentle and caring young men, some of whom had described themselves as pacifists or Vietnam War 'doves,' soon began mistreating their peers and were indifferent to the obvious suffering that their actions produced. Several of them devised sadistically inventive ways to harass and degrade the prisoners, and none of the less actively cruel mock-guards ever intervened or complained about the abuses they witnessed. Most of the worst prisoner treatment came on the night shifts and other occasions when the guards thought they could avoid the surveillance and interference of the research team. Our planned two-week experiment had to be aborted after only six days because the experience dramatically and painfully transformed most of the participants in ways we did not anticipate, prepare for, or predict.

What appears to be clear from this study is that if individuals are placed in defined roles they will behave accordingly. Many criticisms of this piece of research have been raised, including ethical ones, which are discussed in Chapter 11, and there were also issues regarding the volunteers. Carnahan and McFarland (2007, p.603) have suggested that it was participant self-selection that led to the cruelty witnessed in the Stanford Prison experiment (SPE). The authors set out to investigate 'whether students who selectively volunteer for a study of prison life possess dispositions associated with behaving abusively. Students were recruited for a psychological study of prison life using a virtually identical newspaper advertisement to that used in the Stanford Prison experiment; . . . volunteers for the prison study scored significantly higher on measures of the abuse, elated dispositions of aggressiveness, authoritarianism, Machiavellianism, narcissism, and social dominance and lower on empathy and altruism, two qualities inversely related to aggressive abuse. Although implications for the SPE remain a matter of conjecture, an interpretation in terms of person-situation interactionism rather than a strict situationist account is indicated by these findings.' Zimbardo and Haney (1998, p.710) have rejected this explanation, countering, 'the negative, anti-social reactions observed were not the product of an environment created by combining a collection of deviant personalities, but rather the result of an intrinsically pathological situation which could distort and rechannel the behaviour of essentially normal individuals. The abnormality here resided in the psychological nature of the situation and not in those who passed through it.' Regardless of what viewpoint you choose to take this piece of research is considered relevant, including in discussions regarding American soldiers' behaviour in Abu Ghraib, which saw the torture and humiliation of prisoners by their guards.

Conformity and obedience

Norms can influence behaviour only if people conform to them. Without conformity – the adjustment of individual behaviours, attitudes and beliefs to a group standard – some suggest we would have social chaos. Two main hypotheses have been suggested as to why people conform:

- *Normative social influence* – we conform to obtain rewards that come from being accepted by other people, while at the same time avoiding their rejection.
- *Informational social influence* – we may conform to the opinions and behaviours of other people because we believe they have accurate knowledge and what they are doing is 'right'.

Soloman Asch's (1951, 1956) conformity experiments

Factors that affect conformity

1. Group size: conformity increased from about 5 to 35 per cent as group size increased from one to four confederates, but contrary to common sense, further increases in group size did not increase conformity.
2. Presence of a dissenter: When one confederate (according to the plan) disagreed with the others, this greatly reduced real participants' conformity. Apparently when someone dissents, this person serves as a model for remaining independent from the group.

Obedience to authority

Milgram's study (1974) of the dilemma of obedience, when conscience confronted Malevolent Authority, demonstrates the familiar cry of 'I was only following orders'. The gist of the study was that participants were instructed to administer electric shocks to other people even though they screamed and begged for them not to. Sixty-five per cent of participants obeyed the instructor's orders.

Factors that influence destructive obedience

- remoteness of the victim
- closeness and legitimacy of the authority figure
- cog in a wheel syndrome
- personal characteristics.

Milgram concluded that 'often, it is not so much the kind of person a man is as the kind of situation in which he finds himself that determines how he will act' (1974, p.205).

Group interaction and dynamics

Crowd behaviour and deindividuation

In New York several years ago, a man was perched on the ledge of a building threatening to jump. A crowd of nearly 500 people gathered below chanted at him to jump. Leon Mann (1981) found that in 10 of 21 cases where a person threatened to jump, the crowd had encouraged the person to jump.

A process of deindividuation, where a loss of individuality leads to disinhibited behaviour, has been implicated. This process has been applied to diverse types of antisocial behaviour, from cheating and stealing to riots and acts of genocide. Key to deindividuation is the anonymity to outsiders; conditions which make an individual less identifiable to people outside the group reduces feelings of accountability.

PREJUDICE

What is prejudice? Is it a social phenomenon with cognitive, affective and behavioural components, or rather is prejudice an affective component, stereotyping the cognitive, and discrimination a behavioural response with all three components making up the whole? Personally I prefer the latter approach to considering prejudice.

Research in the area of prejudice began in earnest in the 1940s and 1950s and was characterised by an emphasis on the individual in the creation and perpetuation of prejudice. The authoritarian personality theory emphasised the individual, reflecting the popularity of Freud, and was influenced by the anti-Semitism witnessed to such great effect in the Holocaust. It maintained that prejudice was the result of a parenting style rather than a class model, even though it maintained that working-class parents with aspirations towards middle-class conventions demanded blind submission to authority and adherence to convention and tradition. Children brought up under this parenting style became adults who internalised this hostility and directed it against any grouping viewed as non-traditional or different.

By the 1960s this approach had fallen from favour to be replaced by the 'subtle racism' and 'dissociation' models. These models emphasised internal conflict between the consciousness and unconsciousness and between culturally learned and internalised values. Movement away from prejudice is the result of internalised egalitarian values triumphing over social learned responses. Another alternative has been advocated in an attempt to reduce prejudice, grounded in social change. This approach took a more cognitive, context-driven approach than its predecessors.

Categorisation became the key term in this approach to understanding the dynamics of prejudice. Categorisation has adaptive functions that have ensured its continuance; the categorisation of people allows us to attempt to predict their behaviour quickly. Further, the categorisation of both people and objects has enabled us to make sense of and adapt to our environments. These positive aspects of categorisation, however, appear to have come at a price, as categorisation can lay the foundations for prejudice and, from that, discrimination. In his *The Nature of Prejudice*, Allport was at the forefront in arguing for the role of social categorisation in prejudice and its solution through constructive inter-ethnic contact. Allport further argued that the capacity to categorise was inherent and quite normal. As we categorised chairs as furniture, we would categorise people as 'in-group' and 'out-group', and go one step further into loving one or hating the other. This assertion of Allport's has remained popular, though modified over time.

The 'us–them' attitude, or 'in-group' and 'out-group', has been studied in laboratory experiments and it has been established that common biases occur. In-group favouritism refers to the tendency to prefer and attribute more positive characteristics towards members of the 'in-group' and conversely to attribute negative traits to the 'out-group'. Further, people display an 'out-group homogeneity bias'; in-groups can recognise diversity within their own group but consider members of 'out-groups' as all the same, ignoring that many sub-groups exist. For example, when we identify an individual as Asian we ignore the many subgroups of Asians that exist. If one has a negative bias towards the 'out-group' it is more likely that these perceived group biases will be attributed towards an individual of that group. Pettigrew (1979) found that when a stereotype is challenged, that is, a member of the 'out-group' is seen to behave in a way that is opposite to that of the stereotype, this will be written off as an exceptional case or down to luck. For example, if an individual has a stereotype of women as passive and weak and is then confronted by a strong and independent woman they are likely to describe the woman as a 'feminist'. In the case of Margaret Thatcher, a commentator contended that she had more 'male' genes to explain her position of power and strength. In doing this the general stereotype remains intact.

Motivational aspects have been considered as possible roots of prejudice. Fein and Spencer (1997, in Passer, 2001) suggested those with poor self-esteem use prejudice against others in order to enhance their own self-esteem. The term 'social-identity theory' was coined to refer to this phenomenon. Another motivational factor considered was the realistic-conflict theory forwarded by Pettigrew. This view maintained that in times of economic hardship and scarcity intense competition for limited resources leads to prejudice.

Attempts to reduce prejudice

Fiske (1998) maintains that since the 1970s social psychological research has assumed the importance of information or the lack of it as a facilitator of prejudice. Certainly information can aid the breaking down of misinformed and negative stereotypes, but another approach taken to reduce prejudice has its origins arguably in Allport's work.

The contact hypothesis, as its name suggests, advocates contact to challenge negative and prejudicial stereotypes. Race is one of the most powerful categories an individual is placed in, and it is frequently the grounds upon which prejudice is formed. The contact hypothesis can be seen potently in the desegregation of schools in America in the 1950s. Until the 1954 judgment of the American Supreme Court that segregation violated African-Americans' constitutional rights, black children had been segregated from white children. Testimony in the case from psychologists maintained that segregation was damaging the outcomes and self-esteem of African-Americans, and further that it increased hostility and prejudice. Did contact decrease prejudice? Studies have been divided, though overall the results appear to be disappointing. Stephan's (1990, as cited in Paluck and Green, 2009) review of 80 evaluation studies of desegregation programmes involving African-American and Caucasian children concluded that direct contact had not appeared to reduce prejudice. Only 13 per cent reported a reduction in prejudice among whites while 53 per cent actually reported an increase.

Several possible explanations could lie behind this result and need to be taken into account in attempting to reduce prejudice through the contact hypothesis. Firstly, both groups should be of equal status, as this has been found effective in reducing prejudice. 'One-on-one' interactions by members from the groups challenges 'out-group homogeneity bias', as an individual often confronts the group stereotype that has been attached; sub-grouping is also more clearly recognised. When groups are forced to work together towards some common goal, results appear to suggest this to be effective in breaking down the stereotypes that lead to prejudice.

Sherif *et al.*'s (1961) research entitled 'the robber cave experiment' is an example of this principle at work and also arguably of the realistic conflict theory. A group of 11-year-old boys was divided by researchers into two groups which were given the names 'the Eagles' and 'the Rattlesnakes'. While they lived in different cabins, the groups took part in activities together and were getting along well until an element of competition was introduced into the activities they were taking part in. Very quickly hostility and conflict began and prejudice was seen with members of both groups now refusing to form friendships with members from the other group. Researchers attempted to reduce this hostility and prejudice by increasing contact through activities, but increased contact was found to increase the hostility. Finally, hostility and prejudice was reduced by forcing both groups to co-operate in order to achieve mutually beneficial goals. This type of co-operative learning programme has found great favour in school settings.

In defence of the findings of Stephan, the findings must be considered in light of the importance of support by social norms; that is, that significant others also share the same goal orientation. For example, the poor result reported by Stephan could be a reflection of the views held by many of the white children's parents, who remained racist and thus at odds with the aims of desegregation.

Another approach theorised by social psychologists to reduce prejudice is that of 'interactive problem solving'. This has been applied in an attempt to reduce inter-group conflict and has been utilised in the new field of international conflict resolution. Both these approaches emphasise a more inter-group conflict approach in reducing prejudice.

Of course, all these hypotheses and theories have an aim: to construct effective methods to reduce prejudice and discrimination. One such piece of work was conducted by Margo Monteith (1993), who devised a programme that attempted to reduce prejudice against gay people. Monteith describes the common phenomenon of prejudice-related discrepancies. These are responses that are more prejudiced than an individual's personal standards for responding suggest are appropriate. Monteith concludes this to be unsettling when an individual has a genuinely internalised low-prejudiced (LP) belief. Monteith tested individuals with low prejudice and results indicated that 'low-prejudiced subjects' violations of their LP and well-internalised attitudes produced compunction, self- and discrepancy-focused thoughts, attention to discrepancy-relevant information and a slowing of responses' (p.469). Monteith found self-regulation to be effective and insists that the modern fatalistic idea that prejudice is inevitable due to the evolutionary nature of categorisation is flawed. She points to this study and its findings regarding self-regulation as a way forward in attempts to reduce prejudice. Is prejudice learned, therefore? One can ask the same of aggressive and prosocial behaviour. This section will explore these behaviours and the theories that attempt to explain them.

AGGRESSIVE AND PROSOCIAL BEHAVIOUR

Why do some people help others, sometimes at great risk to themselves and for no apparent benefit, while others display aggressive and antisocial behaviours? Are genes to answer, or the family environment we are raised in, our peer group or perhaps our culture? Many researchers have grappled with these issues. Both behaviours have very practical consequences and implications for our understanding of human nature.

What is prosocial behaviour?

The term refers to helping, caring, sharing, co-operation and sympathy (Hay, 1994). What processes or influences motivate prosocial behaviour? The empathy-altruism hypothesis was proposed by C. Daniel Batson. Empathy refers to the ability to put oneself in the place of another and to share what that person is experiencing, while altruism relates to the desire to help another without concern for oneself.

Hoffman identified four stages in the development of empathy (Hoffman, 1987, cited in Schaffer, 1999, p.271):

Stage 1: global empathy begins at the start of the first year. The baby does not see others as distinct and separate from themselves; therefore, the baby behaves as though what has happened to another has actually befallen them.

Stage 2: egocentric empathy starts in the second year. The child is now aware that it is a separate entity but continues to internalise the other's state.

Stage 3: empathy for another's feelings is found in children between the age of two to three years. The child now recognises that others have distinct feelings.

Stage 4: empathy for another's life condition is the final stage in the development of empathy and is seen in early childhood. Here affect (feelings) is twinned with mental representation of the other's general condition. Thus, a concern for others in the form of an emotional response or behaviour can be seen from the second year onwards.

Bystander intervention

One of the best known phenomena in social psychology, 'bystander effect', was identified by John Darley and Bibb Latané (1968) in the aftermath of the murder of Kitty Genovese. Kitty Genovese arrived home to the block of apartments where she lived in New York, and suffered an attack there which lasted for over half an hour. Despite her screams for help and the fact that allegedly 38 witnesses admitted to hearing her screams, it took 30 minutes before anyone called the police. This tragic case illustrates what has come to be known as the 'bystander effect'; the more people are present the less likely an individual is to act, the inference being that they are waiting for, or expect, another to act instead. Can you remember the radio announcements warning of gas leaks in the street? In the announcement you are asked to phone Bord Gáis to alert them to the leak; 'don't assume that someone else has already reported it'. This message highlights the phenomenon that people are less likely to act if others are present, and that the more people present the less likely it is that an individual will act themselves.

Social exchange theory

- We want to maximise our benefits and minimise our costs:
  - we examine the costs and rewards of helping and not helping
- Three rewards of helping:
  - reciprocity: they will owe us when we need help (or at least it eventually balances out)
  - relieves distress: we don't like to see others suffer
  - social approval.

Other different theoretical approaches to understanding prosocial behaviour consider the possible influence of nature (biology, genetics) and nurture (culture) elements.

Genetics

While genetic influences can help explain acts of prosocial behaviour towards family members according to the principle of kin selection (Buck and Ginsberg, 1991), this does not explain examples of this behaviour towards non-kin. Sociobiologists have suggested the concept of reciprocal altruism; that one helps another in the belief that this will increase the likelihood of help being received (Trivers, 1971). This obviously does not satisfactorily explain differences in prosocial behaviour. Evidence has also been found in studies of identical twins and fraternal twins pointing to the greater similarity of the behaviour in the former compared to the latter (Rushton *et al.*, 1986).

Culture

Cultural differences have been proposed as an explanation for the development and individualisation of prosocial behaviours. Beatrice and John Whiting (1975) conducted studies of 3–10 year olds in six small communities in the Philippines, America, Mexico, India, Kenya and Japan. They found that Kenyan, Philippino and Mexican children scored highest on altruistic behaviours, with the American children scoring lowest. A possible explanation for this result is that children from poorer backgrounds have more child-minding and other responsibilities as the mother often has to work in the fields. These children can witness the importance and genuine contribution altruism makes to their survival and that of their family. American culture tends to be more individualistic and the importance of altruism is not as pressing. Hindus were found to feel more obligated to behave prosocially than their American counterparts (Miller *et al.*, 1990), which gives another aspect to the cultural influence.

Aggressive behaviour

In recent times increasing numbers of people seem to hold the opinion that our society is becoming more violent. Particular concern has been voiced regarding the behaviour of pre-teens and adolescents. Psychologists have forwarded many explanations for the development of aggressive behaviour. First we need to clarify what aggression is and difficulties inherent in defining it.

Problems with defining aggression

To define aggression creates many difficulties, especially when dealing with intentionality. If a person does harm when under the influence of drugs, does this differ from the actions of a soldier on the battlefield? If a child pulls a toy away from another because they want to play with it and the other child is hurt in the process, did the child intentionally mean to cause harm?

There appears to be a schism in how the study of aggression is approached; whether aggression is defined by intentionality or by result.

Schaffer (1996, p.279) suggests dividing the categories of aggression into:

- hostile aggression, where the intention of the act is to harm another
- instrumental hostility, which could be used in the example of the child and the toy, where the action is aggressive but the motivation is non-aggressive.

Distinction is also helpful especially when dealing with gender difference between physical aggression and relational (relationships) aggression. Research into relational aggression is helpful in explaining the differences in levels of aggression between boys and girls and perhaps presenting a more complete picture of female aggression. Thus far gender difference has been accredited to hormonal and socialisation differences.

In the past adult aggressive behaviours were studied without reference to childhood aggressive behaviours. It has now been proposed that aggressive behaviour in childhood can become stable and persist into adulthood.

Eron's studies

One of the most influential studies relating to the stability of aggression was carried out by Eron *et al.*, (1971), sampling 600 eight year olds over a period of 22 years. The children were first rated at eight years of age, based on peer perception and their own perception of their aggression. Researchers contacted the sample again (modal age 19) and managed to re-interview 427 of the original group. Eron reported that one of the most impressive findings was the stability of the aggression over time, and also noted that intellectual ability was negatively related to aggressive behaviour. Finally, Eron and his team contacted the sample (modal age 30) and re-interviewed 295 of the group in person and 114 by mail. They also interviewed the spouses and children of some of the sample. What they discovered was the continued stability of aggression but also that those who displayed aggressive behaviour as children were, as parents, more likely to punish their own children severely and be aggressive towards their spouses. Eron concluded that: 'By the time the child is 8 years old, characteristic ways of behaving aggressively or non-aggressively have already been established' (1971, p.34).

Farrington (1991) supports this study through his similar research in England and found that with males, aggressiveness in mid-childhood was an important predictor of antisocial activities in adulthood.

Theories of aggression

Many theories have been forwarded in an attempt to shed light on the determinants of aggressive behaviour.

Cognitive: It has been argued that aggressive children have a greater inability to solve problems on a cognitive level and also to understand others' intentions and motives, resulting in an inappropriate aggressive response.

Temperament and emotional regulation: Children who are reported by their parents as having difficult temperaments are more likely to experience behavioural problems and aggressiveness (Kingston and Prior, 1995). Naturally the parent–child relationship would have to be factored into the parents' perception that their child was difficult.

Parenting and family environment: The family environment and relationships, as witnessed with Eron's findings, play an influential role in the development of aggressiveness. Several types of parenting have been associated with increased levels of aggressive in children (see Olweus' types of parenting style in Chapter 4).

Culture: Cultural factors have a part to play in the development of aggression and its maintenance. The Great Whale River Eskimos' emphasis on peace and abhorrence of violence and aggressiveness is reflected in their child-rearing practice, where they actively discourage aggressive behaviour (Honigmann and Honigmann, 1954); whilst in other cultures and subcultures toughness and aggressiveness are behaviours often revered and encouraged.

From the perspective of social psychology, the following theories have been advanced:

Ethological
Lorenz's ethological theory posits that humans are inherently or naturally aggressive and have learned ways to control these tendencies. Lorenz emphasised the evolutionary value of aggressiveness with regard to survival. Kalikow (2000) outlines that, in *On Aggression* (1966), Lorenz claimed that intraspecies aggression, normally an adaptive phenomenon in animals, has turned deadly in humans because our development of new weapons that can kill at a distance has outrun our innate inhibition against killing.

Social learning
In Chapter 2 Bandura's theory of social learning was examined. Bandura argues in his social-learning theory that humans *learn* to aggress. Bandura's research was centred on children's imitation of aggression, particularly from those they admire. Bandura witnessed this in his study of hyper-aggressive boys. Further research confirmed to Bandura that we learn to aggress through social learning, that is, through modelling by others. Bandura found that parental modelling of aggressive behaviours played a significant role in the familial transmission of aggression. However, Bandura's main interest lay in the role of violence on television in the development of aggression.

The Bobo experiment
In order to test his idea that children copy and imitate violence, Bandura designed an experiment to clarify the processes governing observational learning. In basic terms, children watched a programme where an adult continually hit a life-size doll (Bobo doll). The children were then left in a room with a Bobo doll and their behaviour was observed. It was found that the majority of children copied what they had previously seen on the television; they hit the Bobo doll as they had seen the adult do. This confirmed for Bandura the relationship between violence on television and its imitation by children.

Bandura identified four major effects of exposure to televised violence. It can

- teach novel aggressive styles of conduct
- weaken restraints over interpersonal aggression by legitimising, glamorising and trivialising violent conduct
- desensitise and habituate viewers to human cruelty
- shape public images of reality.

Bandura relates that the television industry launched an attack on his findings and the suggestion that television was responsible for encouraging violence and aggressive behavior in children. This issue was taken so seriously that the American Congress convened a special committee to examine the issue in closer detail (the Surgeon General's Scientific Advisory Committee on Television and Social Behavior, 1972). Because this is such a pertinent issue, especially with the increased television viewing of children and access to video games (some quite violent), we are going to delve into this topic a little more.

The role of media in violence

- 60–70 per cent of all TV programmes contain violence
- 70–80 per cent show no remorse, criticism, or penalty for the violence
- by the time the average American child graduates from elementary school they have witnessed on TV
  - more than 8,000 murders
  - more than 100,000 other acts of violence (e.g., assaults, rape)
- more recently, video games have become children's favourite form of media
  - 90 per cent of children age 2–17 play regularly
- the majority of popular games are violent

The American Psychological Association outline the following issues they identify in the role of television and video games in aggression.

- Decades of social science research reveals the strong influence of televised violence on the aggressive behavior of children and youth.
- Psychological research reveals that the electronic media play an important role in the development of attitude, emotion, social behavior and intellectual functioning of children and youth.
- There appears to be evidence that exposure to violent media increases feelings of hostility, thoughts about aggression, suspicions about the motives of others, and demonstrates violence as a method to deal with potential conflict situations.
- Perpetrators go unpunished in 73% of all violent scenes, and therefore teach that violence is an effective means of resolving conflict. Only 16% of all programs portrayed negative psychological or financial effects, yet such visual depictions of pain and suffering can actually inhibit aggressive behavior in viewers.
- Comprehensive analysis of violent interactive video game research suggests such exposure:

a) increases aggressive behavior
b) increases aggressive thoughts
c) increases angry feelings
d) decreases helpful behavior
e) increases physiological arousal

- Studies further suggest that sexualized violence in the media has been linked to increases in violence towards women, rape myth acceptance and anti-women attitudes. Research on interactive video games suggests that the most popular video games contain aggressive and violent content; depict women and girls, men and boys, and minorities in exaggerated stereotypical ways; and reward, glamorize and depict as humorous sexualized aggression against women, including assault, rape and murder.

- The characteristics of violence in interactive video games appear to have similar detrimental effects as viewing television violence; however based upon learning theory (Bandura, 1977; Berkowitz, 1993), the practice, repetition, and rewards for acts of violence may be more conducive to increasing aggressive behavior among children and youth than passively watching violence on TV and in films. With the development of more sophisticated interactive media, such as virtual reality, the implications for violent content are of further concern, due to the intensification of more realistic experiences, and may also be more conducive to increasing aggressive behavior than passively watching violence on TV and in films.

- Studies further suggest that video games influence the learning processes in many ways more than in passively observing TV:
  a) requiring identification of the participant with a violent character while playing video games
  b) actively participating increases learning
  c) rehearsing entire behavioral sequences rather than only a part of the sequence facilitates learning
  d) repetition increases learning.

- The data dealing with media literacy curricula demonstrate that when children are taught how to view television critically, there is a reduction of TV viewing in general, and a clearer understanding of the messages conveyed by the medium. Studies on media literacy demonstrate when children are taught how to view television critically, children can feel less frightened and sad after discussions about the medium, can learn to differentiate between fantasy and reality, and can identify less with aggressive characters on TV, and better understand commercial messages.

Source: www.apa.org

This synopsis doesn't outline methodological or other weaknesses of the research that was considered in drafting these points; as always, when reading any finding one should use a critical eye. However, many psychologists would feel strongly that there is a plethora of evidence illustrating the powerful link between media and violence. Sometimes I can't help but feel that it is common sense; surely it is not a good idea for children and teenagers to watch and interact with violent games detached from any kind of reality. With the increasing popularity of games such as *Grand Theft Auto*, which includes having sex with prostitutes and then murdering them and stealing money back, what kind of message are we sending out? I think it's only fair that I am clear that I support the position taken by the APA, so I can be accused of bias in this issue. Of course, aggression, as with all things, is a complex issue with many different factors at play; nonetheless, the role of media as a powerful factor is difficult to dispute. There are those who feel that the relationship is exaggerated and this is harmless entertainment. Naturally it is up to you what you think is the relationship between television and video games and aggression. Look at evidence and weigh it up in forming your opinion.

Representation and portrayal of people with disabilities in Irish broadcasting

The following piece is an example of stereotyping at play in the media and the representations created and ascribed to individuals. In this particular piece of research, the National Disability Authority (NDA) note that researchers were able to assign the representation of individuals with disabilities to more than one of the 11 stereotype categories employed in the research. Hence, although there were 88 individuals with disabilities in the programme sample, the researchers noted 119 instances of stereotyping. In 23 of the 88 representations (26 per cent of the total), no stereotype was noted. The stereotype categories were:

- pitiable and pathetic; sweet and innocent; a miracle cure
- victim or an object of violence
- sinister or evil
- faking injury; lazy
- atmosphere – curios or exotica
- 'super-crip'/ triumph over tragedy/noble warrior
- laughable or the butt of jokes
- having a chip on their shoulder/aggressive avenger
- a burden/outcast
- non-sexual or incapable of a worthwhile relationship
- incapable of fully participating in everyday life.

Think about the last time you saw a person with a disability in the media. Do you agree that there is a tendency to ascribe stereotypes to people? When was the last movie you saw that portrayed a person with disability, and how were they portrayed?

For more information: www.nda.ie

SUMMARY

In this chapter social psychology is described as studying social influence, thinking and behaviour. Issues such as prejudice, discrimination and social roles have an immediate relevance in the field of social care. A study of some of the concepts addressed in this chapter should provide an opportunity to reflect on how we perceive others and relate to them.

10
Counselling

The aim of this chapter is to provide a brief introduction to the theories of three of the leading psychotherapeutic approaches: Freudian (psychoanalytic), Rogers (humanist/person-centred therapy) and cognitive behavioural therapy (CBT). Other approaches do exist, such as Gestalt, reality and existential therapy, and many therapists will use an amalgam of these approaches in their practice. To be clear, this introduction is not meant to be exhaustive nor does it equip an individual to become a counsellor. Rather, you will learn through the counselling theories outlined and the skills suggested how to support service users. After dealing with the theory, we will look at issues including the role of the counsellor and ethical considerations. Research including the use of psychotherapy with children in care and the efficacy of counselling will be considered. Finally, we will examine practical applications, such as interpersonal skills and the provision of person-centred social care.

Freud and psychoanalysis

Before reading this section on Freud, it is preferable to have read the section on Freud in Chapter 3 where his conceptualisation of personality, psychosexual development and defence mechanisms are discussed.

Freud is credited by many as the founder or father of psychotherapy. He certainly developed what one of his clients described as the 'talking cure', or what we in the present day would term psychotherapy or counselling. Freud's approach is referred to as 'psychoanalysis', capturing the analytical nature of the interaction between therapist and client. Freud's theories have fallen from grace, reflecting perhaps an unease with the sexual elements of his theory. His formulations surrounding psychosexual stages, including the Oedipal and Electra complexes, have been rejected by many, including his followers, such as Carl Jung and Erik Erikson. However, to disregard the work and importance of Freud would be a mistake. The idea of an unconscious is widely accepted and key concepts such as defence mechanisms are prominent in psychotherapeutic work. Certainly, his assertion that early experiences affect our later development and the importance of the parental relational bond are cornerstones of psychological discourse. Perhaps the best thing to do is to decide for yourself what you think of his work and its relevance.

Freud's early years were to prove instrumental in his development of psychoanalysis. He was influenced by the work of Janet and Charcot, who demonstrated the use of hypnosis. This suggested to Freud that the emotional distress he was witnessing in his clients had its roots in the unconscious, and in order to alleviate the distress the unconscious must be accessed. He developed techniques to access and interpret the unconscious, including dream interpretation, free association and transference, which we will look at more closely below. His work as a psychiatrist dealing with women suffering from 'hysteria' was pivotal to the development of his ideas. Freud found that the symptoms of hysteria eased once the women had reported unpleasant and frightening sexual experiences. Freud conceptualised that these childhood sexual experiences, which he did not believe had actually occurred in reality, were the result of the individual's own childhood sexual needs (libido or sexual energy). This energy passes through the psychosexual stages: oral, anal, phallic, latent and genital, as discussed in Chapter 3. If the individual does not successfully transition through a stage they become 'fixated', and this leads to psychopathology in later life.

Another potential area for psychopathology was in the development of personality, which involved three structures: the id, the ego and the superego. The id is the only element present at birth and is governed by the 'pleasure principle', the ego as it develops is governed by the 'reality principle' and is the rational part of personality development. Finally, the superego or conscience reflects the input of familial and cultural moral mores which shape the individual's sense of morality. Healthy personality development, according to Freud, is based on the resolution of psychosexual and psychosocial issues at the appropriate stages. Unsuccessful resolution such as fixation, or not meeting a critical development task, leads to psychopathology. Anxiety (Hall, 1962, as cited in Passer, 2001) is a painful emotional experience resulting from internal or external stimulation. When the ego is unable to produce realistic coping mechanisms in times of anxiety it resorts to what Freud termed 'defence mechanisms' to relieve the anxiety in a safe manner by denying, distorting or falsifying reality. A number of defence mechanisms exist, including repression, projection, reaction formation, denial, displacement and regression, and these are covered in Chapter 3.

The Freudian approach is considered to be deterministic, meaning that a person's development is determined by factors over which they have no control and certainly no free will. As outlined in Chapter 3, Freud believed that human nature was motivated by irrational forces, unconscious elements and instinctual drives (such as the id). Freud had followers who disagreed with aspects of his theory, especially the psychosexual elements, and broke away. These include Carl Jung (his approach is analytical psychology) and Erik Erikson (psychosocial approach). Those who followed Freud are often described as neo-Freudian and consider social and cultural factors in development. Other important figures include Margaret Mahler and her theory of 'object relations' and Bowlby, who was a member of the British Psychoanalytical Society until he was expelled by Freud's daughter, Anna. A distinction between Freud and his followers is that Freud's focus was on the 'id', whereas those who followed are often labelled 'ego psychologists' as they are more interested in this element of development.

Therapeutic relationship and techniques

As referred to earlier, several techniques were employed by Freud to bring repressed material to the surface in order for the client to gain a better insight into their difficulties and allow for personality reorganisation. The main techniques in psychoanalysis included:

- relationship between therapist and client
- free association
- analysis of resistance and transference
- dream analysis.

Relationship between therapist and client

The relationship between therapist and client offers opportunities for the therapist to understand the roots of the client's difficulties. In traditional psychoanalytic practice the therapist sits with their back to the client who lies on a chaise longue or couch, so that the therapist can remain a blank slate on which the client can 'project' their true feelings, desires and assumptions. It is through this process that the client will increasingly project their feelings of repressed anger or despair towards others (for example, parents, authority figures) onto the therapist. If the client behaves in a disgruntled way towards the therapist, this could indicate that this is how the client behaves towards others. Transference and counter transference also involve the therapist–client relationship. Transference is when the client redirects their feelings from a significant other onto the therapist. Examples of transference can include erotic feelings towards the client, as happened in one of Freud's earliest cases, or feelings of anger, distrust or dependency. Freud came to realise that analysis of the transference relationship allowed him to explore the meaning behind it, which aided the client's treatment. Counter-transference involves the redirection of a therapist's feelings towards the client; in other words, it is when a therapist becomes emotionally entangled with a client. For example, a client might remind the therapist of an important figure and this can affect how the therapist relates to the client. Or as happened to Freud, the therapist can develop sexual feelings for the client. In research conducted by Pope and Tabachnik (1993), 87 per cent of therapists reported having been sexually attracted to at least one if not more of their clients.

Free association

This involves saying whatever comes into the mind; if hesitation occurs in responding, the therapist interprets this as significant as it indicates that the unconscious is attempting to block material from coming into consciousness.

Dream analysis

This technique can allow the therapist to gain access to deeper parts of the client's personality through unlocking and interpreting the meaning of their dreams and fantasies. Dreams symbolically represent the client's inner feelings, motivations and desires.

Traditional psychoanalysis is not commonly practised nowadays as it involves seeing the psychoanalyst every day or at least three times a week. This is not only a time-consuming endeavour for most but a costly one, making it almost prohibitive. Further, the therapist doesn't talk much during the session, only occasionally offering an interpretation if required. From Freud's initial approach of psychoanalysis have come others branches of psychotherapy. An umbrella term that can be used for these branches is psychodynamic psychotherapy, which refers to therapy that uses some of the same theories and principles of psychoanalysis but differs in the techniques and the client–therapist relationship. With this approach, the therapist sits face-to-face with the client; the therapist will talk and the process is far more interactive. Clients will generally see their therapist once a week. While the unconscious is considered, it is not given the same importance as in psychoanalysis. Other issues including social and cultural factors are taken into account in formulating the roots of the client's difficulties.

Strengths and limitations of the psychoanalytic approach

Aspects of Freud's theory have been adopted by other therapists in their work with clients. The importance of defence mechanisms is recognised as are the concepts of transference and counter-transference. Essentially, Freud has offered a comprehensive system of personality and cemented the role of the unconscious in behaviour. Most importantly, his theory emphasises the profound effect of childhood development on later development.

Limitations of the psychoanalytic approach include not just the expense but the long-term nature of this type of counselling, which is particularly unsuited to crisis counselling. Further, in classic psychoanalysis the role of culture and social factors are not considered, making this approach unsuitable for work with culturally diverse client groups or in social work. Freud's formulation was based on his work with neurotic people; he generalised his observations to others. Further, it is very hard to scientifically test many of Freud's central concepts, which by modern standards is considered a weakness.

In a review of studies examining the effectiveness of long-term psychoanalytic therapy (including psychodynamic therapies which are rooted in psychoanalytic theory), de Maat et al. (2009) found that this form of therapy was effective for a large range of pathologies with success rates of up to 71 per cent.

As we have seen, Freud can rightly be seen as the father of the talking cure, however, his psychoanalytic formulation of therapy was to fall from favour and was replaced by newer approaches, one of which was developed by Carl Rogers.

Carl Rogers and person-centred therapy

While Freud's approach to psychotherapy was deterministic, Rogers rejected this view of human nature, believing in the inherent goodness of humans and their desire to move towards self-actualisation (see Chapter 3). Rogers' formulation of a more humanistic therapy was a reaction against Freud's psychoanalytic approach. In keeping with the tenets of humanism, Rogers wished to develop a therapy that emphasised the client's own resources for becoming self-aware. Rogers believed that the client had the capacity for self-growth and to resolve obstacles to achieving this growth. With this form of therapy, the therapist does not 'direct' the client, instead believing the client has the personal 'resources' or capacity to become aware of the obstacles that exist in their life. The role of the therapist is supportive rather than directive. In his seminal book *On Becoming a Person*, Rogers says: 'It is the client who knows what hurts, what directions to go, what problems are crucial, what experiences have been deeply buried.'

One of the most important tenets of Rogers' theory was the quality of the client–therapist relationship. Studies continue to find that the most important variable in therapy outcomes is the client–therapist relationship. Qualities in the therapist that affect this relationship include empathy, congruence (genuineness), unconditional acceptance and respect for the client. Unlike the psychoanalytic approach, Rogerian therapy does not rely on techniques as such, rather emphasis is placed on the client–therapist relationship and creation of an atmosphere of trust, warmth and security which will enable the client to explore the difficulties they are experiencing. If techniques do exist, it could be argued that these involve listening skills, reflection of feelings and clarification. Another difference to Freud's approach is the emphasis placed on the 'here and now' rather than exclusively focusing on childhood events and relationships. Rogers' approach in therapy considers the client's sense of self as crucial. As discussed in Chapter 3, the self is the reference point for how an individual perceives the world and behaviour and also for self-evaluation. Divergence can exist between an individual's sense of self and reality; a person who is perceived by others as successful and competent may privately suffer from self-loathing or low self-esteem. Anxiety is created when a gulf exists between reality and self-concept. Self-evaluation plays a key role in Rogers' therapeutic discourse and is tied to self-esteem through the approval we look for from others, such as parents or friends. Thus, psychological difficulties can manifest as a result of having suppressed inner needs in order to try to satisfy the perceived standards of such dependency figures. The goal of therapy from this perspective is the awareness of inner desires in order to 'self-actualise'.

The following terms are instrumental to Rogers' theory and his therapeutic work:

- congruence
- empathy
- unconditional positive regard
- presence.

Rogers considered congruence or genuineness of vital importance. Unlike psychoanalysis where the therapist remains a blank slate for the client to project onto, the Rogerian therapist allows the client to see the 'real' them as they really are. In other words, the therapist's internal and external experiences are the same; the therapist is authentic.

Empathy is seeing the client's world as they do, of having a subjective understanding of the client. According to Rogers, empathic understanding is:

> If I am truly open to the way life is experienced by another person, . . . if I can take his or her world into mine, then I risk seeing life in his or her way . . . and of being changed myself, and we all resist change. Since we all resist change, we tend to view the other person's world only in our terms, not in his or hers. Then we analyse and evaluate it. We do not understand their world. But, when the therapist does understand how it truly feels to be in another person's world, without wanting or trying to analyse or judge it, then the therapist and the client can truly blossom and grow in that climate. (Rogers, 1961)

Unconditional positive regard is the expression of fundamental respect for the person as a human being. The therapist accepts the individual's right to their feelings.

Presence is the capacity to 'be with' the client fully and in the moment or present. The therapist is engaged and immersed in the relationship with the client.

Strengths and limitations of person-centred therapy

The greatest strength of Rogers' person-centred therapy is the importance he places on the client–therapist relationship. Studies have found that this relationship and the quality of it is one of the most important variables in determining the outcome of therapy. This approach recognises the inner and subjective world of the client and emphasises the importance of the 'person' within the therapeutic dynamic rather than therapeutic techniques or outcomes.

As this approach is so non-directive, the therapist engages in mirroring back content; for example, if a client says she hates men because of a relationship breakdown, a Rogerian therapist will mirror back what she has said: 'So you hate all men.' A potential criticism of this technique is that it brings little of the therapist's own self into the relationship. Also, the past is not considered particularly relevant, with the emphasis on the present, which can be viewed as a shortcoming when dealing with certain clients or contexts.

Ask yourself

What factors might interfere with your being genuine with a service-user? Person-centred practice is of fundamental importance in social care work. Below we will examine the provision of person-centred care and the role of relationships in service-users' lives.

Cognitive behavioural therapy

Cognitive behavioural therapy (CBT) is a therapeutic approach that recognises the relationship between thinking patterns or systems (cognitive) and behaviour or action. In Chapter 3 we examined behaviourism, principles of reinforcement and learned behaviour, and saw the application of behaviourism to changing individual behaviour in the form of applied behavioural analysis (ABA). CBT is an umbrella term for therapies that use behavioural and cognitive techniques. To define CBT very simply, how we think about ourselves and situations determines how we feel, act and behave. Maladaptive or dysfunctional behaviour is the result of cognitive distortions or maladaptive thinking. CBT emphasises the ability of people to make changes in their lives without having to understand why the change occurs. This differs from the psychodynamic approach, which delves into the 'why'. With CBT, clients are give 'homework' to help them change. The popularity of CBT lies in its effectiveness but also in the brevity of treatment, which makes it less costly.

Two figures are associated with this style of therapy: Albert Ellis, who was the founder of an early form of this approach, called rational emotive behaviour therapy (REBT), and, more recently, Aaron Beck, who developed cognitive therapy. First let's examine the work of Albert Ellis.

Albert Ellis and rational emotive behaviour therapy

Though Ellis was originally a psychoanalyst, he became convinced that irrational thought processes, not unconscious forces, were responsible for maladaptive behaviour. Ellis believed that in challenging these irrational thoughts one could effect change and restore the person to healthy functioning. He devised an ABCD model in which his theory is reflected:

A Activating event that is the trigger
B Belief that is activated by A
C Consequences that follow the belief (these can be emotional and behavioural)
D Disputing or challenging the belief system to change the maladaptive consequences.

Dryden (1999) outlines that rational and irrational beliefs lie at the heart of REBT. Rational beliefs are associated with healthy psychological functioning. The primary goal of REBT is to enable clients to change their irrational beliefs to rational ones.

Dryden (1999) outlines the four basic types of irrational beliefs:

- demands
- awfulising or catastrophising beliefs
- low-frustration-tolerance (LFT) beliefs
- beliefs where the self, others and/or life conditions are depreciated.

The four contrasting types of rational beliefs are

- preferences
- anti-awfulising beliefs
- high-frustration-tolerance beliefs
- beliefs where the self, others and/or life conditions are accepted.

Irrational beliefs are defined through their inconsistency with reality; that is, they are illogical, which leads to unhealthy results for the individual. The role of the therapist is to challenge the irrational beliefs.

The following table illustrates the irrational ideas and the alternative or challenges that a rational-emotive therapist may offer:

Table 10.1: Irrational ideas that cause disturbance and alternatives that might be offered by a rational-emotive therapist

Irrational belief	Rational alternative
It is a dire necessity that I be loved and approved of by virtually everyone for everything I do.	Although we might prefer approval to disapproval, our self-worth need not depend on the love and approval of others. Self-respect is more important than giving up one's individuality to buy the approval of others.
I must be thoroughly competent and achieving to be worthwhile. To fail is to be a *failure*.	As imperfect and fallible human beings, we are bound to fail from time to time. We can control only effort; we have incomplete control over outcome. We are better off focusing on the process of doing rather than on demands that we do well.
It is terrible, awful and catastrophic when things are not the way I demand that they be.	Stop catastrophising and turning annoyance or irritation into a major crisis. Who are we to demand that things be different from what they are? When we turn our preferences into dire necessities, we set ourselves up for needless distress. We had best learn to change those things we can control and accept those that we can't control (and be wise enough to know the difference).
Human misery is externally caused and forced on us by other people and events.	Human misery is produced not by external factors but rather by what we tell ourselves about those events. We feel as we think, and most of our misery is needlessly self-inflicted by irrational habits of thinking.
Because something deeply affected me in the past, it must continue to do so.	We hold ourselves prisoner to the past because we continue to believe philosophies and ideas learned in the past. If they are still troubling us today, it is because we are still propagandising ourselves with irrational nonsense. We *can* control how we think in the present and thereby liberate ourselves from the 'scars' of the past.

Source: Passer and Smith, 2001, p.581

Aaron Beck and cognitive therapy

Aaron Beck, like Ellis, started his career as a psychoanalyst and also became disillusioned with the psychoanalytic approach. Beck, like Ellis, recognised the cognitive role (thought processes) in his client's continuing difficulties. Beck saw that his clients demonstrated self-critical cognitions and termed this maladaptive thinking 'automatic thoughts'.

Beck became convinced that emotional disturbances were the result, not of the actual event, but of the client's interpretation of it. For example, if I wave at a friend as I pass her by in my car and she doesn't reciprocate I would assume it was because she hadn't seen me. However, another person who might be depressed or suffering from low self-esteem might interpret that same situation as evidence that they were being ignored. So it is the interpretation that an individual ascribes to a situation that can cause the feelings and behaviour. Beck concentrated on encouraging his clients to pay attention to their 'internal dialogue' or the voice in their head that guided their behaviour.

Cognitive behavioural therapy

Cognitive behavioural therapy (CBT) is an umbrella approach encapsulating many of the ideas of Ellis and Beck. MacLeod (2003) relates that historically CBT is the most recent of the major therapy orientations with new elements being added to it, including strategies for cognitive intervention. The following is an example of how a CBT programme might look:

1. Establishing rapport and creating a working alliance between counsellor and client. Explaining the rationale for treatment.
2. Assessing the problem. Identifying and quantifying the frequency, intensity and appropriateness of problem behaviours and cognitions.
3. Setting goals or targets for change. These should be selected by the client and should be clear, specific and attainable.
4. Application of cognitive and behavioural techniques.
5. Monitoring progress, using ongoing assessment of target behaviours.
6. Termination and planned follow-up to reinforce generalisation of gains.

Source: MacLeod (2003), p.138

According to the Royal College of Psychiatrists, CBT is used successfully to treat anxiety, phobia and bi-polar disorder, to name just a few. Further, it is considered the most effective psychological treatment for moderate and severe depression. For many types of depression it has been found to be as effective as anti-depressants.

Ten key principles of CBT

Homework: ——————➤ practice makes perfect

Action: ——————➤ don't just talk, do!

Need: ——————➤ pinpoint the problem

Goals: ——————➤ move towards them

Evidence: ——————➤ show CBT can work

View: ——————➤ events from another angle

I can do it: ——————➤ self-help approach

Experience: ——————➤ test out your beliefs

Write it down: ——————➤ to remember progress

Strengths and limitations of CBT

Cognitive behavioural therapy has a wide applicability from phobias to depression. Beck's work in particular has proven very effective in the treatment of mild and moderate depression. This approach is short-term and focuses on challenging present thinking to change behaviour and improve affect. It encourages the client's belief in their own capacity to change and discourages dependence on the therapist.

CBT has been nicknamed by some therapists the 'band-aid' therapy, quick and convenient. This approach does not explore the 'why' of how a person feels or has developed their thought processes; it treats the manifestation rather than the root, it could be argued.

Factors involved in therapeutic outcomes

Rogers' identification of the importance of the relationship between therapist and client has been further elaborated upon by Carr, who outlined the following client characteristics

> that have been associated with therapeutic outcome: personal distress; symptom severity; functional impairment; case complexity; readiness to change; early response to therapy; psychological mindedness; ego-strength; capacity to make and maintain relationships; the availability of social support, and socio-economic status (SES).
>
> Therapist characteristics that have been associated with therapeutic improvement: personal adjustment; therapeutic competence; matching therapeutic style to clients' needs; credibility; problem-solving creativity; capacity to repair alliance ruptures; specific training; flexible use of therapy manuals; and feedback on client recovery. (2007, vi)

Effectiveness of psychotherapy

Professor Alan Carr was commissioned by the Irish Council for Psychotherapy to examine the effectiveness of psychotherapy. The report argues for the need for a fully funded national psychotherapy service. According to Carr, one in four people suffer from mental health problems; psychotherapy offers a success rate of between 65 and 72 per cent and can be applied to a range of disorders. It is argued that the provision of an effective, accessible psychotherapeutic service would reduce the numbers presenting to hospital with chronic mental health problems. Carr further argues that 'Within the HSE and other health service organizations, service delivery structures should be developed to facilitate the development of psychotherapy services in primary, secondary and tertiary care. This recommendation is consistent with the policy document – 'A Vision for Change' Report of the Expert Group on Mental Health Policy, Dept. of Health and Children (2006, p.74). What appears to be clear is that at present there is a paucity of psychotherapeutic services and long waiting lists. This results in an escalation of the mental health problems experienced by individuals and increased pressure on hospital services. Implementing a national service delivered at not just primary but tertiary sites would improve the outcomes for individuals suffering from mental health problems and also alleviate pressure on the hospital system.

The UK National Institute for Clinical Excellence (NICE) advises on best practice in ensuring outcomes. It outlines some of the benefits that result from the provision of an effective psychotherapeutic programme at national level:

> The potential benefits of robustly commissioning an effective service providing CBT for the management of common mental health problems include:
>
> - reducing the risk of people proceeding to a more severe form of their condition
> - reducing the suicide risk
> - reducing the number of antidepressant medications prescribed
> - reducing referrals to secondary care services
> - providing access to coping strategies and support as an alternative to taking sick leave from work because of depression
> - retaining employment, even where the individual may suffer from stress, anxiety or depression, and enabling people on benefits to return to work more quickly
> - reducing inequalities and improving access to CBT
> - increasing patient choice, and improving partnership working, patient experience and engagement
> - better value for money, through helping commissioners to manage their commissioning budgets more effectively – this may include opportunities for clinicians to undertake local service redesign to meet local requirements in novel ways.
>
> Source: www.nice.org.uk

What is evident from this is the interplay of factors that contribute to an individual's mental health. Within an ecological approach (Bronfenbrenner) one can see that policy and funding issues at a national level have a direct effect upon the experiences of an individual experiencing mental health problems. The lack of availability and accessibility of psychotherapy causes further family distress, employment difficulties and additional pressure placed on an already overstretched and under-resourced hospital system. It is clear that psychotherapy is an effective treatment for many types of mental health problems.

This completes our introduction to some of the counselling approaches that exist. Each of the three theories presented offer something unique: in the psychoanalytic construct the notion of defence mechanisms and transference are considered by therapists nowadays to be relevant. Carl Rogers' 'person-centred' approach took the emphasis away from technique and placed it firmly on the client, revealing the essential nature of the therapist–client relationship in therapeutic outcomes. Finally, it can be argued that CBT has revolutionised psychotherapy, introducing an effective yet short treatment for the various difficulties individuals face. The brevity of the treatment and resulting cost-effectiveness of CBT compared with other longer and more costly forms of therapy have made it an attractive alternative for health and social-care services.

In the next part of the chapter we will look at skills, specifically counselling and interpersonal skills, which underpin how we interact with service users.

COUNSELLING SKILLS

An essential element of social care involves relating to other people. More often than not, these people can be experiencing difficulties in their lives and as such you, as a care practitioner, must be equipped to relate to them sensitively and supportively. Understanding the origins and manifestations of personal difficulties and distress that people face and, in addition, developing certain counselling skills, will help you support service users. While social care practitioners are not qualified as a counsellors or therapists, often, due to the relational nature of social care, we find ourselves needing to develop and improve skills to help us in our work. We will begin by looking at the skills involved in counselling and then examine the person-centred approach and its implications for you as care practitioners.

For Cournoyer (1991, p.3) a skill, from a social work perspective, can be thought of as a 'set of discrete cognitive and behavioural actions that derive from social work knowledge and from social work values, ethics, and obligations; are consistent with the essential facilitative qualities and comport with a social work purpose within the context of a phase of practice'.

Microskills needed in counselling

- listening
- questioning
- silence
- non-verbal behaviour.

Listening
- use eye contact (where culturally appropriate)
- demonstrate attention, e.g. by nodding
- offer encouragement, e.g. 'Mm-hmm', 'Yes'
- minimise distractions, e.g. television, telephone, noise
- do not do other tasks at the same time
- acknowledge the client's feeling, e.g. 'I can see you feel very sad.'
- do not interrupt the client unnecessarily
- ask questions if you do not understand
- do not take over and tell your own 'story'
- repeat back the main points of the discussion in similar but fewer words to check you have understood the client correctly (paraphrase, reflect feelings, clarify, summarise).

Questioning
There are different types of question:

- A **closed question**, for example, 'Are you on medication?' limits the response of the client to a one-word answer. Closed questions may not require clients to think about what they are saying. Answers can be brief and often result in the need to ask more questions.
- An **open question** requires more than a one-word answer. Open questions generally begin with 'what', 'where', 'how' or 'when'. They invite the client to continue talking and to decide what direction they want the conversation to take.
- With **leading questions** the counsellor guides the client to give the answer they desire. These questions are usually judgemental. For example 'You do practice safer sex, don't you?', 'Do you agree that you should always use a condom?'

Silence
- gives a client time to think about what to say
- gives a client space to experience their feelings
- allows a client to proceed at their own pace
- provides a client with time to deal with ambivalence about sharing
- gives a client freedom to choose whether or not to continue.

Non-verbal behaviour
- body language
- gestures
- facial expressions
- posture
- body orientation
- body proximity/distance
- eye contact
- mirroring
- removing barriers (e.g. desks)

The following skills are used specifically in the counselling relationship:
- paraphrasing content and reflecting feeling
- reframing.

Paraphrasing content and reflecting feeling
These two techniques are rooted in the Rogerian approach to counselling and were used extensively by Carl Rogers. Paraphrasing content involves repeating back what the client has said in simple terms so the client knows they are being listened to and heard. Reflecting feeling is a similar process except that it focuses on the emotional content of what or how the client is feeling. For example, if I was to say to a therapist that I had started a new course in college and was finding the work difficult, leaving me crying often; the content aspect of that statement is that I've started college, but the feeling part is that I'm stressed and overwhelmed. A therapist would paraphrase and reflect this back to me.

Example of reflection of content and feeling
Client statement: I keep expecting my mother to show more interest in me. Time and again I've asked her to come over to see me, but she never does. Yesterday it was my birthday and she did come to visit me, but do you know she didn't even remember it was my birthday. I just don't think she cares about me at all. (Said slowly in a flat tone of voice.)

Counsellor response: You're disappointed by your mother's behaviour (or) You feel hurt by your mother's apparent lack of caring.

Reframing
Each of us has a unique perspective on how we 'view' situations; you and I may see the same event and yet give different descriptions of it reflecting that our perspective is a product of our beliefs and life experiences. When a client presents a perspective or 'picture', the counsellor will attempt to put a different 'frame' on the 'picture', thus giving them another way of viewing the situation. This is called

reframing. Geldard (2005, p.149) explains, 'The idea behind reframing is not to deny the way the client sees the world, but to present them with an expanded view of the world. Thus, if the client wishes, they may choose to see things in a new way.'

Example of reframing

The client has explained that she seems unable to relax because as soon as she turns her back her young son misbehaves and she has to chase after him and punish him. The counsellor has reflected back her feelings about this and now the client is calmer. At this point, the counsellor decides to offer the client a reframe concerning the behaviour of her son.

Counsellor reframe: I get the impression that you are really important to your son and that he wants lots of attention from you.

This statement presents the client with a more positive approach to viewing her son's behaviour; not as an attempt to irritate her but instead seeking attention from her. Should the client decide to accept this reframe and view her son's behaviour differently, this may bring a new direction to their relationship.

Professional practice guidelines – ethical considerations

An essential element of the therapeutic relationship is that of ethical considerations in dealing with clients. See Appendix 3, which outlines the British Psychological Society's guide to ethical issues in the counselling relationship.

Person-centred practice

Rogers, as we have seen, introduced the concept of the person-centred approach in his theoretical work and practice as a psychotherapist. The quality of the relationship between therapist and client has been identified as a crucial factor in the outcome of therapy. The notion of the person-centred approach has been embraced by those in the caring professions from nursing to (child-centred) education to social work.

The National Disability Authority (NDA) states that person-centred planning may be defined as a way of discovering:

- how a person wants to live their life and
- what is required to make that possible.

The overall aim of person centred planning is good planning leading to positive changes in people's lives and services.

Person-centred planning is not so much a new technique for planning as a new approach to – or new type of – planning that is underpinned by a very exacting set of values and beliefs that is very different to the current norm.

It is planning that takes as its primary focus a person – as opposed to a disability or a service or some other particular issue.

The NDA suggest the following as the key principles of person-centred practice:

- Person-centred planning is planning from an individual's perspective on his or her life
- Person-centred planning entails a creative approach to planning which asks 'what might this mean?' and 'what is possible?' rather than assuming common understandings and limiting itself to what is available
- Person-centred planning takes into consideration all the resources available to the person – it does not limit itself to what is available within specialist services
- Person-centred planning requires serious and genuine commitment and co-operation of all participants in the process
- Person-centred planning is an art – not a science: It is best viewed as an organic, evolving process which emphasizes taking time to really get to know people and build relationships and rapport over time; encouraging open and flexible attitudes in all participants in the planning process; listening carefully, acknowledging and exploring various and, in particular, opposing perspectives
- The development of a plan is not the objective of person centred planning: making real, positive differences to someone's life is.

Source: www.nda.ie

Talerico (2003) offers another interpretation of person-centred planning which is more relationally based:

- Knowing the person as an individual and being responsive to individual and family characteristics
- Providing care that is meaningful to the person in ways that respect the individual's values, preferences and needs
- Viewing care recipients as biopsychosocial human beings
- Fostering development of consistent and trusting caregiving relationships
- Emphasising freedom of choice
- Promoting physical and emotional comfort
- Appropriately involving the person's family, friends and social network. (p.14)

The person-centred approach offers a framework, in keeping with Rogers' work, that places the individual at the centre of practice, representing not a simplistic individualised care concept but instead a fundamental shift of philosophy in the social-care arena. Communication forms an essential element in supporting people using a person-centred approach. The following piece suggests how to do just that.

Using person-centred thinking to listen and respond to people

To enable people to have real choice and control over their lives and services, it is suggested that practitioners need to know the answers to the questions set out in the table below. Providers need to know this information and consistently act on it in order to meet the needs of the people being supported. It is not just what staff members do, but the way in which they do it. The quality of the relationship and the interaction between the staff member and the person being supported is essential in ensuring quality services overall. The experiences people have when they interact with professionals are what matter most to the people who use services. The quality of this interaction can create a positive sense of well-being and a desire to take increasing control of their life. Conversely, a poor-quality interaction can cause a person to feel anxious, less confident and consequently less independent.

Table 10.2: Person-centred thinking skills

What do providers need to know about each individual they support?	Person-centred thinking skills that can help
What is important to the person, so that services can be built around what matters to them as an individual.	What is important to the person?
How, when and where the person wants support or services delivered.	How can we best support the person?
What people want today, tomorrow and in the future and how to move towards this.	What is important in the future?
How the person communicates the way in which they want their services personalised.	Communication charts. Decision-making agreements.
How to enable people to be part of their communities as contributing citizens.	Presence to contribution. Planning how to move from being present to contributing.
How well are services being delivered, and are they being delivered in the way people want. What do individuals think of the services they receive and how can services be improved.	What is working? What is not working? These questions can be part of a person-centred review.

Source: www.puttingpeoplefirst.org.uk

Communication

Communication forms an integral part of our interaction with service users. We are going to explore two pieces of research; the first, communication and social work from an attachment perspective, deals with the psychological perspective of communication and discusses 'reflective function' as a method to improve communication, not just between practitioner and service user but also within a multi-agency situation.

The second piece of research examines how communication within health and social care can enhance or jeopardise older people's dignity. This research was based on focus groups conducted in six countries, including Ireland.

Communication and social work from an attachment perspective

Jim Walker charts the role of attachment (and attachment experiences in early relationships) and how these can affect whether communication is effective within social work. Walker suggests that our early relationships form the template for future relationships and that, in the sphere of social work, our ability to communicate and interact effectively with service users is a reflection of these early templates. Therefore it is essential for those working in social care to be aware of and reflect on the feelings and needs not just of service users, but also their own. Walker proposed reflective function as a construct to enable practitioners to improve how they communicate with service users. Walker (2008, p.8) defines reflective function as 'the ability to go beyond immediately known phenomena to give an account of one's own or other's actions in terms of beliefs, desires, plans etc. More simply, . . . it is the ability to think flexibly about thoughts and feelings in both oneself and others.' Reflective function is more than just empathy which is concerned with 'other'; an important aspect is that you can consider 'other' but also yourself. It is important that you think about your own emotional reactions to clients and to the work, rather than focusing purely on the client.

An example of a failure of reflective function is to take the position of 'knowing best' and of disregarding others' opinions. Walker explains other instances of a failure of reflective function in clients he worked with. During his work with teenage girls who had been sexually abused he noticed that the girls were very attuned to his emotional state. When Walker asked them how they thought he was feeling they were able to offer an opinion, yet when he reciprocated and asked them how *they* felt, the girls were unable to tell him. Walker surmises that; 'in the process of focusing on other people they seemingly had been unable to retain any focus on their own mental processes; they were completely unaware of their own feelings; . . . they had some empathy for my state of mind but nevertheless lacked reflective function and an understanding of their own internal processes' (p.9). Walker believes that for the communication process to be effective, both practitioners and agencies need to adopt this approach. Walker describes the importance of 'reflective function' in the area of child protection, suggesting that breakdowns in communication hamper the delivery of services. He cites the case of Victoria Climbie: Lord Laming's report into her death identified a breakdown in communication between the agencies charged with her protection which contributed to her death at the hands of an abusive aunt and the aunt's boyfriend. Reflective practice has relevance in the practitioner/service–user interaction but also between agencies. For students studying social care, Walker emphasises the importance of keeping a journal in order to analyse and improve the skills of reflective function.

Walker demonstrates the importance of reflective function for communication in social care. While his piece is theoretical, the following piece of research examines the impact of how we communicate on older people's sense of dignity.

'Tu' or 'Vous?': A European qualitative study of dignity and communication with older people in health and social care settings

This study gathered qualitative data from six countries, including Ireland, through focus groups and interviews. The older people (65 plus) included those in residential care (e.g. nursing homes) and those who were not. Professionals working with older people (including care workers, nurses and psychologists) also participated in discussions on the role of communication.

Woolhead et al.(2006, p.363) report that different styles of communication between professionals and older people were found to be capable of enhancing or jeopardising dignity. The use of appropriate forms of address, listening, giving people choice, including them, respecting their need for privacy and politeness, and making them feel valued, emerged as significant ways to maintain older people's sense of self-worth and dignity. The authors continue that despite being aware of good communication practices, health and social care professionals often failed to implement them, citing lack of time, staff, resource scarcity, regulation and bureaucracy as barriers. A lack of awareness and effort also emerged as factors. In relation to the impact of communication on dignity, four major categories emerged from the analysis, including

- forms of address
- politeness and privacy
- feeling valued
- inclusion and choice.

Forms of address

The use of first names was identified as an area of contention, with the majority of older people responding that they found the use of first names and pet names ('dear' or 'love') disrespectful and patronising and only appropriate in close relationships. Interestingly, difference did exist between those in residential and non-residential settings, with the former group preferring to be addressed on a first-name basis, possibly reflecting the importance of the relationship between care professional and client. Another element identified as disrespectful was the labelling of individuals as 'tasks', for example, 'I have got three bed baths left to do.' The participants in the study believed that it was a sign of respect to at least ask them how they wished to be addressed. From the professional perspective, a lack of communication was identified as a contributory factor. Where an older person gave their consent to one professional to address them by their first name, this resulted in an assumption by other professionals that they could also use the client's first name. The professionals who participated in the study acknowledged that older people should be given choice in how they wished to be addressed, however, some admitted to being lax in putting this into practice.

'Sometimes we might be very casual about calling older people by their first names, instead of Mr or Mrs, the old-fashioned way. All those things have gone for us, but not necessarily for them' (nurses, Ireland).

Politeness and privacy

Politeness, kindness and privacy were identified as being not just important but appreciated by older people. Involving older people in decision-making was recognised as integral to maintaining their dignity, for example, asking their permission to examine them. The following practices were also identified as supporting the older person's privacy: 'Simple actions, such as knocking on a door before entering, or maintaining eye contact, were aspects of care that older people responded to. Other examples included acknowledging the need for privacy when performing bed baths' (p.368). The following is an account given by an older person living in a nursing home:

> One [caregiver] came in with a list to check who had to go to the toilet. People don't have to go to the toilet by list. They have to go when they need to. Someone asked her to take them. She looked at the list and said, 'It's not your turn'. That's not treating someone with dignity. (p.368)

Feeling valued

The role of person-centred practice became evident from the findings of this study. Participants identified being listened to, acknowledged as a person and given time as supporting their sense of being valued. Barriers that hindered communication between professionals and their clients included lack of staff, financial resources, awareness and increased bureaucracy and these reduced the feeling of value experienced by individual patients.

Inclusion and choice

'I went into this particular specialist and he had an assistant. Instead of talking to me, he was writing all the time. I could have been an elephant. He said, "Take her in there and tell her to strip down," and I just said, "Am I invisible?"' (Social Club, Ireland) (p.369)

The above example given by a participant reflects a fear expressed by many of the older people, of being treated as an 'object'. Not being included in decision-making created a sense that the older person was not seen as a person and their opinions and outlook were not respected. This damaged the older person's sense of worth and left them feeling little more than an object. Woolhead *et al.* (2006, p.369) state that 'It was further acknowledged that it was easy to put one's own values onto older people. Often health professionals were accused of deciding what was best for patients without considering their views.'

This last point is interesting if seen in relation to the previous research on reflective function; applying your own values to another indicates that you have not considered the other person's beliefs and wishes in the decision-making. This is an example of a clear failure of reflective function.

This study highlights the importance of quality communication in supporting the dignity of the older person. It reminds us of the necessity to remain aware and vigilant to ensure that we do not lapse into forgetfulness or laxity in our daily practice. This study also links up with the research on reflective function as it gives real-life examples of failures of reflective function. Practical suggestions can be gleaned from this study, from knocking on doors before entering a person's room to involving the older person in decision-making.

This study forms part of an international endeavour exploring dignity and the older person. The Irish partner in this research project is Age Action.

For more details and for specifically Irish data: http://medic.cardiff.ac.uk

Communication passports for people with intellectual disabilities

The following was developed by the Mental Health Commission as a guide on how best to communicate clearly with service users who have an intellectual disability, and serves as a very practical suggestion for improving and supporting effective communication.

At a service level, communication for all can be supported by:

- using plain language
- preparing easy to read summaries of written documents
- using visual and audio formats to aid communication
- listening
- creating a relaxed environment and allowing adequate time for people to process information and formulate their response
- enabling one to one communication if preferred.

Source: National Institute for Mental Health, 2004; cited in Mental Health Commission, *Code of Practice*

Example – communication passport

Communication passports are designed to support those who are unable to communicate in a conventional way, so that their preferences and views are expressed through the communication passport. Every individual with intellectual disability and/or mental health issues should have a personalised communication passport, relating to all aspects of their life. In this regard, communication passports are often linked in with behaviour support plans and individual care and treatment plans. To ensure best practice, the individual, their family and significant others must be consulted when drawing up a communication passport.

The outcome should be:

- ethical
- promote rights and quality of life
- be current and accurate
- be owned by the individual, rather than professionals.

Source: Mental Health Commission, 2009, p.23

To summarise, we have looked at research examining the role of communication in social work from a theoretical stance in Walker's work on reflective function. The European study demonstrates how an older person's dignity can be enhanced or jeopardised depending on how social care professionals communicate with them. Finally, a very practical example of how to support and encourage effective communication for service users with intellectual disabilities was outlined.

11

Research methods

This chapter provides an introduction to the area of research, in particular, research into psychology and social care. Research as a tool to inform policy and shape practice has become paramount in recent times. Effective interventions can only occur if grounded in good theory and research. We will examine what makes for a good theory and explore the scientific approach to research, which is the dominant force at present. We will examine research methods, points to consider when devising a research proposal and, finally, the role of ethics. Examples of Irish research as illustration are given and further reading is recommended.

A GOOD THEORY

A **theory** is an interrelated, coherent set of ideas which aims to explain and make predictions. **Hypotheses** are predictions and testable assumptions. A hypothesis is a statement that makes an assertion about what is true in a particular situation; often, a statement asserting that two or more variables are related to one another. A **prediction** is a statement that makes an assertion concerning what will occur in a particular research investigation; for example: 'Autism is caused by a virus', prediction or hypothesis?

That a theory must have testable assumptions reflects the scientific approach which is dominant in psychology and social sciences. A good theory acts as a bedrock from which to design and test interventions, such as parenting programmes or psychosocial interventions. It is important to understand the relationship in psychology between theory and applied psychology (its application).

The scientific approach

The essence of the scientific method is that all propositions be subjected to an empirical test. Empiricism within psychology refers to the philosophical idea that all knowledge is derived from sense experience. An empirical approach within research determines that an idea must be studied under conditions in which it may be either supported or refuted. Secondly, the research should be done in a way that can be observed, evaluated and replicated by others. Empiricists would argue that the scientific approach increases the validity of a theory through statistical quantitative methods and the opportunity to replicate results.

In its simplest form, research has goals which are:

- a description of behaviour
- a prediction of behaviour
- to find causes of behaviour
- an explanation of behaviour.

Criteria for judging research within the scientific approach include the following:

- **Objectivity**; as defined by the conclusions rationally, reasonably and rigorously reached by the scientific method (or verified by peer review);
- **Parsimony**; where the most useful explanation is the one which produces the most reliable predictions (has largest scope) from the fewest argumentative or unprovable assertions or axioms (from the 'simplest' theory);
- **Falsifiability**; Karl Popper forwarded the argument that a theory must be falsifiable. This may seem counter-intuitive, but in the example of Freud's psychoanalytic theories, the fact that by their nature they are insufficiently precise to have negative implications is in fact their weakness, which in Popper's view left them more aligned to primitive myth than to proper science.
- **Reproducibility**; that the results and arguments can be replicated and thus tested for validity.

Put more simply, when designing research in accordance with the scientific method the following steps are invoked:

1. observation, gathering and ordering of data
2. induction of generalisations, laws
3. development of explanatory theories
4. deduction of hypotheses to test theories
5. testing of the hypotheses.

RESEARCH METHODS

What are the practicalities of research? Different methodological approaches are used in research, particularly within social care. Qualitative and quantitative approaches are explained, along with the different research methods that accompany these approaches. Examples are given of Irish research that correspond to some of the different research methods discussed. Ethical considerations are considered. Statistics are not part of the scope of this book, however, suitable reading will be suggested.

What methods do we choose when designing research? The first step in scientific research is to identify a question and seek evidence to answer it. Four basic steps in scientific research are:

- formulate a research question
- develop a hypothesis
- test the hypothesis
- draw conclusions.

Once we have decided on the research question we can start to build a research design. So let's look at the field of research methodology.

Quantitative or qualitative approach

According to Coolican (2009, pp.40–41), quantification means to measure on some numerical basis, if only by frequency. Whenever we count we quantify and putting people into categories is a prelude to counting. Quantitative methods can include:

- correlational study
- meta-analysis
- cross-sectional study
- longitudinal study.

Qualitative research, by contrast, emphasises meanings, experiences (often verbally described), descriptions and so on. Raw data will be exactly what people have said (in interview or recorded conversations) or a description of what has been observed (p.41).

Qualitative methods include:

- open-ended questionnaires
- unstructured or semi-structured interviews
- individual case studies
- qualitative observation
- the diary method.

Research that combines both qualitative and quantitative elements is referred to as a mixed-methods approach.

Qualitative methods: Observation

Observation has played an important role in psychology from its early roots to the modern day. Its beginnings were in the practice of 'introspection' (observing and reporting on one's own mental process and emotional content), to Piaget's observations of his own children in formulating his theory of cognitive development. Observation was used by Piaget to formulate his ideas and then to test them. Observation can provide the first-stage data or information through which hypotheses are formed. Three types of observation exist:

- controlled observation
- naturalistic observation
- participant observation.

Controlled observation is generally carried out in a laboratory setting under closely controlled conditions and is closely aligned to the conditions of experimentation.

Naturalistic observation, also referred to as field observation, was the method used by Piaget when he observed his three children in their own usual environments. Thus, unlike controlled observation, participants are not observed under laboratory conditions but in their natural setting, and their behaviour noted.

Participant observation is similar except that the researchers themselves become part of the group being observed. In Chapter 6 we looked at Rosenhaun's 'Trap experiment' where researchers had themselves committed to mental hospitals to observe the patients' behaviour; this was an example of participant observation.

According to Malim and Birch (1997, p.33), strengths and weaknesses of observation are:

Strengths
- There is less chance of the dehumanisation and distortion that can occur with other research methods.
- This type of approach tends to be more holistic and less reductionist than the experimental method. Observational methods tend to deal with the whole situation whereas experimental methods are usually concerned with a narrower aspect.
- That observation provides data to form hypotheses is arguably its greatest strength.

Weaknesses
- Observer bias can be a real difficulty for this method as it is difficult to be certain that value judgements have not been made.
- Cause and effect is more difficult to imply within the observational approach, compared with more quantitative approaches.
- Sampling bias: it can be a challenge to ensure that the samples observed are representative of a bigger population, in other words that the findings based on a sample can be generalised to a wider group.

Observation provides an avenue to research where it would be considered unethical to intervene or manipulate behaviours as part of the research process, for example, manipulating a baby's feeding pattern.

Surveys

A survey involves asking a relatively large number of people for information. In the informal, loosely structured interview, each respondent's answers form a small case study. A survey can consist of a set of such small case studies. More often than not, it involves the use of a structured questionnaire, with answers open or closed.

Strengths
- Surveys allow for a large amount of data to be collected relatively easily.
- Surveys, as with observations, may provide areas or data for further research to be developed from.

Weaknesses
- Design difficulties: a poorly thought-out and designed survey is not worth the paper it's written on.
- Distortions occur when people do not respond truthfully. Malim and Birch (1997, p.37) outline some reasons why this occurs:
  - they are simply not sufficiently interested to think carefully about their answers
  - the wording of written questions or the use of nonverbal cues, tone of voice and so on by interviewers may influence responses.

The following is a good example of qualitative research and illustrates that qualitative research can be as valid and useful as quantitative research, that is sometimes seen as weightier or more 'scientific'.

Irish children's and adolescents' concepts of family

Nixon, Greene and Hogan (2006) conducted research exploring Irish children's and adolescents' concepts of family. The authors (2006, p.79) note that 'childhood as an experience is socially, culturally and historically situated, and not simply a natural or universal state arising out of children's biological condition'. In other words, children are a part and product of their environment. Children also impact on their environments and shape them so it is important to ascertain how children construe 'family'.

Ninety-nine children were drawn from three schools in Dublin. Their ages ranged from 9 to 16 years of age. The first part of the research involved a focus group to examine children's concept of family. Five vignettes which portrayed different types of family were presented to the children with the question, 'Are they a family?' The second part of the research involved the use of open-ended questions to explore children's definitions of family. The five vignettes were taken from O'Brien et al. (1996). The vignettes used and the responses given by the children were as follows:

Vignette 1: 'John and Susan are a married couple without any children.'
* Almost two-thirds of the children endorsed this grouping as a family.
* The authors report that the most frequent reason given for not considering this grouping as a family was the absence of children. They believe this highlights the important role children attached to themselves within the family unit.
* 'If they have a dog they are; . . . it's like they're not part of a family yet because they need something to commit their life to.' (12-year-old girl)

Vignette 2: 'Janet and Dave are a married couple with a son called Ben.'
* All the children endorsed this grouping as a family unit primarily because of the role of the members to care for each other.
* The authors relate that other reasons given for its endorsement as a family unit were presence of a child, the parents are married and the family members live together.
* 'They are a family because, like, they all take care of each other and they have – they have more responsibility to take care of more people.' (10-year-old girl)

Vignette 3: 'Jim and Sue live together with their six year old called Paul. They are not married.'
* The authors found that over 80 per cent of the children believed this grouping represented a family.
* One-eighth of the children indicated that they did not believe this grouping constituted a family. This appears to be related to the lack of marriage and the children's perceived sense of insecurity and instability that entailed.
* 'Because like when them two have committed their lives to him [the son] but the mam and dad haven't committed their lives to each other; . . . the dad can walk out any day now but, like, if they're married, they have to stay together or get a divorce.' (12-year-old girl)

Vignette 4: 'Sally is divorced with a 10-year-old daughter, Karin. Karin lives with Sally.'
* Ninety per cent of the children responded that this grouping constituted a family.
* The main reason given was the emotional ties that connect family members. The authors surmise that 'children were able to distinguish between the inter-parent relationship and the parent-child relationship, and also understood that the quality of the two relationships were independent'.
* Six children were unsure if this grouping did represent a family: 'They are a family but a bit of the family has broken off, so it's not fully a family.' (12-year-old girl)
* The authors continue, 'there was a sense that the divorced family was less than a proper family and represented a deviation from the ideal form'. The authors continue that for a minority the findings highlight that the concept of a nuclear two-parent family remains central.

Vignette 5: 'Karin's father, Tom, lives at the other end of town.'

- Eighty per cent of the children endorsed this grouping as a family.
- Six children were uncertain, citing that the father and daughter did not live together.
- 'I don't think they are at all. I'd say they're just related, like when you don't live with one of your parents. It seems as if they're just somebody you go to see sometimes. It doesn't seem like they're your family at all.' (15-year-old girl)
- The authors remark, 'the importance of the quality of family relationships emerged in the discussion of this vignette; . . . a family was dependent upon the levels of contact and the nature of the relationship'.

Open-ended questions

The research also made use of open-ended questions whose aim was to explore how children define family and also how children view their role and the parental role within the family. The main finding of the research 'that emerged was that a family was defined in terms of the roles and relationships within the family'. Age differences were present, with younger children perceiving family as, 'people who love you and take care of you, a group of people all born from the same person, and a group of people who live in the same house'. The adolescents used the following terms when defining family: 'closeness', 'a safe place to be' and 'people who comfort each other'.

Parental role: for the children, the parents' main role was to look after the children. Age differences were visible in how the parental role in the family was understood: younger children's perceptions of the mother's and father's role within the family were quite stereotypical: the mother was considered the primary caregiver and the father provided financial support. The children related that the father was more willing to take part in play activities than the mother.

Older children, while acknowledging the nurturing and 'breadwinner' roles, mentioned that they saw the role of both parents as one of 'protector' and 'confidant'.

Child's role: the researchers found that 'overall children believed they had an active and important role to play in family life'. This included taking part in decision-making and caring roles such as looking after a sick parent.

The authors conclude that the 'main finding that emerged from their responses was that Irish children and adolescents were accepting of a variety of family forms: they conceptualised "family" in an inclusive and flexible way'.

Source: Nixon *et al.*, 2006

As you can see, through the use of open-ended questions and focus groups discussing the vignettes provided, this piece of research used qualitative methodology. It demonstrates the innovative way qualitative methodology can be used and the information that can be gleaned, which quantitative research would not have been as able to pick up on. This illustrates the strength of qualitative research in that it provides an opportunity to identify new patterns or data that only a more open approach allows to be heard.

Quantitative methods

Correlation is 'the measurement of the extent to which pairs of related values on two variables tend to change together or co-vary. It also gives a measure of the extent to which values on one variable can be predicted from the values on the other variable' (Coolican 2009, p.346). Put simply, 'correlation' describes the strength of the relationship between two or more events or characteristics. A positive correlation exists where, as one variable increases, so does the other (for example, the more time you spend studying the better grades you get). A negative correlation occurs where, as one variable increases, the other variable decreases (for example, the more alcohol I consume the slower my reaction times become). It is very important to remember that a correlation does not mean or prove causation, only that a relationship exists.

Meta-analysis is a method of combining findings across studies on the same subject. The term 'meta-analysis' was coined in the 1970s by Glass, who described it as 'the statistical analysis of a large collection of analysis results for the purpose of integrating the findings' (1976, p.3).

In a systematic review, eligible research studies are viewed as a population to be systematically sampled and surveyed. Individual study characteristics and results are then abstracted, quantified, coded and assembled into a database that, if appropriate, is statistically analysed much like any other.

The following two research methods are comparison studies which look at either the same people as they age over an extended period (longitudinal) or several sub-group samples (such as age, class, sex) studied over a longish period (cross-sectional). Both give information on changes over time. Comparisons can highlight age-related changes and developmental trends.

Longitudinal studies

Longitudinal studies use repeated measures on the same group of people over a substantial period, often many years. According to Coolican (2009, p.181) this approach allows for 'genuine changes and the stability of some characteristics to be observed. If intervals between observations are not too long, major points of change can be identified.'

Strengths
* A major advantage is that in studying individuals over a period of time one gathers information regarding stability and change.

- The method allows for the importance of early experience for later development.
- Longitudinal studies are especially useful when following through the effect of a 'treatment' (for example, educational intervention) and comparing with a control group.

Weaknesses
- Longitudinal studies are very expensive and time-consuming to run.
- Attrition – loss of subjects during the course of the study – is inevitable.

Growing up in Ireland: The National Longitudinal Study of Children in Ireland

The National Longitudinal Study of Children in Ireland (also known as 'Growing up in Ireland') is an example of a longitudinal study currently running in Ireland. According to the Office of the Minister for Children and Youth Affairs, who commissioned the study, the aim of the study is 'to examine the factors that contribute to, or undermine, the well-being of children in contemporary Irish families, and, through this, contribute to the setting of effective and responsive policies relating to children and to the design of services for children and their families'.

The study is monitoring the development of more than 18,000 children – an infant cohort of 10,000 and a nine-year-old cohort of over 8,500 children – yielding important information about each significant transition throughout their young lives.

The specific objectives of the study can be summarised as follows:

- to describe the lives of children in Ireland in order to establish what is typical and normal as well as what is atypical and problematic
- to chart the development of children over time in order to examine the progress and well-being of children at critical periods from birth to adulthood
- to identify the key factors that, independently of others, most help or hinder children's development
- to establish the effects of early childhood experiences on later life
- to map dimensions of variation in children's lives
- to identify the persistent adverse effects that lead to social disadvantage and exclusion, educational difficulties, ill health and deprivation
- to obtain children's views and opinions on their lives
- to provide a bank of data on the whole child
- to provide evidence for the creation of effective and responsive policies and services for children and families.

For more information: www.growingup.ie

TILDA, the Irish Longitudinal Study on Ageing, is another longitudinal study worth investigating: www.tcd.ie/tilda

Cross-sectional studies

Cross-sectional studies, according to Coolican (2009, p.180), 'capture several groups, usually of different ages, at one specific point. The general goals are to map developmental stages or to compare differences across groups on a psychological variable.'

Strengths
- Low attrition rates: unlike in longitudinal studies there is less likelihood of 'losing' people.
- According to Coolican (2009), cross-sectional studies are less time-consuming and relatively inexpensive. Support for theories can be achieved more quickly.

Weaknesses
- It is not possible to observe changes within the same individuals.
- The cohort effect – 'if age difference between the groups studied is large then any difference found might be the result of different experiences by one group and not of, e.g. maturation or stage development.' (Coolican, 2009, p.183)

The Health Behaviour in School-aged Children (HBSC) study is an example of cross-sectional research. As we saw in Chapter 7, the HBSC is a cross-national research study conducted in collaboration with the World Health Organization's Regional Office for Europe. The study aims to gain new insight into, and increase our understanding of, young people's health and well-being, health behaviours and their social context. In addition, the findings from the HBSC surveys are used to inform and influence children's policy and practice at national and international levels.

HBSC was initiated in 1982 and a survey is conducted every four years. HBSC 2010 involves more than 200,000 children from 43 countries. The target age groups for the HBSC study are 11-, 13- and 15-year-old children attending school. Thus every four years HBSC Ireland surveys a sample of Irish children (age categories 10–11, 12–14 and 15–16) from randomly selected schools throughout the country. These age groups represent the onset of adolescence, the challenge of physical and emotional changes and the middle years when important life and career decisions are beginning to be made.

Thus, the design of HBSC Ireland is cross-sectional as it covers an extended period, targeting samples based on age in an effort to identify health-related developmental changes.

Measuring populations

In research, when we refer to a population we are not talking about nationalities. Instead, this term refers to the group of people from which a sample is drawn. For example, if I was conducting research on university students with dyslexia, they would be my population. However, it might not be possible to include large numbers in the research process so I would study a sample or group of the population. The findings of the research (depending on the design of the research) could then be generalised to the rest of the population (that is, the remaining students I didn't include in the study). In order to generalise to the remaining population you must ensure that your sample accurately reflects the composition of the population from which it is drawn; this is referred to as a representative sample.

As with the research methods we have just considered, there are also different approaches to sampling.

Random sample is where every member of the population has an equal chance of being represented, for example, picking every fifth name on a list of first year students (who are the population).

Quota sample is a particularly popular approach with research companies and opinion surveys. You choose characteristics which you consider important to your research question. You then systematically choose individuals who possess these characteristics in the same proportions as the population as a whole. For example, in terms of gender, if you knew that the proportion of males and females in a population was 50:50, you would need to ensure your sample had 50 per cent males and 50 per cent females. You would stop interviewing once you had reached your 'quota', for example, 50 per cent males.

Opportunity sample: unlike the previous two examples, this is not a 'representative' sample; it is, as the name suggests, opportunistic. This sampling approach is based on accessibility. The sample consists of whoever happens to be free to participate at the time of the research. This method is one often used by students. The difficulty with this type of sampling is that it doesn't lend itself to generalisation as it is not representative.

THE RELATIONSHIP BETWEEN RESEARCH AND SOCIAL CARE

In this section we are going to explore applied research and its relationship to policy and practice. How does research support policy and inform practice? Research can provide specific information for policy-makers and practitioners. Through research we can assess outcomes of particular courses of actions or interventions. Finally, research can add to our knowledge and understanding of individual development and the conditions under which it takes place. The importance of evidence-based research and random controlled trials (RCT) will be examined below along with examples of interventions such as 'youngballymun'. Firstly, let us consider theory and applied research.

Applied research

There is nothing so practical as a good theory.
– Lewin

This often-cited quote underscores the relationship between basic and applied psychological research. While the primary goal of basic research is to expand the knowledge base, applied research aims to inform or to solve issues that can be put to particular use (Zigler and Finn-Stevenson, 1999, p.5). What is essential, as emphasised by Lewin, is that interventions must be based upon good theory. If one considers the example of autism; one theoretical psychoanalytic explanation suggested that autism was caused by 'maternal coldness'. As knowledge increased this theory was dismissed. However, the theory was originally given credence and any intervention based on such assumptions would have been misguided and ineffectual to say the least.

While Lewin's observation is valid, it raises certain questions. What is a good theory? As the example of autism suggests, theories are temporally and contextually bound and what is accepted as a good theory can be later be rejected through increased knowledge, vigorous methodologies and, more insidiously, changes in contextual or political forces. It is increasingly being recognised that while human behaviour does not exist in a vacuum, neither does psychological research. To clarify, many, especially in the field of critical psychology, are questioning the objectivity of research. Factors from the individual researcher's beliefs can (consciously or unconsciously) affect what is 'observed' or 'reported'; public and academic opinion can hold influence, as can the political ideology of the day. Research is contextual, but does that mean we can never claim that a theory is good or valid? While it may be tempting to attach so many caveats that it renders any research suspect or transient, many theories have endured and interventions based upon them succeed in ameliorating the issues addressed.

The increasing awareness of the necessity for good research and effective interventions has led to increased scrutiny and demands that interventions are monitored to ascertain if they are beneficial.

Evidence-based interventions and randomised controlled trials

As mentioned earlier in this chapter, interventions should be based on sound research and theory. Evidence-based interventions require that evidence must be forthcoming when instigating and evaluating interventions. The 'youngballymun' project, explored below, is an example of an evidence-based intervention.

Randomised controlled trials (RCTs) address questions about whether and to what extent interventions might work. 'Controlled' refers to the inclusion of one or more study groups, while 'randomised' relates to the method of allocation of participants into control or comparison groups. This, according to Roberts and Dicenso (1999, p.2), 'is the strongest design for questions of whether healthcare interventions are beneficial (i.e. do more good than harm). An RCT is a true experiment in which people are randomly allocated to receive a new intervention (experimental group) or to receive a conventional intervention or no intervention at all (control group). Because it is the play of chance alone that determines the allocation, the only systematic difference between the groups should be the intervention.'

RTC design

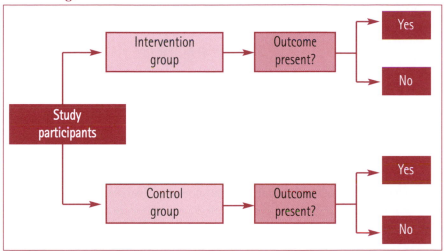

The figure above illustrates the design of a randomised controlled trial. Roberts and Dicenso elaborate that researchers follow participants forward in time (follow up) and then assess whether they have experienced a specific outcome. The two most important strengths of RCT are:

1. the random allocation of participants into groups, which helps to ensure that the groups are similar in all respects except exposure to the intervention
2. the longitudinal nature of the study, whereby exposure to the intervention precedes the development of the outcome.

These two features ensure that any differences in outcome can be attributed to the intervention.

Why are RCTs considered important in research?
Lewis-Beck et al. (2003) note that a major challenge facing researchers and policy-makers is assessing the effectiveness of different types of interventions; for example, does intensive social work input for children with behavioural problems actually help these children and their families? Lewis-Beck et al. (p.918) comment, 'answering such questions requires the use of a research design that permits the

impact of the intervention in question to be disentangled, so far as is possible, from other influences, including social characteristics of the intervention recipients and whatever else is going on in the social context at the time'. RCT can produce rigorous evidence to inform policy and practice decisions about the relative effectiveness of different interventions. There are those in social sciences that have dismissed the relevance of RCT in their arena, possibly due to the association of RCT with medicine. However, what is clear is that RCT design with its emphasis on evaluation of the effectiveness of interventions has a growing and essential role to play in social-care research. While the benefits of RCT design have been outlined, disadvantages also exist, including:

- the cost of conducting a trial
- the long period of follow-up before patients experience the outcome (in the case of health-care interventions)
- the possibility that participants who agree to participate in a trial may differ from those to whom the results would be applied (generalisability).

Evidence-based interventions: Youngballymun

Youngballymun is an excellent example of evidence-based interventions, and highlights perhaps the importance of ensuring interventions are effective.

Youngballymun, the Childhood Development Initiative Tallaght and Northside Partnership Preparing for Life Programme, are the projects that make up the Prevention and Early Intervention Programme whose aim is to support and promote better outcomes for children in areas designated as disadvantaged, through more innovation, effective planning, integration and delivery of services. The programme provides for the introduction and evaluation of a range of integrated interventions for children and their families and tests whether they make a positive difference to children.

The focus of the programme is on supporting interventions which fit with national policy objectives and have been developed in conjunction with the local community. Learning and evaluation are important components of the programme and individual services, area projects and the overall programme are subject to ongoing and robust review and evaluation. Research and planning on prevention and early intervention measures, sponsored by Atlantic Philanthropies, had been undertaken in these areas and they were considered to be in an excellent position to test new models of service delivery. If these models prove successful, the results of these projects may provide the basis for enhanced resource allocation processes and policy changes.

Youngballymun aims to provide a culture where research and evaluation is undertaken not only to demonstrate the success, or otherwise, of the strategy and the individual services therein, but to support the cycle of 'supposition-action-evidence-revision' that characterises good science and good management.

As you can see, an emphasis is placed on evidence-based research. The actual programme running in Ireland itself has been informed by the following research and interventions developed in America:

- The Highscope Perry Pre-School Project (www.highscope.org)
- The Incredible Years programmes, which are research-based, proven effective programmes for reducing children's aggression and behaviour problems and increasing social competence at home and at school (www.incredibleyears.com).

So you can see how the youngballymun project illustrates the importance attached to evidence-based interventions. It will be interesting to see how youngballymun and the other two projects fare and whether they will inform policy and resources allocation.

For more information: www.youngballymun.org

ETHICAL CONSIDERATIONS

Ethics and ethical considerations form an important part of the research process nowadays. We are going to look at an example of ethical guidelines and the levels of risk attached to research. Ethical issues that should be considered when conducting research with children or vulnerable populations are examined, as are examples of questionable research conducted in the past. We will end with some practical points to take into account when devising a research project and also writing it.

Table 11.1: Example of ethical guidelines

Informed consent	Participants should be informed of the objectives of the research, so that they may give informed consent for their participation.
Deception	It is unacceptable to withhold information or give misleading information to research participants; intentional deception should be avoided.
Debriefing	Participants should be fully debriefed to allow them to complete their understanding of the nature of the research.
Withdrawal	Investigators should emphasise the participant's right to withdraw from the research at any time.
Confidentiality	All data obtained should be treated as confidential unless an agreement to the contrary was made in advance.
Protection from harm	Investigators must protect participants from physical and mental harm including distress, either during or arising from investigations.
Privacy	Studies based on observation must respect the privacy and psychological well-being of the people studied.

Source: Giles, 2002, p.27

Levels of ethical risk

No-risk research:
- educational tests – cognitive tests such as aptitude and achievement measures
- surveys and observation of public behaviour, except in cases in which subjects might be identified and/or sensitive behaviour is being studied
- archival research using existing data.

Minimal-risk research:
- standard psychological measures that do not involve any danger to subjects
- studies of cognition and perception that do not involve stress
- fully informed consent is generally not necessary, but debriefing and other ethical concerns are important.

Full-review research:
- research that may involve:
    - physical stress
    - psychological stress
    - invasion of privacy
    - measures of sensitive information in which subjects might be identified.

In such circumstances approval would have to be sought from an ethics or review committee or other relevant body.

Informed consent: participants agree to participate after being informed about:

- the purpose of the study
- potential risks and benefits
- their rights to refuse or terminate participation.

The importance of informed consent increases with increasing risks to participants.

Special populations: increased ethical sensitivity may be called for when participants:

- are younger than 18
- have a disability
- have an illness or are hospitalised
- are imprisoned.

Research with children poses particular ethical considerations. Children are developmentally immature and not fully equipped to make informed consent; an important element when participating in research. The following document, prepared by the Children's Research Centre, outlines some of the ethical considerations at play when carrying out research with children.

Ethical issues in research with children

The Children's Research Centre at Trinity College has proposed in its draft document *Notes on Ethical Issues in Research with Children* (Nixon *et al.*, 2006) that these principles be derived from a set of core values as follows:

- having a commitment to the well-being of those participating or involved in the research process (beneficence)
- having a commitment to doing no harm (non-maleficence)
- having a commitment to respect the rights of those involved, including the rights of individuals to take responsibility for themselves (autonomy).

To these core values the Children's Research Centre adds the following:

- being child-centred in the approach to research, listening to children and treating them in a fair and just manner as individuals in their own right (fidelity).

And, specifically with reference to children with disabilities, we would also add:

- having a commitment to inclusiveness and to facilitating the equal participation of those for whom obstacles might make participation difficult without additional support (inclusivity).

Source: www.nda.ie

Questionable research

Ethics play a vital part in the research process as ensuring the safety (physical and psychological) of participants must be paramount. Throughout this book we have seen examples of research conducted in the past when ethical considerations were not considered or scrutinised. The Milgram and 'Little Albert' experiments are two examples of research where one can question whether damage was done in the pursuit of research. We will first explore the ethical issues with the 'Little Albert' experiment (Chapter 3). The goal of the experiment conducted by Watson and Raynor was to show that an emotional response (fear) of a stimulus could be conditioned in an organism (nine-month-old baby Albert). They were successful, not only in inculcating fear of a white rat but then generalising that fear to other stimuli. We don't know what became of Albert, only that his mother removed him from the hospital. There is no indication that the researchers reversed this 'fear' they had instilled in the baby. Was it ethical that they should instil or provoke a fear response in a child? What do you think? Are there instances when this might be acceptable in your opinion?

A more controversial piece of research that is considered ethically unsound is Milgram's Obedience Study and more particularly the Stanford Prison experiment.

In Milgram's study (Chapter 9), participants were encouraged to increase the electrical voltage being administered to a person in another room. These persons (who were actors, unbeknownst to the participants) begged for them to stop, yet many didn't. The premise of the study was to test whether people would act 'under orders' or obey even though to do so was causing another person harm. The main difficulty of this experiment was its potential to cause harm (emotionally and mentally) to those participants who did obey and believed they had injured and possibly killed another person. Arguably, by today's ethical standards this experiment would not be allowed; participants in experiments should not be deceived and must be aware of any consequences of their participation. As it happened, the participants in the Milgram study did not suffer any long-term psychological distress. The same cannot be said of the Stanford Prison experiment.

As we saw in Chapter 9, the aim of the Stanford Prison experiment was to demonstrate the power of the immediate social situation in shaping individuals' behaviour. Volunteers were divided into two groups, prisoners and wardens. The experiment had to be stopped because of the violence and aggression that developed. What is fascinating is that the people who become cruel and aggressive 'wardens' were ordinary people with no criminal pasts. However, in the context of ethics in research, it is arguable that this experiment crossed the line, as it caused actual distress to the participants. The research had to be halted just six days into the proposed two-week duration of the experiment. Some volunteers were begging to be released and those who didn't suffered psychological distress. The behaviour of the 'wardens' arguably went unchecked with behaviours such as toilet facilities becoming a privilege, prisoners stripped and forced to clean toilets with their bare hands. Amazingly, it was the reaction of a fellow psychologist, Christina Maslach, that brought the experiment to a halt. She was brought in to interview some of the wardens and was horrified by what she was witnessing. She was the only person to challenge what was going on. Zimbardo and the other researchers apparently had so internalised the experiment that they lost their perspective. It was after being challenged by Maslach that the experiment was stopped. It is interesting that even the researchers observing what was going on did not seem to recognise the totality and horror of what had spiralled into degrading and cruel treatment of the 'prisoners'.

Think back over the examples of research you have read in this book: do any stand out as ethically superior, in your opinion, to others? And if so, why?

When are ethics more than codes?

Tjeltveit (2000, p.243) relays that, 'Bersoff . . . argues that APA's current code "builds an ethical floor but hardly urges us to reach for the ceiling". It is a minimalist code that is "conservative, protective of its members, the product of political compromise, restricted in its scope, and too often unable to provide clear-cut solutions to ambiguous professional predicaments".'

HOW TO! A GUIDE TO RESEARCH

Research cycle diagram

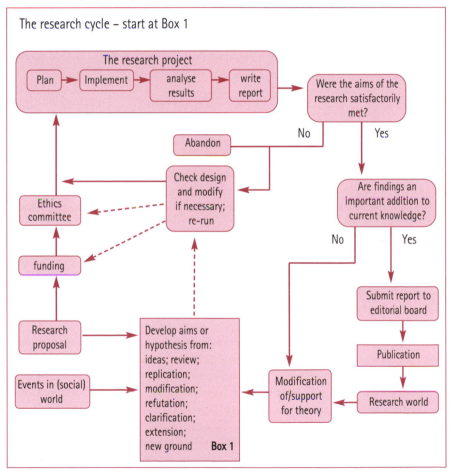

Steps in empirical research

The ideal research proposal should be comprehensive enough to enable the reader to know everything that could be expected to happen if the project were actually carried out – including anticipated obstacles as well as anticipated benefits. In order to design a research project, you may wish to ask yourself the following questions:

1. **Problem statement, purposes, benefits:** What exactly do I want to find out? What is a researchable problem? What are the obstacles in terms of knowledge, data availability, time, or resources? Do the benefits outweigh the costs?

2. **Theory, assumptions, background literature:** What does the relevant literature in the field indicate about this problem? To which theory or conceptual framework can I link it? What are the criticisms of this approach, or how does it constrain the research process? What do I know for certain about this area? What is the history of this problem that others need to know?

3. **Variables and hypotheses:** What will I take as given in the environment? Which are the independent and which are the dependent variables? Are there control variables? Is the hypothesis specific enough to be researchable yet still meaningful? How certain am I of the relationship(s) between variables?

4. **Operational definitions and measurement:** What is the unit of measurement? How will the research variables be measured? What degree of error in the findings is tolerable? Will other people agree with my choice of measurement operations?

5. **Research design and methodology:** What is my overall strategy for doing this research? Will this design permit me to answer the research question? What other possible causes of the relationship between the variables will be controlled for by this design? What are the threats to internal and external validity?

6. **Sampling:** How will I choose my sample of persons or events? Am I interested in representativeness? If so, of whom or what, and with what degree of accuracy or level of confidence?

7. **Instrumentation:** How will I get the data I need to test my hypothesis? What tools or devices will I use to make or record observations? Are valid and reliable instruments available, or must I construct my own?

8. **Data collection and ethical considerations:** Are there multiple groups, time periods, instruments, or situations that will need to be co-ordinated as steps in the data collection process? Will interviewers, observers or analysts need to be trained? What level of inter-rater reliability will I accept? Do multiple translations pose a potential problem? Can the data be collected and subjects' rights still preserved?

9. **Data analysis:** What combinations of analytical and statistical process will be applied to the data? Which will allow me to accept or reject my hypotheses? Do the findings show numerical differences, and are those differences important?

10. **Conclusions, interpretations, recommendations:** Was my initial hypothesis supported? What if my findings are negative? What are the implications of my findings for the theory base, for the background assumptions or relevant literature? What recommendations can I make for public policies or

programmes in this area? What suggestions can I make for further research on this topic?

Once you have answered all these questions and conducted your research you must write it up. Before looking at how a report is structured, let us consider what kind of language is used. The following points are suggested by Malim and Birch (1997, p.143):

- First, remember that much of the report will be written in the past tense. You are describing what has been done, how and why. This seems obvious, but it can be easy to forget in the early stages of report writing.
- Write in simple, clear, concise sentences, using 'businesslike' language. The purpose of a report is to convey information and ideas. It is not the same as an essay, so there is no need to include long and elaborate descriptive passages. Also, it is rarely necessary to use highly technical language.
- As far as possible, use impersonal language, for example, 'The participants were shown the stimulus card' rather than 'I showed the stimulus card to the participants', or 'It seems likely that . . .' rather than 'I believe that . . '.
- Use non-sexist language, for example, 'he or she' rather than 'he', unless of course the participants are all of the same sex.
- Do not include names of participants, and avoid anything by which they might be easily identified. Use initials, perhaps, or simply 'participant A' or 'participant B'.

The following is the structure that is expected within psychology when writing up work:

STRUCTURE OF A RESEARCH PAPER

Abstract
- provides an overview of the whole report.

Introduction section
- general overview of literature
- specific research questions and expectations.

Method section
- participants
- research design
- procedure.

Results section

Findings of the study described in:

- narrative
- tables and figures
- statistical analyses.

Discussion section

- summary of findings
- relate results to past research and theory
- future research.

The following link discusses what makes a good proposal and offer tips on getting it right: www.cardi.ie/researcherstoolkit.

This chapter is intended only as an introductory guide to research. The following texts are particularly useful for more in-depth discussions on all aspects of research.

Recommended books

T. Malim and A. Birch, *Research Methods and Statistics* (Introductory Psychology Series), London: Palgrave Macmillan 1997.

H. Coolican, *Research Methods and Statistics in Psychology*, 5th ed., London: Hodder Education 2009.

Child and family interventions and services

INTRODUCTION

This Section describes twenty-six current child and family interventions and services. As outlined in the Introduction, the information was supplied by health boards, who were asked to nominate models that they experienced to be good practice. In profiling the models, particular reference is made to aspects of the intervention that practitioners have found to work well. The intention is not to portray these services as ideal embodiments of the good practice principles just outlined, but rather to give a flavour of current strategies, actions and approaches. In Section 4, aspects of all the profiles are discussed in relation to the principles of good practice.

For presentation purposes, the profiles have been separated into eight categories that describe a central focus of the intervention. Common features and approaches from each of the categories are summarized at the end of each section. These eight areas are:

1. Early childhood development
2. Parent support
3. Community based family support
4. Work with 'at risk' young people
5. Therapeutic approaches
6. Promoting partnership
7 Work with children in care
8 Policy and service development.

It will become apparent to the reader that the categories are not mutually exclusive. For example, services that offer community-based family support also offer early intervention, social support and therapeutic approaches. Early childhood development services have a strong focus on parent support.

Likewise, promoting partnership is something that is not confined to the three profiles in that category, but it is a common feature across the range of models. The categorical division is used to emphasise and clarify particular approaches and aspects of the interventions, in order to make it easier for the reader to relate to and make sense of the breadth and diversity of information.

Profiles included under each category are as follows:

1. Early childhood development

Three profiles of intervention with children and parents in the early years are:

- Kilkenny Community Early Years Project provides quality childcare to help break the cycle of disadvantage for pre-school children in Kilkenny city.
- Sligo Family Support promotes early childhood development and parent support through home visiting (Lifestart) and centre-based activities in Sligo town.
- The Marte Meo Project, Dublin 7 uses a therapeutic approach to strengthen parents' capacity to promote child development and build relationships.

2. Parent support

Strategies to enhance parental capacity through social support are the focus of the three profiles in this category:

- Home-Start, Tullamore, Co. Offaly matches the skills and interests of volunteers to the needs of isolated families with its home visiting programme.
- The Post-Natal Distress Group, Tallaght, Dublin was a pilot initiative that sought to mobilise peer support to help women cope with post-natal depression.
- The Mid-Western Health Board developed a universal strategy for parent support to meet parents' support and information needs 'from the cradle to the grave'.

3. Community-based family support

These four profiles relate to the work of community based family resource centres:

- Whitefriar St. Community Education and Development Project, Dublin 2 is a community education project providing education, childcare and developmental opportunities to an inner-city community.
- Geraldstown House, Ballymun offers a holistic response to the needs of children, adolescents, adults and families, through group work, education, social support and other means.

- The Family Resource Centre, Tallaght is a preventative social work service that works on a proactive basis in a community setting with vulnerable families.
- Muirhevnamor Springboard Project, Dundalk is a community based Springboard project working closely with schools, community and families to develop an integrated response to family needs.

4. Work with 'at risk' young people

These four services provide a diverse set of interventions targeting 'at risk' children and adolescents:

- The 'Big Deal' Contract – Westside Community Services, a Galway-based Springboard project, developed this child-led approach to dealing with difficult behaviour.
- Gorey Youth Needs Group, Co. Wexford, as well as its core youth work services, works with home, school, community and state agencies for the benefit of young people at risk.
- The C.R.I.B Youth Project and Café in Sligo town, offers universal and targeted services to young people.
- Granard Action Project, Co. Longford is an example of a family support service working with children and young people in a rural town.

5. Promoting partnership

The three profiles in this category are pro-active regarding the development of partnership with service users:

- The Family Welfare Conference Project, Dublin mobilises the support of the extended family to develop a plan for family support.
- The Family Rights Group, Limerick was established by the Mid-Western Health Board to address the powerlessness of parents who have children in care.
- The Western Health Board developed a strategy to promote parental participation at child protection conferences.

6. Therapeutic approaches

Two examples of therapeutic approaches used in child and family interventions are:

- 'Back to Basics', Midland Health Board is a social model of occupational therapy/speech and language therapy for children with autism and their families.

- The Integrated Model of Self Regulation (IMSR) for children in care, NWHB, Donegal has been operational for more than two decades and combines sensory integration with attachment theory.

7. Work with children in care and aftercare

The four profiles in this section relate to assessment of children's needs, approaches to working with children in care and a model of aftercare support:

- The Airne Villa Resource and Assessment Unit, Co. Kerry is an example of a dedicated unit that assesses the needs of children entering care.
- The Amiens St. Childcare Centre, Dublin has several decades experience of caring for children in their own community, while maintaining the child's links with home, community and their sense of identity.
- Gleann Alainn, Glanmire, Co. Cork uses a behavioural approach to deal with difficult behaviour.
- The Aftercare Programme was developed by the Mid-Western Health Board to provide planning, support and guidance for young people leaving care and includes a supported lodgings scheme.

8. Policy and service development

This final set of profiles relate to Health Board policy initiatives designed to develop more effective service provision:

- The Children Services Forum, Carlow is an inter-disciplinary South Eastern Health Board initiative developed to tackle the issue of non-attendance at early years services and generally improve the co-ordination of such services.
- The North Eastern Health Board strategy in relation to developing a comprehensive Family Support Policy Framework is outlined.
- A Quality Management System, accredited by ISO 9002 was implemented by the Roscommon Social Work Team of the Western Health Board.

Source: Department of Health and Children, *Working for Children and Families: Exploring Best Practice*, 2003: http://www.nuigalway.ie/childandfamily research

Classification of personality disorders

People may display the signs of more than one personality disorder.

CLUSTER A: 'SUSPICIOUS'

Paranoid

- suspicious
- feel that other people are being nasty to you (even when evidence shows this isn't true)
- sensitive to rejection
- tend to hold grudges

Schizoid

- emotionally 'cold'
- don't like contact with other people, prefer your own company
- have a rich fantasy world

Schizotypal

- eccentric behaviour
- odd ideas
- difficulties with thinking
- lack of emotion, or inappropriate emotional reactions
- can see or hear strange things
- related to schizophrenia, the mental illness

CLUSTER B: 'EMOTIONAL AND IMPULSIVE'

Antisocial, or dissocial

- don't care about the feelings of others
- are easily frustrated
- tend to be aggressive
- commit crimes
- find it difficult to make intimate relationships
- impulsive – do things on the spur of the moment without thinking about them
- don't feel guilty
- don't learn from unpleasant experiences

Borderline, or emotionally unstable

- impulsive
- find it hard to control emotions
- feel bad about yourself
- often self-harm, e.g. cutting yourself or making suicide attempts
- feel 'empty'
- make relationships quickly, but easily lose them
- can feel paranoid or depressed
- when stressed, may hear noises or voices

Histrionic

- over-dramatise events
- self-centered
- show strong emotions, but which change quickly and don't last long
- can be suggestible
- worry a lot about your appearance
- crave new things and excitement
- can be seductive

Narcissistic

- have a strong sense of your own self-importance
- dream of unlimited success, power and intellectual brilliance
- crave attention from other people, but show few warm feelings in return
- exploit others
- ask for favours that you do not then return

CLUSTER C: 'ANXIOUS'

Obsessive-compulsive

- worry and doubt a lot
- perfectionist – always check things
- rigid in what you do
- cautious, preoccupied with detail
- worry about doing the wrong thing
- find it hard to adapt to new situations
- often have high moral standards
- judgemental
- sensitive to criticism
- can have obsessional thoughts and images (although these are not as bad as those in obsessive-compulsive disorder)

Avoidant (aka Anxious/Avoidant)

- very anxious and tense
- worry a lot
- feel insecure and inferior
- have to be liked and accepted
- extremely sensitive to criticism

Dependent

- passive
- rely on others to make their own decisions
- do what other people want you to do
- find it hard to cope with daily chores
- feel hopeless and incompetent
- easily feel abandoned by others

Source: Royal College of Psychiatrists

British Psychological Society Practitioners' obligations and responsibilities to self and to clients

1.1 COMPETENCE

Following Section 2 of the Society's Code, practitioners will offer their best practice while recognising their current limitations in terms of training and ability and not practise beyond them. They will continue throughout their careers to maintain and develop their knowledge and skills by undertaking and recording continuing professional development, including keeping abreast of the literature, broadening professional and personal experience, consulting with colleagues, participating in workshops, courses and conferences as well as regularly reviewing their own needs and performance. The supervision relationship . . . is a key element in this process. Accredited (chartered) practitioners will ensure that they are in possession of a current practising certificate irrespective of the amount or context of their practice. Practitioners will ensure that they accurately represent their current level of training and competence.

1.2 FITNESS TO PRACTISE

Practitioners will:

- continually monitor and maintain an effective level of personal functioning; i.e. should a practitioner feel unable to work effectively, he or she will seek advice from the supervisor or professional consultant. If necessary, the practitioner will withdraw for a time period considered appropriate;
- respond to concerns about the fitness of a colleague to practise safely. In order to safeguard both the client and the profession, they have a duty to discuss their concerns with their colleague or to share their concern with a senior colleague so that safe practice is maintained. The safety of the client is paramount;
- ensure that they hold adequate, professional indemnity insurance and maintain their personal safety;

- always seek to support clients' control over their lives and their ability to make appropriate decisions;
- be mindful of the power dynamics of the professional/client relationship;
- respect the diversity of beliefs and values held within society and will continually review their practice with due regard to changing societal norms;
- respect clients' autonomy.

In view of the personal and often intense nature of the therapeutic relationship practitioners must actively avoid any exploitation of their clients financially, sexually, emotionally or in any other way.

Special regard will be paid to the Society's statement (in the Code of Conduct) on Sexual Harassment and Dual Relationships. With respect to the latter, therapeutic relationships expressly preclude sexual relationships and all boundary issues will be carefully considered. Any concerns must be discussed with the supervisor as a matter of urgency. It is the practitioner's responsibility to define and maintain clear and appropriate boundaries. Regardless of the theoretical orientation or approach adopted, practitioners will always endeavour to gain clients' agreement to engage in their counselling psychology practice. (See also the discussion of informed consent in the Division of Counselling Psychology's Guidelines on Confidentiality and Record Keeping.)

1.3 CONTRACTING

Practitioners will:

- be responsible for making clear and explicit contracts;
- inform clients of any financial liabilities before they are incurred;
- inform clients of issues of confidentiality, including those pertaining to record keeping, supervision, research and continuing professional development, during the contracting process.

Contracts must be subject to regular review.

1.4 CONFIDENTIALITY

For further detailed information refer to the Division of Counselling Psychology's Guidelines on Confidentiality and Record Keeping. Rigorous respect for issues of confidentiality is fundamental to the ethical practice of counselling psychology. Practitioners will clarify and explain the nature and extent of confidentiality from the start of the contract. All circumstances in which confidentiality may be breached will be identified. Client records must be held securely at all times. The nature and purpose of records kept and the client's rights of access will be made clear at the outset of the contract. Practitioners will make provision for appropriate access to records and appropriate notification of clients in the event of their own death or incapacity. Agreements about confidentiality will continue after a client's death unless legal or ethical considerations demand otherwise.

1.5 CONFIDENTIALITY IN THE LEGAL PROCESS

It is a fundamental responsibility of the practitioner to be aware of the specific legal implications of their work, including the general legal requirements concerning the giving and withholding of information, and the obligation to seek professional support and guidance when necessary. The practitioner will establish channels for discussing legal issues with appropriately qualified people, in advance of the specific need.

Source: www.bps.org.uk

References

Aarts, P. and Op den Velde, W., 'Prior traumatization and the process of aging: Theory and clinical implications' in B.A. van der Kolk *et al.*, eds, *Traumatic Stress: The effects of overwhelming experience on mind, body, and society*, New York: Guilford 1996.

Abkarian, G. G., 'Communication effects of prenatal alcohol exposure', *Journal of Communication Disorders* 25 (1992), 221–40.

Abramson, L. Y., Seligman, M. E. P. and Teasdale, J. D., 'Learned helplessness in humans: Critique and reformulation', *Journal of Abnormal Psychology* 87 (1978), 32–48.

Ainsworth, M. D. S., Blehar, M. C., Waters, E. and Wall, S., *Patterns of Attachment: A psychological study of the strange situation*, Hillsdale, NJ: Erlbaum 1978.

Allport, G., *Handbook of Social Psychology*, Worcester, MA: Clark University Press 1954.

Allport, G., *The Nature of Prejudice*, Reading, MA: Addison-Wesley 1954; 1979.

American Psychiatry Association, *Diagnostic and Statistical Manual of Mental Disorders DSM-IV-TR*, 4th ed., APA 2000.

Asch, S. E., 'Effects of group pressure upon the modification and distortion of judgment' in H. Guetzkow, ed., *Groups, Leadership and Men*, Pittsburgh, PA: Carnegie Press 1951.

Asch, S. E., 'Studies of independence and conformity: A minority of one against a unanimous majority', *Psychological Monographs* 70 (1956) (Whole no. 416).

Atkinson, J. W., 'Motivational determinants of risk-taking behavior' (1957) in *Personality, Motivation, and Action: Selected papers*, New York: Praeger 1983.

Ayuso-Mateos, J. L., Pereda, A., Dunn, G., Vazquez-Barquero, J. L., Casey, P., Lehtinen, V., Dalgard, O., Wilkinson, G. and Dowrick, C., 'Predictors of compliance with psychological interventions offered in the community', *Psychological Medicine* 37(5) (2007), 717–25.

Babyak, M. A., Blumenthal, J. A., Herman, S., Khatri, P., Doraiswamy, P. M., Moore, K. A., Craighead, W. E., Baldewicz, T. T. and Krishnan, K. R., 'Exercise treatment for major depression: Maintenance of therapeutic benefit at 10 months', *Psychosomatic Medicine* 62 (2000), 633–8.

Bandura, A., 'Autobiography' in M. G. Lindzey and W. M. Runyan, eds, *A History of Psychology in Autobiography*, Vol. IX, Washington, DC: American Psychological Association 2006.

Bandura, A., 'The evolution of social cognitive theory' in K. Smith and M. Hitt, *Great Minds in Management: The process of theory management*, Oxford: Oxford University Press 2001.

Baron-Cohen, S., *The Essential Difference: The extreme male brain*, London: Penguin 2004.

Baumrind, D., 'Effects of authoritative parental control on child behavior', *Child Development*, 37(4) (1966), 887–907.

Beardslee, W. R., 'The role of self-understanding in resilient individuals: The development of a perspective', *American Journal of Orthopsychiatry*, 59 (1989), 266–278.

Beck, A. T., Rush, A. J., Shaw, B. F. and Emery, G., *Cognitive Therapy of Depression*, New York: Guilford 1979.

Beck, A. T., 'Cognitive therapy of depression: New perspectives' in P. J. Clayton and J. E. Barrett, eds, *Treatment of Depression: Old controversies and new approaches*, New York: Raven Press 1983.

Becker, E., *The Denial of Death*, New York: Free Press 1973.

Beecher, B., 'The medical model, mental health practitioners, and individuals with schizophrenia and their families', *Journal of Social Work Practice*, 23(1) (2009), 9–20.

Benson, C., 'The unthinkable boundaries of self: The role of negative emotional boundaries for the formation, maintenance, and transformation of identities' in R. Harré and F. M. Moghaddam, eds, *The Self and Others: Positioning individuals and groups in personal, political and cultural contexts*, Westport, CT: Praeger 2003.

Berger, P. L. and Luckmann, T., *The Social Construction of Reality: A treatise in the sociology of knowledge*, New York: Anchor 1967

Best, D., Day, E., McCarthy, T., Darlington, I. and Pinchbeck, K., 'The hierarchy of needs and care planning in addiction services: What Maslow can tell us about addressing competing priorities?', *Addiction Research and Theory*, 16(4) (2008), 305–7.

Bishop, S. and Leadbeater, B., 'Maternal social support patterns and child maltreatment: Comparison of maltreating and nonmaltreating mothers', *American Journal of Orthopsychiatry*, 69 (1999), 172–81.

Black, M. M., 'The roots of child neglect' in R. M. Reece, ed., *Treatment of Child Abuse: Common ground for mental health, medical, and legal practitioners*, Baltimore, MD: Johns Hopkins University Press 2000.

Blatt, S. J. and Zuroff, D. C., 'Interpersonal relatedness and self-definition: Two prototypes for depression', *Clinical Psychology Review*, 12 (1992), 527–62.

Blyth, D. and Traeger, C., 'Adolescent self-esteem and perceived relationships with parents and peers' in S. Salzinger, J. Antrobus and M. Hammer, eds, *Social Networks of Children, Adolescents and College Students*, Hillsdale, NJ: Erlbaum Associates 1988.

Bowlby, J., 'Maternal care and mental health', World Health Organization Monograph (1951) (Serial No. 2).

Bowlby, J., *Attachment and Loss*, Vol. 2., London: Hogarth 1980.

Boyd, D. and Bee, H., *Lifespan Development*, 4th ed., New York: Allyn and Bacon 2005.

Breese, J. R. and Feltey, K. M., 'Role exit from home to homeless', *Free Inquiry in Creative Sociology*, 24 (1996), 67–76.

Brewin, C. and Andrews, B., 'Psychological defence mechanisms: The example of repression', *The Psychologist*, Special Issue: Freud in a Modern Light, 13(12) (2000), 615–17.

Bronfenbrenner, U., *The Ecology of Human Development*, Cambridge, MA: Harvard University Press 1979.

Brooker, D., 'What is person-centred care in dementia?', *Reviews in Clinical Gerontology* 13 (2004), 215–22.

Brooks-Gunn, J., Petersen, A. C. and Eichorn, D., 'The study of maturational timing effects in adolescence', *Journal of Youth and Adolescence* 14(3) (1985), 149–61.

Bruch, H., Czyzewski D. and Suhr, M. A., *Conversations with Anorexics*, New York: Basic Books 1988.

Buck, R. and Ginsburg, B. E., 'Emotional communication and altruism: The communicative gene hypothesis' in M. Clark, ed., *Altruism: Review of Personality and Social Psychology*, Vol. 12, Newbury Park, CA: Sage 1991.

Bugental, J., 'The third force in psychology', *Journal of Humanistic Psychology* 4(1) (1964), 19–25.

Buskist, W. and Miller, H., 'The analysis of human operant behavior: A brief census of the literature, 1958–1981', *The Behavior Analyst* 5 (1982), 137–41.

Cain, D. J., 'Advancing humanistic psychology and psychotherapy: Some challenges and proposed solutions', *Journal of Humanistic Psychology*, 43(3) (2003), 10–41.

Carnahan, T. and McFarland, S., 'Revisiting the Standford Prison Experiment: Could self-selection have led to the cruelty?', *Personality and Social Psychology Bulletin* 33(5) (2007), 603–14.

Carr, A. and Byrne, J., 'Psychosocial profiles of Irish children with conduct disorders, mixed disorders of conduct and emotion and emotional disorders' in A. Carr, ed., *Clinical Psychology in Ireland: Empirical studies of problems and treatment processes in children and adolescents*, Vol. 3, New York: Edwin Mellen 2000.

Carr, A., *The Handbook of Clinical and Adolescent Clinical Psychology: A contextual approach*, New York, Brunner-Routledge 2003.

Carr, A., *Positive Psychology: The science of happiness and human strengths*, London: Brunner-Routledge 2004.

Carr, A., 'Effectiveness of Psychotherapy', 2007; http://www.psychotherapy-ireland.com/wp-content/uploads/2007/09/recommendations.pdf.

Carter, R., *Mapping the Mind*, London: Phoenix Publishers 1998.

Carter, R., *The Brain Book*, London: Dorling Kindersley 2009.

Cattell, R. B. and Horn, J. L., 'Age differences in fluid and crystallized intelligence', *Acta Psychologica* 26 (1967), 107–29.

Central Statistics Office, *Ageing in Ireland*, Dublin: Stationery Office 2007.

Cianciolo, A. T. and Sternberg, R. J., *Intelligence: A brief history*, Malden, MA: Blackwell 2004.

Clarke, A. M. and Clarke, A. D. B., *Early Experience: Myth and Evidence*, London: Open Books, 1976.

Cohen, D. J. and Volkmar, F. R., *Handbook of Autism and Pervasive Developmental Disorder*, 2nd ed., New York: John Wiley and Sons 1997.

Commission on the Status of People with Disabilities, A *Strategy for Equality: Report of the Commission on the Status of People with Disabilities*, Stationery Office, Dublin 1996.

Connolly, G., Kennelly, S., Conroy, R. and Byrne, P., 'Teenage pregnancy in the Rotunda Hospital, 1992–1996, A review', *Irish Medical Journal* 91 (1998), 209–12.

Coolican, H., *Research Methods and Statistics in Psychology*, 5th ed., London: Hodder Education 2009.

Costa, P. and McCrae, R., 'A five-factor theory on the Rorschach', *Rorschachiana*, 27 (2005), 80–100.

Cournoyer, B., *The Social Skills Workbook*, London: Wadsworth 1991.

Cowie, H., Smith, P. and Blacks, M., *Understanding Children's Development*, 3rd ed., Oxford: Blackwell 2003.

Cozolino, L., *The Neuroscience of Psychotherapy: Building and rebuilding the human brain*, New York: W. W. Norton 2002.

Crockett, L. and Petersen, A., 'Pubertal status and psychological development: Findings from early adolescence studies' in R. M. Lerner and T. T. Foch, eds, *Biological-psychosocial Interactions in Early Adolescence: A lifespan perspective*, Hillsdale NJ: Erlbaum 1987.

Crosse, S., Kaye, E. and Ratnofsky, A., A *Report on the Maltreatment of Children with Disabilities*, Washington, DC: National Clearinghouse on Child Abuse and Neglect 1993.

Curtiss, S., *Genie: A psycholinguistic study of a modern day 'wild child'*, London: Academic Press 1977.

Daichman, L. S., 'Elder abuse in developing countries' in M. Johnson, ed., *The Cambridge Handbook of Age and Ageing*, Cambridge: Cambridge University Press 2005.

Damasio, A., *The Feeling of What Happens: Body and emotion in the making of consciousness*, New York: Harcourt Brace 1999.

Darley, J. M. and Latané, B., 'Bystander "apathy"', *American Scientist* 57 (1969), 244–68.

Davidson, L., 'Philosophical foundations of humanistic psychology', *The Humanistic Psychologist* 28(1–3) (2000), 7–31.

De Maat, S., de Jonghe, F., Schoevers, R. and Dekker, J., 'The effectiveness of long-term psychoanalytic therapy: A systematic review of empirical studies', *Harvard Review of Psychiatry*, 17 (2009), 1–23.

De Raad, B. and Perugini, M., eds, *Big Five Assessment*, Göttingen, Germany: Hogrefe and Huber 2002.

De St. Aubin, E., McAdams, D. P. and Kim, T.-C., eds, *The Generative Society: Caring for future generations*, Washington, DC: American Psychological Association 2004.

De Ward, S. and Moe, A., 'Like a prison: Homeless women's narratives of surviving shelter', *Journal of Sociology and Social Welfare*, 37 (1) (2010) 115–35.

De Wolff, M. S. and van Ijzendoorn, M. H., 'Sensitivity and attachment: A meta-analysis on parental antecedents of infant attachment', *Child Development*, 68 (1997), 571–91.

Dekovic, M. and Janssens, J. M., 'Parents' rearing style and child's sociometric status', *Developmental Psychology*, 28 (1992), 925–932.

Department of Health and Children, *Children First: National guidelines for the protection and welfare of children*, Dublin: Department of Health and Children 1999.

Department of Health and Children, *Working for Children and Families: Exploring Best practice*, Dublin: Department of Health and Children, 200???

Diaz-Laplante, J., 'Humanistic psychology and social transformation: Building the path towards a livable today and a just tomorrow', *Journal of Humanistic Psychology*, 47(1) (2007), 54–72.

Drewes, A., 'Bobo revisited: What the research says', *International Journal of Play Therapy* 17(1) (2008), 52–65.

Dryden, W., 'Some reflections on rational beliefs' in M. Neenan and W. Dryden, *Rational Emotive Behaviour Therapy: Advances in theory and practice*, London: Whurr 1999.

Dubas, J. S., Graber, J. A. and Petersen, A. C., 'The effects of pubertal development on achievement during adolescence', *American Journal of Education* 99 (1991), 444–60.

Elder, G. H., 'Human lives in changing societies: Life course and developmental insights' in R. Cairns, G. H. Elder and E. J. Costello, eds, *Developmental Science*, Cambridge: Cambridge University Press 2001.

Elkind, D., 'Egocentrism in adolescence', *Child Development* 38 (1967), 1025–33.

Elkins, D., 'Why humanistic psychology lost its power and influence in American psychology: Implications for advancing humanistic psychology', *Journal of Humanistic Psychology*, 49 (3) (2009), 267–91.

Ellis, B. J. and Garber, J., 'Psychosocial antecedents of variation in girls' pubertal timing: Maternal depression, stepfather presence, and marital and family stress', *Child Development*, 71 (2000), 485–501; http://ag.arizona. edu/fcs/fshd/people/ ellis/CD%20Ellis%20and%20Garber%202000.pdf [Accessed 17.8.2010]

Eron, L. D., Walder, L. O. and Lefkowitz, M. M., *Learning of Aggression in Children*, Boston: Little Brown 1971.

Farrington, D. P., 'Childhood aggression and adult violence: Early precursors and later outcomes' in D. J. Pepler and K. H. Rubin, eds, *The Development and Treatment of Childhood Aggression*, Hillsdale, NJ: Erlbaum 1991, 5–30.

Fein, S. and Spencer, S. J., 'Prejudice as self-image maintenance: Affirming the self through derogating others', *Journal of Personality and Social Psychology*, 73 (1997), 31–44.

Field, H. and Domangue, B., *Eating Disorders Throughout the Lifespan*, New York: Praeger 1987.

Fischoff, B., 'Hindsight ≠ foresight: The effect of outcome knowledge on judgement under certainity', *Journal of Experimental Psychology: Human Perception and Performance* 1975, 1 (1975), 288–99.

Fiske, S. T. and Taylor, S. E., *Social Cognition*, Reading, MA.: Addison-Wesley 1984.

Fiske, S., *Stereotyping, Prejudice, and Discrimination: The handbook of social psychology*, Vol. 2, 4th ed., New York: McGraw-Hill 1998.

Fitzmaurice, E., *Applied Social Care*, 2nd ed., Dublin: Gill and MacMillan 2009.

Fitzpatrick, C. C., Fitzpatrick, P. E. and Turner, M. J., 'Profile of patients attending a Dublin adolescent antenatal booking clinic', *Irish Medical Journal*, 90 (1997), 96–7.

Fox, E. and Riconscente, M., 'Metacognition and self-regulation in James, Piaget, and Vygotsky', *Educational Psychology Review*, 20 (2008), 373–89.

Freud, S., *An Outline of Psychoanalysis: The standard edition of the complete psychological works of Sigmund Freud, Vol. 23*, London: The Hogarth Press and the Institute of Psychoanalysis 1964.

Frith, U., *Autism: Explaining the enigma*, Oxford: Blackwell 1996.

Furnham, A., 'Belief in a just world: Research progress over the past decade', *Personality and Individual Differences*, 34 (2003), 795–811.

Gardner H., *Frames of Mind: The theory of multiple intelligence*, New York: Basic Books 1983.

Garmezy, N., 'Stressors of childhood' in N. Garmezy and M. Rutter, eds, *Stress, Coping and Development in Children*, New York: McGraw-Hill 1983, 43–84.

Garnefski, N. and Arends, E., 'Sexual abuse and adolescent maladjustment: Differences between male and female victims', *Journal of Adolescence*, 21 (1998), 99–107.

Geldard, K. and Geldard, D., *Practical Counselling Skills*, London: Palgrave Macmillan 2005.

Giedd, J., 'What makes teens tick?', *Time*, 10 May, 2004.

Giles, Bridget, ed., *Social Psychology*, London: Grange Books 2002.

Gilligan, R., 'Family support and child welfare: Realising the promise of the Child Care Act' in H. Ferguson and P. Kenny, eds, *On Behalf of the Child: Child welfare, child protection and the Child Care Act*, Dublin: Farmer 1995.

Gilligan, R., 'Promoting resilience in children in long-term care: The relevance of roles and relationships in the domains of recreation and work', *Journal of Social Work Practice* 22(3) (2008), 37–50.

Glass, G., 'Primary, secondary and meta-analysis of research', *Educational Researcher*, 5 (1976), 3–8.

Goffman, E., *Asylums: Essays on the Social Situation of Mental Patients and Other Inmates*, New York: Doubleday Anchor 1961.

Government of Ireland, *Disability Act 2005* (2005a); Available: http://www.oireachtas.ie/documents/bills28/acts/2005/a1405.pdf.

Greening, T., 'Five basic postulates of humanistic psychology', *Journal of Humanistic Psychology* 47 (2007), 1.

Griffin, S. and Shevlin, M., *Responding to Special Educational Needs: An Irish perspective*, Dublin: Gill and Macmillan 2007.

Gross, R., *Psychology: The science of mind and behaviour*, 6th ed., London: Hodder Education 2009.

Hall, D., 'Technical note: Extreme deprivation in early childhood', *Journal of Child Psychology and Psychiatry*, 26(5) (1985), 825.

Harter, S., 'Causes, correlates and the functional role of global self-worth: A life-span perspective' in R. J. Sternberg and J. Kolligian, eds, *Competence Considered*, New Haven, CT: Yale University Press 1990.

Hartman, D., 'Oppositional defiant disorder', 2007; http://www.sess.ie/categories/emotional-disturbance-and/or-behavioural-problems/oppositional-defiant-disorder [Accessed 17.6.2010].

Hay, D. F., 'Prosocial development', *Journal of Child Psychology and Psychiatry*, 35 (1994), 29–71.

Health Service Executive, *Protecting Our Future*, Dublin: Stationery Office 2002.

Herbert, M., *Typical and Atypical Development: From conception to adolescence*, Oxford: BPS Blackwell 2006.

Hetherington, E. M. and Parke, R. D., *Child Psychology: A contemporary viewpoint*, 5th ed., New York: McGraw-Hill 1999.

Hoffman, M., 'The origins and development of empathy', *Motivation and Emotion* 14 (2) (1990), 75–80.

Holt, S., Manners, P. and Gilligan, R., *An Evaluation of the Naas Child and Family Project: A Springboard initiative*, Kildare Youth Services and South Western Health Board 2002.

Honigmann, I. and Honigmann, J., 'Child-rearing patterns among the Great Whale River Eskimo' (1954) in H. R. Schaffer, *Social Development*, Oxford: Blackwell 1996.

Horkan, M. and Woods, A., *This Is Our World: Perspectives of some elderly people on life in suburban Dublin*, Report no. 12, National Council for the Aged, 1986; http://www.ncaop.ie/publications/research/reports/This_Is_Our_World12.pdf [Accessed 11.9.2007].

Hruby, G., 'Sociological, postmodern, and new realism perspectives in social constructionism: Implications for literacy research', *Research Reading Quarterly* 36(1) (2001), 48–62.

Irish College of Psychiatrists, *A Better Future Now: Position statement on psychiatric services for children and adolescents in Ireland*, 2005; http://www.rcpsych.ac.uk/files/pdfversion/op60.pdf [Accessed 12.7.2010].

Jablensky, A., Sartorius, N., Ernberg, G., Anker, M., Korten, A., Cooper, J. E., Day, R. and Bertelsen, A. (1992), 'Schizophrenia: Manifestations, Incidence and Course in Different Cultures. A World Health Organization Ten-Country Study' in *Psychological Medicine Monograph Supplement* 20, Cambridge: Cambridge University Press 1992.

Jahoda, M., *Current Concepts of Positive Mental Health*, New York: Basic Books 1958.

Janoff-Bulman, R., *Shattered Assumptions: Towards a new psychology of trauma*, New York: Free Press 1992.

Janoff-Bulman, R. and Frantz, C. M., 'The impact of trauma on meaning: From meaningless world to meaningful life' in M. Power and C. Brewin eds, *The Transformation of Meaning in Psychological Therapies: integrating theory and practice*, Chichester, Sussex: John Wiley & Sons 1997.

Kalikow, T. J., 'Konrad Lorenz' in Alan E. Kazdin, ed., *Encyclopedia of Psychology*, Vol. 5, Washington, DC: American Psychological Association 2000.

Karau, S. J., 'Deindividuation' in A. E. Kazdin, ed., *Encyclopedia of Psychology*, Vol. 2, Washington, DC: American Psychological Association 2000.

Kelly, B. D., 'Penrose's law in Ireland: An ecological analysis of psychiatric inpatients and prisoners', *Irish Medical Journal*, 100(2) (2007), 373–4.

Kingston, L. and Prior, M., 'The development of patterns of stable, transient and school-age aggressive behavior in young children', *Journal of American Academy of Child and Adolescent Psychiatry* 34 (1995), 348–58.

Kirk, S., Gallagher, J. J., Coleman, M. R. and Anastasiow, N., *Educating Exceptional Children*, Boston: Houghton Mifflin 2000.

Klein, M., 'The mutual influences in the development of ego and id', *Psychoanal. Study Child* 7 (1952), 51–3.

Kolb, B. and Whishaw, I. Q., *Fundamentals of Human Neuropsychology* (5th edition), New York: Freeman-Worth 2003.

Lalor, K. and Share, P., *Applied Social Care: An introduction for students in Ireland*, Dublin: Gill and Macmillan 2009.

Larson, R., 'Toward a psychology of positive youth work', *American Psychologist* 55(1) (2000), 170–83.

Latané, B. and Darley, J. M., 'Group inhibition of bystander intervention in emergencies', *Journal of Personality and Social Psychology* 10 (1968), 215–21.

LeClerc, G., 'The self-actualization concept: A content validation', *Journal of Social Behaviour and Personality* 13(1) (1998), 69–84.

Lee, B. J. and Goerge, R. M., 'Poverty, early childbearing, and child maltreatment: A multinomial analysis', *Child and Youth Services Review* 21(9–10) (1999), 755–80.

Lerner, M. J., 'Evaluation of performance as a function of performer's reward and attractiveness', *Journal of Personality and Social Psychology* 1 (1965), 355–60.

Levinson, D., 'A conception of adult development', *American Psychologist* 41(1) (1986), 3–13.

Lewis-Beck, M. S., Bryman, A. and Liao, T. F., *The Sage Encyclopedia of Social Science Research Methods*, London: Sage, 2003.

Luthar, S. and Zigler, E., 'Vunerability and competence: A review of research on resilience in childhood', *American Journal of Orthopsychiatry* 61(1) (1991), 1–22.

MacLeod, J., *An Introduction to Counselling*, London: Open University 2003.

Magnusson, D., Stattin, H. and Allen, V. L., 'Biological maturation and social development: A longitudinal study of some adjustment processes from mid adolescence to adulthood', *Journal of Youth and Adolescence* 14(4) (1985), 267–83.

Maldonado, J. R., Butler, L. D. and Spiegel, D., 'Treatments for dissociative disorders' in P. E. Nathan and J. M. Gordon, eds, *A Guide to Treatments that Work*, New York: Oxford University Press 1998.

Malim, T. and Birch, A., *Research Methods and Statistics* (Introductory Psychology Series), London: Palgrave Macmillan 1997.

Malina, R. M., Bouchard, C. and Bar-Or, O., *Growth, Maturation and Physical Activity*, 2nd ed., Human Kinetics Europe 2004.

Mann, L., 'The baiting crowd in episodes of threatened suicide', *Journal of Personality and Social Psychology*, 41(4) (1981), 703–9.

Marcia, J., 'Identity in adolesence' in J. Adelson, ed., *Handbook of Adolescent Psychology*, New York: Wiley 1980.

Maslow, A., 'A theory of human motivation', *Psychological Review*, 50 (1943), 370–96.

Maslow, A., 'Humanistic science and transcendent experiences', *Journal of Humanistic Psychology* 5 (1965), 219–27.

Maslow, A., *Motivation and Personality*, 3rd ed., New York: Harper & Row 1970.

Masten, A. S., 'Ordinary magic: Resilience processes in development', *American Psychologist*, 56 (2001), 227–38.

McAvoy, H., Sturley, J., Burke, S. and Balanda, K., 'Unequal at birth: Inequalities in the occurrence of low birthweight babies in Ireland', The Institute of Public Health in Ireland (2006); http://www.publichealth.ie/ index.asp?locID=489 anddocID=689 [Accessed 1.6.2010].

McKay, S., 'Ireland and rape crises' in W. Balzano and M. Sullivan, eds, *The Irish Review* 35 (Summer 2007), 92–9.

Meltzoff, A. and Moore, M., 'Imitation of facial and manual gestures by human neonates', *Science* 198 (1977), 75–8.

Meltzoff, A. and Moore, M., 'Infant imitation and memory: nine month olds in immediate and deferred tasks', *Child Development* 59 (1988), 217–25.

Mental Health Commission, *Code of Practice: Guidance for persons working in mental health services with people with intellectual disabilities*, 2009; http://www.mhcirl.ie/Mental_Health_Act_2001/Mental_Health_Commission_Codes_of_Practice/People_with_Intellectual_Disabilities/Code_of_Practice_

Guidance_for_Persons_working_in_Mental_Health_Services_with_People_with_Intellectual_Disabilities.pdf.

Milgram, Stanley, *Obedience to Authority: An experimental view*, London: Harpercollins 1974.

Miller, J. G., Bersoff, D. M. and Harwood, R. L., 'Perceptions of social responsibilities in India and in the United States: Moral imperatives or personal decisions?', *Journal of Personality and Social Psychology* 58 (1990), 33–47.

Miller, P., *Theories of Developmental Psychology*, 4th ed., New York: Worth Publishers 2002.

Monteith, Margo, 'Self-regulation of prejudiced responses: Implications for progress in prejudice-reduction efforts', *Journal of Personality and Social Psychology* 65(3) (1993), 469–85.

Moody, H., 'Ethical dilemmas in old age care' in Johnson, M., ed., *The Cambridge Handbook of Age and Ageing*, Cambridge: Cambridge University Press 2005.

Morse, B. A., 'Fetal Alcohol Syndrome in the Developing Child', paper presented at the Fetal Alcohol Syndrome and Other Congenital Alcohol Disorders: A National Conference on Surveillance and Prevention, Centers for Disease Control, Atlanta, GA, 1991.

Mraovick, L. and Wilson, J., 'Patterns of child abuse and neglect associated with chronological age of children living in a midwestern county', *Child Abuse and Neglect* 23(9) (1999), 899–903.

Mrazek, P. and Mrazek, D., 'Resilience in child maltreatment victims: A Conceptual exploration', *Child Abuse and Neglect* 11 (1987), 357–66.

Nanson, J. L., Hiscock, M., 'Attention deficits in children exposed to alcohol prenatally', *Alcoholism: Clinical and Experimental Research* 14 (1990), 656–61.

Nasser, M., 'The rise and fall of the anti-psychiatry movement', *The Psychiatrist* 19(12) (1995), 743–6.

National Children's Bureau, *Promoting the Health and Well-being of Young People in Supported Housing: A practical guide and training manual*, National Children's Bureau 2006.

National Institute of Mental Health, 'Schizophrenia'; http://www.nimh.nih.gov/health/publications/schizophrenia/complete-index.shtml [Accessed 6.7.2010].

Nevin, J., 'Analyzing Thorndike's law of effect: the question of stimulus-response bonds', *Journal of the Experimental Analysis of Behaviour* 72 (1999), 447–50.

Nixon, L., Greene, S. and Hogan, D., 'Concepts of family among children and young people in Ireland', *The Irish Journal of Psychology*, 27(1–2) (2006), 79–87.

O'Brien, M., Alldred, P. and Jones, D. (1996), 'Children's constructions of family and kinship' in J. Brannen and M. O'Brien (eds.) *Children in Families: Research and Policy*, London: Falmer Press 1996.

O'Donovan, M.-A. and Doyle, A. 'Measure of Activity and Participation (MAP): Participation and ageing: The experience of people 'on the NPSDD', *MAP*

Bulletin, 4 (2009); http://www.hrb.ie/uploads/tx_hrbpublications/ MAPBulletin Issue4.pdf.

Ochberg, F., 'Post-traumatic Therapy' in G. Everly, and J., Lating, *Psychotraumatology*, London: Plenum Press 1995.

Okumura, Y., Tanimukai, S. and Asada, T., 'Effects of short-term reminiscence therapy on elderly with dementia: A comparison with everyday conversation approaches', *Psychogeriatics* 8 (2008), 124–33.

Paluck, E. L. and Green, D. P., 'Prejudice reduction: What works? A critical look at evidence from the field and the laboratory', *Annual Review of Psychology* 60 (2009), 339–67.

Pancer, M., 'Social psychology: The crisis continues' in Dennis Fox and Isaac Prilleltensky, eds, *Critical Psychology: An introduction*, Thousand Oaks, CA: Sage 1997.

Papalia, D. E., Olds, S. W. and Feldman, R. D., *Human Development*, 10th ed., New York: McGraw-Hill 2005.

Passer, M. and Smith, R., *Psychology: Frontiers and applications*, New York: McGraw-Hill 2001.

Pearson, E. and Podeschi, R., 'Humanism and individualism: Maslow and his critics', *Adult Education Quarterly* 50(1) (Fall 1999), 41–55.

Peterson, C. and Seligman, M., *Character Strengths and Virtues: A handbook and classification*, Washington, DC: Oxford University Press 2004.

Pettigrew, T. F., 'The ultimate attribution error: Extending Allport's cognitive analysis of prejudice', *Personality and Social Psychology Bulletin* 5(4) (1979), 461–76.

Pipher, M., *Reviving Ophelia: Saving the selves of adolescent girls*, New York: Ballantine Books 1994.

Pope, K. and Tabachnick, B., 'Therapists as patients: A national survey of psychologists' experiences, problems and beliefs', *Professional Psychology: Research and Practice* 25(3) (1993), 247–58.

Radke-Yarrow, M., Cummings, E. M., Kuczinsky, L. and Chapman, M., 'Patterns of attachment in two- and three-year-olds in normal families and families with parental depression', *Child Development* 56 (1985), 884–93.

Revelle, W., 'Personality structure and measurement: The contribution of Raymond Cattell', *British Journal of Psychology* 100 (2009), 253–7.

Robbins, B., 'What is the good life? Positive psychology and the renaissance of humanistic psychology', *The Humanistic Psychologist*, 36 (2008), 96–112.

Roberts, B. W. and Del Vecchio, W. F., 'The rank-order consistency of personality traits from childhood to old age: A quantitative review of longitudinal studies', *Psychological Bulletin*, 126 (2000), 3–25.

Roberts, J. and Dicenso, A., 'Identifying the best research design to fit the question: Part 1: quantitative designs', *Evidenced-based Nursing* 2 (1999), 4–6.

Rochat, P., 'Origins of self-concept' in G. Bremner and A. Fogel, eds, *Blackwell Handbook of Infant Development*, Oxford: Blackwell 2001.

Rogers, Carl, *On Becoming a Person*, 1961.

Rolland, J.-P., 'Cross-cultural generalizability of the five-factor model of personality' in R. R. McCrae and J. Allik, eds, *The Five-Factor Model of Personality across Cultures*, New York: Kluwer Academic/Plenum 2002.

Rosenberg, M., 'Self-concept and psychological well-being in adolescence' in R. L. Leahy, ed., *The Development of the Self*, Orlando, FL: Academic Press 1985.

Rushton, J. P., Fulker, D. W., Neale, M. C., Nias, D. K. B. and Eysenck, H. J., 'Altruism and aggression: The heritability of individual differences', *Journal of Personality and Social Psychology* 50 (1986), 1192–8.

Rutter, M. and Bartak, L., 'Special education treatment of autistic children: A comparative study: I. Follow-up findings and implications for services', *Journal of Child Psychology and Psychiatry* 14 (1973), 241–70.

Rutter, M., 'Pathway from childhood to adult life', *Journal of Child Psychology and Psychiatry* 30 (1989), 23–51.

Rutter, M., 'Practitioner review: Routes from research to clinical practice in child psychiatry: Retrospect and prospect', *Journal of Child Psychology and Psychiatry* 39(6) (1998), 805–16.

Rutter, M., 'Resilience concepts and findings: Implications for family therapy', *Journal of Family Therapy* 21 (1999), 119–44.

Rutter, M., Bailey, A., Simonoff, E. and Pickles, A., 'Genetic influences in autism' in D. J. Cohen and F. R. Volkmar, eds, *Handbook of Autism and Pervasive Developmental Disorders*, 2nd ed., New York: Wiley 1997.

Rutter, M. and the English and Romanian Adoptees (ERA) study team, 'Developmental catch-up, and deficit, following adoption after severe global early privation', *Journal of Child Psychology and Psychiatry* 39(4) (1998), 465–76.

Schaffer, H. R., *Social Development*, Oxford: Blackwell 1996.

Schaie, K. W. and Willis, S. L., 'A stage theory model of adult cognitive development revisited' in R. Rubenstein, M. Ross and M. Kleban, eds, *The Many Dimensions of Ageing: Essays in honor of M. Powell Lawton*, New York: Springer 2000.

Schilling, R. and Schinke, S., 'Personal coping and social support for parents of handicapped children', *Child and Youth Services Review* 6 (1984), 195–206.

Schlundt, D. G. and Johnson, W. G., *Eating Disorders: Assessment and treatment*, Boston: Allyn and Bacon 1990.

Schorr, L. and Marchand, V., 'Pathway to the prevention of child abuse and neglect'(2007); http://www.dss.cahwnet.gov/cdssweb/entres/pdf/Pathway.pdf [Accessed 11.7.2010].

Sedlak, A. and Broadhurst, D., *Third National Incidence Study of Child Abuse and Neglect: Final report*, Washington, DC: US Government Printing Office 1996.

Seligman, M., *Helplessness: On depression, development, and death*, New York: Freeman 1992.

Seligman, M. and Csikszentmihalyi, M., 'Positive psychology: An introduction', *American Psychologist* 55 (2000), 5–14.

Shaffer, D. R., *Developmental Psychology: Childhood and adolescence*, 4th ed., Pacific Grove, CA: Brooks/Cole 1999.

Sherif, M., Harvey, O. J., White, B. J., Hood, W. R. and Sherif, C. W., *Intergroup Conflict and Cooperation: The Robbers Cave experiment*, Norman: University of Oklahoma Book Exchange 1961.

Singh, N. A., Clements, K. M., Fiattarone, M. A., 'A randomized controlled trial of progressive resistance training in depressed elders', *Journal of Gerontology* 52 (1997), 27–35.

Skinner, B. F., 'A brief survey of operant conditioning'; http://www.bfskinner.org/BFSkinner/SurveyOperantBehavior_files/A_brief_survey_of_operant_behavior.pdf [Accessed 6.6.2010].

Skinner, B. F., *The Behaviour of Organisms: An experimental analysis*, New York: Appleton 1938.

Skinner, B. F., *Science and Human Behavior*, New York: Macmillan 1953.

Skuse, D., 'Extreme deprivation in early childhood – I. Diverse outcomes for three siblings from an extraordinary family', *Journal of Child Psychology and Psychiatry* 25(4) (1984), 525–41.

Skuse, D., 'Extreme deprivation in early childhood – II. Theoretical issues and a comparative review', *Journal of Child Psychology and Psychiatry*, 25(4) (1984), 543–72.

Slattery, M., *Key Ideas in Sociology*, UK: Nelson Thornes 2003.

Smith, P., Cowie, H., Blades, M., *Understanding Children's Development*, 4th ed., London: Blackwell 2003.

Stark, L. R., 'The shelter as "total institution"', *American Behavioral Scientist* 37 (1994), 553–62.

Steiner, Jean-François, *Treblinka*, New York: Plume 1966.

Sternberg, R. J., *The Triarchic Mind: A new theory of human intelligence*, New York: Viking 1988.

Stratton, K., Howe, C. and Battaglia, F., eds, Institute of Medicine, Fetal Alcohol Syndrome: Diagnosis, Epidemiology, Prevention, and Treatment, Washington, DC: National Academy Press 1996.

Sunderland, M., *The Science of Parenting*, London: Dorling Kindersley 2006.

Szasz, T., *The Myth of Mental Illness: Foundations of a theory of personal conduct*, New York: Harper Row 1974.

Talerico, K., 'Person-centred approach: An important approach for 21st century health care', *Journal of Psychosocial and Mental Health Services*, 14(11) (2003), 14.

Thomas, D., Leicht, C., Hughes, C., Madigan, A. and Dowell, K., 'Emerging practices in the prevention of child abuse and neglect' (2003); http://www.childwelfare.gov/preventing/programs/whatworks/report/report.pdf [Accessed 10.8.2010].

Tiet, Q. Q., Bird, H. R. and Davies, M., 'Adverse life events and resilience', *Journal of the American Academy of Child and Adolescent Psychiatry* 37 (1998), 1191–200.

Tjeltveit, C., 'There is more to ethics than codes of professional ethics: Social ethics, theoretical ethics and managed care', *The Counselling Psychologist* 28(2) (2000), 242–52.

Trivers, R. L., 'The evolution of reciprocal altruism', *Quarterly Review of Biology* 46 (1971), 35–57.

Tzeng, O., Jackson, J. and Karlson, H., *Theories of Child Abuse and Neglect: Differential perspectives, summaries, and evaluations*, New York: Praeger 1991.

Vygotsky, L. S., *Mind and Society: The development of higher psychological processes*, Cambridge, MA: Harvard University Press 1978.

Walker, J., 'Communication and social work from an attachment perspective', *Journal of Social Work Practice*, 22(1) (2008), 1–22.

Waller, M., 'Resilience in an ecosystemic context: Evolution of the concept', *American Journal of Orthopsychiatry*, 71(3) (2001), 290–7.

Wasco, S. M., 'Conceptualizing the harm done by rape: Applications of trauma theory to experiences of sexual assault', *Trauma, Violence, and Abuse*, 4 (2003), 309–22.

Watson, J. and Rayner, R., 'Conditioned emotional reactions' (1920); http://psychclassics.yorku.ca/Watson/emotion.htm [Accessed 14.8.2010]

Weber, J. A. and McCormick, P., 'Alateen members and non-members understanding of alcoholism', *Journal of Alcohol and Drug Education*, 37(3) (1992), 74–84.

Weinstein, R., 'Goffman's asylums and the social situations of mental patients', *Orthomolecular Psychiatry*, 11(4) (1982), 267–74.

Werner, E. E., 'Risk, resilience, and recovery: Perspectives from the Kauai longitudinal study', *Development and Psychopathology*, 5 (1993), 503–15.

Whiting, B. and Whiting, J., *Children of Six Cultures*, Cambridge, MA: Harvard University Press 1975.

Windholz, G., 'Pavlov, psychoanalysis, and neuroses', *Pavlovian Journal of Biological Science*, 25(2) (1990), 48–52.

Woolhead, G., Tadd, W., Boix-Ferrer, J., Krajcik, S., Schmid-Pfahler, B., Spjuth, B., Stratton, D. and Dieppe, S., '"Tu" or "vous?" A European qualitative study of dignity and communication with older people in health and social care settings', *Patient Education and Counseling* 61 (2006), 363–71.

World Health Organization, *The Ottawa Charter for Health Promotion* (1986); http://www.who.int/healthpromotion/conferences/previous/ottawa/en/index.html [Accessed 14.6.2010].

World Health Organization, *Promoting Mental Health: Concepts, emerging evidence and practice*, Geneva: WHO (2005); http://www.who.int/mental_health/evidence/MH_Promotion_Book.pdf [Accessed 11.7.2010].

World Health Organization, *Child Maltreatment* (2010); http://www.who.int/topics/child_abuse/en/ [Accessed 15.8.2010].

Wyatt, R. C. and Livson, N., 'The not so great divide? Psychologists and psychiatrists take stands on the medical and psychosocial models of mental illness', *Professional Psychology: Research and Practice* 25 (1994), 120–31.

Zahn-Waxler, C., Radke-Yarrow, M. and King, R. A., 'Child-rearing and children's prosocial initiations toward victims of distress', *Child Development* 50 (1979), 319–30.

Zigler, E. F. and Finn-Stevenson, M., 'Applied developmental psychology' in M. H. Bornstein and M. E. Lamb, eds, *Developmental Psychology: An advanced textbook*, 4th ed., Mahwah, NJ: Earlbaum 1999.

Zimbardo, P. and Haney, C., 'The past and future of American prison policy: Twenty-five years after the Stanford Prison Experiment', *American Psychologist* 53(7) (1998), 709–27.

Zimbardo, P. G., 'Does psychology make a significant difference in our lives?', *American Psychologist* 59 (2004), 339–51.

WEBSITES

http://bfskinner.org/BFSkinner/SurveyOperantBehavior_files/A_brief_survey_of_o perant_behavior.pdf

http://childabusecommission.ie/rpt/05-03A.php]

http://medic.cardiff.ac.uk/archive_subsites/_/_/medic/subsites/dignity/projectfindin gs/index.html

http://www.rccp.cornell.edu/tcimainpage.html

www.aamr.org/content_100.cfm?navID=21

www.aamr.org/news/news_item.cfm?OID=1314

www.alzheimer.ie/eng/Media-Centre/Facts-About-Dementia/Irish-Statistics

www.apa.org/pubs/journals/releases/resolutiononvideoviolence.pdf

www.barnardos.ie/policies_and_campaigns/our-policy-priorities/child-protection.html

www.childmentalhealthcentre.org/index.html

www.cssp.org/major_initiatives/pathways.html

www.dohc.ie/press/releases/2007/20070907.html

www.dohc.ie/publications/pdf/children_first.pdf

www.dohc.ie/publications/pdf/hpstrat.pdf?direct=1

www.dohc.ie/publications/protecting_our_future.html)

www.dohc.ie/publications/springboard.html

www.drcc.ie/about/savi.pdf

www.enableireland.ie/sites/enableireland.ie/files/SPARCLE_-_a_multi-centre_European_study_of_the_relationship_of_environment_to_participation _and_QoL_in_children_with_CP.pdf

www.healthyminds.org/Document-Library/Brochure-Library/Lets-Talk-Facts-Warning-Signs-of-Major-Mental-Illnesses.aspx

www.healthyminds.org/Main-Topic/Schizophrenia.aspx

www.hse.ie/portal/eng/services/Publications/services/Older/openyoureyes.pdf

www.icsg.ie/Library/documents/Community%20Profile%20of%20SS%20for%20O lder%20People%20in%20Galway.pdf

www.irishhealth.com/index.html?level=4andid=10063andvar=print

www.mhcirl.ie/Publications/Mindmap_Teamwork.pdf

www.nacd.ie/publications/34482FamilySupport.pdf

www.ncbi.ie

www.nda.ie/cntmgmtnew.nsf/0/CE957ED7DA23464B802576CB005B809A/$File/
SexualAbuse2008_11.htm

www.nda.ie/cntmgmtnew.nsf/0/12AF395217EE3AC7802570C800430BB1/$File/0
6_principles.html

www.nda.ie/cntmgmtnew.nsf/0/588299199D4C28C7802575F500296134?OpenDo
cument

www.nda.ie/cntmgmtnew.nsf/0/851DE72FE32677F0802571CB005A165B/$File/re
search_children_disabilities_09.htm]

www.nda.ie/website/nda/cntmgmtnew.nsf/0/419BBFC356BC438A80257705003F
A51D/$File/mwd_litreview_12.htm

www.nhs.uk/conditions/hydrocephalus/Pages/Introduction.aspx

www.nhs.uk/video/pages/medialibrary.aspx?Id={D095EF23-B14E-4CA9-A6DB-
1490147F68A9}&Uri=video/2009/May/Pages/Personalitychangerealstory.aspx

www.nice.org.uk/media/187/2B/2009004AntisocialPersonalityDisorder.pdf

www.nice.org.uk/media/878/F7/CBTCommissioningGuide.pdf

www.nuigalway.ie/childandfamilyresearch/documents/exploring_good_practice.pdf

www.nrh.ie/LIVE_Docs/Brain per cent20Injury per cent20Inpatient per
cent20Programme.pdf

www.omc.gov.ie/documents/child_welfare_protection/Report_of_Special_Rapport
eur_on_Child_Protection_Geoffrey_Shannon.PDF

www.omc.gov.ie/documents/publications/ODTC_Full_Eng.pdf

www.omc.gov.ie/sonc2008/part3/abuse-and-neglect.asp]

www.omc.gov.ie/viewdoc.asp?fn=/documents/policy/natrecpol.htm

www.omc.gov.ie/viewtxt.asp?fn=/documents/Child_Welfare_Protection/OMCYA_
Child_Protection_Policy_Jan2009.doc

www.psihq.ie/DOCUMENTS/MILDpaper.PDF

www.psihq.ie/TRAINING_CAREERGUIDE.ASP]

www.puttingpeoplefirst.org.uk/_library/Resources/Personalisation/EastMidlands/W
orkstreams/PCP/newguidance/Person_Centred_Planning_-_Advice_
for_Providers.pdf]

www.tcd.ie/childrensresearchcentre/assets/pdf/Publications/gardaspecialprojects.pdf

www.tcd.ie/childrensresearchcentre/assets/pdf/Publications/socialandpsychological.
pdf

www.tcd.ie/funding-priorities/priority/health/neuroenhancement.php

www.tcd.ie/research/ageingconsortium/projects/pdf/Ageing_irobertson.pdf

www.youngballymun.org

www.youtube.com/watch?v=OJs-4cncGmk

Index